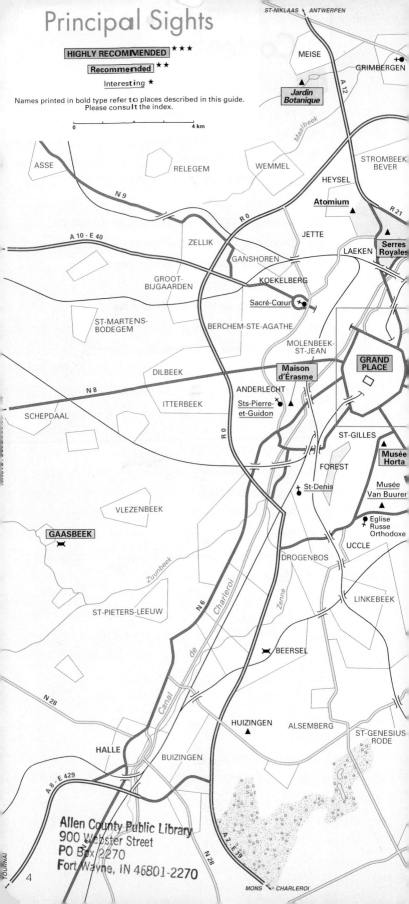

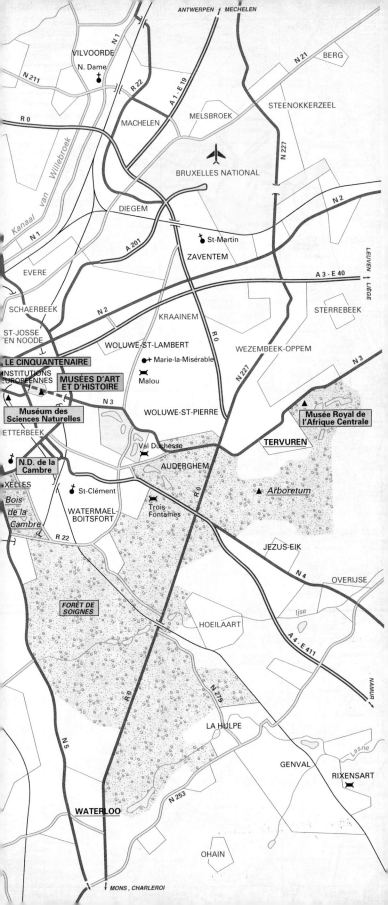

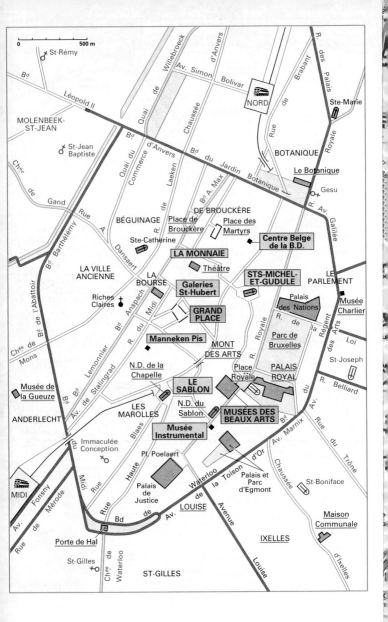

THE ORIGINAL TOWN WALLS

The original town walls stretching over 4 000m - 2 1/2 miles included seven gates and some fifty defensive towers. It was the walls that made Brussels a real town. It was probably Lambert II (1041-1063) who first ordered the construction of the walls rising to an average height of 7m - 23ft and built of square-hewn sandstone ashlar. They were completed by Henry II (1063-1079). The original purpose was to provide protection for the Coudenberg ducal residence (now Place Royale). A few sections have survived and some can still be seen today including the Tour Anneessens, Tour de Villers, Tour Noire, Tour de Pléban (towers) and the curtain wall in the Hôtel S.A.S.

Travelling in Brussels

The *Société des Transports Intercommunaux de Bruxelles* (STIB) was set up in 1954. It is the largest urban public transport company in Belgium, with routes totalling a length of 430km - 267 miles and covering the nineteen towns within the Greater Brussels area as well as a few other towns on the periphery of the conurbation.

The *Centre d'Informations Téléphonées* (CIT) provides information, by phone, on routes and timetables (☎ (02) 515 20 00).

Le Roy/GLOBAL PICTURES

Public transport runs from about 0600 to midnight and you can use the same tickets however you travel. Maps and brochures can be obtained in certain bus or underground stations and in the Tourist Office (TIB).

There are also passes for one to five trips throughout the STIB network; the ten-trip pass is only valid on urban routes. A one-day pass gives unlimited travel. Tickets are valid for one hour, including a free link-up with another route or even with a train, in which case the ticket is valid for two hours. Remember to stamp your ticket or pass in the machine each time you get on a bus or go into a station.

Passes and tickets are on sale on trams or buses, in booking halls and in certain shops (bookshops). They are also available from automatic ticket machines in various stations.

Travelling by Underground

The underground was built in Brussels in 1976 and the stations have been decorated by some sixty different contemporary artists, making the network one huge art gallery *(see Introduction, Living in Brussels)*.

The main line (33km - 21 miles long) crosses the city from east to west and has four termini (Heysel, H Debroux, Stockel and Bizet). The name of the terminus is indicated on the carriages to make the lines more user-friendly.

The second line (7.5km - almost 5 miles long) is the "inner ring" *(petite ceinture)* which cuts across the main line in two places - Arts-Loi and Simonis.

Like the Rogier, Bourse and Gare du Midi stations, the one at Porte de Namur includes an information and ticket office. It also has a Lost Property office.

The entrances to the underground are indicated by a blue sign bearing a white letter "M".

Trams

Trams are an integral part of the urban landscape in Brussels; there are some fifteen routes. They travel either at street-level or in tunnels. This enables them to escape the often heavy traffic in the city. The underground trams are known as the *prémétro* and they run on two routes - one along a north-south line linking, for example the Gare du Nord and Gare du Midi (railway stations) and the other following the outer ringroad *(grande ceinture)* in the suburbs of Woluwe and Schaerbeek. The trams running through the streets cover the entire conurbation. One of them, no 94, is also used for sightseeing trips from Jette to Boitsfort. At each stop, there is a sound commentary on the city presented by the *ADépartementier de Recherche et d'Action Urbaines* (ARAU, Urban Action and Research Workshop). For further information, contact the OPT (☎ 504 03 90) or the Tourist Office (☎ 513 89 49).

Bus

The bus service covers many of the streets within Brussels and in the suburbs, enabling passengers to link up with underground routes into the city centre.

The STIB has published an interesting brochure entitled *Art Nouveau en transports en commun*. The corresponding public transport routes are listed and three suggestions are given for routes that take passengers through the city streets past some of the outstanding Art Nouveau buildings.

A practical guide to Brussels

Embassies

Canadian Embassy: 2 Avenue de Tervuren, 1040 Brussels. ☎ 741 06 11
British Embassy: 85 Rue d'Arlon, 1040 Brussels. ☎ 287 62 11
United States Embassy: 27 Boulevard du Régent, 1000 Brussels. ☎ 508 21 11
Australian Embassy: 6 Rue Guimard, 1040 Brussels. ☎ 231 05 00

Banks

Most banks are open from 0900 to 1600. Some of them close between 1230 and 1330 but stay open later during the week or are open on Saturday mornings.

Post Offices

Normal opening hours during the week are 0900 to 1700. The post office on the first floor of Centre Monnaie (Place de la Monnaie) is open on Saturdays from 0900 to 1500. The office at 48A Avenue Fosny near Gare du Midi is open twenty-four hours a day (stamps and postal services).

Credit Cards

Travellers cheques and the main international credit cards (Visa, Eurocard, American Express) are accepted in nearly all shops, hotels and restaurants. Some of the cash lines also take international credit cards.

Emergency phone numbers to report lost credit cards: American Express. ☎ 676 21 21
Visa, Eurocard. ☎ 070 344 344

Local Currency

The currency of Belgium is the Belgian franc. There are 50 centime, 1 franc, 2 franc, 20 franc and 50 franc coins; 100 franc, 200 franc, 500 franc, 1 000 franc, 2 000 franc and 10 000 franc notes.

Bank Holidays

1 January
Easter Day
Easter Monday
1 May
Ascension Thursday
Whitsun
Whit Monday
21 July (national holiday)
15 August
1 November
11 November
25 December

Chemist's

Most are open from 0830 to 1830. There is a rota system for on call at night, or on Sundays and bank holidays. A list is displayed in the windows of all chemist's.

Shops

Most shops are open from 0900 to 1800.

Places of Interest, Churches, Museums

Usually open from 1000 to 1700. Most museums are closed on Mondays.

Telephone

Phone cards for use in public phone boxes, covering calls to subscribers in Belgium or abroad, can be obtained from post offices, railway stations and in most paper shops. Some phone boxes operate with 5 franc, 20 franc and 50 franc coins. The Belgacom office at 17 Avenue de l'Impératrice (near the central railway station) is open daily from 0800 to 2200.
If you want to phone the United Kingdom from Belgium, dial 00 44 and the subscriber's number (including the area code). To phone the United States or Canada, dial 00 1. For Australia, the code is 00 61.
To take advantage of cheap-rate calls, phone between 1830 and 0800.

Guided Tours

ARAU (*Atelier de Recherche et d'Action Urbaines* - Urban Action and Research Workshop): 55, boulevard A Max, 1000 Brussels, Tel 219 33 45. Nearly all the members of this association are local people who have been fighting the rampant property development or destruction of the city since the end of the 1960's. They offer a number of tours-on-a-theme in the city centre including Brussels 1900 (Art Nouveau), Brussels 1930 (Art Deco), A Different View of Brussels etc.

Arcadia: 58 Rue Henri Wafelaerts, 1060 Brussels, ☎ 534 38 19. This association organises theme tours.

De Boeck Sightseeingtours: 8 Rue de la Colline, 1000 Brussels, ☎ 513 77 44. Coach tours of the city.

La Fonderie: 27 Rue Ransfort, 1080 Brussels, ☎ 410 99 50. Industrial sightseeing tours on foot, by coach or by boat. Tours of Brussels Harbour and companies at work.

Itinéraires: 157 Rue Hôtel des Monnaies, 1060 Brussels, ☎ 539 04 34. Guided tours-on-a-theme.

Pro vélo: 32A Rue Ernest Solvay, 1050 Bruxelles, ☎ 502 73 55. Sightseeing tours by bike (high season only).

TIB (Brussels Tourist Office): Town Hall, Grand-Place, 1000 Brussels, ☎ 513 89 40. Guided tours for individual sightseers in the summer months.

Taxis: The main taxi firms are: Taxis Verts, ☎ 349 49 49 - Taxi Orange, ☎ 513 62 00.

The 19 communes of Brussels

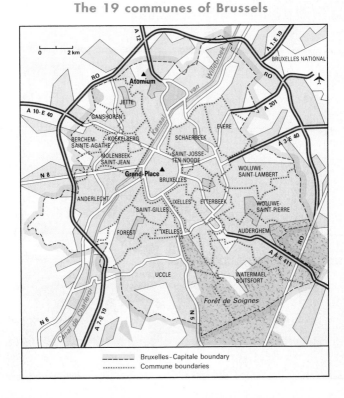

_ _ _ _ _ _ _ Bruxelles-Capitale boundary
.... Commune boundaries

Introduction

A long-standing cosmopolitan tradition

A great many historians disagree as to the origins of Brussels. The meaning of the name, "settlement in the marshes", summarises almost all that is known of the period prior to the 10C, although the first mention of the town, in 695 AD, indicates that *Brosella* was part of the bishopric of Cambrai.

The Foundation of the City – Brussels belonged to Lotharingia which Emperor Otto of the Holy Roman Empire divided into Upper and Lower Lotharingia in 959 AD. In 977, his son Otto II entrusted Lower Lotharingia (the region bounded by the Meuse, Champagne and Scheldt) to a Duke who was a descendent of Charlemagne, Charles of France. The duke set up his *castrum* in Brussels *c*977-979 and this is the official date of the founding of the city although, in those days, it was nothing more than a sort of county. The geographical position of the settlement on the River Senne, on the largest of the three islands, Saint-Géry, was to lead to the development of its role as a military stronghold of some economic importance. It also ensured that the settlement was in a position of strength compared to the County of Flanders. On the death of Charles of France's son in 1005, though, it was the Count Lambert I of Louvain who inherited Brussels and thereafter the House of Louvain governed it for some four hundred years.

The Ducal Fortress – Lambert II's role in the history of the city was of major importance because he moved the fortress to the Coudenberg (now Place Royale) and probably took the decision to have town walls erected. This construction project was completed by his successor, Henry II. In 1106, Godefroid I was granted the title of Duke of Lotharingia and the Counts of Louvain were then referred to as Dukes of Brabant. Godefroid introduced the hereditary charge of Castellan (ie military guardian of the castle) and the function of amtman or mayor. It was also in the early years of the 12C that the town enjoyed an initial period of economic expansion, encouraged by the newly-developing cloth industry.

After a period of instability, indeed of violence, the town's middle classes took a firm hold on the town's affairs and began to lay claim to privileges and franchises. In 1229, Henry I granted Brussels its first written charter. By then, Lotharingia was something of a historical oddity, the emperor had abandoned Brabant, and the town was gradually moving ahead of Louvain. Brussels became a trading centre which benefited from the breakdown of trading relations between Flanders and England on the one hand and, on the other, from the decisive victory won by Duke John I in 1288 over Reinald of Guelders. The victory ensured a link between Brabant and the Rhine and led to the control of the trade routes linking Bruges, the largest port on the North Sea coast, and Cologne, the most powerful trading centre in Germany.

The Expansion of the Town and Development of the Guilds – In the 14C, trades and crafts gained their independence. The famous Battle of the Golden Spurs (1302) at which the Flemish people inflicted a crushing defeat on Philip the Fair's French cavalry finally made the craftsmen and urban militia aware of their political clout. In Brussels, a popular revolt broke out in 1303 against the dynasties or wealthy middle-class families who controlled the town's economy. The main event, however, took place in 1356 after the town was occupied by Louis de Male, Count of Flanders, during his dispute with Duchess Jeanne and her husband, Wenceslas, regarding their respective rights to inherit the duchy. Assisted by the people of Brussels, and in particular by the butchers from the streets around Grand-Place, the patrician leader, Everard 't Serclaes, routed the Flemish troops. When Jeanne returned, swearing an oath of loyalty to the charter of liberties known as the *Joyeuse Entrée* (a law laying down the rights and duties of princes and their subjects), crafts were given official recognition and guild members became more closely involved with political life. Despite these periods of public disorder, the 14C was a prosperous time owing to the success of the cloth industry across Europe as a whole. The town underwent demographic expansion and building began outside the walls, especially along the roads leading into the town where suburbs began to spring up. The events of 1356 led to the hasty construction (1357-1379) of a second town wall which encircled the area of town protected by eight kilometres - almost five miles of ramparts with seven fortified gateways. This pentagonal expansion is still evident in Brussels city centre today.

Towards the end of the century, the cloth industry entered a slump as a result of competition from England. Moreover, the political climate was distinctly unhealthy during the first few years of the 15C. The consequence of this twofold situation was a revolt by craftsmen in 1421. From then on, the town was managed by seven aldermen (one per dynasty), six counsellors (representing the crafts), four receivers and two burgomasters. This form of management lasted until 1795.

Burgundian Splendour – In 1430, Philippe de Saint-Pol died without an heir. Brabant then became part of the Burgundian provinces under the control of Duke Philip the Good who had a large number of official residences but who spent most of his time in Dijon. He instigated a policy of openness which met with hostility from the craftsmen who had been burdened with high levels of taxation since the beginning of the century. Industrial activity went into a decline but the town nevertheless became a major administrative centre within the Duke's vast complex territory and it sought to enter the Duke's good graces by increasing the number of new prestigious buildings. Under Mary of Burgundy, Charles the Bold's daughter, Brussels finally became the capital of the very rich Burgundian state and luxury crafts enjoyed a boom (altarpieces, tapestries, illuminated books and manuscripts, gold and

ROGER-VIOLLET

Philip the Good

silverware, leather etc.). The development was based, of course, on the presence of the Court but it was also encouraged by the incessant coming-and-going of ambassadors, noblemen and travellers. It was, then, quite natural for the town to attract the most brilliant artists of the day, in particular Rogier van der Weyden (Rogier de la Pasture) who became the town's official artist.

Decadence during the Days of the First Hapsburgs – The politics of splendour had its downside. The town had been left financially ruined and, moreover, the war against Louis XI was an expensive business. Currency was devalued, prices rocketed, and the area was in the grip of famine and utter poverty when Maximilian of Austria came to power after his wife was killed in a riding accident in 1482. With resources in short supply, civil war soon broke out. In 1488, Brussels joined Flanders in revolting against Maximilian – a worthless gesture as it turned out because the town was decimated by plague two years later. The community had been bled white, and in 1503, Philip the Fair decided to impose financial control and cut out urban expenditure. Then, as if to worsen an already catastrophic situation, Margaret of Austria, having been appointed Governess of the Netherlands, moved the capital from Brussels to Malines, a town that had already been favoured by Charles the Bold.

Finding Favour with Charles V – Charles of Hapsburg, a Burgundian prince, was born at the beginning of the century and made his official entry into Brussels at the age of 15. He mounted the throne of Spain one year later and was elected Emperor of Germany in 1519 under the title of Charles V. The man "on whose States the sun never set" was a frequent visitor to the capital of Brabant. His presence was essential

ROGER-VIOLLET

Emperor Charles V

for the town since it was then seen as the capital of the Netherlands and the Empire since the Emperor had no main residence in either Spain or Germany. Even more importantly, his abdication in 1555 did not deal a death blow to the town. On the contrary, the princes and officials responsible for governing the Netherlands then made it their place of residence. The town had a Court and was a seat of government and Brussels regained its past splendour by attracting courtiers and families with close links to the monarchy. It was also visited by all the great merchants, high ecclesiastical dignitaries and men of arts and letters such as Holbein, Dürer or Erasmus. The chroniclers of the day described it as "a beautiful and great city". The arrival of a large number of immigrants led to considerable urban expansion and even Antwerp, a metropolis of international trade, was soon unable to rival the city in Brabant. The direct consequence of this development was a lessening of the power of the craftsmen and a gradual increase in the authority of the town's governors.

Revolt against Spain – When Charles V abdicated, he granted his Austrian possessions to his brother, Ferdinand I, and his Spanish possessions and the Netherlands to his son, Philip II. This was a tragedy for the Netherlands.

Heresy, which had already gained a foothold among the misery and abject poverty of the working classes, began to spread through the Reformation which appeared in Brussels in the guise of Calvinism. At the same time, opposition to the tyrannical policies of Philip II began to gather momentum and it found its leader in William of Orange, a prince who had been brought up Brussels and had been one of Charles V's protégés. This political and moral opposition led to the Noblemen's Compromise. In 1566, their resistance was given the backing of the ordinary townsfolk and violent clashes occurred throughout the town. In the following year, Philip II responded to the rebellion by sending in the Duke d'Albe, Alvarez of Toledo, who set up a *Conseil des Troubles* (Commission of Civil Unrest) also known as the *Conseil du Sang* (Commission of Blood) because of the pillaging and numerous executions that it instigated. Belgian schoolchildren all know about the execution of the Counts of Egmont and de Hornes, one of the main events in the history of the nation. The violence of the Inquisition was powerless in the face of the rebellion and the Reformation. In 1577, William of Orange, nicknamed William the Taciturn, made a triumphant entrance into the state capital which was governed by the Calvinists until 1585. Acting on the orders of Philip II, Duke Alessandro Farnese of Parma finally captured the town. He gave even greater impetus to his victory by granting a general amnesty to the townspeople and by promising to uphold the town's privileges. Philip II's authority was re-established and this paved the way for the triumph of the Counter-Reformation at a time when the very Catholic Archduke Albert and Archduchess Isabella became the sovereigns of the Netherlands.

Religious Fervour – At the dawn of the 17C, Brussels was literally invaded by religious Orders. There were Apostolics, Augustinian friars, Brigittines, Capuchins, Carmelites, Jesuits, Minim Brothers, Oratorians etc, all of them forming large communities. This was also the century of censorship and control by an all-powerful Church. People could not find work if they were not Roman Catholics. Meanwhile, further communities of Apostolics, Ursulines, Visitandines and English Dominicans arrived and settled near the Town Hall. This religious fervour was accompanied by a period of relative calm since the Archduke and his spouse had been successful in guaranteeing the prosperity of Brussels. Yet this period of peace was to be short-lived; it ended with the death of Archduke Albert in 1621.

Threats and Destruction from France – Cardinal-Infant Ferdinand governed in the name of his brother, King Philip IV, and was respected by all. He had to withstand pressure from King Louis XIII of France who had decided to invade the Netherlands, encouraged by the anti-Spanish policies of Richelieu and, later, Mazarin. Further campaigns were launched during the reign of Louis XIV who came in person to inspect the recent reinforcement of the second town wall before laying siege to Maastricht in 1673. Incursions became increasingly numerous in the last quarter of the 17C until the Sun King finally decided to bombard Brussels, knowing that its defences were weak. His aim was to draw off the Dutch and English troops besieging the French forces entrenched in the citadel of Namur. As a result of the total war concept recommended by Louvois during the destruction of the Palatinate in 1689, the bombardment ordered on 13 August 1695 by Maréchal de Villeroy was terrifying and terrible *(see the history of Grand-Place).*

The Urban Economy – from Guild to Capitalism – The expansion in luxury trade resulting from the presence of the Burgundian Court and the rule of Charles V was under serious threat during the reign of Philip II. It finally went into a total slump owing to the events of 1695. However, as proved by the townspeople immediately after the French bombardment when they began to rebuild the fabulous Grand-Place that is so well-known today, Brussels could shake off a particularly precarious economic situation and regain its former glory. This rebirth led to the digging of the Willebroek Canal linking the town to the sea. The manmade stretch of water was the result of a bitter struggle with Malines and Vilvorde yet after its inauguration in 1561 it profoundly changed city life. By digging out basins in the very heart of the city, Brussels gradually became a port in which goods could be loaded and landed.

The guilds had gained an outlook that was somewhat protectionist and, in the Middle Ages, had left their mark on the town's economy but they were suffering from a regime that had become obsolete. Although as political and social forces they were still active, they were unable to withstand for long the arrival of the factories that began to see the light of day in the 17C. How could a group of craftsmen subject to crippling expenditure by their guilds offer any real resistance to modern industry which employed a large work force and made use of machinery? The days of local markets were over. Brussels and its harbour acquired cloth mills, leather works, soap factories and chemicals plants and the major concern of all of them was to produce cheap goods for export. While the guilds were busy rebuilding a Grand-Place that was even more beautiful than before, the town was becoming a centre of international trade in a wide range of products including new foodstuffs from the colonies.

The Austrian Period – When Charles II died in 1700, it was discovered that he had designated Philip of Anjou to succeed him, a man who was none other than the grandson and possible successor of King Louis XIV of France. The risk of the unification of Spain and France under a single sovereign led to the War of Spanish Succession. This period of tension ended in the Treaties of Utrecht and Rastadt in 1713 and 1714. The main conditions laid down in these treaties were that Philip V of Anjou should waive his rights to the throne of France and that the Netherlands should pass to Emperor Charles VI.

Austrian domination was clement towards the Netherlands and its most densely-populated city, Brussels (57 854 inhabitants in 1755, 74 427 in 1783). The governors, however, were faced with the last few revolts on the part of the guilds in their attempts to re-establish their former privileges. In 1731, when Archduchess Marie-Elisabeth was Governor, the ducal palace on Coudenberg, which dated back to the 11C, was totally destroyed by fire. Then came the death of Charles VI, which provided another pretext for a war of succession, and Maurice of Saxony captured Brussels in 1746 on behalf of King Louis XV of France who was later forced to return it to Maria-Theresa of Austria under the terms of the Treaty of Aix-la-Chapelle. The Empress sent her brother-in-law Charles of Lorraine to Brussels and he set up one of the most dazzling Courts of the day there.

During the second half of the 18C, Brussels was an industrial town with a very large working-class population. The crafts were gradually dying out. Meanwhile, workers' trades unions were coming into being, initially in the form of occult sickness benefit associations, in an economy that was a precursor of 19C capitalism as far as its structure was concerned. Local decision-making was, of course, subject to agreement from Vienna and the city was administered by a group of high-ranking civil servants. This powerhouse attracted leading merchants, intellectuals and philosophers. University studies were very highly-considered and patrons of the Arts at the Court had their own artists. Although the city was bilingual, the cultural language was French. The textile and tobacco industries drew in leading financiers with colossal fortunes, interested in the transit trade. Poverty, however, was also spreading, at a time when neo-Classical avenues and boulevards were being rigorously planned and drawn with a ruler through the heart of the town. Modern Brussels was born.

Revolution in Brabant and France – When, on 7 January 1789, Joseph II decided to cancel the charter of liberties dating back to 1356, it aroused such a sense of frustration that an unusually violent rebellion broke out. The popular uprising removed the Austrians from power and led to the creation of the Republic of the United Belgian States on 10 January 1790. It was a complex episode. The basic forces and leaders were Democrats but the financiers who backed the revolt were radically opposed to the ideas being put forward by the French Revolution. It is a little-known episode but it lasted for 11 months until the Austrians, supported by European nations that looked askance at the turn of events in France, came back and wiped out a revolution that went just one step too far.

King Joseph II

After the successes in the battlefield at Jemappes (1792) and Fleurus (1794), the southern part of the Netherlands was integrated into France in 1795 and Brussels was no more than the "county town" of the *département* of Dyle. Craft guilds were suppressed and the guildhalls were sold off as national property. Numerous buildings in Brussels were subjected to pillaging; indeed, the situation continued until Bonaparte was appointed Consul in 1799. Later, on 18 June 1815, it was not far from the former county town of Dyle, in Waterloo to be precise, that Napoleon's ambitions came to an abrupt and irreversible halt.

Dutch Rule – The Kingdom of the Netherlands was unusual in that it had two capital cities – The Hague and Brussels. The Court travelled from one to the other but the diplomatic corps decided to remain in Brussels. This had the advantage of preserving the dazzling social life to which Brussels had become accustomed and it attracted the young Crown Prince, William of Orange, who was said to be only too willing to rebel and get into scrapes. He was a liberal thinker, frequenting even the most progressive circles of society.

Tension, however, grew up between north and south on questions relating to educational policies which were ill-accepted by the Roman Catholics. The evident Dutch hold on public life and the limitations placed on the freedom of the press by a multitude of court cases were also areas of concern. William I was soon to fail in the southern part of his kingdom but, to give praise where due, he was instrumental in bringing the industrial revolution to Belgium.

Independence – The city's history then followed the same course as the history of the kingdom but it was in Brussels that the revolutionary movement really took shape. The population was already stirred by news of the uprisings in Paris in July 1830 and it gave its monarch a very frosty welcome on his arrival in the following August. Police reports of the day give an eloquent description of the explosive situation in the half-capital of the Netherlands. On 25 August, during a performance of *The Mute Girl of Portici* in the Théâtre de La Monnaie, the audience began a rebellion when the tenor sang the first few notes of the famous aria *Amour sacré de la Patrie* (Sacred love of one's fatherland). People left the auditorium and joined the crowds of workers outside. The throng was enlarged by a number of uncontrollable elements and, together, they went on the rampage through the building belonging to the Orangist newspaper, *Le National*, before going on to smash windows in the Law Courts where the trials involving the various newspapers and journals were being held.

On the following day, the mass resignation of all the forces of law and order accelerated the process of revolution. Some shouted *Vive la France* while others wore the cockade of Brabant. Confusion was at its height. The city was subject to generalised pillaging, windows were smashed then, gradually, the riot took on more radical overtones. King William hesitated to intervene. The moderates travelled to The Hague to find the parliamentary solution that the sovereign believed would put a stop to events. However, as ill-luck would have it, at the same time, the province sent several companies of volunteers to Brussels and they were resolutely extremist in their views and actions. The regional recruits in the Dutch Army, unable to pass through the city gates, decided to enter the city on 23 September and were convinced that they would win the day. In fact, a skirmish halted them in their tracks on the outskirts of the town's park. Most of the soldiers were Belgian and they sought refuge inside the park. They were then encircled for four days (known as the September Uprising) by volunteers who had quickly formed groups of combatants, but the Army managed, in some cases at least and despite the poor quality of its leadership, to escape. It was too late! News of the Army's defeat had spread like wildfire and caused all the towns in the province to rally to the cause. Taking advantage of this unexpected good fortune, a provisional government was soon set up. The revolution had just created a new State – Belgium. On 21 July 1831, Prince Leopold of Saxe-Coburg-Gotha officially entered the city and took the oath which was to make him King of the Belgians.

Urban Development – In 1830, the capital and its suburbs included some 3% of the total population of the country; by 1914, the figure had risen to 10%. In the meantime, the industrial revolution had totally changed the city and its size had increased considerably. Rural communities were rapidly becoming towns throughout Europe. The city was expanding and, at the same time, was changing. In 1850, it had twice as many cul-de-sacs as streets and, like most large towns, the housing conditions were generally unhealthy. When Leopold II came to power, the Senne was covered over, new districts were created and the land was levelled.

At the same time, the city's industrial vocation (textiles, building, publishing, mechanical engineering and luxury products) was given greater impetus with the setting-up of a more organised banking sector. Stimulated by the *Société Générale*, a bank founded by William I and known in those days as the *Banque de Bruxelles*, private bankers began to act as sleeping partners in industrial firms. The banks and their subsidiaries provided the basis of what we now know as industrial loans. Moreover, the Franco-Prussian War of 1870 turned Brussels, indirectly at least, into an international financial centre by attracting businessmen and capital from neighbouring countries.

On 5 May 1835, the first Continental train left from Malines station for the station in Allée Verte, a trip that was then fashionable through an area to the north of the Porte d'Anvers. The capital city of the kingdom was about to become a major railway junction within the heart of a country whose heavy industry (mining, metal working) was famous for its excellence and productivity far beyond its national borders. The city benefited of course from this development in communications and by 1870 it had four railway stations.

King Leopold II

Ideas, too, were on the move, stimulated by the question of education which, for many years, divided Catholics who wanted to regain their monopoly of this sector and liberal thinkers determined to give people an opportunity to climb the rungs of the social ladder through learning. This is why, even today, "free" education in Belgium refers to state-run lay institutions, unlike France where the term is used for church schools. This contradiction can be explained by the diametrically-opposed regimes in the two countries. The monarchy and the Republic each granted freedom of conscience to ideas that were opposed to mainstream thinking. As far as liberty was concerned, Belgium could give as good as it got in the 19C. Its capital city opened its doors to many an exile, thereby attracting some of the sharpest minds of the day from all over Europe. In just a few years, the Café des Mille Colonnes, which had already seen Cambacérès puff out his chest in defiance at the beginning of the century, became a favourite haunt of Giuseppe Mazzini, organiser of Republican putsches; he was followed by Karl Marx and Victor Hugo.

Brussels' main handicap rapidly became the administrative situation of its suburbs, all of which were independent towns. This raised enormous problems of management after the population explosion of the second half of the 19C. The city provided education, civil engineering projects, health amenities, police services etc. but received nothing in return. It even went so far as to consider annexing the outlying towns which were taking advantage of all that the city had to offer. Not surprisingly, the towns refused but, within a decade, a joint intercommunity committee had been set up to solve problems of common interest such as the provision of an adequate water supply. This infrastructure undoubtedly led to an increased awareness and, much later, to the status of the Brussels conurbation.

Wars and Crises before Major Transformation – At the beginning of the century, the capital was a large, liberal, progressive city at the head of a conservative country. Intellectual life was flourishing, as were the daily papers which accounted for more than one-half of national circulation. Trade, which was already dynamic, was further encouraged by the organisation of several international exhibitions ranging from the one to celebrate the Jubilee in 1880 to the World Fair in 1910 for which the poster showed Grand-Place with an airship flying over it. This picture travelled right round the globe. After the deep slump which led to the setting up of the Belgian Workers' Party in 1885, the turn-of-the-century was marked by an industrial boom whose leading figure was, without doubt, Ernest Solvay. The town centre became filled with the incessant comings-and-goings of trams and omnibuses, the Stock Exchange was filled with the tumult of youth, the large department stores filled their shelves with a huge range of items, and Art Nouveau came to the fore amid a plethora of swirls and curves. A smiling yet intimidated crowd walked past the first cameras operated by cinematographic reporters.

Unfortunately, the enthusiasm of Brussels was dampened twice by German occupation, from 1914 to 1918 and again from 1940 to 1944. From September 1944 to April 1945, the city was even subjected to air raids by the infamous V1 flying bombs which missed its main buildings, although the damage was such that it would be wrong to add "fortunately". In the interwar years, the main question on everybody's lips in Brussels was again the unification of the suburbs and the city. Laeken was annexed in 1921 so that the harbour installations, which were still thriving owing to the Willebroek and Charleroi Canals, could be extended (machine-building, power plants, chemicals, pharmaceuticals and textiles, food-processing including biscuits and chocolate etc.). However, the solution to the problem of Greater Brussels was delayed by the 1929 crisis, the period of national mourning in 1934 following the accidental death of the much-loved monarch, Albert I, the emergence of extremists in 1936, and the occupation of 1940.

After the Second World War, the capital city was the scene of a royal crisis during which the various political parties were split on the appropriateness of Leopold III's return. In March 1950, the impasse led to a referendum and 57.5% of the population gave their support to the king thereby putting an end to the regency of Prince Charles. However, it was the arrival of Baudouin I on the throne in August that same year which finally calmed the situation. Heated arguments then began again almost immediately over the question of language and they continued throughout the 1950's.

New laws attempted to solve the difficulties opposing the French- and Dutch-speaking communities and Brussels, of course, posed the greatest problem of all. The solutions all tended towards regionalisation and the bilingual Bruxelles-Capitale district including 19 towns and villages was set up in 1963.

In 1958, the city also became the headquarters of the **European Economic Community** (EEC), now known as the **European Union** (EU), and of EURATOM (European Atomic Energy Community). Since 1967, it has also played host to NATO (North Atlantic Treaty Organisation) and, since 1954, to the WEU (Western European Union). This confirmed the deeply international and cosmopolitan vocation of the city of Brussels, as if any confirmation were needed.

Brussels Today – The political problems arising from the city's status are as complex as they were long to resolve. In 1970, Section 107 (d) was added to the Constitution indicat-

King Baudouin I

19

ing that Belgium included the regions of Wallonia, Flanders, and Brussels. The Brussels conurbation officially includes 19 towns within an area of 62sq miles – 161.78sq km. They are Anderlecht, Auderghem, Berchem-Sainte-Agathe, Brussels, Etterbeek, Evere, Forest, Ganshoren, Ixelles, Jette, Koekelberg, Molenbeek-Saint-Jean, Saint-Gilles, Saint-Josse-ten-Noode, Schaerbeek, Uccle, Watermael-Boitsfort, Woluwe-Saint-Lambert and Woluwe-Saint-Pierre. Since 1989, these towns have formed a region in their own right called Bruxelles-Capitale and they have their own Council consisting of 75 directly-elected members with a 5-year mandate constituting one French-speaking group and one Dutch-speaking group. Since the reform of the Belgian state in 1980, the city has also been the headquarters of the offices of the Flemish Region; Wallonia chose Namur as its headquarters. Brussels has both Flemish and French communities. Last but not least, Brussels is still a major industrial centre. Its main characteristic is the wide range of sectors of activity (metal working, car assembly, chemicals, printing, publishing, clothes, leather goods, gold and silverware, technological research etc.). Although the secondary sector is regressing slightly at the present time, the tertiary sector is continuing to develop. This is easily explained by the city's function as a national and European capital. The economic consequences of its internationalisation are considerable. Just think of the number of companies that have chosen Brussels for their commercial or administrative head offices. Perversely, this has led to a decrease in the population which fell below the symbolic bar of one million in 1982 as a result of the exodus of many former city dwellers to towns on the periphery. In 1990, the Bruxelles-Capitale region had a population of 964 385.

Brussels, a city of European institutions

Since 1 January 1958, the Belgian capital has been the seat of the European Economic Community (EEC) and the European Atomic Energy Commission (EURATOM), both of which were set up on 25 March 1957 by the Treaty of Rome. The founder members of these communities were West Germany, Belgium, France, Italy, Luxembourg, and the Netherlands. The Europe of the 6 was later extended to include the following countries – Denmark, Ireland and the United Kingdom in 1973, Greece in 1981, Spain and Portugal in 1986. The Europe of the 12 opened its doors to still other nations in 1995 – Austria, Finland and Sweden. The Europe of the 15 that we know today will doubtless be extended further in the future.

THE MAIN DATES

1851 Victor Hugo mooted the idea of a United States of Europe.

1919 The League of Nations was set up.

1926 The European Economic and Customs Union was founded.

1929 Aristide Briand laid before the League of Nations a draft proposal for a United States of Europe.

1941 The United Nations Organisation (UNO) was founded.

1943 Winston Churchill proposed a Council of Europe.

1945 The International Monetary Fund (IMF) was set up.

1948 The Benelux Union came into being. It was a Customs & Excise agreement between Belgium, the Netherlands and Luxembourg. The General Agreement on Tariffs and Trade (GATT) was also set up.

1949 The Council of Europe came into being and the North Atlantic Treaty Organisation (NATO) was founded.

1950 The European Payments Union was founded.

1951 The ECSC (European Coal and Steel Community) was set up.

1954 Benelux suggested setting up a common market. The WEU (Western European Union) was founded.

1955 A European monetary agreement was signed.

1957 The Treaty of Rome set up the EEC and Euratom.

1958 The EEC set up its headquarters in Brussels.

1959 The European Free Trade Association (EFTA) was founded. Its members were Austria, Denmark, the United Kingdom, Norway, Portugal, Sweden and Switzerland.

1961 The United Kingdom sought membership of the EEC.

1962 Agreement was reached on the Common Agricultural Policy (CAP).

1963 An agreement was signed aimed at establishing an association between 18 African countries and the EEC.

1965 The EEC, EURATOM and ECSC were merged.

1967 Denmark and Ireland sought membership of the EEC. The United Kingdom sought membership for the second time.

1968 Full Customs Union was established between Member States.

1972 The European Monetary System (EMS) came into being.

1973 Denmark, the United Kingdom and Ireland became members of the EEC.

1979 The European Currency Unit (ECU) came into being and the first elections were held for the European parliament.

1981 Greece became a member of the EEC. The Single Market was set up within the EEC.

1984 A project was tabled by Italian MEP, Altiero Spinelli, for a European Union.

1985 Greenland (Danish territory) left the EEC.

1986 Spain and Portugal became members of the EEC. The Single European Act was signed.

1989 The European Bank for Reconstruction and Development (EBRD) was set up.

1990 Free circulation of capital was authorised throughout the EEC and the Community was extended further to the reunification of Germany. The Schengen Accord was signed.

1992 The European Economic Area (EEA) was set up between the EEC and EFTA. The Maastricht Treaty was signed, setting up the European Union.

1995 Austria, Finland and Sweden became members of the European Community.

FROM COMMUNITIES TO THE EUROPEAN UNION

Since 1958, the European Communities have included the ECSC, the EEC and EURATOM. A treaty signed on 8 April 1965 decided to merge the three bodies and the merger took effect on 1 July 1967, although the three treaties that had set up the individual organisations remained in existence.

The **ECSC** (European Coal and Steel Community) was aimed at political rapprochement through a common market in coal and steel and the removal of all obstacles to the circulation of goods. The treaty that set up this body will expire in 2002.

The **EEC** (European Economic Community), otherwise known as the Common Market, was designed to provide continuous, well-balanced expansion of standards of living in Member States through the free circulation of goods, people and capital and the implementation of common policies in sectors such as farming, trade, competition, energy and transport. Since 1991, the EEC has been called the European Community and it has been commissioned to seek ways of setting up economic and monetary union by the end of the 20C with the launch of a single currency known as the Euro.

EURATOM (European Atomic Energy Commission) was set up to promote the development of nuclear energy within Member States.

The Treaty of Maastricht, which was signed on 7 February 1992 and took effect on 1 November 1993, instituted the **European Union**. The EU is required to seek political co-operation on a European scale and co-operation in the fields of justice and internal affairs of individual States.

THE FIVE INSTITUTIONS

Five institutions work to ensure that the European Community operates smoothly.

The European Parliament – *Its headquarters are in Strasbourg but a large number of committee meetings and meetings of political groups are held in Brussels. Most of the administrative staff (general secretariat) are posted in Luxembourg.* Since 1979, the parliament has been directly elected for a 5-year term of office by universal suffrage, except in the United Kingdom where votes are cast for a single name in a first-past-the-post system of voting. Since the last elections in June 1994, the parliament's 567 members have been subdivided as follows – Luxembourg (6), Ireland (15), Denmark (16), Belgium, Greece and Portugal (25), Netherlands (31), Spain (64), France, the United Kingdom and Italy (87), and Germany (99). Sweden will be sending 22 members of parliament, Austria 21 and Finland 16. This subdivision does not lead to the setting up of national groups but, instead, to the coming together of groups of the same political colour. The Parliament functions through committees responsible for monitoring the activities of the executive. These committees invite representatives of the executive to explain the Commission's proposals and decisions and are, at the same time, spokespersons for the Parliament as far as its opinion on proposals submitted by the Commission to the Council is concerned. The Parliament is firstly a means of democratic scrutiny. It regulates the operating costs of the various bodies and makes known its observations regarding the implementation of the budget. It also intervenes in the Community's legislative activity and benefits from a system of joint decision making in certain fields. Finally, it has a say in certain pertinent questions of the day through emergency debates or the setting up of ad hoc committees. It was because of its role that the Maastricht Treaty commissioned this high-ranking institution to appoint a mediator or ombudsman who would be required to look into complaints from any citizen or resident within the Community.

The Council of Ministers – *Headquarters in Brussels. A few sessions are held in Luxembourg.* The Treaty of Maastricht has given the Council a central purpose, ie it is the decision-making body of the Community. The heads of State or heads of government of the Member States and the President of the Commission meet regularly at sessions attended solely by politicians. These are the famous European summits. The Council itself brings together the representatives of governments (1 per country) and its President is designated in turn for a period of

The "Cheese Box" building

Ch. Bastin et J. Évrard

6 months in order to avoid any risk of hegemony. During sessions, decisions are taken by simple majority, by qualified majority or unanimously depending on the subject under discussion. For example, the Council can only amend Commission proposals by unanimous decision. The composition of the Council, then, varies depending on the subject being discussed – social matters, agriculture, economics and finance, environment, industry, fishing, transport etc. But it is the Ministers of Foreign Affairs who are actually considered as the main representatives of their countries. They are assisted in their task by a committee of permanent representatives who rank as ambassadors and who are themselves assisted by some one hundred or more working parties consisting of diplomats and high-ranking civil servants seconded from ministries in the Member States.

The European Commission – *10 000 of its 13 200 statutory civil servants (to which should be added a vast number of fixed-duration contracts signed with experts in various fields) work in Brussels.* This body has a threefold purpose. Firstly, it is the guardian of the treaties and, as such, it is required to ensure that they are correctly applied. This task makes the Commission a body of enquiry and board of control. Secondly, it is the Community's executive body and it therefore draws up the legal texts, orders and regulations in addition to managing Community funds. Thirdly, it instigates Community policies in order to guarantee its coherence which means that it draws up the European laws under discussion before tabling them in the form of a proposal to the Council. It consists of 17 members appointed by the governments of Member States for a 4-year term. The members are independent as regards their governments or the Council and only the Parliament is empowered to seek their automatic resignation by voting on a censure motion.

The Court of Justice – *Headquarters in Luxembourg.* The Court consists of 13 judges and 6 prosecutors designated by the governments of Member States for a 6-year term of office. The Court monitors the legality of Community legislation and gives rulings on the interpretation and validity of legislation laid down under Community law. Its procedures are in many ways similar to those used in all High Courts of Justice in Member States. It has the power to inflict ordinary fines or fines for contempt on a State if it does not comply with a ruling. A lower Court was set up in 1989 and has special competence with regard to the ECSC Treaty, rules on fair competition, and cases instigated by private individuals against public bodies and the authorities set up by the European Community. It cannot rule on commercial cases.

The Court of Auditors – *Headquarters in Luxembourg.* Set up in 1975, the Court of Auditors is required to exercise budgetary controls on the legality, accuracy and financial management of the income provided by European taxpayers and managed by the

European Union. Its 12 members are appointed for a 6-year period by the Council of the European Community. The Court draws up an annual report at the end of each financial year and the report is published in the Official Journal, accompanied by the replies from official bodies to the observations and comments made by the Court.

In addition to these five institutions, there is the **Economic and Social Committee** (ECOSOC) and the **Committee of the Regions.** ECOSOC has 189 members and represents various sectors of economic and social life (employers, workers, self-employed, farmers etc.). The Regional Committee also has 189 members but is more politicised inasmuch as it reflects regional and local authorities in Member States. It can give an opinion on any proposal forwarded to the Economic and Social Committee.

EUROPE IN QUESTION

1. What are the symbols of the European Community? Firstly, an azure blue flag with 12 gold stars (the number is invariable) set out in a circle. It was selected in 1955.

Secondly, the European anthem which is the prelude to the *Ode to Joy* in Ludwig van Beethoven's 9th Symphony. The version used is an arrangement by Herbert van Karajan adopted in 1972.

2. Are the Union's citizens in favour of the unification of Western Europe? Yes, to a very large extent. According to a survey carried out in 1993, ie when the Community had 12 Member States, 73% of citizens questioned declared themselves in favour of unification and 9% had no opinion. The least favourable to unification (this comes as no surprise) are said to be the British (only 59% in favour) and the Danes (62% in favour). These figures should not, of course, be confused with the results of the referenda carried out in Denmark, Ireland and France concerning the Maastricht Treaty signed in 1992.

3. What were the implications of the Maastricht Treaty? The Treaty of Maastricht, which was signed on 7 February 1992 and which took effect on 1 November 1993, set up the European Union. Its main innovations were as follows: (1) the strengthening of the Community's powers; (2) the setting-up of a common defence policy; (3) a social policy based on common principles; (4) a common foreign policy; (5) common rules relating to political asylum and immigration; (6) the limiting of the Community's responsibility to matters that could not be dealt with on a national level; (7) a single European currency; (8) regional participation in decision-making; (9) closer co-operation in the fight against drugs and organised crime; (10) the ability to vote in municipal elections for citizens resident in another Member State; (11) legislative power granted to the European Parliament; (12) monetary stability in an effort to combat inflation.

4. What does the Single Market imply? The removal of checks on goods at national borders and a guarantee that individuals will not be required to pay the same tax twice when purchasing goods for their own use. Common security for citizens and the right to settle freely in any other Member State. Recognition of professional qualifications by all Member States. Extension of competition.

5. What can be taken from one country to another with no restrictions? With the exception of Denmark: 800 cigarettes, 400 cigarillos, 200 cigars, 1 kg tobacco, 10 litres spirits, 20 litres aperitifs, 90 litres wine (including 60 litres sparkling wines), 110 litres beer. These figures can be increased on condition that the person transporting the goods can prove they are destined solely for private use.

6. How is the European Union financed? Member States make over the income from Customs & Excise duty and agricultural duties. They also pay a percentage of the income from VAT. The remainder of a State's financial contribution depends on its ability to pay. In 1994, the budget amounted to 70 billion ecus.

7. What was the Schengen Accord? It was signed on 19 June 1990 and aims gradually to remove controls at border crossings between Member States who were signatories of the Accord (Germany, Belgium, France, Luxembourg, and the Netherlands in 1985, Italy in 1990, Spain and Portugal in 1991 etc.). The Accord came into effect in 1995 but the Schengen Space has met a few problems as regards its application (especially on the part of France) due mainly to the fight against drugs (this has been made difficult because of the distinctive policies implemented by the Netherlands) and to certain particular situations such as, for example, the ease with which people can claim naturalisation and the attractiveness of the benefits system in certain countries. EU citizens have total freedom of movement within the Schengen Space.

Any request for asylum is looked at by an individual State which was a signatory of the Accord, ie the one in which relatives of the applicant are already living, the one which issued him/her a visa or the first one in which the applicant arrived, even as an illegal immigrant.

8. How large is the European Union's share of the world market? In 1992, not taking into account the level of trade between Member States within the Community, the European Union achieved export levels of 20.7% as against 16.4% for the United States, 12.4% for Japan, 4.9% for Canada and 45.7% for the rest of the world.

9. Is the Council of Europe part of the European Community? No. It should not be confused with the European Council. The Council of Europe was set up in 1949 and has its headquarters in Strasbourg, with offices in Paris and Brussels. In 1993, it had 28 members. Its aim is to strengthen the ties between members in order to promote the ideals and principles that make up their common heritage. This was why it recently developed the Demosthenes programme, in an attempt to help Central and Eastern European countries to implement their constitutional, legislative and administrative reforms.

10. What does European citizenship mean? It means that a citizen of a European country can enjoy the protection of any diplomatic and consular authority of another Member State if his/her own country is not represented in the country in which he/she finds himself/herself. It also means that the citizen can vote and be elected in the municipal election in the Member State in which he/she is resident.

11. Which countries have applied to join the European Union? In 1987, Morocco asked to become a member of the EEC but was refused by virtue of Section 237 of the Treaty of Rome (members must be European States). Members must also be democratic States. Turkey, Cyprus, Malta, Hungary and Poland have all applied for membership at the present time. A national referendum was held recently in Switzerland and Norway, where the population voted against joining the Union.

12. What are the conditions demanded of applicants for membership? Countries wishing to join the EU are required to accept unconditionally the terms of the Treaty of Rome and the modifications made to it by the Treaty of Maastricht. A transitional period is, however, provided for so that new members can adapt existing structures. This period also enables the Community to revise its own standards if the applicant country has standards which are higher in a given sector than the Community's own. Special conditions are laid down during negotiations prior to membership; they vary from one country to another.

13. Are Europeans in favour of a common defence policy? Yes. 77% of them are in favour according to a survey carried out in 1993. The Italians would appear to be the most favourable (83%); the Danes the least enthusiastic (45%).

14. Who have been the Presidents of the Commission? Walter Hallstein from Germany (1958-1967), the Belgian Jean Roy (1967-1970), the Italian Franco Malfatti (1971-1972), the Frenchman François-Xavier Ortoli (1973-1976), Roy Harris Jenkins from the UK (1977-1980), Gaston Thorn from Luxembourg (1981-1984), Jacques Delors from France (1985-1994) and Jacques Santer from Luxembourg (1995-).

Wysocki/EXPLORER

Reigns of successive Royal Families

Carolingians

977-991	Charles of France, Duke of Lower Lotharingia
991-1005	Otto I, Duke of Lower Lotharingia

House of Louvain

1005-1015	Lambert I, Count of Louvain, known as the Elder
1015-1038	Henry I, Count of Louvain
1038-1041	Otto of Louvain
1041-1063	Lambert II, Count of Louvain, called Balderic
1063-1079	Henry II, Count of Louvain
1079-1095	Henry III, Count of Louvain
1095-1140	Godefroid I the Bearded
1140-1142	Godefroid II the Younger
1142-1190	Godefroid III the Valiant
1190-1235	Henry I the Warrior
1235-1248	Henry II the Magnanimous
1248-1261	Henry III the Merciful
1261-1294	John I the Victorious
1294-1312	John II the Peace-Loving
1312-1355	John III the Triumphant
1355-1406	Jeanne
1406-1415	Anthony (Valois of Burgundy)
1415-1427	John IV
1427-1430	Philip I of Saint-Pol

House of Burgundy

1430-1467	Philip the Good
1467-1477	Charles the Bold
1477-1482	Mary of Burgundy
1482-1493	Maximilian of Austria
1493-1506	Philip I the Handsome (Habsburg of the Low Countries)
1506-1515	Margaret of Austria

Spanish rule

1515-1555	Emperor Charles the Fifth
1555-1598	Philip II (Habsburg of Spain)
1598-1621	Isabel of Austria and Albert
1621-1633	Isabel of Austria
1633-1665	Philip IV
1665-1700	Charles II
1700-1706	Philip V of Anjou (Bourbon)

Austrian rule

1713-1740	Charles VI (Habsburg of Austria)
1740-1780	Maria Theresa
1780-1790	Joseph II (Lorraine)
1790-1792	Leopold II
1792-1795	Francis II

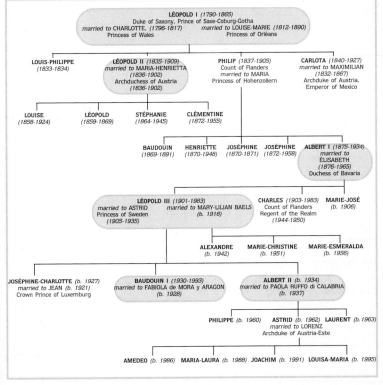

King Albert II and Queen Paola

French rule

1795-1799	Directoire: Commissaire Bouteville
1799-1804	Consulate: Napoleon Bonaparte
1804-1815	Empire: Napoleon I

Dutch government

1815-1830	William I of Orange-Nassau

Independence

1830-1831	Regency of Baron Surlet de Chokier
1831-1865	Leopold I of Saxe-Coburg-Gotha
1865-1909	Leopold II
1909-1934	Albert I
1934-1951	Leopold III
1944-1950	Regency of Prince Charles
1951-1993	Baudouin I
1993-	Albert II

MICHELIN GUIDES

The **Red Guides** (hotels and restaurants)

Benelux - Deutschland - España Portugal - Main Cities Europe - France - Great Britain and Ireland - Italia - Suisse

The **Green Guides** (fine art, historical monuments, scenic routes)

Austria - Belgium and Luxembourg - California - Canada - Chicago - England: the West Country - France - Germany - Great Britain - Greece - Ireland - Italy - London - Mexico - Netherlands - New England - New York City - Paris - Portugal - Quebec - Rome - Scotland - Spain - Switzerland - Tuscany - Washington DC

...and the collection of regional guides for France.

The arts in Brussels

Some people may be surprised not to find the names of several great Belgian artists in this chapter. A number of old masters worked in Bruges, Antwerp and Liège and cannot, therefore, be included in a chapter dealing with art in Brussels. Moreover, although Art lost its restrictive regional aspects after the 1830 revolution, the inclusion of every tendency and trend that manifested itself in Belgium would not be representative of art in the capital city.

ARCHITECTURE

Romanesque Architecture (early 11C - early 13C) – Romanesque architecture did not result in the creation of a Belgian School as such. It did not appear in the Brabant region until the 11C and its introduction was due to the influence of the Rhenish School for Brabant had been part of the Holy Roman Empire since the Treaty of Verdun, signed in 843 AD. Brussels has 4 complete Romanesque buildings and a few traces of Romanesque architecture in some of its churches – the crypt of Saint-Guidon in Anderlecht, the church of Saint-Lambert in Woluwe, the Sainte-Anne chapel in Auderghem and the church of Saint-Clément in Watermael-Boitsfort. These buildings are all part of the so-called Mosan tradition, constructed of sandstone from Lède except in Auderghem where there is a decorative combination of materials. The churches are all designed to a basilica-type layout with side entrance and huge bell tower. The one exception is the church of Saint-Clément which is built in the shape of a Latin Cross.

Romanesque-Ogival Architecture (early 13C - mid 13C) – This was a transitional style which reflected the political economy of its day. It was influenced by the style prevalent in the north of France and was introduced via Flanders. Its main characteristics are semi-circular arches, pointed arches and columns. Two major buildings of this type are Notre-Dame-de-la-Chapelle (chancel and transept) and the cathedral church of Saints-Michel-et-Gudule (chevet).

Early Gothic (mid 13C – early 14C) – Although the decoration on the capitals still bears traces of the Romanesque style, Early Gothic was marked by the introduction of vertical lines, an example of which is the inclusion of tall towers. Arches, doors and windows became ogival and were subdivided into sections. Balustrades and pinnacles added a decorative touch to the building. The embellishments changed to include garlands round the cornice and crockets and finials on the gables. The cathedral church of Saints-Michel-et-Gudule is a fine example of Pointed Gothic; others include the church of Saint-Denis in Forest and the former church in Laeken (chancel).

Radiating Gothic (early 14C – late 14C) – There are very few examples of this style in Brussels. It is characterised by the richness and realism of the decorative features. Capitals were decorated with the famous Brabant crocket and engaged columns rose to a vaulted roof with elliptical ribs. Windows were widened and the tracery included the use of geometric designs.

Flamboyant Gothic (early 15C – early 16C) – The finest buildings in the capital date from this period of Gothic architecture. They include the church of Saints-Pierre-et-Guidon in Anderlecht, the cathedral church of Saints-Michel-et-Gudule (towers,

Gothic Architecture in Brabant

Gothic architecture provided a solution to an essential need of medieval builders faced with the requirement to construct buildings that were vast, tall and full of light. The main features of the style are the vaulted roof over intersecting ribs and external support in the form of piers which gradually became lighter and more ethereal until they formed flying buttresses. In Brabant, architects sought inspiration in the great French cathedrals but lessened the height. However, the modifications they made to their models created a specific style which then spread to places outside the province.

Churches in Brabant have a nave, two aisles, and an ambulatory with radiating chapels. They also feature a massive tower forming a porch on the west front and side chapels topped with triangular gables set in a row like terraced houses. In many instances, there is no transept and the rose windows have been replaced by large bays. The interior is very different to the interiors of churches built in other styles. The nave has robust cylindrical pillars with capitals decorated, originally at least, with a double row of crockets. Later, large statues of the Apostles were placed against the pillars. The chapels in the side aisles were interconnected, forming further aisles. In some instances, the triforium was replaced by a very ornate open-work balustrade.

north aisle, nave, transept), Notre-Dame-de-la-Chapelle (nave, aisles and tower) and Notre-Dame-du-Sablon. Stellar vaulting was brought to Brussels by Mathieu Keldemans (chapel of Saint-Guidon in Anderlecht) and Pierre van Wyenhove (chapel of the Holy Sacrament in the cathedral of Saints-Michel-et-Gudule). Capitals became narrower before disappearing altogether. Decorative features were more complicated and, in some cases, exuberant. Windows were designed in the shape of a flame and rose windows became more complex. There was a plethora of pinnacles but flying buttresses became less important and smaller. French influence waned while the Brabant School was at the height of its popularity.

Vernacular Architecture – Town Halls were also characteristic of Brabant architecture whereas Flanders gave expression to the power and might of its

Ch. Bastin-J. Evrard.

Church of Notre-Dame-de-la-Chapelle

urban authorities through the construction of belfries. The Town Hall in Brussels is a magnificent public building on which work began in 1401. Its design is unusual. It resembles a large house decorated like a reliquary with canopied niches. Other outstanding features include the arcades on the ground floor and the corner turrets similar to those seen on older fortified buildings. In the vicinity of the Town Hall, the houses are built in a pleasing combination of brick and stone, the latter being used as window surrounds, cross-bars and string-courses that add emphasis to the various storeys. The façades are decorated with a pointed gable combining Flemish-style tiers and the stepped tiers common in Germany (none of the gables was built before the late 15C).

16C – The Renaissance had very little impact in Belgium and there are very few Renaissance buildings in Brussels where the churches were designed in the Flamboyant Gothic style, even during this period. The final stage of the cathedral church of Saints-Michel-et-Gudule made use of this style (north chapel) and the only building reminiscent of the Roman *palazzi* was the Palais Granvelle (c1550 but it no longer exists) designed by Sébastien van Noye who sought inspiration in the Palazzo Farnese in Sangallo.

Italianate-Flemish Architecture (17C – mid 18C) – It was Wenceslas Cobergher who introduced the Italian Baroque style into the Netherlands. Two years after his return from Rome, in 1607, he built a church for the Carmelites (it was destroyed in 1785) based on the designs of Giacomo della Porta. However, it was not until Jacques Francart that the creativity of the Italian style was combined with the traditionalism of Gothic architecture. The true Italianate-Flemish style expresses the renewal of Roman Catholicism and is best seen in churches such as Saint-Jean-Baptiste-au-Béguinage, Notre-Dame-des-Riches-Claires, Notre-Dame-de-Bon-Secours, the west front of the church of La Trinité and the church built for the Brigittine Order. The main features of the style are the return of semi-circular arches, the superposition of architectural Orders (Doric, Ionic, Corinthian, Tuscan and composite), the basilica-type, or central, layout, and exuberant ornamentation consisting mainly of scrolls, rustication, cartridges, and statues. Vernacular architecture included highly-ornate façades which reached something like stylistic perfection in the Maison de la Bellone and the houses lining Grand-Place. Built in the period following the reconstruction of the famous square, the church of Notre-Dame-du-Finistère and the church built for the Order of Minor Brothers are transitional constructions which are the precursors of the Classical Age.

Brussels, Capital of Art Nouveau (1893-1910)

Belgium was one of the first countries to become involved in the Art Nouveau Movement and the first buildings to be designed in this style were the Hôtel Tassel (**Victor Horta**, 1861-1947) and the house belonging to **Paul Hankar** (1859-1901).

Palais Stoclet

Art Nouveau is undoubtedly connected with a small progressive group of lay people, all of them young intellectuals who expressed enthusiastic support for this radically new style of architecture. Thanks to them, Art Nouveau was able to develop. Traditional building materials (stone, glass and timber) were still used but new materials (steel and concrete) were also included in designs that were created rationally. Horta was resolutely innovatory in the layout of private housing, creating a well of light on which all the rooms are centred. The interiors of his own home (now the **Musée Horta**) and of private mansions such as the Hôtel Van Eetvelde or the Hôtel Solvay are a remarkable example of a total work of art in which curves are the predominant feature.

Paul Hankar, whose most outstanding designs were the Hôtel Ciamberlani and the window of the De Backer flower shop, belonged to the more geometric tendency of Art Nouveau.

Henri van de Velde (1863-1957) built his own villa, "Bloemenwerf" in 1895 on Avenue Vanderaey in Uccle, in a style reminiscent of an English cottage.

Among the major buildings of this period, there is also Saintenoy's **Old England** which is soon to house the **Musée instrumental**, the **Maison du St-Cyr** designed by Strauven (this building is remarkable for its narrow frontage), the houses in Rue Vanderschrick designed by Ernest Blérot, the poster-façade of the **Maison Cauchie** and the Hôtel Hannon designed by Jules Brunfaut.

The very famous **Palais Stoclet** designed by Joseph Hoffmann, an Austrian architect, was, like Dr. Van Neck's orthopaedic clinic designed by Antoine Pompe, a precursor of the modern style.

Neo-Classical Architecture (late 18C – mid 19C) – Neo-Classical architecture was a reaction against the ornamental exaggeration of the Italianate-Flemish style and it had its heyday in Brussels when Charles of Lorraine was Governor. Place Royale and the church of Saint-Jacques-sur-Coudenberg (architects: Nicolas Barré and Barnabé Guimard), the Palais de la Nation and the area round about, the Palais des Académies (architects: C van der Straeten and T-F Suys), the Théâtre Royal de la Monnaie, the Galeries Saint-Hubert (architect: J-P Cluysenaar), the Hospice Pachéco, Place des Barricades and the pavilions in the botanical gardens are the most outstanding examples of the style. The architecture of this period was undoubtedly influenced by the Louis XIV style but it has been combined with Austrian features to produce a style which is particularly evident on Place des Martyrs (C-A Fisco). The decorative features are austere, the façades include a single architectural Order instead of the former plurality, and barrel vaulting enjoyed a major comeback.

Eclecticism (2nd half of 19C) – A small number of architects were exponents of the neo-Gothic (Maison du Roi designed by Pierre-Victor Jamaer and Notre-Dame in Laeken designed by Joseph Poelaert) or Romanesque-Byzantine style (Sainte-Marie designed by L van Overstraeten) but gradually the buildings became more and more like wedding cakes. Examples of this can be seen in the Banque nationale (F Beraert) or the Stock Exchange (L Suys). This period ended with two almost opposing trends – the exaggerated monumentalism of Joseph Poelaert (Law Courts) and the austere Classicism of Alphonse Balat (Musée d'Art ancien and the glasshouses in Laeken). It was also during this period that the boulevards were laid out in the city centre, that

Gédéon Bordiau built the gigantic complex known as the Cinquantenaire, and that Charles Girault designed the Musée de Tervuren. In short, this was the reign of the great King Leopold II who left the imprint of his personality on everything connected with architecture and town planning in the capital city.

As well as this eclectic architecture, the end of the 19C saw the development of the **Flemish neo-Renaissance style** seen at its best in the Théâtre flamand (K.V.S.) designed by J Baes.

20C – After Victor Horta, a number of Belgian architects began to make use of the modernist style and attempted to resolve the problem of collective housing. This was the 1920's, the era of the garden-cities, among them **Le Logis** and **Floréal** designed by J-J Eggerickx and L-M van der Swaelmen in Watermael-Boitsfort and the **Kapelleveld** garden city in Woluwe-Saint-Lambert designed by the architects Pompe, Hoste, Van der Swaelmen, Rubbers and Hoeben. Also during this period, **Louis-Herman de Koninck** designed several geometrically-shaped houses in Uccle bringing innovation to the private housing market by introducing reinforced concrete shells. This was the time of **Art Deco**, a style that can be seen in the Résidence Palace (1923-1926), the Palais des Beaux-Arts (1920-1928), the superb interior of the Musée Van Buuren (1928) in Uccle and in the Palais de la Folle Chanson (1928), an apartment block in Ixelles.

After the Second World War, it was decided to renovate the city centre after creating the north-south junction (Jonction Nord-Midi). This railway line, which runs partly underground, was inaugurated in 1952 and was designed to link two stations – Gare du Midi and Gare du Nord. It was a major project, leading to a complete facelift for the area between the **Lower end of the town** (boulevards in the city centre and Grand-Place) and the **Top end of the town** (the hills around the town's park). In 1958, when the underpasses were built for the **inner ring road** (petite ceinture), Brussels hosted its second World Fair (it attracted 41 500 000 visitors) with the **Atomium** as its symbol and the motto, Building the World for Mankind. The key word was definitely "building", indeed architectural conferences today now refer to the "Brusselisation" of a city. It took ten years of intensive work to change the entire look of the capital and a large number of public or private buildings continued to spring up within its boundaries in the years following the World Fair. Among them are the Cité Administrative (1958-1984, public sector offices), the Banque Bruxelles Lambert (1959), the Tour du Midi (1962-1967), the Centre Berlaymont (1967), the Bibliothèque royale (1969, royal library), the central post office and the local government offices for the city of Brussels (1971), and the Musée d'Art moderne (1978-1984). The renovation of the Théâtre de la Monnaie (1985-1986) must also be included in this list. On the outskirts of Brussels are the superb Glaverbel building (1963), the Royale belge (1966-1967 and 1985) and the head offices of the CBR company (1968) in Watermael-Boitsfort; and the Maison médicale (1975) on the campus of the Université Catholique in Woluwe-Saint-Lambert.

PAINTING

15C – The Primitives played a vital role in the history of painting in Flanders. One of them, Rogier de la Pasture, was named (1436) as the official painter of the town of Brussels where he took the name of **Rogier van der Weyden**. His presence encouraged the development of a veritable Brussels School but Vrancke van der Stockt, Pierre van der Weyden, Colin de Coter and the Master of the View of Sainte-Gudule were not on a par with the great "Master Rogier" and the town decided not to replace him after his death.

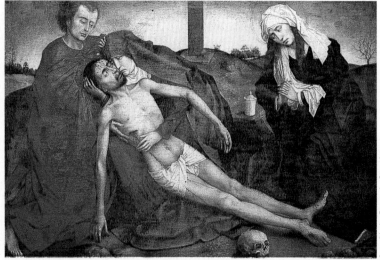

Pietà, Rogier van der Weyden

16C – This century was marked by a trend towards the Italianate style. Jean Gossart who was summoned to Brussels by Margaret of Austria travelled to Brussels from Rome as did **Bernard van Orley**, an artist greatly praised by his contemporaries. He met Raphael and then handed on his skill and artistry to Michel Coxie and Pieter Coecke whose daughter was to marry the greatest Flemish artist of the century, **Pieter Brueghel the Elder.** Brueghel settled in Brussels in 1563 and, although he also visited Italy, it was his observations of the morals and lifestyle of villages in the Brabant region which provided some of the finest works in the history of painting.

17C – The Brussels School lost some of its influence to Antwerp, home of Peter Paul Rubens, Anthony van Dyck and Jacob Jordaens. In the capital of Brabant, Gaspard de Crayer, the painter of religious themes was particularly productive and David Teniers the Younger, a genre painter, proved to be a genius in moving from the realism of the century in which he lived to the pastoral scenes of the 18C. Finally, the city boasted a myriad of landscape artists, the most eminent being Jacques d'Arthois and Denis van Alsloot.

18C – Output increased but quality dropped, mainly for reasons relating to speculation and many an artist made use of an art form that was "Rubens-like". Two artists stood out from the others – Victor Janssens, who painted mainly religious subjects and scenes from mythology, and André Corneille Lens who introduced neo-Classicism.

19C – The French artist Jacques Louis David was exiled to Brussels where he acted, in some ways, as the leader of a school that was to develop with the revolution. In fact, it was a man from Wallonia who took over from David in Brussels and became the father of the Belgian School. He was François Joseph Navez, who painted numerous portraits, genre scenes, and religious or historical works. Several tendencies followed each other or existed side by side – Romanticism with Gustave Wappers, Louis Gallait and **Antoine Wiertz,** both of whom were followed by a whole army of secondary artists, genre painting with Jean Baptiste Madou, a new wave of landscape artists such as François Roffiaen, Paul Lauters and Jean-Baptiste Kindermans, portrait painting with Liévin de Winne, animal paintings with Joseph Stevens, the Tervuren School whose finest exponent was Hippolyte Boulanger, Realism with **Charles de Groux** and **Constantin Meunier** (they owed much to Jean Portaels). Alfred Stevens was very famous in Paris during his lifetime. He specialised in paintings of women. Eugène Smits, on the other hand, cultivated a fashionable form of eclecticism. Guillaume Vogels was a great landscape artist and the precursor of Impressionism in Belgium. This movement was represented by two students from the Académie de Bruxelles, Henri Evenepoel and Théo van Rysselberghe. Towards the end of the century, several trends and new styles co-existed in Brussels. George Lemmen and Auguste Oleffe were neo-Impressionists, Léon Frédéric worked in the same style as the Primitives, and **Fernand Khnopff's** work was influenced by the British Pre-Raphaelites although he used the style prevalent in Symbolism. Eugène Laermans painted works that were already Expressionist, and Xavier Mellery used the chiaroscuro techniques in his drawings. In doing so, he showed affinities with the charcoal sketches created by Seurat. Brussels, then, was bubbling over with avant-garde artistic talent, as shown by **Les XX,** a movement which was founded in Brussels in 1893. It organised exhibitions, inviting French artists such as Rodin, Signac, Pisarro, Seurat, Toulouse-Lautrec and Gauguin and Dutch artists (Toorop and Van Gogh). It placed the emphasis on individualism and its primary aims were to break away from the Academic style of earlier years and instigate an artistic revival.

20C – The paintings of **Rik Wouters** let a ray of sunshine into the early years of the century. Classed as a Colourist, his work is reminiscent of Cézanne's and the paintings created by the early Fauvists. He paved the way for **Fauvism in the Brabant area** and the style was to produce such famous names as Fernand Schirren, Edgard Tytgat and Jean Brusselmans. The last two then gradually changed their style and adopted Expressionism.

Le Flûtiste by Rik Wouters

Musées Royaux des Beaux-Arts

Surrealism was very active in Belgium, particularly in Brussels. It first appeared in 1926 and the movement included **René Magritte** whose technique was used to represent the imaginary, although his works remained understandable by everybody. The most outstanding artists of this time were Paul Nougé, E.L.T. Mesens, Raoul Ubac and, of course, **Paul Delvaux** whose figures are shown wandering through scenes like stage sets. The main exponents of abstract art were Victor Servranckx and Jo Delahaut. In 1948, after the Second World War, Christian Dotremont from Belgium created the **COBRA group** in Paris (COpenhagen, BRussels, Amsterdam) led by the Dane Asger Jorn, the Dutchman Karel Appel and **Pierre Alechinsky** from Brussels. From 1960 onwards, artists in Brussels followed the main international trends. Among them were Roger Somville (Expressionism). One artist stands out from the others. He is **Marcel Broodthaers** who was originally known as a poet before imagining a conceptual art form that criticised the mechanisms surrounding major works of art. Finally, no description of Art would be complete without a mention for the career of **Jean-Michel Folon** the illustrator from Brussels whose simple pictorial language is eloquent for everybody.

SCULPTURE

13C and 14C – In Brabant, sculpture showed a marked taste for the grotesque (gargoyles on Notre-Dame-de-la-Chapelle).

15C – As wars led to a decrease in the population in towns in Meuse, a Brabant School of sculpture developed and reached its height in Brussels c1450 (galleries and the entrance to the Town Hall). In addition to the carvings in stone which were used as architectural decoration, the artists, drawing inspiration from painting, produced countless wooden **altarpieces** which are remarkable for the finesse of the carving and their realism. The reredos was a speciality of the Brabant area. It was usually rectangular and fitted with shutters that were painted in bright, vibrant colours. Inside, in a frame of architectural design were scenes painted in the round which became gradually more realistic and more intricate as time passed (see the magnificent St George Reredos by **Jan Borman** in the Musées royaux d'Art et d'Histoire). The same picturesque trend is evident in the carvings on the choir stalls. The armrests and misericords in various churches were decorated with satirical figures full of imagination, providing a pitiless illustration of human vice.

16C – Sculpture was an extension of medieval art and workshops continued to produce altarpieces which were full of pathos. Later, there was a return to greater simplicity. At the same time, a number of outstanding figures came to the fore, especially in Flanders. **Jean Mone**, sculptor to Charles V and a native of Metz, was strongly influenced by Italy. He settled in Malines near Brussels where his influence was clearly felt (reredos in Sainte-Gudule).

17C – Single statues began to appear owing to "Jesuit art". **Luc Fayd'herbe**, one of Rubens' pupils, introduced the Italian Baroque style then gave it his own personal touch, but local sculpture retained its characteristics (realism, veracity and naturalism). **Jérôme Duquesnoy the Elder**, whose works are reminiscent of those of Corneille Floris, made *Manneken Pis*. His son, François, a friend of Nicolas Poussin, was so talented that Pope Urban VIII commissioned him to decorate the canopy created by Bernini. Jérôme, François' brother, was an outstanding portrait artist (St Thomas, St Paul, St Matthew and St Bartholomew in the cathedral church of Saints-Michel-et-Gudule).

St George Reredos

18C – Between the Baroque and Classical periods sculptors produced a plethora of fine wood carvings (choirstalls in Grimbergen and the pulpit in the cathedral of Saints-Michel-et-Gudule). Figures are shown in movement and the clothing is attractively draped. This can be seen in the *Fontaine de Minerve* (Place du Grand Sablon) by Jacques Bergé who also produced a large number of terra cotta pieces. In addition to Pierre-Denis Plumier (courtyard of the Town Hall), the main figures of the day were Laurent Delvaux from Ghent (Palais de Lorraine), and Gilles-Lambert Godecharle (pediment on the Palais de la Nation), a talented artist who had an unfortunate, and rather too frequent, tendency to copy Canova or Houdon.

19C – At the dawn of the new century, Mathieu Kessels paved the way for a return to Classicism (*Le Lanceur de disques* on the Palais de l'Académie). The century was strongly influenced by the French School with the arrival of François Rude, Albert Carrière-Belleuse and Auguste Rodin. Romanticism had its outstanding figure in the person of Willem Geefs who produced an enormous number of pieces with his four brothers overseeing the work of his assistants. Charles Fraikin and Eugène Simonis were part of this movement. Halfway through the century, three trends became apparent. Firstly, there were those who worked in the Italianate style, among them the amazing Paul de Vigne, Thomas Vinçotte, Julien Dillens and Charles van der Stappen. Then came the sculptors who claimed to be part of the Flemish Renaissance such as Jef Lambeaux. Finally, there was a Realist tendency headed by **Constantin Meunier** whose works are too little-known. The "Italians" were replaced by Charles Samuël, Jules Lagae or Victor Rousseau. Georg Minne and his neo-Primitive art form took the Realist tendency into the following century.

20C – The art of movement and the Baroque plasticity of Rik Wouters' work make him part of the great tradition of Flemish artists who have provided so many strong, daring pieces over the years despite the fact that he is usually classified among the Impressionists. Following in the footsteps of G Minne, Oscar Jespers and Joseph Cantré represented Expressionist concepts. Among the pioneers of the post-war years are Maurice Carlier and Félix Roulin. The works of **Jacques Moeschal**, inventor of the "signals", can be

Denille.EUREKA SLIDE

Fountain designed by Pol Bury

seen along the motorways and in towns and cities. They are made of concrete and steel. **Pol Bury,** a Walloon who is nevertheless close to the COBRA Movement, has been producing kinetic works since the 1950's. These are works in which there is always movement (sculptures fitted with motors, balls, hydraulics etc.). Finally, André Willequet, Olivier Strebelle and André Ghysels have been among the leading sculptors of the last few decades.

TAPESTRY

Background Facts – Tapestries were designed to decorate the walls of castles, churches and the homes of the wealthy; sometimes they provided the background decoration for festivities and special events. Series (ie several tapestries illustrating the same theme) travelled with princes and high-ranking dignitaries so that they could enjoy privacy wherever they stopped. In Europe, tapestry developed mainly from the second half of the 14C onwards and became particularly important, especially in Brussels. The first tapestries were mainly religious compositions. Later, they represented historical tableaux, hunting scenes, allegories, and scenes from mythology. In 1526, a decree required tapestry-makers to weave their mark into the border, with the emblem of the city or town. In Brussels, this consisted of a double "B" (for Brussels and Brabant) flanking a small red shield.

The Technique – Tapestries are made on looms on which two rows of thread (the brightly-coloured warp and neutrally-coloured woof) are crossed to form a motif. The patterns are based on a painted pattern or "cartoon". If the warp is horizontal, the tapestry is described as being low-warp; if it is vertical, the tapestry is high-warp (low-warp tapestry is commonest in Belgium). The woof consists of woollen threads often combined with silk, gold or silver.

Brussels – The oldest known Brussels tapestries date from the second half of the 15C. The technique used was sophisticated and the compositions were still Gothic in style. In 1466, the Dukes of Burgundy put in their first commission and this marked the beginning of the heyday of the industry in Brussels. At the end of the 15C and during the early years of the 16C, interest in the Italian Renaissance led to the development, encouraged by the Humanists, of a characteristic highly-decorative style. Compositions became huge, reproducing depth and perspective, and the scenes were presented with great attention to detail. They represented only one subject at a time. The many figures were dressed in lavish costumes, draped like pieces of sculpture, the landscapes were dotted with Renaissance buildings, and plants were depicted in meticulous detail. The borders were filled with flowers, fruit and masks, ani-

Tapestry, Notre-Dame-du-Sablon

Musées Royaux d'Art et d'Histoire

mals or scrolls. In or about 1516, Pieter van Aelst, alias d'Enghien, completed a commission from Pope Leo X for the Sistine Chapel. The *Actes des Apôtres* was made to drawings by Raphael. From then on, all the great princes of the western world commissioned tapestries from Brussels and the Italian style triumphed in Flanders. **Bernard van Orley** was considered to be the greatest exponent of this art form. He made the series of *Honneurs* created *c.* 1520 for Charles V, the *Légende de Notre-Dame du Sablon* (1516-1518) and *Les Chasses de Maximilien*, a tapestry that was actually made by Guillaume de Pannemaker, one of a talented family of tapestry-makers. Charles V's Court painter, Pieter Coecke, produced the cartoons for the *Péchés capitaux* and the *Histoire de Saint-Paul*. In the early 17C, Brussels lost its supremacy but commissions continued to flood in. Numerous tapestries were made to sketches by Rubens *(Les Triomphes du Saint-Sacrement)* and Jordaens *(Proverbes, Vie à la campagne)*. They differ from others for their sense of the dramatic, the use of perspective, and the width of their borders. In 1712, Josse de Vos made *La Conquête de Tunis* for Vienne and *Les Campagnes du général duc de Marlborough* for Blenheim Palace in England. However, the number of master tapestry-makers fell sharply and at the end of the 18C the last of the workshops in Brussels finally closed its doors.

LACE MAKING

This art form probably came originally from Venice, although Flanders claims to have discovered bobbin-lace. It is made on a cushion or pillow. The threads are stretched on bobbins and crossed over to form either a net or a pattern. The piece of lace is pinned onto the pillow. The original form of lace was purely geometric (mid 15C) and used to decorate clothing. Flemish painters show people wearing lace collars and cuffs. The craft was taught to young girls in schools and soon became popular. Once the period of wars and conflicts was over, the craft became a source of prosperity again and, in the 17C, Flanders lace enjoyed an unrivalled reputation. Brussels was one of the main centres of lace making at that time, along with Bruges, Malines and Antwerp. The schools each had their own characteristics but, until the end of the 17C, the term "Flanders lace" was used to describe output from the southern part of the Netherlands, ie Antwerp, Ghent, Liège, Malines, Valenciennes and Brussels where most of the lace was needle-point.

During the early years of the 18C, Brussels lace became a net based on round stitches. The finer "drochel" net consisting of small, hexagonal stitches took pride of place as of 1760 in order to fit in with the ornate requirements of the Louis XV style. In those days, Brussels lace was the most highly sought-after and it was also the most expensive because it took a long time to make and required a great deal of care and attention. This explains why it was reserved almost exclusively for royal families.

LETTERS

The presence of French intellectuals in Brussels after the *coup d'état* of 2 December 1851 stimulated intellectual life in the capital and encouraged such local talents as André van Hasselt (1805-1874) who was little-known when he died and, more especially, **Charles de Coster** (1827-1879) whose masterpiece *The Glorious Adventures of Tyl Ulenspiegel* was considered by liberals and freemasons as a basic principle for life. The main character, Till Eulenspiegel, was portrayed on the silver screen by Gérard Philipe. Another of Brussels' authors was **Camille Lemonnier** (1844-1913) who was nicknamed the "Marshal of Belgian Letters". His best-known works were *Un Mâle* and *La Belgique*, his famous epitome. Under the impetus of Jules Destrée, the literary movement gained momentum again after the First World War but, like most of their compatriots, the writers of Brussels chose to work outside their own country. They included **Fernand Crommelynck** *(The Splendid Cuckold)*, the Rosny brothers or Charles Plisnier, a native of Mons who won the literary Goncourt Prize for his work *Faux Passeports*. **Michel de Ghelderode,** on the other hand, a daring dramatist who wrote a great many works, lived in Ixelles. Although most of these writers were French-speaking, the Romantic writer Henri Conscience was a Dutch-speaker as was the great Catholic poet Guido Gezelle (1830-1899), both of whom lived in Brussels. Stanislas André Steeman, the father of the humorist Stéphane Steeman, won success with the publication of his book *L'Assassin habite au 21*. At the present time, **Pierre Mertens** (winner of the Prix Médicis in 1987 and writer of *Eblouissements*) is the best-known of all Brussels' authors.

The Belgian forgery business

In a letter sent to Countess Hanska, Honoré de Balzac wrote "I am thirty years old and more than 200,000 francs in debt. Belgium possesses the million I have earned." According to local legislation at the time, and until the Franco-Belgian Agreement in 1852, forgery was a lawful business. This accounts for the huge number of books by French authors that were published in Brussels. On a visit to the city, François-René de Chateaubriand deemed the procedure to be unscrupulous and complained to Louis XVIII who made an unsuccessful protest to King William I. In fact, the King of the Netherlands purposefully encouraged the liberal ideas that were being refused and refuted by the restored Bourbon monarchy and he even offered subsidies to the forgers. He later had cause to regret his action however, for the industry popularised the French language which he had banned from use in public instruments.

COMIC STRIPS

Belgium has two schools of thought in this respect – Brussels has **Tintin** and Charleroi has Spirou. The latter of the two towns has boasted a number of leading authors such as Charlier, Franquin, Tillieux, Roba or Leloup. Brussels, for its part, is indissoluble from the famous Tintin, who was born on 10 January 1929 in *Le Petit Vingtième*. He was the brilliant creation of Georges Rémi, alias **Hergé,** who also gave us the faithful Snowy, the irascible Captain Haddock and the loony scientist Professor Calculus, all of them involved in the young reporter's many adventures across the globe.

The *Tintin* comic grew out of the legendary comic strip from Brussels; it was first published on 26th September 1946. Hergé was not alone. He worked, among others, with E P Jacobs who was to gain fame with his own heroes Blake and Mortimer. The comic has sadly disappeared in recent times but it defended what might be called the "clear line school" ie particularly meticulous graphics. From the mid 60s onwards this school was develop and change, producing a realistic, more adult and somtimes violent form of comic strip. The comic gradually acquired an international fame that kept pace with its success and it had dozens of heroes. Here is just a short list of some of them, with the dates on which they first appeared – Alix l'Intrépide by Martin (1948), Lefranc reporter by Martin (1952), Dan Cooper by Weinberg (1954), Chick Bill by Tibet (1955), Michel Vaillant by Graton (1957), Oupah-Pah le peau-rouge by Uderzo and Goscinny (1958), Ric Hochet by Tibet (1959), Zig et Puce by Greg (1963), Isnogoud le Vizir by Tabary (1966), Bruno Brazil by Vance (1968), Cubitus by Dupa (1969), Jonathan de Cosey (1975) etc. This brief overview would be incomplete without a mention for the role of the press in the development of comic strips in Brussels. The main national Belgian newspapers traditionally included weekly supplements, usually printed in black and white but occasionally with one additional colour. It was in supplements such as these that readers first made the acquaintance of Quick et Flupke the Brussels kids by Hergé *(Le Petit Vingtième)*, Jehan et Pistolet by Uderzo and Goscinny *(La Libre junior)*, Poussy by Peyo *(Le Soir jeunesse)*.

© SPRL Jean Roba/Dargaud Benelux

ROBA. Boule et Bill

© Dargaud Editeur Paris, 1971

PEYO.
The Astrosmurf

MORRIS ET GOSCINNY
Lucky Luke - Les collines Noires

© Peyo 1970. Licence IMPS, Bruxelles, 1995

WILLY VANDERSTEEN
Bob and Bobette

© Editions Standaard

E.P. JACOBS. Les 3 formules du Professeur Sato

SCHUITEN-PEETERS. La route d'Armilia

FRANQUIN - Gaston Lagaffe

THORGAL - La gardienne des clés

Foreign celebrities in Brussels

Brussels has always attracted men of letters, scientists and artists, just as it has for many years provided asylum for celebrities whose political opinions forced them to leave their native land. This was the case after Louis Napoleon's *coup d'état* of 2 December 1851 which resulted in some sixty members of parliament being sent into exile, among them Victor Hugo, and some 200 refugees arriving in the capital of Brabant (Marcel Duprat, Edgar Quinet, Jules Valles, François Raspail etc.). The exiles chose Belgium and more particularly Brussels because the liberal constitution in this parliamentary monarchy provided them with guarantees that they could not find anywhere else.

Here is an open-ended list of those who left their mark on the city.

Charles Baudelaire (1821-1867): He fled his creditors in Paris, hoping to find an editor for his works in Brussels where he arrived on 24 April 1864. The poet and art critic, disappointed by the failure of a lecture tour, became very bitter and wrote a number of cutting epigrams which were published under the title *Amoenitates Belgicae*. He fell ill and finally left the Hôtel du Grand Miroir for Paris in July 1866.

Hector Berlioz (1803-1869): In 1842, the great Romantic musician personally conducted his *Symphonie Fantastique* in the Église des Augustins (then on Place de Brouckère).

Général Georges Boulanger (1837-1891): The General had been Minister of War and his reforms had made him very popular. He was hoping to be appointed President for life when he was forced to flee Paris in conditions that were little short of farcical. Sentenced in his absence to life imprisonment, he settled in Rue Montoyer. He was unable to bear the death of his mistress, Marguerite de Bonnemain, and committed suicide on her grave in the cemetery in Ixelles where he is buried next to the woman he loved.

Charlotte Brontë (1816-1855): In 1842, she came to teach English to the pupils of the Institut Héger. Her book *Villette* describes the Brussels of the day. She described Leopold I's forehead as having "a strange, painful frown" caused by "constitutional melancholia".

Lord George Gordon Byron (1788-1824): In the spring of 1816, the poet stopped here for 10 days on his way from England to Switzerland. He is said to have written the verses of the Third Song of *Childe Harold* at 51 Rue Ducale which skirts the city park.

Albert Carrier-Belleuse (1824-1887): In 1871, just after the civil war and the Paris Commune, he won the contract for the sculptures decorating the Stock Exchange. He also produced a few more personal works.

Edith Cavell (1865-1915): An English nurse whose patriotism caused her death during the First World War.

François-René de Chateaubriand (1768-1848): Dressed in the uniform of the Regiment of Navarre in order to serve in the Princes' Army, the writer travelled to Brussels where the Counts of Provence and Artois, Louis XVI's brothers, wore the white cockade and showed a certain arrogance despite the warm welcome from the Belgians (the Prince de Ligne had put at their disposal the Château de Beloeil). His name was mentioned as a possible contender for the throne of Belgium.

Paul Claudel (1868-1955): From 1932 to 1935, the author of *The Satin Slipper* was French Ambassador to Belgium. The country made him a gift of his ceremonial sword when he entered the *Académie Française*.

Jacques Louis David (1748-1825): David was a regicide and the second period of Restoration of the Monarchy forced him into exile. He was invited by King William I of the Netherlands and settled in Brussels in 1816. He refrained from taking part in any political activity. He lived in Rue Léopold behind the Mint and had a workshop in Rue de l'Evêque. In 1821, one of the rooms in the City Hall was put at his disposal so that he could paint a copy of *The Coronation of Napoleon I*. He is buried in the city's cemetery.

Alexandre Dumas (1802-1870): He became a political refugee after Louis Napoleon II's *coup d'état* but he fled France mainly to escape from his creditors. He settled in Boulevard de Waterloo where he wrote his *Memoirs*, completed *Ange Pitou*, added a few finishing touches to *The Queen's Necklace*, and wrote a play entitled *La Tour Saint-Jacques*. He invited a constant stream of dinner guests and organised a number of lavish receptions. By the time he left Brussels, his name was synonymous with luxury and affluent living.

Erasmus (1469-1536): In 1521, the universal author of *The Praise of Folly* spent a few months in Anderlecht before moving permanently to Basel. The superb house where the Dutch Humanist lived now bears his name.

Victor Hugo (1802-1885): After being forced to flee from France, he settled in The Pigeon (26-27 Grand-Place) on the day he arrived, 12 December 1851. He lived out his exile at 4 Place des Barricades, and it was from there that he was expelled from Belgium after daring the Belgian government not to accept the new refugees, those who had fought during the Commune and who were demanding recognition as political refugees. In June 1871, he left for Vianden in the Grand Duchy of Luxemburg, after declaring, "The Belgian government has expelled me but it has complied with my wishes. I cannot personally enjoy the asylum extended in Belgium to those who have lost their battle in the political arena but I have won it for them. I am therefore satisfied."

La Malibran (1808-1836): After beginning her career in London at the age of 16, the Spanish soprano Maria Felicia Garcia, who had married a man named Malibran in New York, came to Brussels to marry her second husband, the Belgian violinist, Charles de Bériot. She died in London in 1836 as a result of a riding accident and was buried in Laeken Cemetery.

Karl Marx (1818-1883): He was expelled from France with Michel Bakounine at the request of Prussia and on 1 February 1844 booked into the Hôtel de Saxe in Rue Neuve under the name of Charles Marx, Doctor of Philosophy, Aged 26, From Treves. He made a formal undertaking not to publish any works on the politics of the day and lived in Rue du Bois Sauvage, Place du Petit Sablon and, later, at 42 Rue d'Orléans in Ixelles where his second daughter was born. He published *The Poverty of Philosophy* (1847) and *The Communist Manifesto* (1848) which he wrote with Engels.

Wolfgang Amadeus Mozart (1756-1791): He was invited to the Court of Charles of Lorraine at the age of 7. The great genius gave a harpsichord concert in the drawing rooms of the Palais de Lorraine on 7 November 1763.

Félix Tournachon, alias Nadar (1820-1910): After his exhibitions in Paris and London, the famous photographer who had patented an aerial photography process took a ride in a hot-air balloon over Brussels in 1864. In order to hold back the crowds who were jostling to see the balloon, barriers were set up; they were named after the celebrity.

Napoléon (1769-1821): The future emperor stayed in Brussels on several occasions, firstly in February 1798 when he lodged at the Hôtel d'Angleterre in Rue de la Madeleine and again in July 1803 when he stayed at the Hôtel de la Préfecture in Rue de Belle-Vue. During the Napoleonic Empire, Bonaparte developed a few town planning projects of which the largest was the ring road on the site of the former town walls.

Gérard de Nerval (1805-1855): The poet came to Belgium three times. In 1840, he came to Brussels to attend the first night of his play, *Piquillo*, and see Jenny Colon, the young actress with whom he had fallen in love in 1834 and who began her career at the Théâtre de la Monnaie on 14 September (she provided inspiration for the character of *Aurelia*). There are those who claim that de Nerval really came to investigate copyright infringements on French books by Belgian publishers.

Auguste Piccard (1884-1962): The Swiss physicist who developed the bathyscaphe taught at the Université Libre de Bruxelles between 1922 and 1954.

Pierre-Joseph Proudhon (1809-1865): Proudhon went into voluntary exile in 1858 (as he had in 1849) after being sentenced to 3 years' imprisonment for his work *De la Justice dans la Révolution et dans l'Église*. He stayed in Rue du Méridien then in Saint-Josse, under the name M Durfort, and claimed to be a mathematics teacher. He returned to Paris after the 1860 amnesty.

Giacomo Puccini (1858-1924): The creator of *Tosca* and *Madame Butterfly* died in a clinic at 1 Avenue de la Couronne in Ixelles. He had been taken to hospital after falling ill during a performance of one of his own works.

Arthur Rimbaud (1854-1891): See insert.

Auguste Rodin (1840-1917): The famous sculptor spent six years in Brussels (1871-1877) when he was young and totally unknown.
He lived at 36 Rue du Pont Neuf then at 111 Rue Sans Souci. He designed *The Age of Bronze* here and worked on the sculptures for the Stock Exchange.
"Those were the days when I lived on ten centimes' worth of mussels and ten centimes' worth of chips per day."

Auguste Rodin

François Rude (1784-1855): The famous sculptor who created the statue of the *Departure of the Volunteers* on the Arc de Triomphe in Paris settled in Brussels after the downfall of the Empire and left the city again in 1827. Most of the work he completed in Brussels, especially his low reliefs for the Prince of Orange's pavilion in Tervuren, have unfortunately disappeared.

Jean-Baptiste Rousseau (1671-1741): His diffamatory verses took him into exile in 1712, and he was to remain abroad for 30 years. He lived in Rue aux Laines and Rue de l'Arbre-Bénit before residing in the castles in Enghien and Héverlé (Brabant). He was buried in the Église des Carmes déchaussées (Discalced Carmelite Church) but his remains were moved to the church in the Sablon District in 1813.

Paul Verlaine (1844-1896): See insert.

François-Marie Arouet, alias Voltaire (1694-1778): He came to Brussels often but his comments on the city were unfair. In honour of his friends, including the Duke of Arenberg, he gave a memorable reception based on the theme of Utopia in Rue de la Grosse Tour where he lived and where he finished his play, *Mahomet*.

Verlaine and Rimbaud

July 1873: Paul Verlaine (1844-1896) arrived in Brussels and wrote to Arthur Rimbaud (1854-1891) to tell him that he was going to enlist in the Spanish Army. Rimbaud, author of *Le Bateau ivre*, arrived with all due speed. The two poets argued as they went from one café to another. Verlaine threatened to commit suicide and bought a revolver in an armoury in the Galeries Saint-Hubert. At no 1 Rue des Brasseurs, he fired two shots at Rimbaud, wounding him in the wrist. Rimbaud lodged a formal complaint with the police and returned to Paris. Meanwhile, his impetuous friend was locked up in the Petits-Carmes. He was sentenced in the Court of Petty Sessions to 2 years' imprisonment.

Living in Brussels

Brussels is much appreciated by foreigners for its tranquillity and lifestyle and it willingly reveals its charms to visitors who take the time to try and understand it. This is a city full of contrasts, paradoxes, and contradictions. Brussels itself is a compact city yet Greater Brussels covers a vast area.

It may, indeed, be the only large European city not crossed by a river making its way to the sea. Yet it has much to offer. It is up to you, the visitor, to find it – and up to us to help you on your way.

VISITING BRUSSELS

The City – The city centre corresponds to the pentagon historically encircled by the town walls and most of the sights are to be found between the Boulevards Lemonnier and Anspach on the one hand and the boulevards forming the inner ring road (*petite ceinture*) on the other from Porte de Hal to Place Madou. A few of the sights constitute the high points of any visit and are ideal focal points from which to tour the surrounding areas – **Place de Brouckère** which featured in of one of Jacques Brel's songs, **Grand-Place** described by Victor Hugo, **Place du Grand-Sablon** which is so popular with the young and wealthy, and **Place Royale** lined with magnificent neo-Classical pavilions. Brussels may not have the dense traffic jams common to other European cities but it is still difficult to find a car parking space here during the day. It is therefore advisable to visit the city on foot, even if some of the areas are rather hilly. And when you get tired, there is always a bus, tram or underground that will take you to any of the districts described in this guide quickly and safely. A stroll through the streets of the city centre is the only way to soak up the very special atmosphere of the old town. **Manneken Pis** is not very far from the **cathedral** and the magnificent **Musée d'Art ancien** is close to the wide avenues that radiate out from the **Parc de Bruxelles**. In fact, in Brussels, you are never very far from the next sight on your list. The city centre lies in a dip and is known as the lower end of the town. It is flanked by the upper end of the town which runs from the Law Courts to the Botanique district. The unusual lie of the land is obvious as soon as you arrive in the city centre. The best **panoramic views** are to be had from the following places:

– **Place Poelaert** at the foot of the enormous Law Courts overlooking the Marolles and Sablon districts.

– **Basilique du Sacré-Cœur** in Koekelberg. There is a breathtaking view from the dome.

– **Atomium** in Heysel, in which the top sphere stands at a height of 102m – 332ft above ground level.

Basilica Church - Panoramic view of Brussels

The steps in Mont-des-Arts, like Place Royale, Place du Congrès, the *cité administrative*, the top end of Boulevard du Jardin Botanique, and, soon, the terrace in the Old England building also provide some delightful **views** of parts of the city.

The Conurbation – Several bus, tram and underground routes run to the outlying towns and villages within the conurbation (Bruxelles-Capitale). However, it is easy to reach them by car because, with the exception of a few main roads that are very busy at peak times, driving is not a problem here. In fact, the further you move from the city centre, the more advisable it is to use your car. The network of public transport is highly centralised and it is difficult to travel from one suburban town to another. Brussels stretches out a few tentacles beyond its historic boundaries. Laeken, Heysel, and the districts named after **Avenue Louise, Bois de la Cambre**, the **Institutions européennes** and **Le Cinquantenaire** all belong to Brussels, territorially at least. The city is surrounded by a string of towns and villages which make up the Greater Brussels conurbation (population: one million). It took a very long time to define its status. The western end has little to attract tourists apart from **Anderlecht** which has more than just industries and **Koekelberg**, which is famous for its basilica church. The north developed around the harbour but it also includes the royal estate of **Laeken**, a district full of sights. There is also the **Heysel** plateau, used for major trade fairs. The south is generally residential but this is not immediately obvious to visitors arriving from **Saint-Gilles, Forest**, and **Ixelles**, all of which include districts where Art Nouveau has pride of place. The residential character of the very select town of **Uccle** on the other hand leaves nobody in any doubt. The eastern side covers a wide area with residential suburbs such as **Woluwe-Saint-Lambert, Woluwe-Saint-Pierre, Auderghem**, and **Watermael-Boitsfort** and the added attraction of the nearby Soignes Forest.

Outlying Districts – There are a few bus routes (the buses are few in number and slow) out to the suburbs described in this guide but we strongly advise you to drive to them. Traffic is not a problem except at peak times. The area around Brussels is very attractive and residential. This is green countryside where the living is fairly easy. Foreign tourists may be surprised to see road signs indicating here and there that they are entering Flemish or Walloon territory, just as they are surprised to see quick splashes of paint covering up information on road signs in French and Dutch. This is the visible part of the community problem. It is the only disadvantage for visitors for, whatever supporters of one or other of the linguistic communities may say, tourists are warmly welcomed by both groups. **Beersel** and **Gaasbeek** to the west have a few reminders of medieval Brabant and they lead to the gentle Payottenland that was so beloved of Brueghel the Elder. The Bouchot Estate in **Meise** to the north is a very attractive destination for an excursion and **Grimbergen** has a Norbertine minster which is of particular interest. To the south lies **Waterloo**, which still seems to be trembling to the clash of arms between Napoleon's troops and Wellington's army. The **Forêt de Soignes** to the east has superb beech groves stretching into the Walloon and Flemish

41

countryside within the Brabant area. **Tervuren** has its museum-palace and delightful park and the castle in **Rixensart** stands in a very pleasant area dotted with vast estates.

BRUSSELS, A CAPITAL FULL OF PARKS AND GARDENS

The capital of Belgium is dotted with trees, parks and gardens. If you need convincing, just look at the statistics. In Paris, parks and gardens are equivalent to 1sq m – 10.76sq ft per inhabitant. In London, the figure is 9sq m – 97sq ft. It rises to 13sq m – 140sq ft in Berlin and 25sq m – 269sq ft in Vienna but in Brussels it is almost 40sq m – 430sq ft. If you want to make the best of the open spaces, you have to walk. At the beginning of this chapter, we mentioned contrasts and this is obvious in the city's parks. There are very few of them in the centre of the

Soignes Forest

Ch. Bastin-J. Evrard

town but the further out you travel, the more parks and gardens you will find. They include the **Parc de Bruxelles**, the **Jardin du Monts des Arts**, the **Square du Petit Sablon**, and the **Parc d'Egmont**. The towns and villages that make up Greater Brussels, on the other hand, are full of open spaces, and there is, of course, the vast **Forêt de Soignes** (4 386 hectares – 10 838 acres) stretching south-eastwards from the city. The list that follows is open-ended but it has the advantage of including all the main parks and gardens open to the public. Anderlecht: **Parc de la Pede, Parc Astrid, Parc de Scherdemael,** and the country park. Auderghem: **Etangs du Rouge-Cloître.** Bruxelles-Extension: **Square Ambiorix, Parc du Cinquantenaire, Parc Léopold.** Forest: **Parc de Forest, Parc Duden.** Ixelles: **Etangs d'Ixelles** and gardens in the **Abbaye de la Cambre, Jardin du Roi, Parc Tenbosch, Bois de la Cambre.** Jette: **Bois de Dieleghem, Bois du Laerbeek.** Koekelberg: **Parc Elisabeth.** Saint-Josse-ten-Noode: **Jardin du Botanique.** Schaerbeek: **Parc Josaphat.** Uccle: **Parc Brugmann, Parc de Wolvendael, Parc Raspail, gardens in the Musée Van Buuren.** Watermael-Boitsfort: **Parc Ter-coigne, Parc Tournay-Solvay.** Woluwe: **Parc communal Roodebeek, Parc Meudon, Parc Malou, Parc des Sources, Etangs Mellaerts, Parc de Woluwe.**

THE REAL BRUSSELS

Brussels has gradually become a city full of offices (national centralisation and European bodies *obligent*) and has lost a lot of the charm that it must have had at the beginning of the century.
It has been overrun by a desire for the functional. Working-class districts have been expropriated and many of the local people have left the city to settle in the suburbs or in towns and villages on the periphery of the conurbation, in the Flemish or French-speaking areas of Brabant. The city, though, has not lost its heart. Indeed, the shape of the pentagonal old town is not unlike a heart and there is much that pleads in favour of a delightful city with an eventful if little-known past that continues to make itself heard and felt within the walls. It is not always at the entrance to museums or in the best-known places that the soul of the city is to be found. It is easier to spot beside a stall selling *caricoles* or in a bar in the Marolles district or in the vicinity of Place de Brouckère. The real Brussels man, the authentic *brusseleer*, has a very strong accent and his speech is full of the truculent joviality that has, fortunately, maintained the true character of the city.
Grand-Place, Jacques Brel, Art Nouveau, René Magritte, Manneken Pis, the Atomium, or even Europe are all words that conjure up images of Brussels in the eyes of many non-local people, and quite rightly so. But it would be a pity to stop there rather than expanding on these few basic concepts because Brussels has so much more to offer.

Among the typical specialities are the **caricoles** that we have just mentioned. There are still some street-vendors selling them under the green and red striped awnings (the city's colours) above their handcarts. They are sea snails, eaten piping hot off a small plate. These street vendors are becoming increasingly rare and are seen mainly in working-class districts (Marolles, Sainte-Catherine, market round the Gare du Midi). A number of tiny shops sell hot **waffles** (especially round Place de Brouckère and Porte de Namur). The **spekuloos** is a biscuit made with candied sugar which all the cafés serve (unfortunately wrapped in cellophane) with a cup of coffee. The best place to buy the biscuits is 31 Rue au Beurre near Grand-Place. Dandoy the confectioner has his shop there and has the original recipes, as well as moulds that are several centuries old.

A caricole seller

While on the subject of sweets, visitors should sample the famous **Belgian pralines** which are something of an art form in Brussels. The Léonidas shops are the least expensive, and there are several of them but Godiva, Neuhaus, Mary, Corné and Wittamer are without any doubt the most refined and elegant makes. Most bakers and cake shops also make chocolates and they sell their own pralines. People are rarely disappointed with what they buy. Bakers also sell **pistolets**, small round rolls that are as popular in Brussels as croissants in Paris. Other bakery products include the **cramique** (a currant roll) and **craquelins** (a type of *cramique* sprinkled with sugar candy). All these specialities, as you will have noticed, are edible. Yes, the people of Brussels enjoy their food. A number of restaurants will serve you an **américain** (steak tartar) and chips, an eminently local dish, or you can enjoy the traditional **mussels and chips** in Rue des Bouchers and Place Sainte-Catherine *(see the chapter entitled Good Food)*. If you're hungry for a snack, try a **tartine de fromage blanc** (cheesecake) washed down with a beer. In Brussels, people drink **gueuze, lambic, faro,** or **kriek** which are as delicious as they are surprising. Of course, if you prefer, you can order a **blanche** or a draught **pils**.

Spekuloos biscuits

There are a number of cafés and pubs that have retained their own special charm:
– *Adrienne Atomium* (Square Atomium), a restaurant with a panoramic view of Brussels.
– *L'Amadeus* (13 Rue Veydt), a Brussels wine bar quite unlike any other.

43

– *L'Archiduc* (6 Rue A. Dansaert) which is a superb example of 1930's decoration.
– *Aux Armes de Bruxelles* (13 Rue des Bouchers), a restaurant with an atmosphere that could only exist in Brussels.
– *Le Bar* in the *Hôtel Astoria* (103 Rue Royale), a chic venue in which to taste any of the wide selection of whiskies, in surroundings recreating the railway sleeping cars of the 1920's.
– *Le Bar Dessiné* (Hôtel Radisson SAS, 47 Rue du Fossé-aux-Loups) in which the interior decoration is based on Belgian comic strips.
– *A la Bécasse* (11 Rue Tabora) and its draught lambic.
– *La Brouette* (3 Grand-Place) for its exceptional setting.
– *Le Café Métropole* (31 Place de Brouckère) for its superb decoration and magnificent patio.
– *La Chaloupe d'Or* (24-25 Grand-Place) for its exceptional setting.
– *Le Cirio* (18-20 Rue de la Bourse) which first served the redoubtable speciality that is still served in a few of the city's bars, **the half en half**, half sparkling wine and half white wine.

Le Cirio

– *L'Espérance* (1-3 Rue du Finistère), a former brothel with a wonderful Art Deco interior.
– *Le Falstaff* (17-19 Rue H. Maus) for its attractive Art Nouveau decoration.
– *La Fleur en papier doré* (53-55 Rue des Alexiens), once frequented by the Surrealists and now used once a month for poetry meetings.
– *La Grande Porte* (9 Rue Notre Seigneur), an old pub serving typical Belgian fare.
– *Henry J. Bean's* (40 Rue Montagne aux Herbes Potagères), a very busy place on concert evenings.
– *A L'Imaige Nostre-Dame* (Impasse des Cadeaux, between 6 and 8 Rue du Marché aux Herbes), which is fairly quiet because it has a reputation for discreteness but which still has its original decoration.
– *'t Kelderke* (15 Grand-Place), a Brussels pub in a vaulted cellar.
– *Café Leffe* (46 Place du Grand-Sablon) sells specialities such as the four types of Leffe beer. It also serves a limited bill of fare based on special beers.
– *La Manufacture* (12 Rue Notre-Dame du Sommeil), a restaurant housed in the former workshops of the famous leather goods firm Delvaux.
– *Mok ma Zwet* (93 Rue des Carmélites, Uccle), a restaurant with a typical Brussels atmosphere.
– *A la Mort subite* (7 Rue Montagne aux Herbes Potagères), more typical than this you cannot get!
– *L'Ogenblik* (1 Galerie des Princes), a restaurant with a wonderful interior like an old café.
– *Le Paradoxe* (329-331 Chaussée d'Ixelles), a vegetarian restaurant that stages musical and jazz evenings.
– *La Porteuse d'Eau* (48 Avenue J. Volders) has a magnificent set of Art Nouveau style stained-glass windows.
– *Rick's Café Américain* (344 Avenue Louise), a fairly noisy bar and restaurant which is always full of hustle, bustle and crowds.
– *Le Roi d'Espagne* (1-2 Grand-Place), very much a tourist venue but the waiters and setting are absolutely unique.
– *La Roue d'Or* (26 Rue des Chapeliers) is a restaurant with a superb Surrealist interior referring to René Magritte and his characters with their bowler hats and umbrellas.

- *Au Soleil* (Rue du Marché au Charbon) where the clientele is young and trendy.
- *Sounds* (28 Rue de la Tulipe) organises jazz concerts.
- *In 't Spinnekopke* (1 Place du Jardin aux Fleurs), said to be the oldest bar in Brussels.
- *Taverne du Passage* (30 Galerie de la Reine), a restaurant with an Art Deco interior.
- *Toone VII* (21 Petite Rue des Bouchers) upholds tradition with its old-fashioned interior and small puppet theatre. There are performances throughout the year.
- *Le Travers* (11 Rue Traversière), the favourite haunt of jazz buffs.
- *De Ultieme Hallucinatie* (316 Rue Royale) for its Art Nouveau interior.
- *Le Vieux Pannenhuis* (317 Rue Léopold Ier, Jette) is a 17C coaching inn.
- *Vincent* (8-10 Rue des Dominicains) is a typical Brussels restaurant. Large paintings on ceramics depict various aspects of life at sea.

STREET ART

Sgraffiti

At the end of last century, the authorities encouraged the development of art by organising competitions for the decoration of house fronts. The most commonly-used technique, because of its visibility from some distance away, was sgraffito which bears a resemblance to fresco painting. The surface is covered with a light-coloured base, then parts of the base are scratched away while still wet, leaving the support medium to show through and form a pattern or drawing. Some of the most fashionable sgraffiti from the Art Nouveau period are still visible today in Brussels:
- The house that belonged to Paul Hankar the architect, 71 Rue Defacqz, St-Gilles *(qv)*. The sgraffiti were created by A Crespin.
- The private mansion that belonged to Albert Ciamberlani the artist, 48 Rue Defacqz, St-Gilles *(qv)*. The sgraffiti were the artist's own work.
- The house belonging to Edouard Ramaekers the architect, 35 Rue Le Corrège, Bruxelles-Extension *(see Quartier des Institutions européennes)*. The work was created by an anonymous artist.
- A private house at 83 Rue Faider, Ixelles *(see St-Gilles)*. The sgraffiti have been attributed to Privat Livemont.
- Houses in Rue Vanderschrick in St-Gilles *(qv)*. The work was created by an anonymous artist.
- The house belonging to the sgraffiti specialist Paul Cauchie, 5 Rue des Francs, Etterbeek *(see Cinquantenaire)*.

Cauchie House, Sgraffiti under the cornice

Comic strips

People with a love of comic books will be delighted to find a trail referring specifically to the Ninth Art. For the past while, a number of characters from comic strips have decorated a number of gable ends in the city:
- Boule and Bill by Roba, Rue du Chevreuil.
- Brousaille by Frank Pé, Plattesteen.
- Le Chat by Philippe Geluck, Boulevard du Midi.
- Néron by Marc Sleen, Place St-Géry.
- Ric Hochet by Tibet and Duchâteau, Rue des Bons Secours.
- Bob and Bobette by Willy Vandersteen, Rue de Laeken.

A brochure indicating the exact location of these murals can be obtained from the Tourist Information Office, Grand-Place, 1000 Bruxelles, ☎ Tel 513 89 40.

Art underground

Brussels has 58 underground stations on 3 métro and "prémétro" (underground tramway) lines.

The stations were decorated by 54 different Belgian artists. Tourists interested in the subject (and armed with a great amount of patience) can of course cover the entire underground network in order to see all the art displayed beneath the city's pavements but for those who are more likely to take the underground only to go from one point to another in the city, the most outstanding pieces of work are to be seen at the following stations:

– **Anneessens:** Christian Dotremont and Pierre Alechinsky, both members of the COBRA group.

– **Botanique:** Jean-Pierre Ghysels who worked with Zadkine in Paris and who produced *The Last Migration* (1977).

– **Bourse:** Paul Delvaux for *Nos Vieux Trams Bruxellois* (1978) and Pol Bury for *Moving Ceiling*, a kinetic work consisting of 75 tubes which move in the draught.

– **Gare du Midi:** Jacques Moeschal, architect and sculptor, for his work on the structure of the station.

– **Gare de l'Ouest:** Guy Vandenbranden for his luminous stained-glass window entitled *Compositie* (1982).

– **Hankar:** Roger Somville, leader of the Belgian Expressionist movement, for a fresco entitled *Notre Temps* (1976).

Notre Temps, by Roger Somville, Hankar Station

– **Horta:** The wrought ironwork comes from the Maison du Peuple (the People's Palace) which was destroyed in 1965. The stained-glass windows were designed in warm tones. They come from the former Hôtel Aubecq and pay homage to Victor Horta the architect.

– **Montgomery:** Jo Delahaut for the geometry of his *Rythme bruxellois* (1975) and Jean-Michel Folon for a fresco entitled *Magic City* (1979).

– **Porte de Hal:** *Le Passage Inconnu* (1993) by François Schuiten is reminiscent of the atmosphere in his album, Brüsel.

– **Stockel:** for its reminiscences of the world of Hergé, creator of Tintin.

BRUSSELS – SHOPS AND MARKETS

People in Brussels go "shopping" in "shopping-centres". It is, perhaps, the linguistic quarrel which is still posing everyday problems in Brussels that has led people, in some instances, to have recourse to English. This, though, is only a minor exception because, in many cases, people speak better French in Brussels than they do in Paris, apart from having a very strong accent. Just think – this was the mother country of Maurice Grevisse, Joseph Hanse and Albert Doppagne, grammarians and linguists who were among the most fervent defenders of the French language.

The lower town

Boulevard Anspach, Place de Brouckère and Boulevard Adolphe Max — Department stores (including the Virgin Megastore in the Anspach Center), travel agents, cafés and restaurants are strung out along this line of streets running through the centre of the city.

City 2 — This multi-storey shopping centre stands at one end of Rue Neuve. Numerous shops (including the FNAC book and record store).

Galerie Agora — Cheap boutiques (clothes, accessories).

Galerie Bortier — Bookshops.

Galeries Saint-Hubert — Three arcades under one roof (Galeries du Roi, de la Reine and des Princes). Luxury stores and boutiques, a superb bookshop (Tropisme), cinemas, tearooms, restaurants and a theatre.

Passage 44 — Shopping precinct on Boulevard du Jardin Botanique, frequented mainly for its theatre, temporary exhibitions, and the Médiathèque de Belgique (media library where you can hire records and videos).

Place du Grand Sablon and surrounding streets — Antique shops, art galleries and cafés. "Antiques and Book Market" on Saturdays and Sundays, starting at 0900.

Rue Blaes — The street is intrinsically working-class. It opens onto Place du Jeu de Balle where the most traditional flea market in the city is held every morning.

Rue Dansaert — Trendy fashion in a few boutiques.

Rue des Fripiers — A small shopping street between the Stock Exchange and Place de la Monnaie.

Rue Haute — A very popular street that is slowly being influenced by Place du Grand-Sablon.

Rue du Marché aux Herbes — Department stores and the Belgian Tourist Information Office. Craft market on Saturdays and Sundays from 1000 to 1800.

Rue du Midi — Heaven for philatelists and collectors of coins or musical instruments.

Rue Neuve — The main shopping street with department stores (L'Inno, Marks & Spencer, P&C) and off-the-peg clothes shops. Chock-a-block with people on Saturday afternoons.

Rue Sainte-Catherine — Coin market on Saturdays from 0800 to midday.

The upper town

Avenue Louise — A traditional avenue lined with elegant shops (Bouvy, Cartier, Dean, New D, Dujardin, Old England, Vuitton etc.). Off-the-peg and haute couture clothes (Belgians Strelli and Watelet, Féraud, Ferré, Rech, Valentino, Mugler etc.).

Avenue de la Toison d'Or — Between Porte de Namur and Place Louise. This avenue is mainly pedestrianised and has become an esplanade. The Galerie of the same name opens onto Chaussée d'Ixelles and the Galerie Louise opens onto the avenue of the same name. This is a very busy shopping area.

Boulevard de Waterloo — Luxury shops, haute couture houses (including Chanel, Armani, Delvaux, Versace, Gucci and Saint-Laurent) and cafés.

Galerie Louise — Situated between Avenue de la Toison d'Or and Avenue Louise. Recently extended, this gallery is a very popular shopping area. It includes one of the city's large bookshops (Libris).

Porte de Namur — A "must" on any visit. This is the real centre of activity in the upper town.

Rue de Namur — Upmarket off-the-peg boutiques (Kenzo, Laura Ashley, Natan).

Rue Royale — A few shops and the Rossel bookshop (from the name of the group which controls the daily newspaper, *Le Soir*).

The Conurbation

Anderlecht — The main shopping street is Rue Wayez. A bric-à-brac sale is held at the Westland Shopping Centre every Sunday from 0800 to 1300. The main market takes place on Sunday morning near the Gare du Midi (there are a lot of Mediterranean products on sale). Bric-à-brac market in the Abattoirs on Saturdays and Sundays from 0900 to 1600.

Auderghem — Chaussée de Wavre is the town's main shopping street especially between Square De Greef and Boulevard du Souverain. Bric-à-brac market on the first Sunday in the month on Place Pinoy from 0630 to 1300, on the second Sunday in the month on Boulevard du Souverain from 0600 to 1400, on the third Sunday in the month on the car park of Maxi G.B. from 0700 to 1300, and on the last Sunday in the month beneath the Viaduc Hermann-Debroux (A4-E411 motorway flyover) from 0700 to 1300.

Etterbeek – There are two shopping areas, Carrefour de La Chasse and Rue des Tongres, plus the Galerie du Cinquantenaire not far from the park of the same name (Mérode underground station).

Forest – Bric-à-brac market on Sundays from 0800 to 1300 on Place Saint-Denis, and from 0700 to 1300 on Parvis Saint-Antoine.

Heysel – "Old paper" market (books, post cards etc.) in Bruparck on the second Sunday of the month from 1000 to 1800.

Ixelles – Two main shopping streets run from Porte de Namur, Chaussée d'Ixelles and Chaussée de Wavre. Between them is the pleasant Rue Saint-Boniface. Place Flagey has a market on Saturday mornings. Near the cemetery in Ixelles is the Boondael district where there are several shopping streets. Place du Châtelain et Rue du Bailli contain numerous restaurants, cafés, shops specialising in interior decoration and off-the-peg boutiques.

Jette – The shopping area centres on Place Reine Astrid and Rue Léopold.

Koekelberg – The Basilix Shopping Center stands in Avenue Charles Quint.

Laeken – A post card market is held on the fourth Saturday in the month at 26 Rue Schildknecht from 0800 to 1200.

Molenbeek-Saint-Jean – Computer market on Sundays from 0900 to 1500 (Rue de l'Intendant).

Saint-Gilles – Numerous shops in Chaussée de Waterloo on each side of the Barrière de Saint-Gilles.

Schaerbeek – Chaussée de Louvain and Place Dailly where there is a bric-à-brac market on the first Saturday of the month from 0800 to 1800.

Uccle – There are numerous shops in the Bascule district (junction of Chaussée de Waterloo and Chaussée de Vleurgat), in Chaussée d'Alsemberg and in the long Rue Vanderkindere where a bric-à-brac market is held on Sundays from 0800 to 1400.

Watermael-Boitsfort – This very residential town has a few shops around Place Keym. Small market on Sunday mornings on and around Place Gilson.

Woluwe-Saint-Lambert – Avenue George Henri is the busiest shopping street in the town. The shopping centre on Boulevard de la Woluwe was the largest in Europe when it was first opened in the early 1970's (Habitat, l'Inno, C & A etc.). A collectors' market is held there on the third Sunday in the month from 0730 to 1300. A bric-à-brac market takes place on the first Sunday in the month on Place Saint-Lambert from 0600 to 1330.

Woluwe-Saint-Pierre – Most of the shops are on Place Dumon. Books and old papers market in the Musée du Transport urbain bruxellois (364b Avenue de Tervuren) on the first Saturday in the month from 0900 to 1600.

Only the markets held throughout the year have been included in this list. There are additional opportunities to look for the unexpected bargain at fairs, markets, bric-à-brac sales or car boot sales held in one or other of the capital's districts on occasional weekends. Additional information can be found in the magazine called Kiosque.

BRUSSELS FOR CULTURE

The city marks the linguistic divide between the Dutch-speakers and French-speakers. It is also the city of international institutions such as the European Union, NATO, WEU etc. and Brussels has been chosen as the marketing platform for Europe by numerous multinational companies. It is estimated that 36% of the city's residents are foreigners. There has been a fairly high level of immigration and the city has a number of foreign communities, especially in some of the districts which cannot be described as "tourist venues".

Brussels is a European city *par excellence* but has no districts linked specifically to any one nationality within the European Union, with the exception of a few streets in Anderlecht, Ixelles or Saint-Gilles which will have large Italian, Spanish and Portuguese populations. However, these people settled in the towns before the EEC was set up. European nationals have blended into the city and prefer to live near the European institutions or in the residential suburbs. In fact, visitors will not immediately notice that they are in a cosmopolitan city but if they listen carefully they will frequently hear people speaking German, English, Spanish, Dutch or even Russian (this is a recent development).

Brussels is a warm-hearted but secretive city and the foreigners who live there seem to like this aspect of it. It is easy to find produce from all the countries in Europe owing to the many specialist grocer's shops. Under the Rond-point Schuman, there is a shopping mall that sells products from every country in the European Union. On the other hand, Brussels has relatively few bookshops and it is not easy to find works in foreign languages: Gutenberg, 34 rue de Louvain, 1000 Bruxelles (German), W.H. Smith, 71-75 Boulevard A. Max, 1000 Bruxelles or The House of Paperbacks, 813 Chaussée de Waterloo, 1180 Uccle (English), Il Libro Italiano, 354 Chaussée de Wavre, 1040 Bruxelles (Italian) or on the first floor of the FNAC store in City 2 (German, English, and Italian works).

Brussels, like any other major city, has an American community. They have a school in Sterrebeek (outside the conurbation) and they do their shopping in their own stores. One of their favourite haunts is *Rick's*, a bar-restaurant on Avenue Louise.

Over the past decade, there has been a constant increase in the number of Japanese businessmen and staff of Japanese firms in Brussels. Most of them live in Auderghem and they have even opened a school there.

Black Africa has its own district, called "Matongué". It is in Ixelles near and in the gallery of the same name (between Chaussée d'Ixelles and Chaussée de Wavre). This area attracts immigrants from Central Africa who are resident in France, Holland and Germany. It is impossible to miss Matongué if you are driving through Ixelles in the Porte de Namur direction for it is like a piece of Kinshasa set down in the land of Tintin. It has everything an African immigrant could wish for ie hairdressers, grocer's shops, fabrics, newsagents, record shops etc. Passers-by can appreciate the custom which encourages peaceful rivalry between young men as they try to outdo each other in sartorial elegance at the end of the day. The district has several African night clubs.

Schaerbeek has a large Turkish community living mainly around Chaussée de Haecht. It has numerous restaurants, cafés and shops steeped in the delightful atmosphere of a bazaar and redolent with the scents of the Mediterranean.

There is no Chinatown in Brussels but there are many Asian restaurants, especially Vietnamese. The main specialist shop is *Sun-Wa* (Rue de la Vierge Noire).

BRUSSELS FOR A NIGHT OUT

The weekly supplement to the *Le Soir* daily paper, entitled *MAD*, and the monthly magazine *Kiosque* both publish a complete programme of what's on in Brussels. The weekly English-language *Bulletin* and the monthly *Tenue de ville* are also good sources of information.

Cinemas

The inauguration of the Kinepolis complex in Heysel has led to serious doubts about the viability of the other cinemas in Brussels. Many of them have already closed and most of the others have been bought up by major distributors. Luckily, there is still a handful of local cinemas left. Brussels' international dimension gives cinema-lovers the great advantage of being able to enjoy films in their original version with sub-titles in two languages.

Lower end of the city – *Actor's Studio*, 2 auditoria (16 Petite Rue des Bouchers, ☎ 512 16 95). *Arenberg-Galeries*, 2 auditoria (26 Galerie de la Reine, ☎ 512 80 63): Total Screen Festival in summer, a delight for cinemagoers. *Aventure*, 3 auditoria (57 Galerie du Centre, entrance via Rue des Fripiers or Rue de la Fourche, ☎ 219 17 48). *Musée du cinéma*, 2 auditoria (9 Rue Baron Horta, ☎ 507 63 70): Belgium's film library. *U.G.C. de Brouckère*, 10 auditoria (Place de Brouckère, ☎ 0900 29 930): weekly festival for young and old alike on Saturday mornings at 0930 (except in summer).

Avenue de la Toison d'Or

Bolcina/GLOBAL PICTURES

Upper part of the city – *Centre culturel de la communauté française de Belgique* ("Le Botanique", 236 Rue Royale, ☎ 218 37 32) for a few previews or festivals. *U.G.C. Acropole*, 11 auditoria (15 Avenue de la Toison d'Or, ☎ 0900 29 830): breakfast shows every Sunday morning at 1000. *Styx*, 2 auditoria (72 Rue de l'Arbre Bénit, ☎ 512 21 02): the seats are hard but the programmes are always top-quality. *Vendôme*, 5 auditoria (18 Chaussée de Wavre, Ixelles, ☎ 502 37 00).

Heysel – *Kinepolis*, 27 auditoria + 1 cinema-in-the-round (Bruparck, Underground line 1A Heysel, ☎ 0900 35 241).

Forest – *Movy Club*, One 1930's style auditorium (21 Rue des Moines, ☎ 537 69 54). *Centre Culturel Jacques Franck* (94 Chaussée de Waterloo, Saint-Gilles, ☎ 538 90 20).

Woluwe-Saint-Pierre – *Le Stockel*, 1 auditorium (Place Dumon, Stockel Underground station or Tram 39. ☎ 779 10 79).

Theatres

The city is particularly fortunate in the number and quality of its theatres which just goes to prove that contrary to preconceived ideas the people of Brussels actually enjoy an evening out.

Atelier Sainte-Anne (75-77 Rue des Tanneurs, ☎ 548 02 60).

Auditorium 44 (Passage 44, Boulevard du Jardin Botanique, ☎ 218 56 30).

Centre Culturel Jacques Franck (94 Chaussée de Waterloo, Saint-Gilles, ☎ 538 90 20).

Centre Culturel d'Auderghem (183 Boulevard du Souverain, ☎ 660 03 03). Usually stages productions by Parisian companies on tour.

Centre Culturel de la communauté française de Belgique ("Le Botanique", 236 Rue Royale, ☎ 218 37 32). The great central rotunda contains a theatre.

Centre Culturel et Artistique d'Uccle (47 Rue Rouge, ☎ 374 04 95).

Centre Culturel de Woluwe-Saint-Pierre (93 Avenue Thielemans, ☎ 773 05 88). Usually stages productions by Parisian companies on tour.

Comédie Claude Volter (98 Avenue des Frères Legrain in Woluwe-Saint-Pierre, ☎ 762 09 63). The father of the young actor Philippe Volter who is enjoying a fine career in films in France directs this theatre with constant success.

Koninklijke Vlaamse Schouwburg or Théâtre flamand (Flemish theatre) (146 Rue de Laeken, ☎ 217 69 37). For bilingual audiences only.

Nouveau Théâtre de Belgique (122 Rue du Viaduc, ☎ 640 84 37).

Rideau de Bruxelles (Palais des Beaux-Arts, 23 Rue Ravenstein, ☎ 507 82 00).

La Samaritaine (16 Rue de la Samaritaine, ☎ 511 33 95). A small, intimate auditorium for shows that are often full of biting humour.

Théâtre 140 (140 Avenue E. Plasky in Schaerbeek, ☎ 733 97 08). Numerous foreign companies stage productions here.

Théâtre de la Balsamine (1 Avenue F Marchal, ☎ 735 64 68).

Théâtre des Galeries (32 Galerie du Roi in the Galeries Saint-Hubert, ☎ 512 04 07). Comedies and farces have been staged here for decades.

Théâtre de marionnettes de Toone (23 Impasse Schuddeveld at the end of the Petite Rue des Bouchers, ☎ 511 71 37). José Géal's wooden puppets maintain the tradition for tenderness and a sense of fun prevalent among the people of working-class Brussels. The shows are performed in dialect, French, Dutch, English and German.

Théâtre National de Belgique (Centre Rogier, Place Rogier, ☎ 203 53 03). This is the best-known of the theatres. It was recently directed by Jean-Claude Drouot who was succeeded by Philippe van Kessel. The large auditorium is used for the Classical repertoire and for international co-productions. The small auditorium is used for one man shows and more marginal productions.

Théâtre de Poche (Bois de la Cambre, 1a Chemin du Gymnase, ☎ 649 17 27). This small theatre is unprepossessing from the outside but is a pleasant venue for an evening out. Moreover, the programme includes some very high-quality productions.

Théâtre Poème (30 Rue d'Ecosse, Saint-Gilles, ☎ 538 63 57).

Théâtre de Quat'Sous (34 Rue de la Violette, ☎ 512 10 22).

Théâtre du Résidence Palace (155 Rue de la Loi, ☎ 231 03 05). The theatre stands almost opposite the "Charlemagne", the seat of the European Council. Superb auditorium in the building designed by Michel Polak.

Théâtre royal du Parc (3 Rue de la Loi, ☎ 511 41 47). The theatre stands almost opposite the Palais de la Nation, seat of the Chamber of Representatives and the Senate. This theatre specialises in light entertainment with a mixture of vaudeville and farce.

Théâtre Varia (78 Rue du Sceptre, Etterbeek, ☎ 640 82 58). Over the last few years, this theatre has acquired an excellent reputation for the quality of its productions.

Opera and Dance

Théâtre royal de la Monnaie (Place de la Monnaie, ☎ 229 12 11). La Monnaie enjoys a reputation for excellence on a European, or even worldwide, scale under the direction of organist Bernard Foccroulle and dancer and choreographer Anne Teresa De Keersmaeker. Thanks to their work, the Opéra Nationale has retained its reputation for excellence, producing and creating very high-quality performances.

La Monnaie - José van Dam in Alban Berg's *Wozzeck*

Classical Music

Brussels has long been renowned for its excellence in the field of classical music. After all, the Concours Reine Elisabeth is one of the most prestigious competitions for budding soloists.

Cathédrale des Saints-Michel-et-Gudule (Parvis Ste-Gudule, ☎ 217 83 45). Sacred and Baroque music.

Conservatoire Royal de Musique (30 Rue de la Régence, ☎ 511 04 27). This is the royal academy of music and, as such, it welcomes small groups of classical instrumentalists and full orchestras.

Église Sts-Jean-et-Etienne aux Minimes (62 Rue des Minimes). Sunday concerts and recitals, music festival in the summer.

Église Notre-Dame-du-Bon-Secours (Rue du Marché au Charbon). A few, rare recitals are given here.

Église Notre-Dame-du-Sablon (Rue de la Régence). Organ works and sacred music.

Église Saint-Lambert (Place du Sacré-Coeur, Woluwe-Saint-Lambert). Baroque music concerts.

La Luna (20 Square Sainctelette, ☎ 201 59 59). Classical works are not heard here very often but, when they are, the performances are usually of a very high quality since they are given by the Société Philharmonique de Bruxelles.

Palais des Beaux-Arts (23 Rue Ravenstein, ☎ 507 82 00, or 11 Rue Baron Horta, Société Philharmonique de Bruxelles, ☎ 511 34 33). The palace is the home of Belgium's national orchestra which performs in the Henry Le Boeuf Auditorium. During the year, the Société Philharmonique invites well-known soloists to play with the national orchestra, as well as foreign orchestras and conductors.
Every two years, the famous Concours Reine Elisabeth is held here.

Variety Shows

Centre culturel d'Auderghem (183 Boulevard du Souverain, ☎ 660 03 03). Singing stars perform here.

Centre culturel de la communauté française de Belgique (Le "Botanique", Rue Royale, ☎ 218 37 32). Le Botanique includes the Rotonde and the Orangerie. Numerous stars give performances here.

Centre culturel de Woluwe-Saint-Pierre (93 Avenue Thielemans, ☎ 773 05 88). Big names from the world of song perform here regularly.

Cirque royal (81 Rue de l'Enseignement, ☎ 218 20 15). This auditorium attracts internationally-famous singers, as well as ethnic song and dance troupes and ballet companies.

Espace Delvaux (Place Keym, Watermael-Boitsfort, ☎ 660 49 60). Little-known artistes with performances ranging from classical music to the most unusual types of variety shows.

Forest National (36 Avenue du Globe, Forest, ☎ 347 03 55). The largest concert hall in Brussels. It has recently been refurbished and attracts internationally-famous pop stars and rock groups.

La Luna (20 Square Sainctelette, ☎ 201 59 59). This has recently become a very fashionable venue. All types of music.

La Samaritaine (16 Rue de la Samaritaine, ☎ 511 33 95). This is the place to hear little-known singers and groups.

Le Travers (9 Rue Traversière, ☎ 218 40 86). Rock and jazz. No glitz but a good evening out.

SPORT

Football

This is the national sport in Belgium, as it is in the countries adjacent to it. The national team plays its matches in the Stade Roi Baudouin (formerly the Heysel Stadium). The capital boasts a prestigious team in Anderlecht, which has been the winner several times over of the European Cups (it plays in Stade Vanden Stock). Nobody local talks about the Anderlecht team; they call them the « mauves and whites » (the club colours). The R.W.D.M. team (Racing White Daring Molenbeek) is less well-known but has a large number of supporters (the team plays at the stadium in Molenbeek-Saint-Jean).

Cycling

This is the other national sport although cycling does not arouse the same passion and fervour in Brussels as it does in Flanders or Wallonia. The capital however constitutes the finishing line in the classic Paris-Brussels road race first run in 1893. Past winners include Merckx (1973), Gimondi (1976), De Vlaeminck (1981) and Sorensen (1992).

Running

The Brussels 20 kilometer race attracts thousands of participants every year from all over Belgium, as well as an international elite. The finishing line is beneath the arches in the Cinquantenaire.

Skating Rinks

Le Poseidon (4 Avenue des Vaillants, Woluwe-Saint-Lambert). Ice skating.

Forest National (36 Avenue du Globe, Forest). Ice skating.

Gymnase (Bois de la Cambre). Roller skating.

Swimming Pools

Aqualibi (Wavre).

Le Longchamp (1 Square De Fré, Uccle). An elegant district and pleasant surroundings.

Le Calypso (60 Avenue Wiener, Auderghem). A family atmosphere and a pool set in the middle of trees and shrubs.

Le Poseidon (4 Avenue des Vaillants, Woluwe-Saint-Lambert). Includes a solarium and a jacuzzi. There is also a separate paddling pool for toddlers.

Centre sportif de Woluwe-Saint-Pierre (2 Avenue Salomé, Woluwe-Saint-Pierre). An olympic pool but its size has been decreased to leave room for a toddlers' paddling pool.

Neptunium (56 Rue de Jérusalem, Schaerbeek). Rather obsolete, but this gives it a certain charm.

Océade (Bruparck).

Tennis

This has become a very popular sport and there are a large number of clubs. The **Royal Léopold Club** (42 Avenue Dupuich, Uccle), **Le Royal Rasante Tennis Club** (56 Rue Sombre, Woluwe-Saint-Lambert) and **Le Primrose Tennis Club** (41-43 Avenue du Gros Tilleul, Heysel) are the most select. If you are an inveterate tennis player and you want a game during your stay in Brussels, contact the Fédération Royale Belge de Tennis on 675 11 40.

The Practical Information section at the end of the guide lists :
– information on travel, motoring, accommodation, recreation
– local or national organisations providing additional information;
– calendar of events
– admission times and charges for the sights described in the guide.

Brussels and its celebrities

The date underlined indicates whether the person was born or died in Brussels. This list is open-ended.

Philosophy: Siger de Brabant (c. <u>1235</u> - between 1281 and 1284), an adversary of Thomas Aquinas and teacher at the Sorbonne in Paris. Dante considered him to be the "greatest mind" of his day.

Painting: Rogier de la Pasture whose name was translated into Van der Weyden (c. 1400-<u>1464</u>); Bernard van Orley (c. <u>1490</u>-<u>1542</u>); Pieter Brueghel the Elder (c. 1527-<u>1569</u>) and his sons, Pieter Brueghel the Younger (<u>1564</u>-1638) and Jan Brueghel (<u>1568</u>-1625) nicknamed Velvet Brueghel; the "Painter of Port-Royal", Philippe de Champaigne (<u>1602</u>-1674); Adam van der Meulen (<u>1632</u>-1690), Painter Ordinary to Louis XIV; François-Joseph Navez (1787-<u>1869</u>), member of the Institut de France; Alfred Stevens (1823-1906); Rik Wouters (1882-1916) who painted in Watermael-Boitsfort; René Magritte (1898-<u>1967</u>); Pierre Alechinsky (<u>1927</u>).

Sculpture: François Duquesnoy (<u>1597</u>-1643) known to the Italians as Francesco Fiammingo; Constantin Meunier (<u>1831</u>-<u>1905</u>).

Architecture: Jacques Francart (<u>1577</u>-1652); Jean-Pierre Cluysenaar (1811-<u>1880</u>); Joseph Poelaert (<u>1817</u>-<u>1879</u>); Victor Horta (1861-<u>1947</u>); Paul Hankar (1861-<u>1901</u>); Frenchman Auguste Perret (<u>1874</u>-1954).

Writers: Charles de Coster (1827-<u>1879</u>); Camille Lemonnier (<u>1844</u>-<u>1913</u>); the Rosny brothers, Joseph Henri (<u>1856</u>-1940) and Séraphin Justin (<u>1859</u>-1948); the comedy writer Francis de Croisset (<u>1877</u>-1937); Franz Hellens (<u>1881</u>-<u>1972</u>); Michel de Ghelderode (<u>1898</u>-<u>1962</u>); Marguerite Yourcenar (<u>1903</u>-1987), member of the Académie Française and whose surname is an anagramme of Crayencour; Françoise Mallet-Joris (1930), member of the Académie Goncourt who recently moved to Ixelles.

Music: Eugène Ysaïe (1858-<u>1931</u>), the famous violinist; Toots Tielemans (<u>1922</u>), jazz composer and musician; the baritone José van Dam (<u>1940</u>).

Medicine: André Vésale (<u>1515</u>-1564), anatomist and official doctor to Charles V; Jan Baptist van Helmont (<u>1577</u>-<u>1644</u>) who discovered carbon monoxide; Jules Bordet (1870-<u>1961</u>), Nobel prizewinner in 1919.

Jacques Brel

D. Frasnay/RAPHO

Films and Theatre: Jacques Feyder (<u>1885</u>-1948), author of *Kermesse héroïque* who was born in Ixelles; Raymond Rouleau (<u>1904</u>-1981); Raymond Gérome (<u>1920</u>).

Singers: Annie Cordie (<u>1928</u>) née Cooreman; Jacques Brel (<u>1929</u>-1978).

And also: Mary of Burgundy (<u>1457</u>-1482), daughter of Charles the Bold and wife of Maximilian of Austria; Charles Joseph, Prince de Ligne (<u>1735</u>-1814), an Austrian Field-Marshal who was a friend of Catherine II of Russia; Prince d'Arenberg (<u>1753</u>-<u>1833</u>), Count Auguste de La Marck, who served as a go-between for Mirabeau and the Court; Maréchal Jean-Baptiste Dumonceau de Bergendael (<u>1760</u>-<u>1821</u>) whose name is carved on the Arc de Triomphe in Paris; the French General Augustin-Daniel Belliard (1769-<u>1832</u>); Paul Deschanel (<u>1855</u>-1922), President of the Third Republic; General Weygand (<u>1867</u>-1965) whose father was a member of the royal family; Jean Capart (<u>1877</u>-1947), Egyptologist; illustrators Georges Rémi (<u>1907</u>-<u>1983</u>) alias Hergé and Pierre Culliford (1928-<u>1992</u>) alias Peyo who created the Smurfs; ethnologist Claude Lévi-Strauss (<u>1908</u>), member of the Académie Française; Ilya Prigogine (1917) chemist and Nobel prizewinner who was born in Moscow but who elected to come and live in Brussels; the artist Jean-Michel Folon (<u>1934</u>) etc.

Arcades St. Hubert

The City
of Brussels

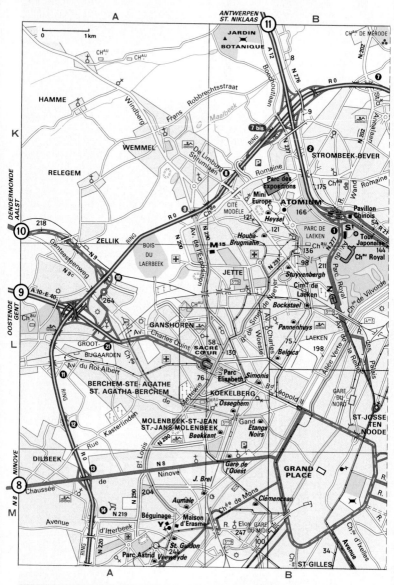

B¹   Bibliotheca Wittockiana
M¹⁵ Demeure abbatiale de Dieleghem

M²⁶ Musée du Transport urbain bruxellois
P¹   Palais Stoclet

The Société des Transports intercommunaux de Bruxelles *(STIB)*
has published an interesting brochure entitled
L'Art Nouveau en transports en commun.
There is a list of corresponding routes and three suggested itineraries
through city streets lined with outstanding Art Nouveau buildings.

STROMBEEK-BEVER

ZAVENTEM

KRAAINEM

VILVOORDE

ZELLIK

S¹ Serres Royales
Y Collégiale des Sts-Pierre-et-Guidon

Z Église N.-D.-de-Laeken
Z¹ Église St-Lambert

If you are a fan of Art Nouveau, don't miss:
- *Musée Horta (museum)*
- *Centre belge de la Bande Dessinée (Belgian comic strip centre)*
- *Maison Cauchie (townhouse)*
- *Hôtel Hannon (townhouse)*
- *Old England*
- *The squares*
- *The lakes in Ixelles*

GREATER BRUSSELS

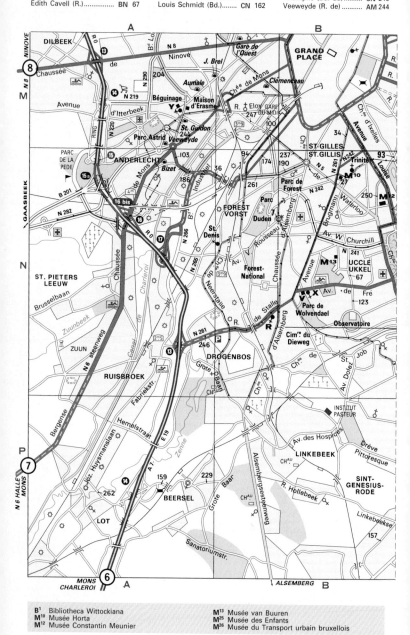

B¹ Bibliotheca Wittockiana
M¹⁰ Musée Horta
M¹² Musée Constantin Meunier

M¹³ Musée van Buuren
M²⁵ Musée des Enfants
M²⁶ Musée du Transport urbain bruxellois

Do you enjoy classical music?
There are regular mid-day concerts in the auditorium of the Musée d'Art Ancien (Wednesdays), the Musée Charlier (Thursdays) and the Théâtre de la Monnaie (Fridays).

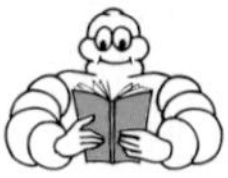

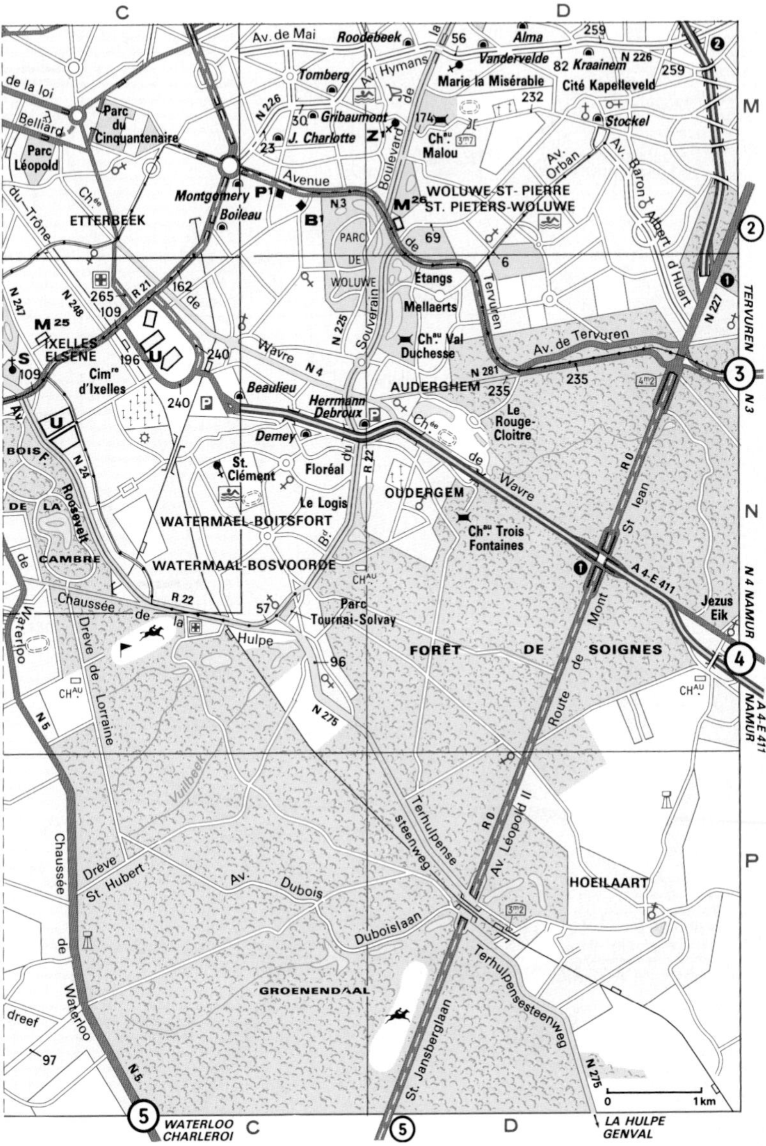

BEERSEL

DROGENBOS

KRAAINEM

LOT

ST-GENESIUS-RODE

P[1] Palais Stoclet
R Église N.-D.-des-Affligés
S Abbaye N.-D.-de-la-Cambre
U Université Libre de Bruxelles
V Le Cornet - X Église orthodoxe russe
Y Collégiale des Sts-Pierre-et-Guidon

*In Brussels, the next place of interest is never far away so,
at the end of each chapter,
you will find several suggestions
to extend your sightseeing tour.*

H¹ Maison communale d'Ixelles
J Palais de Justice
M⁷ Musées royaux d'Art et d'Histoire
M⁸ Musée royal de l'Armée et d'Histoire militaire
M⁹ Muséum des Sciences Naturelles
M¹¹ Musée communal d'Ixelles
M¹⁴ Musée de la Gueuze
M¹⁶ Porte de Hal : musée du Folklore

For information on the exhibitions, shows and fairs in Brussels,
consult the weekly « MAD »
supplement in the daily paper called Le Soir
(the supplement is published on Wednesdays)
or buy the montlhy magazine called Kiosque.

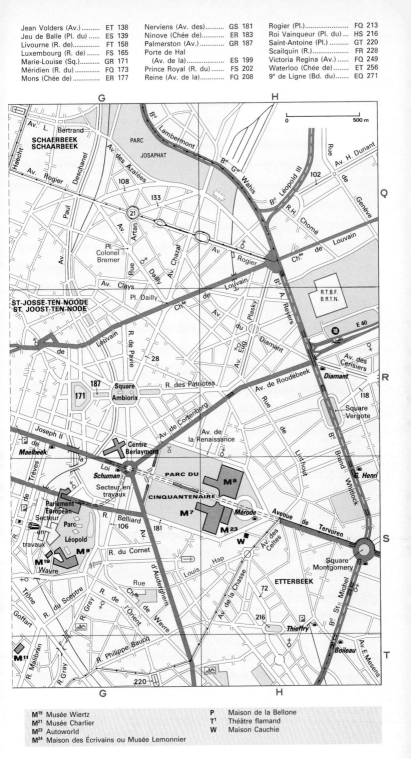

M¹⁹ Musée Wiertz
M²¹ Musée Charlier
M²³ Autoworld
M²⁴ Maison des Écrivains ou Musée Lemonnier

P   Maison de la Bellone
T¹ Théâtre flamand
W   Maison Cauchie

Sightseeing by tram.
The TIB (Grand-Place) or Office du Tourisme belge
(63 Rue du Marché-aux-Herbes) offers a sightseeing trip from
Jette to Boitsfort with sound commentary provided by
ARAU (Atelier de Recherche et d'Action Urbaines).
For information, contact the TIB Tel 513 89 40 or the OPT Tel 504 03 90.

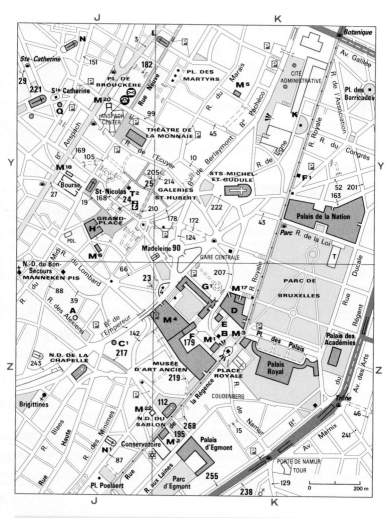

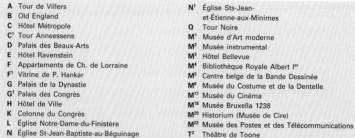

A Tour de Villers
B Old England
C Hôtel Métropole
C¹ Tour Anneessens
D Palais des Beaux-Arts
E Hôtel Ravenstein
F Appartements de Ch. de Lorraine
F¹ Vitrine de P. Hankar
G Palais de la Dynastie
G¹ Palais des Congrès
H Hôtel de Ville
K Colonne du Congrès
L Église Notre-Dame-du-Finistère
N Église St-Jean-Baptiste-au-Béguinage

N¹ Église Sts-Jean-et-Étienne-aux-Minimes
Q Tour Noire
M¹ Musée d'Art moderne
M² Musée instrumental
M³ Hôtel Bellevue
M⁴ Bibliothèque Royale Albert Iᵉʳ
M⁵ Centre belge de la Bande Dessinée
M⁶ Musée du Costume et de la Dentelle
M¹⁷ Musée du Cinéma
M¹⁸ Musée Bruxella 1238
M²⁰ Historium (Musée de Cire)
M²² Musée des Postes et des Télécommunications
T² Théâtre de Toone

Quartier des Musées Royaux des BEAUX-ARTS de Belgique★★★

The Site – After Charles of Lorraine had commissioned the building of Place Royale, the city decided about 1820 to open up a thoroughfare towards Notre-Dame du Sablon; it was called Rue de la Régence. The street name has no connection with the role played by Baron Surlet de Chokier between 1830 and 1831, in the period leading up to the coronation of Leopold I. It is merely a reminder of the form of local government, known at that time as the "Council of the Regency". It was extended during the building of the Palais de Justice (Law Courts) which closes off the end of the street.

Opposite the Musée d'Art ancien is the Palais de la Cour des Comptes, the former residence of the Count of Flanders, brother of King Leopold II and father of King Albert I who was born there in 1875 *(commemorative plaque on the side overlooking Place Royale)*. The Musée d'Art ancien *(see below)* is part of the huge complex known as the Musées Royaux des Beaux-Arts de Belgique which contain a wide range of marvellous collections and which also include the Musée d'Art moderne. Taken together, the two museums give a comprehensive view of the developments in painting and sculpture over a period spanning almost six centuries. The museums are adjacent to each other and are interconnected in the interior by the "forum" or great hall, linking the two sections.

★★★ Musée d'Art ancien ⊙ – *3, rue de la Régence*

The Museum of Ancient Art came into being in the late 18C when an exhibition of works of art was organised in the Former Court in Charles of Lorraine's palace. The works displayed were considered by the French occupying forces as mediocre and the army had therefore left them behind. It was Bonaparte who took the official decision to establish an art gallery in 1801, when he set up the Museum of the Department of La Dyle which he endowed with works of high artistic quality, in order to decrease the stocks being held in the Louvre.

The collections were primarily built up by individual patrons of the arts during the first half of the 19C. Later the museum instigated its own purchasing policy which swelled the collections to such an extent that a new art gallery was built in the neo-Classical style to designs by Alphonse Balat between 1874 and 1880. It was inaugurated in 1887 and extended by the addition of a new wing in 1974.

The façade with its Corinthian columns is decorated with statues personifying Music, Architecture, Sculpture and Painting *(left to right)*. Over the doors are busts of Peter Paul Rubens, Giambologna and Jan van Ruysbroeck. The museum is universally famous for its admirable collection of Flemish primitives but it also contains superb works by the Flemish, Dutch, French, German, Italian and Spanish Schools, and painters from Pieter Brueghel to James Ensor.

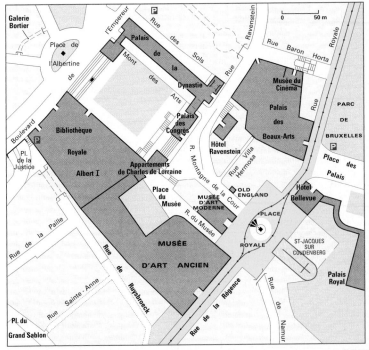

15C and 16C (blue tour) – *Numbers in brackets refer to the room numbers.*

Before beginning a tour of the 15C works, it is useful to take a look at the fragment of wood panel illustrating *Scenes from the Life of the Virgin Mary (room 10)*. It is representative of the final stages in the development of international Gothic in the southern area of the Low Countries and is an excellent example of the new form of pictorial art that was to be introduced a short time later.

In their search for realism the Italian Primitives tended to represent the human body with an accuracy that was almost scientific. In the Low Countries, on the other hand, realism was more concerned with the design and concept of the work. A somewhat heavy elegance is still noticeable in the *Pietà* (11) of **Petrus Christus** (?-*c*1472) whose rare works reflect the influence of J van Eyck. *The Annunciation* (11) by the **Master of Flémalle**, who is thought by some to be Robert Campin, is a variation on the central panel of the *Mérode Triptych* exhibited in the Cloisters (New York). R Campin taught Rogier van der Weyden whose studio produced the *Sforza Triptych* (12). It illustrates the Italian interest in the art of the Low Countries.

ARTIST	SELECTION
Rogier van der Weyden (*c*1400-1464). After the death of J van Eyck, he was the undisputed leader of Flemish painting despite the fact that he was born in Tournai which was French territory at that time. The sculptural forms of his art contain a powerful combination of humility and emotion. He was official painter to the city of Brussels, hence the Dutch translation of his name.	*Pietà* (11) *Laurent Froimont* (11) and *Antoine, Grand Bâtard de Bourgogne* (11) illustrate the extraordinary talent of Van der Weyden as a portrait artist.
Dirck Bouts (*c*1420-1475) produced a more Nordic, even ascetic type of painting, but with an increased sense of luminosity. His elongated figures seem resigned to their fate.	*Calvary* (12) *Justice of the Emperor Otto III* (13) consists of two pictures representing ordeal by fire; they were the work of Dirck Bouts himself. The pictures, which were painted for the courtroom in Louvain Town Hall, depict a miscarriage of justice and serve as a reminder that art also has an educational value.
Hugo van der Goes (*c*1440-1482). This artist had a melancholy temperament and was very much influenced by J van Eyck. He was exceptionally skilled in highlighting the characters of his subjects.	*La Vierge et l'Enfant* (12)
Hans Memling (*c*1435-1494). Memling was a German by birth but he worked in Bruges where he brought one final period of brilliance to a town in which Art was already on the decline. His works were greatly admired in the 19C; they are steeped in the delicate mysticism that characterised Rhenish paintings.	*La Vierge et l'Enfant* (14) *Barbara van Vlaenderberch* (14) *The Martyrdom of St Sebastian* (14), probably painted for a guild of archers.

Towards the end of the century, several anonymous artists were influenced by Memling, among them the **Master of the Legend of Saint Ursula**, *La Vierge et l'Enfant* (12). Others were influenced by Rogier Van der Weyden including the **Master of the Life of Joseph**, *Affligem Abbey Triptych* (16) and **Jean Hey** (?-*c*1505) who worked in the Loire Valley and produced a magnificent *Ecce Homo* (16) dated 1494.

Hieronymus Bosch (*c*1450-1516), a brilliant pictorial genius, who addressed himself to people like Thomas More and Machiavelli rather than to the religious painting of his time.	*The Temptation of St Anthony* (17). The original is in Lisbon. *Calvaire avec donateur* (17). The subject here is still treated in the traditional manner.

The extraordinary miniature of the *Temptation of St Anthony* (17) was painted by an anonymous artist of the Southern Low Countries School.

Lucas Cranach the Elder (1472-1553). This German artist was a friend of Luther. Some of his works were dominated by pathos; others were highly sophisticated.	*Venus and Cupid* (18) *Portrait of Dr. J Scheyring* (18)
Gerard David (*c*1460-1523), the last of the great Primitives. He produced excellent compositions with delicate colours and, in some of his works, deep shadows.	*L'Adoration des Mages* (21) *La Vierge à la soupe au lait* (21), in which the intimacy of daily life is blended with the spirituality of religion.

The innovations characteristic of the Renaissance did not appear suddenly and the works created in the 16C, although still medieval, already showed Humanist tendencies, developing and diversifying the search for innovation in religious painting, portraiture and landscape art.

This is evident in the work of **Ambrosius Benson** (*c*1499-1550) and **Adriaen Isenbrandt** (*c*1500-1551) who continued painting in the style of their master G David, or the paintings produced by **Joos van Cleve** (*c*1464-1540) whose landscapes were influenced by **Joachim Patenier** (?-1524).

Quentin Massys (*c*1465-1530), a friend of Erasmus, has an Italianate style that is a precursor of the Mannerism of the Antwerp School.

La Vierge et l'Enfant (22). This work is reminiscent of works by the Master of Flémalle.
Triptyque du Calvaire (22)

The Little Girl with the Dead Bird (22) which is attributed to the Southern Low Countries School is an appealing work for its disturbing yet moving charm.

Although Antwerp replaced Bruges as a centre of artistic creation, Brabant had two painters of renown whose style was not yet totally Mannerist (distortion of forms, refined backgrounds and delicate colouring). They were **Colin de Coter** (*c*1455-*c*1540), *Saint Michel* (23) and **Aelbrecht Bouts** (*c*1460-1549). Others working in this style included the **Maître de 1518** and **Jan Mostaert** (*c*1475-*c*1556) who was an official painter to Margaret of Austria. The work entitled *Venus and Cupid* (25) by **Jan Gossaert** (*c*1478-1532) also named Mabuse after the town of Maubeuge where he was born, showed a new spirit and the introduction of mythological subjects. In 1508, the artist accompanied Philip of Burgundy to Rome.

The Little Girl with the Dead Bird,
Southern Low Countries School

Cussac/Musées Royaux des Beaux-Arts

The portraits and tryptychs produced by **Bernard van Orley** (*c*1490-1542) are representative of the heyday of Renaissance art in Brussels.

It should be pointed out that the decidedly Mannerist *Mise au Tombeau* (29) by **Maerten van Heemskerck** (1498-1574) was painted during the same period as the *Jugement dernier* (28) by **Pieter Huys** (*c*1515- *c*1581) who again made use of the subject matter and style that characterised the works of Hieronymus Bosch.

In the mid 16C a large number of outstanding artists combined the sacred and the profane. Humanism then attempted to bring together the real and the imaginary in a Realist School that was transcended by Pieter Brueghel the Elder.

Pieter Brueghel the Elder (*c*1527-1569) was one of the great modern artists who subjected his inspiration to a profound metamorphosis. His art is both archaic and modern; it is also masterly, original and varied. The landscape is no longer just a background and the figures are brought to life by the philosphical talent of this undisputed genius.

The Adoration of the Kings (31) is reminiscent of the art of tapestry. This work is a tempera on canvas. *La Chute des anges rebelles* (31) is a striking illustration of the story of the Apocalypse.
The Fall of Icarus (31) illustrates Ovid's fable and an old Flemish proverb: "No plough will stop for a dying man."

Pieter Brueghel the Younger (1564-1638), his son and follower, extended his father's work.

The Massacre of the Innocents (31)
Retour de pèlerinage (34)

At the end of the 16C, when the traditions of Flemish painting existed side by side with the Italian influence, people began to turn to a certain type of Romanticism with **Pieter Pourbus** (*c*1523-1584) and the landscape became a *genre* in its own right. In some cases it was little short of monumental. This trend can be seen in the works of **Jacob Grimmer** (c1526-c1590), *Paysage avec château* (32) and **Paul Bril** (1554-1626) who worked in Rome and more especially in the Vatican. It is also visible in two anthropomorphic landscapes (34) by an anonymous artist from the Southern Low Countries.

An interesting collection of paintings and sculptures by the Brussels and French schools can be seen in rooms 37 to 45 (the Delporte Bequest). It includes the charming group of *Les Quatre Saisons* (39) by **Abel Grimmer** (c1570-c1619), the superb *Paysage d'hiver avec patineurs et trappe aux oiseaux* (44) by Pieter Brueghel the Elder and the *Danse de noce en plein air* (44) by Pieter Brueghel the Younger (1607).

17C and 18C (brown tour)

This remarkable collection which is dominated by the forceful personality of Rubens includes a large number of the genres prevalent in the 17C.

Artists specialising in religious subjects sought inspiration in the Italian masters and worked on such huge canvases that many of their paintings cannot be hung in the museum's rooms. They created well-balanced, almost static, compositions. At the same time, other artists were perpetuating the Flemish tradition by the use of brilliant colours and meticulous attention to detail.

Peter Paul Rubens (1577-1640) was very much in the public eye during his lifetime – he was a diplomat – and he produced an amazing number of works. His powerful style with its use of warm colours was both monumental and precise, and this brought him a measure of fame and prestige that has never dwindled.	*Têtes de nègre* (52) *Hélène Fourment* (52), his wife, who was 37 years younger than he was. *L'Assomption de la Vierge* (62) *Le Martyre de saint Liévin* (62)

Landscapes and still lifes met the requirements of the decorative trends of the day. The *Nature morte avec guirlandes de fleurs* (53) by **Jan Brueghel** (1568-1625), nicknamed Velvet Brueghel, is a first-class picture. The genre gained popularity through what might be called "kitchen sink works" which had a number of outstanding exponents including **Frans Snyders** (1579-1657), *Le Garde-Manger* (54). Superb examples of interiors, especially in collectors' houses, show the extent to which Rubens' contemporaries were forced to specialise. As far as portrait painting was concerned, **Cornelis de Vos** (c1584-1651) showed great subtlety but the undisputed master of the day was Anthony van Dyck.

Anthony van Dyck (1599-1641). This prodigious painter was trained by Rubens but he established his own personality and developed a pictorial style that varied greatly during a number of very productive periods of his life. His work as a portraitist was to exercise a strong influence on Reynolds, Gainsborough and Hogarth.	*A Genoese Lady and her Daughter* (53) *Renaud et Armide* (53) is a sketch that shows a rare degree of talent. *Jean-Charles della Faille* (55)
Jacob Jordaens (1593-1678) was a symbolic figure in Flemish art. He developed a naturalistic form of art in a dense robust style.	*Allegory of Fertility* (57), in which Pomona the nymph is depicted in a less celestial guise than in Rubens' work. *The "King" Drinks* (57)

In the United Provinces, economic prosperity ensured that painting could develop. The region enjoyed democracy within a capitalist system but encountered no political problems as a result. Tradesmen were concerned to decorate their homes and public buildings and they provided new commissions for the artistic community. Moreover Calvinism, which condemned the display of sacred pictures, encouraged the genre paintings (Delft and Leyden Schools) in which **Adriaen van Ostade** (1610-1685) excelled and landscape painting of which **Jacob van Ruisdael** (c1610-1629) was the most outstanding representative.

Before finishing the tour which was deliberately limited to the 17C it is interesting to linger for a moment and study the differences in the works by two contemporary artists, both of whom specialised in portraiture. *Trois Enfants avec une voiture tirée par un bouc* (60) by **Frans Hals** (c1582-1666) seems to have an almost fleeting dynamism whereas *Nicolaas van Bambeeck* (60) by **Rembrandt** reveals a psychological understanding that is impressive for its rigour.

Rooms 50, 51 and 61 contain Italian and French works (Barocci, Tintoretto, Tiepolo, Carracci, Champaigne, Greuze, Vouet, Claude le Lorrain).

19C (yellow tour)

The tour begins with an anachronistic clash between the neo-Classical and Romantic schools. Neo-Classicism is represented by a Belgian artist **François-Joseph Navez** (1787-1869), by Jean-Auguste Dominique Ingres (1780-1867) and by Jacques-Louis David. A new school brilliantly represented in Paris by Eugène Delacroix (1798-1863) and Théodore Géricault (1791-1824) corresponded perfectly to the wind of revolt which was sweeping through Brussels: see the impressive *Épisode des Journées de septembre*

1830 (70) by **Gustave Wappers** (1803-1874) and works by Hendrik Leys, Louis Gallait and Willem Geefs. Note also, in rooms 70 to 68, paintings by Constable, Fromentin, Gros and Raeburn.

Jacques-Louis David (1748-1825). His rather severe art form extolled the ideologies of the French Republic and of the Empire. He was considered as a regicide during the Second Restoration of the monarchy in France and exiled (1815-1825) to the Kingdom of the Netherlands.
The Death of Marat (68), the work most admired by visitors, pays homage to a hero of the French Revolution.
Mars and Venus (69) was painted in Brussels in 1824.

Before entering rooms 72 to 77, note the display cabinets containing interesting sculptures by Bourdelle, Degas, Renoir, Bugatti and Rodin. The rooms house mainly Realist works from the second

The Death of Marat, by J.-L. David

half of the 19C. The most outstanding works are by **Gustave Courbet** (1819-1877) (72), **Louis Artan de Saint-Martin** (1837-1890) (75 and 76) and **Henri Fantin-Latour** (1836-1904) (77). The Belgian School of Realism reflects both the poverty of the working classes and the elegant yet somewhat melancholy life style of the wealthy members of society.

Constantin Meunier (1831-1905). According to Rodin, this painter and sculptor of social realism was "one of the great artists of the century". His talent was expressive and deep-seated. A visit to the museum in his last home is of particular interest *(see Ixelles).*

Le Puddleur (78)
Vieux Cheval de mine (78)
The Fire-Damp Explosion (79), a work which is reminiscent of Zola's book *Germinal* published in 1885.

Note the Intimist paintings of **Henri de Braekeleer** (1840-1888).

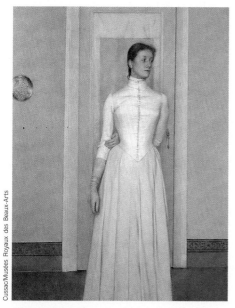

Portrait of Marguerite, by Fernand Khnopff

The museum contains excellent works by the Impressionists, neo-Impressionists and Luminists (the Belgian equivalent of the other two movements) and the visit gives ample opportunity to see numerous paintings by national artists. However, although the works of **Théo van Rysselberghe** (1862-1926), **Guillaume Vogels** (1836-1896) or **Emile Claus** (1849-1924) are of interest, the work entitled *Henriette au grand chapeau* (80) by the fascinating **Henri Evenepoel** (1872-1899) and the *Portrait de paysan* (80) by **Vincent van Gogh** (1853-1890) are even more eye-catching.

A number of different artistic trends appeared in succession *c*1880. An outstanding example of this was Les XX (1884-1893), a group of Belgian artists who were seeking a renewal of art and who invited large numbers of foreign artists (Seurat, Toulouse-Lautrec, Van Gogh, Gauguin etc.) to come and exhibit their works. For some fifteen years, Brussels was a centre of avant-garde art which constantly aroused scandal because of its innovatory tendencies.

Room 85 is dedicated to the works of **Fernand Khnopff** (1858-1921). As the leader of the Belgian Symbolists, he undoubtedly influenced the Secession Movement in Vienna, particularly Klimt. Khnopff created a kind of ambivalent woman who was part angel and part *femme fatale*. Note the enigmatic *Caresses*, the *Portrait of Marguerite* and *Memories*. Room 86 contains works by the first Laethem-Saint-Martin group, including *Dimanche après-midi* by **Gustave van de Woestijne** (1881-1947) and *Le Grand Porteur de reliques* by **George Minne** (1866-1941).

Room 88 contains an extraordinary collection of masterpieces, among them *Conversation dans les prés* by **Paul Gauguin** (1848-1903), *Nude against the Light* by **Pierre Bonnard** (1867-1947), *Les Deux Écoliers* by **Edouard Vuillard** (1868-1940), *The Seine at the Grand-Jatte* by **Georg Seurat** (1859-1891) and *La Calanque* by **Paul Signac** (1863-1935).

James Ensor (1860-1949) was one of those exceptional painters whose visionary work, whether it was Naturalist or Expressionist in style, disconcerted his own contemporaries.

Une Coloriste (89) belongs to his Realist, or "sombre" period. *Scandalised Masks* (89). *Squelettes se disputant un harengsaur* (89) or... Ensor's art.

Visitors pass *Watteau* (87) by **Jean-Baptiste Carpeaux** (1827-1875), *The Thinker* by **Auguste Rodin** (1840-1917) and *La Plage* (90), an Impressionist painting by **Félicien Rops** (1833-1898) before reaching Room 91 which has a delightful collection of small oil paintings by **Auguste Renoir** (1841-1919), **Claude Monet** (1840-1926), **Alfred Sisley** (1839-1899) and **Eugène Boudin** (1824-1898).

Drawings Collection: *Closed.* Collections in the reserve include some 10 000 drawings but only researchers have access to them.

On the floor below is a **sculpture gallery.** The first exhibit is an informative display explaining the techniques of moulding and casting, and giving a brief history of changes in sculpture in Belgium from the 18C to the beginning of the 20C. Also displayed are several works by **Gilles-Lambert Godecharle** (1750-1835).

The Museum of Modern Art lies on the other side of the main foyer or "forum".

★★ Musée d'Art Moderne ⊘ – *1 Place Royale.*

The Museum of Modern Art was inaugurated in 1984 and includes two sections. The building with its main entrance on Place Royale is used for temporary exhibitions (top three floors).

The museum itself is an underground building designed by R Bastin and L Beek the architects. It has eight storeys below street level radiating out around a well of light from Place du Musée. It houses permanent collections of 20C sculptures, paintings and drawings (from Fauvism to contemporary art), set out in more or less chronological order. National works are displayed next to the creations of numerous foreign artists.

The works from the early part of the century benefit from direct daylight; more recent works are lit by high-quality artificial lighting. New acquisitions are exhibited on Levels -2 and -3 where the visit begins.

Since the science of exhibitions is mainly concerned with demonstration by example, the following text, although following the direction of the visit, describes just a few of the main Belgian artists and the most interesting foreign works.

Level − 2 *Subject to change*
Conceptualist and Minimalist art – Ian Hamilton Finlay (United Kingdom), *Monument to Joseph Bara* (1986); Alan Charlton (United Kingdom); Richard Long (United Kingdom); Sol LeWitt (USA), *Walldrawing* (1985); Arnaldo Pomodoro (Italy).

Level − 3
The well of light lies beyond this floor, where the collection consists of works by very different artists and part of the Goldschmidt Bequest. Among the varied works are a wooden statue of *Diane* (1937) by Ossip Zadkine (France); kinetic works by **Pol Bury** (1922) including *Ponctuation molle* (1960); *Red Poles* (1973) by Sam Francis (USA); *Le Pape aux hiboux* (1958) by Francis Bacon (United Kingdom); *Draped Woman on Steps* (1958) by Henry Moore (United Kingdom); a pop-art canvas by Andy Warhol (USA); an amazing composition by Robert Rauschenberg (USA); a creation called *Capella* (1990) by Nam June Paik (USA); *Potato Chips in Bags* (1963) by Claes Oldenburg (USA), and plaster sculptures moulded onto the models themselves by George Segal (USA).

The diversity of works exhibited makes this a particularly interesting visit. There are drawings by Jules Lismonde, sculptures by Reindhoud, Raoul d'Haese and Eugène Dodeigne, abstracts by René Guiette, *La Généreuse* by Olivier Strebelle, and an amazing oil painting by Jan van den Eeckhoudt, *Les Citrons* (1913). One section of the gallery deals with Fauvism in the Brabant area, represented by *Le Portemanteau* (1917) by Thévenet, *Autoportrait à la palette* (c1916) by Paerels, and *Expression de jeune fille* (1932) by H Daeye.

Baigneuse, by Léon Spilliaert

Level — 4

This floor houses a collection of works by Fauvists, Cubists, Abstract artists, and Expressionists. The display begins with paintings representative of "Brabant Fauvism", a movement whose members were influenced by Cézanne in their reaction against Symbolism. They include Auguste Oleffe, Ferdinand Schirren (*La femme au piano*, 1917), and the talented leader of the group **Rik Wouters** (1882-1916) who died too young (*Au soleil*, 1911), *La Dame au collier jaune* (1912), *Le Flûtiste* (1914), and *Les soucis domestiques* (1913).

In some of his works, **Léon Spilliaert** (1881-1971) used a language close to Expressionism. He was a forerunner of Surrealism and Abstract art. Of special interest among his drawings are *Femme sur la digue* (1908) and *Baigneuse* (1910).

Gentil Bernard by Georges Rouault (France); *Le Compotier* by Maurice de Vlaminck (France); *Vue de Marseille* by Raoul Dufy (France); *Portrait de Louis Barthou* (1931) by Kees van Dongen (Netherlands); *Jardin de fleurs* (1926) by Emil Nolde (Germany); *Guitare et compotier* (1920) by Pablo Picasso (Spain); *Le Compotier* (1919) by Georges Braque (France); *Femme lisant* by Henri Matisse (France); *Femme vue de dos* (1930) by Jacques Villon (France).

Abstract art in Belgium developed mainly in Brussels and Antwerp. There was no longer any question of style; instead, artists began talking of a new vision of art including Cubism and Constructivism, Expressionism and Surrealism.

The "pure plasticity" of Belgian art is represented by **Victor Servranckx** (1897-1965), *Exaltation du machinisme* (1923), *Opus 47* (1923); Marcel-Louis Baugniet, *Le joueur de tennis* (1926); Pierre-Louis Flouquet; Félix de Boeck, *Mer abstraite* (1923); and Jozef Peeters. Futurism is represented by Schmalzigaug, *Le baron F. Delbeke* (1917).

Auto-Portrait au "Tefillin" (1928) by Marc Chagall (France); *Le joueur en transe* (1908) by Oskar Kokoschka; *Les hélices* (1918) by Fernand Léger (France); *Mirr* (1936) by Hans Arp.

A Flemish movement known as the Laethem-Saint-Martin second group (named after a small village near Ghent) included several Expressionists whose sometimes stark works are characterised by earthy colours. Among the members of this group were **Constant Permaeke** (1886-1952), *Les Fiancés* (1923), *Niobe* (1951); Joseph Cantré the sculptor; Fritz van den Berghe, *Dimanche* (1924); and Gustave de Smet, *La famille* (1920). Edgard Tytgat should also be

Jeune femme,
by Oscar Jespers

considered as part of this movement. His art underlined his determination to achieve the simplification evident in the works of **Oscar Jespers** (1887-1970) such as *Jeune femme* (1930); Otto Dix (Germany), *Deux enfants (*1921); and Ossip Zadkine in his sculpture *La ville détruite* (1947).

Level – 5

The most outstanding part of the Museum is its Surrealist collection. This was an eminently international movement but it developed and spread in Belgium through an unusually large number of works by artists such as Magritte, Paul Colinet, Marcel Mariën, E L T Mesens, Paul Nougé, Raoul Ubac and Jean Scutenaire. The group first appeared in 1926, barely two years after the movement was founded by André Breton (who broke away from it in 1947). Although **Paul Delvaux** (1897-1994) was never part of the movement, he has to be considered with it. The world he portrayed was often frozen in a rather cold sensuality. Of the six Delvaux paintings exhibited here, *Le Couple* (1929) still belongs to the Expressionist period. Note too *La voix publique* (1948) and *Pygmalion* (1939).

L'Éclipse by Francis Picabia (France); *Le Jongleur* (1940) by Marino Marini (Italy); *L'Ombre de la main* (1929) by Amédée Ozenfant (France); *Uhrpflanzen* (1924) by Paul Klee (Switzerland); *Auto-Portrait* (1943) by Man Ray (USA); *Deux mannequins* (*c*1920) by G De Chirico (Italy).

Display cabinets contain photographs, original editions, printed documents and autographs relating to Belgian Surrealism. The movement used a more optimistic form of expression than the corresponding group in Paris.

Cussac/Musée Royaux des Beaux-Arts © ADAGP 1996

The Empire of Lights, by René Magritte

Level – 6

The Georgette and **René Magritte** (1898-1967) Room contains a remarkable collection of twenty-six of the most important works created by this exceptional artist. Magritte was initially inspired by Cubism and Futurism but he then met Servranckx and, later, De Chirico who exerted a profound influence on him before he finally asserted his own genius to the full. There is one sculpture, *Les Grâces naturelles* (1967) and a number of gouaches and paintings including *Le Démon de la perversité* (1928), *Magie noire* (1945) belonging to the "Full Sun" period, *L'Empire des lumières* (1954) and *Le Domaine d'Arnheim* (1962).

La Mélancolie d'une belle journée (1913) by Giorgio De Chirico (Italy); *L'Avion* (1929) by Yves Tanguy (France); *La Tentation de saint Antoine* (1946) by Salvador Dali (Spain); *L'Année céleste* (*c*1925) by Max Ernst (Germany); *Danseuse espagnole* (1924) by Joan Miró (Spain); *Onze formes du doute* (1957) by Roberto Matta (Chile); *Tauromachie* (1953) by Germaine Richier (France).

Soon after the end of the Second World War, a new wave of Abstract art emerged, called La Jeune Peinture belge. It extolled the virtues of "colour and a return to the human scale".

The movement included Gaston Bertrand; Marc Mendelson, *Toccata et fugue* ; Louis van Lint; and Jean Milo.

The group broke up in 1948 and left the way open for a few individual artists such as Antoine Mortier whose work bore resemblances to "action painting".

New movements were formed as quickly as the old ones disappeared. In 1948 a group called COBRA (COpenhagen – BRussels – Amsterdam) was founded, in Paris. It encompassed any artistic trend based on spontaneity and a total lack of constraint.

The leading members were the Dutchman Karel Appel, *Nu couché* (1957); Asger Jorn from Denmark, *Les Trois Sages* (1955); and **Pierre Alechinsky** (1927-) from Brussels, *Parfois c'est l'inverse* (1970).

Others associated with this group were Christian Dotremont and Henri Michaux. The Phases movement, which worked mainly in the realm of the imaginary and the unreal, appeared in 1952. In Belgium, its main exponents were Jacques Lacomblez, *Prélude* (1955) and Marie Carlier.

Le Burg dévasté (1952) by Jean Dubuffet (France); *Composition* (1963) by Hans Hartung (Germany); *Seigneur frapperons-nous de l'épée* ? (1954) by Alfred Manessier (France); *Sans titre* (1952) by Jean-Paul Riopelle (Canada); *Toile grise* (1933) by Serge Poliakoff (France).

Level – 7

Various artistic trends are displayed in this section – the geometric abstraction of the Frenchman Auguste Herbin and of Jo Delahaut; the German group, Zero, which included among its members the Italian artist Lucio Fontana, *Concetto spaziale* (1965); *Peinture* (1962) by Otto Piene; the op-art of Vasarely (France), a trend that was continued by Walter Leblanc, *Twisting Strings* (1975); the kinetic art of Heinz Mack (Germany), *Silberdynamo (to view the work, press the switch)*; and the "assembly of matter" by the Franco-American artist Arman, *Le Harem du croisé*.

Level – 8

Mobile by Alexander Calder (USA); *Progression* (1974) by Donald Judd (USA); a montage of neon lights without a title (1964), by Dan Flavin (USA); Art and Language (United Kingdom); Christo (USA); *Fragmente* (1987) by Tony Cragg (USA); *Paupière* (1989) by Giuseppe Penone (Italy); Christian Boltanski (France); Bertrand Lavier (France) *Wandskulpturen* (1981) by Bernd Lohaus (Germany).

After 1960, art gained an even greater international dimension that erased all the traditional classifications separating painting and sculpture. Some artists considered that figurative art was dead; others remained unconditional supporters of imagery. Labels such as Minimalism, Hyper Realism, New Subjectivity etc. continued to come into being.

However, when looking at works that express the world we live in, we do not have the benefit of hindsight and it would perhaps be preferable to try to understand them rather than merely to reject them on the grounds that they are "ugly".

Moules rouges casserole, by Marcel Broodthaers

Several contemporary Belgian artists are represented here – Marthe Wery, Didier Vermeiren, Jacques Charlier, Jan Vercruysse, Jacques Lizène, Jef Geys, Wim Delvoye, Paul Gees, Jan Fabre, Panamarenko, Michel Mouffe, Denmark, Dan van Severen, Mark Luyten, and Marie-Jo Lafontaine. The most disconcerting one of all is undoubtedly the poet **Marcel Broodthaers** (1924-1976) whose montages *(Moules rouges casserole)* (1965) consisting of basic materials and whose conceptual representations *(Musée d'Art moderne, dpt des Aigles)* (1971) find their inspirational source in national Surrealism (his video of *The Crow and the Fox* in shown every Thursday at 1500).

On Place Royale, turn right from the museum and pass under the portico separating the two buildings.

Place du Musée – Its harmonious neo-Classical layout is the result of three successive periods of construction – the Lorraine Palace *(see below)* between 1756 and 1766, the central wing in 1825 and the left wing in 1877.

The central and left wings of the building used to house the Royal Library (Bibliothèque royale); they now contain the national art galleries (Musées Royaux des Beaux-Arts de Belgique).

In the centre of Place du Musée is the well of light leading down into the Musée d'Art moderne, designed by Bastin and Beek the architects. A statue of Charles of Lorraine (Jahotte, 1848) used to stand on this spot but it has been moved to a new site near the semi-circular Lorraine Palace.

Place du Musée

Ch. Bastin-J. Evrard

Palais de Charles de Lorraine ⊙ – *1 Place du Musée*. In 1756, Charles of Lorraine bought the Nassau Palace from the Princess of Orange. It had become the residence of the Austrian Governors-General after the Palace of the Dukes of Brabant had been burned down in 1731. Charles of Lorraine ordered the reconstruction of much of the Gothic palace in the Louis XVI style, commissioning an architect from Bruges, Jean Faulte (1726-1766), to carry out the work. He died before it was completed. He was followed by Laurent Benoît Dewez (1731-1812). In 1780, the Austrian Governor's heir, Joseph II, sold almost the entire contents of the palace to pay off his uncle's debts. The palace was no longer lived in and was used, instead, to house a number of bodies and institutions including the Université Libre de Bruxelles *(see Ixelles)* which was set up in 1834. The palace originally consisted of several apartments, chanceries, drawing rooms, libraries and offices. All that remains today is the wing visible from Place du Musée; the remainder has been replaced by the buildings of the royal library (Bibliothèque royale de Belgique) located to the rear on Mont des Arts. This wing used to overlook formal gardens laid out on the site of a lake. A chapel dedicated to

Charles of Lorraine

Duke Charles Alexander of Lorraine and Bar (b Lunéville 1712, d Tervuren 1780), brother-in-law of Empress Maria Theresa of Habsburg, arrived in Brussels in March 1744 but left again in May of the same year to take command of the Imperial Army of the Rhine. On his return in April 1749 he immediately won the support of the people because, unlike many Spanish, Italian and German governors of earlier times, he was viewed as a fellow countryman who spoke the same language.

His Court was famous for its splendour and brilliance. He encouraged patronage, was attentive to prestige but, at the same time, was also something of a rake. He was fascinated by alchemy. His rule brought the area a period of peace that enabled the arts and industry to flourish. Charles of Lorraine was also Grand Master of the Teutonic Order.

St George stood on the lakeside *(see Chapelle de Nassau)*. The palace also had its own botanical garden *(see Quartier du Botanique)* but it was not recreated after the fire that destroyed many of the buildings in 1826.

The façade has been integrated into the present-day Place du Musée. In addition to Charles of Lorraine's apartments, the building contains the engravings room and the chalcography section of the royal library.

The Façade – The decorative features (garlands, trophies, cornices and statues) were cre-ated by **Laurent Delvaux** (1695-1778), an official artist to the Court who was born in Ghent but who also spent some time in England and in Rome. His style is an appealing combination of Baroque and Classicism, with an additional symbolic qual-ity. The balconies to each side of the semi-circular entrance are flanked by four allegorical statues – *(left to right)* War with a shield, Peace with a bee-hive, Pru-dence and a serpent, Religion and an open Bible. On the second floor, four children represent Justice, Tempe-rance, Force and Prudence. At the very top is the Lion of Fame which is said to repre-sent Belgium.

The former chapel royal *(right)* was built in 1760 in the Hallenkirche style and given to the Protestants in 1803 when Brussels was part of the French *département* of La Dyle. King Leopold I, who was a Protestant, attended services there.

Ch. Bastin et J. Evrard

Charles of Lorraine's palace - Close-up

The Governor's Apartments ⓥ – Charles of Lorraine's apart-ments were lavishly restored in 1976 and they bear witness to the governor's taste for splendour and luxury. The abundant use of symbols in the decorative features reflect his interest in the pseudo-science of alchemy *(see insert)*.

The double doors at the entrance enabled carriages to take visitors right into the rotunda so that they were not exposed to the elements. At the foot of the staircase *(left)* is a superb white marble statue by Delvaux (1770) representing **Hercules** but with the Governor's features. Hercules' club bears the Governor's monogram, "C", two Crosses of Lorraine and the Cross of the Teutonic Order. Eleven of the twelve Labours of the demigod of Greek mythology are illustrated on the bronze handrail of the stair-case, made by Adrien Anrion, an artist from Nivelles. It is a copy dating from 1888. The impressive stairwell is surmounted by a cupola painted in 1883 by Joseph Stallaert (1825-1903); the work represents the four seasons. Charles' interest in symbolism is evident on the landing in Cramillon's stucco work (1764), especially above the door where a cherub is depicted riding a sphinx and ordering all those who look at the work to remain silent. This is meant as an example of the Duke's esoteric approach to his research projects. Every detail has a precise elaborate significance. In the four rectan-gular panels are illustrations of the four natural elements surmounted by a tutelary divinity – Water with Neptune (seashell, dolphin), Air with Juno (birds, trumpet), Earth with Cybele (lion, sheaves of wheat), and Fire with Vulcan (anvil, armour).

The rotunda was one of several reception rooms in the palace. The stucco work recalled the Governor's military career which was again immortalised by B Verschoot in the cupola. The splendid Lyons silk curtains in this room and the ones beyond it were made in 1980 to the original designs. The black and white checkerboard **floor** (it was restored in 1885) includes a striking spiral motif. The star pattern is original; it has twenty-eight branches consisting of samples from national marble quarries, as indicated in the central rosette.

Beyond the rotunda is a series of five interconnecting rooms which were used as the summer apartments. Each one has a different colour scheme (gold, green, yellow, blue, and red) and the walls are lined with panelling or silk. Two artists were commissioned to undertake the decoration. The first three rooms were decorated by Jean Augustin

73

Olivier (1739-1788) from Marseilles; the last two by Antonio Moretti from Namur, an extraordinarily talented stucco artist as is evident in the vivid hunting scenes in the fourth room. There is an amusing feature in the first room where the wainscoting has been made with a secret window in the fourth panel. This enabled the Duke to look into the entrance hall and see who his visitors were.

After leaving the palace, take the first turning on the left and go down the short flight of steps to Rue Montagne de la Cour.

Additional sights

On the slopes of the Coudenberg below Place Royale is Rue Montagne de la Cour which used to link working-class Brussels, the lower part of the town, and the aristocratic district including the Counts of Brussels' residence. With Rue Ravenstein, this street marks the boundaries of the northern slopes of the hill, the site of the Jewish ghetto in the 12C, 13C and 14C. It was a very busy street in days gone by but has been greatly reduced in size and has undergone major alteration to make way for the Musées Royaux des Beaux-Arts de Belgique and the Bibliothèque Royale de Belgique (art galleries and library).

From this steeply-sloping street, there is a beautiful **view** of the gardens on Mont des Arts and the elegant tower above the Town Hall.

Walk up to the top of the street and back down again then turn right into Rue Ravenstein.

★ **"Old England"** – *94 Rue Montagne de la Cour. This building is scheduled to house the Musée instrumental (qv) shortly.*

This splendid Art Nouveau building was bought by central government in 1978. It was built in 1899 by the architect Paul Saintenoy (1862-1952). He was commissioned by the British firm, Old England, which had had premises in Brussels since 1886. The recent renovation has restored the old shops to their former glory after the removal of a coat of white paint dating from 1938 which was designed to integrate this whimsical piece of architecture into the neo-Classicism of Place Royale. The delightful corner turret has been rebuilt, after being demolished in 1947, and this will enable the tea-room opening onto the patio to become once more the popular meeting-place for the people of Brussels that it was at the turn of the century.

Old England

Hôtel Ravenstein – *3 Rue Ravenstein.* This superb town-house (late 15C-early 16C) stands downhill from the astonishing neo-Gothic Delacre Pharmacy built by Paul Saintenoy in 1898-1900. The mansion gave its name to the street in which it stood in the middle of the 19C. It was built for the Cleves who were Lords of Ravenstein; their castle was in Tervuren. This is the city's last surviving aristocratic mansion from the Burgundian period. After alterations by Saintenoy *(see above)* in 1893-1894 and by Malfait in 1934-1937, it now has a façade flanked by a small tower, a charming inner courtyard, and a gatehouse which can be

Ch. Bastin-J. Evrard

seen from the narrow Rue Terarken *(go down the flight of steps on the outside of the building)*. The stables and gardens were located on the site now occupied by the Palais des Beaux-Arts. The mansion houses a number of scientific institutions.

Palais des Beaux-Arts – *23 Rue Ravenstein*. This arts centre, which was designed and built (1923-1928) by Victor Horta, is especially noteworthy for its interior. The famous architect was ordered to restrict the size of the building so that it would not cut off the view of Rue Royale. Unfortunately, the adjacent building belonging to the *Société Générale* did not comply with this constraint. Horta did, however, and in order to fulfil the requirements he had to set part of the building below ground level. The geometric façade was designed in the Art Deco style. It has become internationally famous in the music world as a result of the prestigious *Concours Reine Elisabeth* (competition for pianists, violinists, singers and composers). Major cultural events are held on the first three floors (exhibitions, concerts and drama productions). It includes the Henry Le Bœuf Auditorium named after the banker who was the driving force behind the construction of the centre; it seats 2 200 people. There is also a chamber music room which is famous for the excellence of its acoustics, a studio and several exhibition halls. The foyer is in constant use (films, documentaries, lectures, meetings). There is also a shop selling art books and posters.

Theoretically, the centre hosts major events as part of "Europalia", a biennial festival which describes a country through every aspect of its culture.

Musée du cinéma ⊘ – *Rue Baron Horta*. The Belgian film library is much more a film theatre for cinema buffs than an exhibition centre dedicated to the history of the Seventh Art. In addition to some Dickson-Casler mutoscopes and an Edison kinetoscope dating from the end of the last century (all in working order), the museum contains several showcases which explain various attempts to represent movement, illustrate the history of the magic lantern, describe Marey's chronographic experiments, and explain the mechanics of the techniques developed by the Lumière brothers.

A double-flight horseshoe staircase made of blue stone leads to Rue Royale *(see Parc royal)*. It covers one of the few remaining vestiges of the first town wall. Further downhill, on a level with Rue des Douze Apôtres, there is a white marble sculpture called *Maturity* (1922) by Victor Rousseau.

Options from Rue Montagne de la Cour:

▶▶ Mont des Arts by the flight of steps downhill.
Cathedral via Rue Ravenstein as far as the crossroads then Rue des Paroissiens (third right).
Place Royale by going back up the street.
Quartier du Sablon by going back up the street and taking Rue de la Régence (right) from the square.

Quartier du BÉGUINAGE

There were three Beguine convents in Brussels during the Middle Ages, of which Notre-Dame de la Vigne, founded *c*1250, was the largest with some 1 200 Beguines. The convents were a combination of religious and lay communities – the sisters were not bound by perpetual vows. The communities were very popular during the century that followed their establishment, for reasons of piety of course but also because of the saftey they provided at a time when single women, whether widows or spinsters, had a particularly hard life. They followed the example of the Bégards, a monastic order, and began by producing wool and woollen products. From the 16C onwards, they made lace. The Beguine convent of Notre-Dame de la Vigne originally looked very like a Flemish town; it consisted of an enclosure with two gates. It was ransacked during the French Revolution and the community was abolished in 1797 although it survived for some time as a lay institution. After the setting-up of the Grand Hospice and the subsequent changes to the urban landscape, the Beguine community disappeared from the city. Only the church remains.

The streets surrounding the church dedicated to St John the Baptist are particularly peaceful. They form an island of neo-Classical constructions but their uniformity is somewhat spoilt by later buildings of more mediocre quality. The streets surrounding the church dedicated to St Catherine are busier and have older houses. They still have the atmosphere inherent to the quays where all the goods for the city were unloaded. Today the square and quays are lined with restaurants specializing in fish and seafood.

Tour Noire (JY Q) – *Corner of Rue de la Vierge Noire and Place Sainte-Catherine*. The tower is one of the few remains of the first city wall, but unfortunately it cannot be seen to advantage because of its immediate surroundings. It was saved from demolition by the burgomaster Charles Buls, and restored by the architect Jamaer in 1888 in a style reminiscent of Viollet-le-Duc; the semi-conical roof is an addition above the old crenelated platform. It can be seen on one of the panels on a triptych of Philip the Fair and Joan the Mad in the Musée d'Art ancien.

Place Sainte-Catherine (JY 221) – The site has been dedicated to St Catherine since the beginning of the 13C, but contrary to what most people in Brussels think, the square was only laid out in 1870, after the filling in of the great basin of the same name which had been dug in 1565. The square was constructed over the old Salt and Seed quays and has several façades with Flemish Renaissance gables between Rue de Flandre and Quai aux Briques.

The even-numbered side of Rue Sainte-Catherine has a few 16C and 17C houses which show the gradual changes in the design of gables.

Église Sainte-Catherine (JY) – All that remains of the 14C-15C church which was extended in 1629 is the Baroque-style tower (*no 45*). The church on the square today was designed by Joseph Poelaert (*see Law Courts*) and was built from 1854 to 1859 in a combination of architectural styles. The main inspiration was drawn from the church of St-Eustache in Paris. The chevet is indicative of the fairly whimsical design drawn by the architect. Inside, there is a picture by De Crayer entitled *Sainte Catherine reçue au ciel*. The typical Flemish pulpit may have come from the cathedral church in Malines. The two tombs were carved by Gilles-Lambert Godecharle.

On the eastern side of the square, take the street to the right.

Maison de la Bellone (ER P) ⊘ – *46, Rue de Flandre.*
This "house at the back" *(maison de derrière)* as it used to be called in Brussels is not visible from the street. The façade of the beautiful patrician residence dates from the end of the 17C and is thought to have been the work of the sculptor Cosyn. In the centre above the arch over the front door is a statue of Bellona, the goddess of war. In the background, a trophy commemorates the Austrian victory over the Turks at Zenta in 1697. The window ledges are decorated with four medallions representing Roman emperors. The building now houses the Maison du Spectacle (it hosts exhibitions and includes a documentation centre).

Ch. Bastin et J. Evrard

Maison de la Bellone

Return to Place Sainte-Catherine. Before going along the north side towards the quays, stop for a moment in Rue St Catherine beyond Rue de Flandre and look at the beautiful 16C and 17C gables on the even-numbered side.

The quays – The quays were built in two stages (1878 and 1911); between the church (église Sainte-Catherine) and Place de l'Yser lie the quays which serve as reminders of the city's original port. The very name Quai aux Briques (JY 29) (literally Brick Wharf) indicates that from the 16C onwards after the building of the Willebroeck Canal boats used to sail upriver to this point and unload cargoes of bricks from Boom near Antwerp. These were the bricks used to build most of the houses in the city. In 1982 two basins were fitted out, interspersed with an obelisk-fountain by Janlet (1897) on Quai aux Briques in honour of Burgomaster Anspach (*see Place de Brouckère*). At the corner of the quay and Rue du Marché aux Porcs stands the beautiful house called the "Sea Horse" built in 1680 (reconstructed in 1898-1899). It has an attractive façade with crow-stepped gables topped by arched pediments ornamented with small volutes.

The names of the quays still give a pointer to the industries and activities connected with them. They include Quai au Bois à Brûler (firewood), à la Houille (coal), à la Chaux (lime), aux Barques (small boats), au Foin (hay). Some of the quays still have a few old houses, notably the Quai au Bois de Construction (building timber) which has a Hanseatic house (1711) even though Brussels had no direct connections with the Hanseatic League. In any event, the designation of this house as Hanseatic is an improper use of the term since it was built two centuries after the decline of the famous league. The house is actually one of the few examples in Brussels of French-style rebuilding after the French bombardment of the town in 1695. Unfortunately, it is now in a very dilapidated state but it will soon be undergoing restoration.

Beyond Quai à la Houille, turn right onto Quai aux Pierres de Taille.

Théâtre flamand (K.V.S.) (EQ T¹) – *146 Rue de Laeken.* In 1882 Jean Baes the architect was commissioned to alter and enlarge the old warehouse on the quays but his commission required him to keep the façade (1780). He did it by placing it behind the new building. Audience safety played a major role in determining the architecture of the Flemish Theatre. This explains the presence of four exterior metal terraces and their staircase down to the ground floor. Note the eclectic decorative use of building processes and materials.

Turn right into Rue de Laeken and right again into Rue du Grand Hospice.

Hospice Pacheco (EQ) – The dilapidated condition of the houses in the old Beguine convent which had contained the Hospices Réunis since the beginning of the 19C prompted the city administration to commission the architect Henri-Louis-François Partoes (1790-1873) to design a building with the double purpose of helping destitute elderly people and embellishing the city. The construction of this neo-Classical complex took place between 1824-1827. It was re-baptised Institute Pachéco in 1889. The buildings are set out around two courtyards in a fairly Spartan manner. The austerity of the architecture reflected the purpose of the buildings. Daily life was not meant to be joyful there. Any infraction of the rules was punished by confinement to the hospice and a second offence resulted in the wrongdoer being sent to the workhouse. Fortunately times have changed; today the institute includes a corrective training centre and a convalescent home. Only the outer walls were retained after the restoration carrried out between 1976 and 1982.

The **hospice chapel** ⊘ decorated in warm tones, contains four pictures by François-Joseph Navez (1787-1869). There are also sculptures by Pierre Puyenbroeck (1804-1884), *Emperor Charles V,* Charles Fraikin (1817-1893), *Duke Henry I of Brabant* and Willem Geefs (1805-1883), *John I, Maria Theresa, Joseph II and Leopold I.*

Go down Rue de l'Infirmerie opposite the hospice.

Église Saint-Jean-Baptiste-au-Béguinage (JY N) ⊘ – *Place du Béguinage.* This Baroque church was the Beguines' place of worship. Building work began in 1657 and the church was consecrated in 1676. The architect is unknown but in the 19C the design was thought to be by Coeberger and Fayd'Herbe.

Exterior – The exterior of the church is clad in stone. The west front is based on the Jesuit principles evident in the Gesù church in Rome which was built in 1575. Yet the principles have not been followed to the letter. Seen from a distance (this was impossible in the 17C; the square did not exist until the two hundred years later) the church is obviously designed around a soaring upward line. There are no spans to break up the rhythm (the engaged columns on the first floor mark three equivalent spans) and the swirls on the sides have been replaced by gables topped with a ball in a style that reflects the patrician townhouses of the 17C. Because of this, it would be wrong to describe the church as having been built in a true Jesuit style even though the proportions are reminiscent of the Jesuit church in Brussels (Francart, 1621) and the carvings call to mind the Jesuit church in Louvain (Hésius, 1671). In this building, there is a sense of movement in every architectural feature – twin pilasters, capitals of different architectural orders, engaged columns, string-courses, volutes, torcheres, heads of cherubs, or ribbed pediments. All of them project beyond the line of the walls in a particularly eye-catching design.

The exterior of the church includes other Baroque features including the onion-shaped lantern turrets on the side chapels and the richly-ornamented walls of the transept. The hexagonal tower still has a Gothic structure, with bulls' eye windows and ornamental cartridges. The upper section of the tower has a number of amazing pinnacles which Fierens described as "a sort of Baroque interpretation of the tower on the Town Hall". The entire exterior of the church has been carefully built and this is unusual in Baroque churches, even in Italy, because with the exception of the west front the walls were usually concealed by the surrounding buildings.

Interior – The layout combines a Gothic Latin cross and the plan common to contemporary 17C churches which had a nave and aisles ending in an apse. In line with the trend to emphasize the central part of the church, the architect widened the aisles, opened up chapels at the transept and by doing so created a lighter airier space despite the lack of a cupola above the transept crossing.

Church of St John the Baptist

The decoration of the nave is clearly Baroque. This is obvious from the series of winged cherubs on the squinches between the columns and the entablature, the projecting cornices or the coffered transverse ribs separating the bays. This decorative abundance is intensified with angels and ornamental scrolls in the transept. At the top of the apse over the choir, the architrave is elaborately decorated and the niche contains a statue of St John to whom the church is dedicated. This profusion of details and figurative sculptures is typical of the church, and creates an exciting building. Indeed the decoration is arguably excessive and the composition often becomes too complex, especially in the transept.

Among the furnishings in the church the most outstanding item is the typical pulpit (**chaire de vérité**, 1757) which comes from a church in Malines and is attributed to Lambert-Joseph Parant. In testimony to the revival of preaching at that time there is a carving of St Dominic striking out heresy at the foot of the pulpit. The six confessionals (18C) are decorated with the busts of allegorical figures and saints. The plasterwork Stations of the Cross by a neo-Classical sculptor Joseph-Germain Geefs were set up in 1862. There is also a series of paintings by Théodore van Loon (1629-1678) – *Sainte Trinité* (north transept), *Annonciation* (south transept), *Saint Pierre aux liens* (north chapel). Notable also is a *Christ en croix* by Gaspard de Crayer.

Options from Place du Béguinage:

►► Place de Brouckère by taking Rue du Cyprès then Rue des Augustins leading to Place de Brouckère.

La Monnaie by going first to Place de Brouckère then on to Place de la Monnaie via Rue Fossé aux Loups.

Vieux Centre by returning to Place Sainte-Catherine then going along Rue A Dansaert via Marché aux Grains (Grain Market).

La Bourse (Stock Market) by going along Rue A Dansaert to the Stock Market.

Quartier du BOTANIQUE

To tourists, the Botanical Garden district and its immediate vicinity constitute a sort of northern boundary beyond which there is little of any great interest except Laeken. When work was completed on the north-south junction (a new station was built nearby in 1956), the northern part of the capital city, which had once been a hive of activity, became almost fatally isolated. The beautiful royal route that once linked the palace in Laeken to the palace in the town centre (Avenue du Parc Royal, Avenue de la Reine, Rue des Palais, and Rue Royale) is now no more than a memory. Because of this we shall concentrate on the elegant architecture in the Botanical Garden district, to which lawns and flower beds add a touch of extra beauty.

★ **Le "Botanique" (FQ)** ⊘ – *236 Rue Royale*. This building gets its name from the purpose for which it was erected. Although it now houses the **Centre culturel de la communauté française de Belgique,** it was built as a botanical garden because, in 1826, it was decided to do away with the one that had been in the Palais de Lorraine since 1797. This earlier botanical garden had been set up by decree during French rule with the aim of giving each university and college in the city its own botany collection. The design chosen was for a glass and iron building that made full use of the latest techniques. More than 6 hectares – 15 acres of land were added to the project between Porte de Schaerbeek and the square now known as Place Rogier. The choice of designer for the building caused a great deal of controversy from the outset. In 1826, the royal architect Tilman-François Suys presented an initial project but it was deemed to be too expensive. The French architect Gineste then worked on Suys' original design, altering details but keeping most of its basic features. The neo-Classical building was given huge glasshouses and side pavilions which were used as orangeries. After the Second World War, the Belgian National Garden, which was too cramped in its original location, was moved to Meise *(qv)*.

Le "Botanique"

The botanical gardens lie in particularly pleasant surroundings and now host and organise a wide range of special events such as theatrical productions (in the great central rotunda), musical evenings (song, dance), cinema and temporary exhibitions. In July, the gardens play host to the International French Song Contest.
Originally the **gardens,** which were partly laid out by Charles-Henri Petersen, consisted of three terraces overlooking a lake, each in a different style. They have since been altered slightly as a result of the building of the Gare du Nord (railway station), the relocation of the plant collection in Meise, the damage caused during the war, and the building of an underpass which decreased the overall area by one-half. Few of the 52 sculptures that made up the ornamentation designed by Constantin Meunier and Charles van der Stappen, two brilliant late 19C artists, have survived to the present day. Some of them can still be seen in front of the south façade of the building, including *Winter* (Pierre Braccke), *Autumn* (C Meunier), *Summer* (C Meunier) and *Spring* (Hippolyte Le Roy) flanking the central glasshouse. A number of animal sculptures bear

witness to the fashion for this new art form in the 1880's. In preparation for the 1958 World Fair René Pechère was commissioned to turn the old gardens into a city-centre park open to all. It contains a few superb trees which are sure to delight those with a fondness for arboriculture. The iris, the symbol of the Brussels-Capital City region ("region" because Belgium has been a federal state since 17 February 1994), is given pride of place here and from April to June there are almost 40 different varieties to admire.

Rue Traversière is one of the side turnings from Rue Royale to the left of the **église du Gesù** (a church built in 1860 but with a modern west front designed by Antoine Courtens in 1939) almost opposite the entrance to the botanical gardens. The café *(no 11)* called *Le Travers* is famous for its rock and jazz concerts. The café-cum-restaurant called *De Ultieme Hallucinatie (316 Rue Royale)* still has quite amazing Art Nouveau interior decoration.

Continue along Rue Royale.

Église Sainte-Marie (**FQ**) – *Place de la Reine. Closed for restoration.* This church bars the view along Rue Royale. Built from 1845 onwards to designs by an architect from Louvain, Louis van Overstraeten (1818-1849), who was only 26 years of age at the time, it is unusual for its Romanesque-Byzantine style including a few ogival features. The architect sought inspiration in the Church of San Vitale in Ravenna and gave it a central octagonal layout with radiating chapels. For the entrance, he designed a projection consisting of a triple porch (the tympanum above the central porch decorated with a mosaic of the Virgin Mary is especially worthy of note) and a narthex leading into the rotunda surrounded by six side chapels. This central section is topped by a cupola in which the impressive dome is dotted with gilded stars. Like the orderly design, the semi-circular arches and carvings are Romanesque-Byzantine in style. The polygons topping the turrets at the rear of the church and the chancel backed by a tower are Orientalist. The flying buttresses and bellcote-pinnacles are ogival. This strange combination is highly unusual but is quite impressive, although the surrounding area does little to show the building off to advantage.

Opposite the chevet of the church is Rue Royale Sainte-Marie.

Halles de Schaerbeek (**FQ**) – *22A Rue Royale Sainte-Marie. Closed for repair.* The old covered market only a few yards from the church dedicated to the Blessed Virgin Mary was restored in 1985 and is one of the few surviving examples of the city's industrial architecture. The market was saved from demolition when it was purchased by the French Commission for Culture in Brussels *(Commission Française de la Culture de Bruxelles)* and is well-known to city-dwellers for the various artistic events staged there.

Return to the botanical gardens then turn right into Avenue Victoria Regina beyond Boulevard du Jardin botanique.

Place Rogier (**FQ 213**) – This square lies at the end of Boulevard Adolphe Max and Rue Neuve and is constantly undergoing alteration. It is easy to spot because of the Centre Rogier tower block which houses the **Théâtre National de Belgique,** temporary exhibition halls and numerous offices.

At the rear of the square is the area commonly known as the "northern district", a network of streets forming what might be called the "red light area". Beyond it, opposite the Gare du Nord (railway station) is a district that has undergone radical change since 1967. It is the new "Manhattan" district with its tower blocks known as the World Trade Center.

Options from Place Rogier:

▶▶ Place de Brouckère via Boulevard Adolphe Max.
    Quartier du Parlement via Boulevard du Jardin Botanique and Rue Royale *(right).*
    Koekelberg via Boulevard d'Anvers and Boulevard Léopold II.
    Laeken by returning to église Sainte-Marie then going along Rue des Palais. Bear left into Avenue de la Reine which runs under the railway bridge.

Quartier de la BOURSE

Like the nearby districts around Place de Brouckère and the old town, this district underwent extensive changes during and after the covering over of the River Senne between 1867 and 1871 *(see Quartier de la Ville ancienne)*. The Stock Exchange that gives this district its name is set back from Boulevard Anspach and is the most impressive building in the lower end of the city. It backs onto the old streets of medieval Brussels leading to Grand-Place. The Brussels Stock Exchange opened its doors on 8 July 1801 and was housed in a number of different buildings before arriving the heart of the pentagon that is Brussels city centre.

It is a busy district, always full of citydwellers and tourists scurrying here and there. Indeed, Place de la Bourse and the adjacent streets do not go to sleep until the wee sma' hours. The area around Rue du Beurre is famous for its jeweller's shops.

La Bourse de Commerce (JY) – *Place de la Bourse*. This majestic building stands on the site of the former Franciscan Convent dating from the 13C and was erected between 1868 and 1873 to designs by Léon Suys. It bears some resemblance to Charles Garnier's opera house in Paris because L Suys used the same Palladian theme of a flattened central dome preceded by a peristyle. The inspiration may be Classical but the simplicity is overcome by an abundance of decoration which some people describe as Baroque over-exuberance.

Stock Exchange – Close-up

Exterior – This is undoubtedly the most ornate of all Brussels' 19C buildings and many a sculptor worked under the management of Frenchman Albert Carrier-Belleuse and Antoine van Rasbourg to create the decorative carvings.

The sculptures on the top are clearly visible from a short distance away. At the very top of the attic on the façade is a sculpture of *Belgium teaching Commercial and Industrial Expansion* by Jacques Jacquet. He also carved the low relief on the tympanum, *Belgium*, set between Industry and Navigation, and the two lions flanking the staircase (they symbolise *Power Dominated by Intelligence*). The other two lions, on each side of the pediment, were the work of Elias. With the massive portico of six Corinthian columns, the building expresses a degree of triumphalism which is only slightly tempered by the two groups of children by Sterckx *(left)* and Leemans *(right)*. From a point nearer the building, the ornamental profusion of set-backs, genies, garlands of flowers and fruit, processions of cherubs and allegorical figures all become easy to see. Beneath the peristyle are another two winged figures representing *Good* and *Evil*. They were carved by De Haen *(see Quartier de la Place de Brouckère, Hôtel Métropole)*.

Walk round the outside of the building and note the succession of groups, figures and niches. Allegorical figures have pride of place here. Some of them seem rather nonchalant, especially the two figures carved by Samain above the pediment of the first window on the north side (Rue de la Bourse). They are ambiguously realistic and seem to be giving expression to a metaphor which associates the pleasures and power of money in a way that is very definitely end-of-the-century. More noteworthy is the frieze of *putti* which A Carrier-Belleuse placed between two storeys on the east side (Rue Henri Maus) and on the south side (Rue du Midi). It was carved with the assistance of Julien Dillens and Auguste Rodin. The great French sculptor is thought to have carved the groups representing *Asia* and *Africa* (Rue Henri Maus) above the attic.

Interior ⊙ – *Enter from Rue du Midi*. A glass screen separates visitors from the floor of the Exchange where all is agitation and gesticulation. One of the walls is decorated with 4 caryatids, also by Rodin.

81

Bruxella 1238 (JY M[18]) ⊘ – *Rue de la Bourse.*

This small archeology museum stands on the site of a former Franciscan convent founded in 1238. The buildings belonging to this religious order, which included a church, cloisters, brewery, library, vegetable garden and infirmary, used to stretch from Rue Tabora right across Place de la Bourse. The convent was closed during the Wars of Religion in the 16C and damaged during the bombardment of 1695. It finally disappeared altogether at the end of the 18C and the site was taken over by the Butter Market which continued to function until the Stock Exchange was built. During digs that began in 1988 the remains of the former church and convent were uncovered, along with numerous graves including that of Duke John I of Brabant who died in 1294. Bones and pieces of pottery were also found.

Cafés line the street to each side of the Stock Exchange. *Le Falstaff* (17-19 Rue H Maus) has fine turn-of-the-century decoration by E Houbion. *Le Cirio* (18-20 Rue de la Bourse) is a traditional café, typical of the Brussels style.

Go along Rue Tabora behind the Stock Exchange.

In a café called *A la Becasse* (no 11) you can enjoy draught *lambic* (beer one or two years old). The name of the café (literally, *At the Sign of the Woodcock*) is a reminder that brewers have always appreciated bird names. The entrance to the cul-de-sac is indicated by a superb pavement depicting the elegant bird. In days gone by, this was lugubriously known as the "Allée des Morts" (Death Alley) because it lead to the Recollects' cemetery.

Return the way you came and turn left into Rue au Beurre.

Église Saint-Nicolas (JY) ⊘ – *Rue au Beurre.* This church was founded at the same

time as the city itself, or at least it is mentioned in documents dating from the second half of the 12C as one of the chapels dependant on the church of Saints-Michel-et-Gudule *(qv)*. The fact that it is dedicated to St Nicholas, the patron saint of boatmen, made it a market church, which is hardly surprising given the proximity of Grand-Place *(qv)*. The church was almost entirely destroyed during the 1695 bombardment. The tower, which collapsed in 1714, used to stand in front of the building. A rebuilding project for which there is a model in the Musée communal *(see Maison du Roi)* gives an excellent idea of what the church used to be like but the project never came to fruition. In 1956, it was given a new west front in the Gothic style.

The interior consists of three aisles but no transept. The aisles open onto a chancel and a chapel set at an oblique angle (apparently because of an old stream). From the entrance, the remains of the Romanesque narthex are visible to the right; it dates back to the original church. Louis XIV style furniture replaced the original furnishings which disappeared among the ruins of the church after the 1695 bombardment when a cannon ball embedded itself in the third pillar on the left. The choir stalls have medallions carved by J-B van der Haegen telling the story of St Nicholas. The high altar has tall Corinthian columns, a canopy and imperial manteling and was designed by Corneille van Nerven, the architect of the rear of the Town Hall. The chancel is closed off by a superb *repoussé* **wrought-iron grille** that is partially gilded. It was brought here from the abbey in Ninove (18C).

Among the works decorating the church is a gilded copper reliquary of the martyrs of Gorcum who died in the Netherlands in 1572 (German, 1868), a *Descente de Croix* attributed to the Carracci School (*c*1600), *Jésus et le centurion*, a copy of a painting by Paolo Veronese, *Jésus et les docteurs* by Jean van Orley, *La Vierge et l'Enfant endormi*, a small painting attributed to Rubens, and *St Anthony* and *St Francis*, two statues (early 18C) carved by Guillaume Kerrickx. They were brought here from the former Recollects church.

Rue au Beurre is arguably the best way of accessing Grand-Place. The sweet shop called *Dandoy* (*no 31*) is one of the leading specialists for "Spekuloos" and macaroons. It occupies the "De Peerle" House built *c*.1700.

Options from the Stock Exchange:

▶▶ Quartier de la Place de Brouckère by going along the right-hand side of Boulevard Anspach.

Old town by going along the left-hand side of Boulevard Anspach. Turn left into Rue de Bon Secours then right into Rue du Marché au Charbon.

Quartier du Béguinage by going down Rue A Orts opposite and Rue A Dansaert then turning right into Rue Marché aux Grains.

Quartier de la Monnaie by going along the rear of the Stock Exchange and turning left into Rue Tabora which extends into Rue des Fripiers.

Grand-Place.

Quartier de la place de BROUCKÈRE

To tourists the historic centre of Brussels is undoubtedly symbolised by Grand-Place and the picturesque streets round about but for the city's inhabitants the nerve centre of Brussels is Place de Brouckère and the main boulevards which cross the capital from north to south.

The area between Place de Brouckère and Place Rogier is full of stores and local government offices which draw in crowds of civil servants every day from the French- and Dutch-speaking provinces of the country. Calm descends on the district at the end of the working day although the square after which it was named still retains some of its atmosphere and an air of Edwardian charm.

A Touch of Paris – In 1871, after Léon Suys had covered over the River Senne *(see Quartier de la Ville ancienne)*, the burgomaster Jules Anspach decided that the central boulevards should present an architectural interest worthy of a capital city. The competition organised in 1872 selected 20 buildings as prizewinners, and the contract for the construction of the boulevards was awarded to a Parisian building contractor Jean-Baptiste Mosnier. Parisian architects were hired to draw up the plans, and 62 buildings were completed before Mosnier went bankrupt in 1878. The French influence is evident in the façades of the prestigious buildings constructed along the three boulevards converging on Place de Brouckère. The influence of Baron Haussman's urban development of Paris in the days of the Second Empire is obvious here; even the building material was stone imported from France. This was an important new feature for Brussels where brick was commonly used for building. The buildings that were the prizewinners in the competition of 1872 are clearly visible because of the use of blue stone, an eminently national building material. Moreover, between 1872 and 1880, there were numerous French Communards in Brussels and they were frequently hired by French contractors to work on the building sites. Because of this, many façades were ornamented with sculptures by French artists in exile.

★ **The square that features in a Jacques Brel song** (JY) – The square was named after Charles de Brouckère, one of the fathers of the 1831 Constitution and burgomaster of Brussels from 1848 to 1860. Since the last third of the 19C, it has been the point of convergence of the three main boulevards in the city centre. It stands on the site of the Augustinian church but the façade has been moved *(see église de la Trinité)*. The architectural harmony of the square was modified at the end of the 1960s by the construction of two glass buildings and the removal of the Emile Janlet's obelisk-fountain (now partially relocated on Quai aux Briques). The square continues to be one of the busiest places in the capital.

A few superb frontages have survived. The old Hôtel Continental built by Eugène Carpentier in 1874 has a monumental façade. It stands on the north side of the square, where boulevards E Jacqmain and A Max merge. On the west side is a neo-Classical building housing the UGC de Brouckère cinema, in which the largest auditorium, the Grand Eldorado, still has the Art-Deco low reliefs installed by Marcel Chabot in 1933 (the auditorium has been divided into two storeys). The Hotel Métropole on the east side *(see below)* stands adjacent to a building designed by Emile Janlet on which the monumental pilasters seem to be hanging in thin air, a feature that underlines their purely decorative function.

The café in the Hôtel Métropole

Hôtel Métropole (JY C) – *31, Place de Brouckère.* In 1891, the Wielemans brewery bought the building that is now the Hôtel Métropole next to the Passage du Nord and commissioned Alban Chambon the architect to carry out the necessary alterations. It was inaugurated in 1894 and its clientèle has traditionally included outstanding personalities and artists such as Sarah Bernhardt, Artur Rubinstein, Isadora Duncan and various prominent statesmen. In 1911, the Conseil Physique Solvay (it was attended by such famous physicists as Marie Curie and Einstein) was held there. The Métropole has also been used as a set in numerous films (*Le Sang des autres* directed by Claude Chabrol, *Benvenuta* directed by Paul Delvaux, etc.). The adjacent building *(nos 33-35)* was designed by Gédéon Bordiau the architect who also designed the Cinquantenaire *(qv)*. It was bought at the same time by the Wielemans and annexed to the Hôtel Métropole. The figures on the hotel roof were carved by Jacques de Haan the sculptor. They symbolise Progress between Abundance and Peace.

In summer and winter, the Métropole is famous for its beautiful patio.

Passage du Nord (JY 182) – The Passage du Nord running between Boulevard Adolph Max and Rue Neuve is a shopping arcade with an old-fashioned charm. It was built in 1881-1882 to plans by the architect Henri Rieck shortly after the construction of the boulevard and stands between the charming Flemish-style House of Cats designed by Henri Beyaert (it won first prize in the competition organized by Anspach, *see above*) and the Hôtel Métropole. The delightful façade of the Passage du Nord which has lost its upper storey is now adorned with groups of children carved by Albert Desenfans; the sculptures symbolise Day and Night.

Inside, under the glass roof, are 32 **caryatids** carved by Joseph Bertheux. They form a veritable ode to modern mythology – Architecture, Sculpture, Painting, Commerce, Textile Industry, Shipping and Astronomy (each one is repeated four times). The arcade is three floors high. Initially it included a series of rooms one of which was called the Musée du Nord (see the inscription on the façade). It was designed to be a waxworks museum similar to the famous Musée Grévin in Passage Jouffroy in Paris. These rooms were sold and became part of the Hôtel Métropole in 1910.

Rue Neuve (JY) – This pedestrian precinct is undoubtedly the best-known street in Brussels, for the locals at least, and it has been the busiest shopping centre in Brussels since the middle of the 19C. On Saturday afternoons, it is crowded with people. Its purpose was confirmed in 1978 when the CITY 2 complex was opened at the corner of Boulevard du Jardin botanique.

Near the middle of the street *(left)* is the church of Notre-Dame du Finistère opposite the *L'Innovation* department store built originally by Victor Horta but later rebuilt after the dramatic fire of 22 May 1967 in which 254 people died.

Église de Notre-Dame-du-Finistère (KY L) – In days gone by, a chapel was dedicated to Notre-Dame *in finis terrae* because it was located at the very end of the town. It was much frequented by laundresses, many of whom lived in this district. The chapel was later replaced by the present parish church (1708-1730) whose architect is unknown. It contains the statue of Notre-Dame-du-Finistère. Inside, the nave, aisles and apse are decorated with stucco work and panelling. The three white marble altars were made by A Leclerq.

The café called *L'Espérance (nos 1-3 Rue du Finistère)* has a shop window and an attractive Art Deco interior frequently used in films. The best-known film of all was *L'Orchestre rouge.*

Just before L'Innovation, take Rue Saint-Michel to Place des Martyrs.

Place des Martyrs

★ **Place des Martyrs (KY)** – *Restoration in progress.* This beautiful, peaceful square was built in the Classical style by the architect Fisco in 1774-1775 on the site of the meadow where the drapers used to come and lay out their fabrics. Like Place Royale, it bears witness to the latter days of Austrian rule when the arts enjoyed a period of outstanding productivity sometimes referred to as the Third Renaissance *(see Quartier du Palais royal)*.

The central statue (1838) by Willem Geefs represents the Fatherland Crowned. It stands over a crypt surrounded by a gallery containing the inscription of the names of 445 patriots "who died a martyr's death in the September 1830 Uprising". To the south is the monument (Dubois, 1898) to Count Frédéric de Mérode who was also killed in 1830; the great curved memorial was designed by Henry van de Velde. To the north is another memorial (Crick, 1897) in memory of Jenneval, author of the words of the national anthem, la "Brabançonne". He too was killed in 1830.

On the east side of the square, go along Rue du Persil then turn left into Rue du Marais and right straight away into Rue des Sables.

★★ **Centre belge de la Bande Dessinée (KY M⁵)** ⊘ – *20, Rue des Sables.* This magnificent Art Nouveau building in Rue des Sables was built from 1903 to 1906 by Victor Horta as a store for Charles Waucquez (wholesale textile merchant). It is the only remaining example of the series of department stores designed by the famous architect.

The façade of white Euville stone is pleasantly designed. The vast entrance hall is lit from above by a granite and iron street-light which gives the interior the appearance of a public square. Around the hall are a restaurant, book shop, library and small display in memory of Victor Horta. The library is both a reading room open to all *(no charge for holders of admission tickets)* and a study centre equipped with a computerized catalogue of comic strips. The monumental stone staircase has an iron balustrade decorated with charming palmetto motifs; it leads up to the rooms containing the Centre's collections. Temporary exhibitions are held there on a regular basis. The glass roof diffusing soft light and the exposed metal framework are typical features of the Art Nouveau style.

The first exhibition on the mezzanine explains the different stages involved in making a comic strip (script, drawing, colouring, printing, distribution). A small auditorium with 50 seats presents a number of non-stop audio-visual films on Art Nouveau, the Ninth Art or its most illustrious representatives. "Le Trésor" contains more than 3 000 original plates from the greatest comic strips, put on view 300 at a time in rotation. Animated cartoons and the corresponding techniques are described by means of authentic documents.

On the first floor, a clever **Museum of the World of the Imagination** takes visitors on a trip through the world of the great heroes of Belgian comic strips and their creators, thanks to small dioramas and well-planned décors. The museum begins with the very famous Tintin (Hergé) and his faithful companions, followed by Spirou (Rob-Vel), Gaston Lagaffe (André Franquin), Bob and Bobette (Willy Vandersteen), Blake and Mortimer (Edgar Pierre Jacobs), Lucky Luke (Morris), Boule and Bill (Roba), the Smurfs (Peyo), Gil Jourdan (Tillieux), etc. Magazines, plates, sketches, working tools and photographs all help to weave the spell which has captivated young and old alike ever since Hergé first introduced his hero in the pages of *Le Petit Vingtième*, the children's supplement to the newspaper *Le Vingtième Siècle*.

Options from Rue des Sables:

▶▶ Cathédrale Saint-Michel by going up the steps then turning right into Boulevard de Berlaymont which brings you out almost at the Cathedral.

Quartier du Botanique by going down the street and turning right into Rue du Marais then continuing to Boulevard du Jardin Botanique. Go up the boulevard to Rue Royale or down to Place Rogier.

Quartier du Béguinage by returning to Place de Brouckère then going along Rue des Augustins and turning left towards Tour Noire.

Quartier de La Monnaie. Return to Rue Neuve. Place de la Monnaie is located at the end of the street.

The May Tree

The planting of the *Meiboom*, or May tree, takes place each year at the corner of Rue des Sables and Rue du Marais. The tradition dates back to Brussels' victory over Louvain, an event which has been celebrated by the planting of a tree since 1213. It was formerly carried out by the Crossbowmen's Guild in the 14C and later by the Guildsmen of St Lawrence; it is now the local inhabitants who organise the event on 9 August each year (eve of the Feast of St Lawrence). During the ceremonies a guild-member climbs up the tree to fly the town's red and green flag before the eighteenth hour. The deadline was fixed because everything had to be over before evensong.

Sometimes a bush, pole or even a simple plant is used to symbolise the tree, in order to keep the tradition alive.

A JUBILEE UNDER LEOPOLD II
Setting and buildings

To celebrate the golden jubilee of the kingdom of Belgium, Leopold II and Victor Besme decided to make use of a military parade ground which was obstructing the development of new suburbs to the north-east of the capital, and erect a prestigious building to commemorate the event. The building was part of a vast urban project *(see European Institutions: A Tour of the Squares)* masterminded by Gédéon Bordiau who in 1875 proposed the creation of an esplanade (park and museums) which would provide a landmark between the Royal Park and Tervuren Castle. Drawing inspiration from the Victoria and Albert Museum in London and the Palais de Longchamps in Marseille, he designed a complex consisting of two wings connected by a semi-circular colonnade.

Le Cinquantenaire

On 20 June 1880 only the two wings were ready to house the National Exhibition for the Golden Jubilee of the Belgian nation; only one of the two rose windows on the façade remains; the other was destroyed in 1946 when the Pavilion of Antiquity was ravaged by fire; it was rebuilt ten years later in a different style but one which respected the overall symmetry of the building. The colonnade was completed in 1888 and the mosaics added in 1920. In 1897 the site was used for the World Fair. The rear halls, whose metal structure was intended to reflect the technology of the times, were then added. The **arcades** alone only required eight months' work (1904-1905) and were built by the Frenchman, Charles Girault (1851-1932), whom the king had met at the World Fair in Paris in 1900. For this particularly symbolic monument, the architect proposed a triple arcade (30m – 100ft wide) in the Louis XVI style, differing from the commemorative arch of Antiquity in that its three openings are of equal dimensions. The decorative programme is intended to attract attention. In the eyes of the people of Brussels, however, the quadriga alone – *Brabant Raising the National Flag*, by Jules Lagae (1862-1931) and Thomas Vinçotte (1850-1925) is enough to incarnate the Golden Jubilee. Eight allegories of the provinces occupy the base of the monumental arch (the 9th is depicted in the quadriga). The allegories of Fame (winged female figures blowing on a trumpet) in bronzed plaster which once decorated the 4 corners of the upper storey were removed in 1910 and not replaced by the bronzes originally designed to go there.

In 1888, Gédéon Bordiau conceived the idea of a comprehensive museum. The idea naturally appealed to the ambitious views of Leopold II, who wanted to give his country an image in keeping with the European power it had become during his reign. The Jubilee Palace is therefore a place of education and edification which will gradually develop according to the vicissitudes of History. Today, the buildings house the Royal Museums of Art and History (south wing, divided into the Nervian wing and Kennedy wing, added in 1966), the Army Museum (north wing and hall), Autoworld (south hall), a casting shop (south hall), and the laboratories and library of the Institut royal du Patrimoine artistique (IRPA – Royal Artistic Heritage Institute), built in 1962 on the Avenue de la Renaissance side.

Park

The park, designed by Gédéon Bordiau, is the suburban equivalent of the Brussels Park. It consists of a formal garden (in line with the palace) and landscape gardens (along the sides) but is being developed only gradually. Certain parts of the park date back to the 1880 and 1897 exhibitions, while the plantations date from 1888 (elms, oleanders, acacias, chestnut trees). The land was used as a fairground up until 1930, when the Heysel Exhibition Grounds were opened in the northern part of the town. An expressway was built through the park in 1974.

There are various monuments. In 1889 Victor Horta built a temple, the **Pavillon des Passions Humaines,** a small open temple-like construction dedicated to human passions which, although still somewhat removed from Art Nouveau, already shows a certain mastery of this type of architecture which was soon to achieve universal renown. The pavillion was created for the sculpture of the same name by the sculptor Jef Lambeaux. It was however soon walled up, initially at the request of the authorities who considered it to be immoral and secondly, at the request of Lambeaux who believed that his sculpture was not being shown to advantage by the zenithal lighting designed by Horta. Closed after three days, the pavillion has never been finished. Several sculptures lie along the path, including *Le Faucheur* by Constantin Meunier, *Les Bâtisseurs de villes* by Charles van der Stappen, and allegories of the seasons at the western entrance. The small tower, a medieval pastiche from the end of the last century, was built to glorify the architectural qualities of Tournai stone. The former "Panorama of Cairo", built in 1880 by Ernest van Humbeek in the Arabic style, was restored and turned into a mosque in 1978 by the Tunisian architect Boubaker.

★★★ MUSÉES ROYAUX D'ART ET D'HISTOIRE (HS M⁷) ⊙

The museums, which were originally established in 1835 at Porte de Hal, are among the largest on the European continent and offer a panorama of human history from prehistoric times to the present. The collections are extremely rich, particularly with regard to Antiquity, the non-European civilisations and the decorative arts, especially the altarpieces and tapestries which are a brilliant reflection of Belgian art. There are about 140 exhibition rooms, a library containing more than 100 000 books, an educational and cultural service, creative workshops for children and adults, a museum for the blind and a slide library. Temporary exhibitions regularly attract a large public.

Turn left into the circular entrance hall, then left again into room 44 (18C vehicles), and go down to level 0 to begin the tour in room 14.

The numbers in square brackets correspond to the room numbers assigned by the museum.

level 0

The Near East collections cover a vast geographical area which, according to biblical sources, was the Garden of Eden. These regions, with their deserts and mountains and Fertile Crescent, gave birth to various civilisations illustrated here by Cyprus whose art, as a result of its geographical position and trade relations, bears the stamp of Egyptian, Greek and Phoenician influences.

ROOMS		CONTENTS	SELECTION
Near East	14	Cyprus and Palestine: ceramics, sculpture	Woman with a Dove (5C BC) [I].
Near East	15	Cyprus, Palestine, Anatolia: ceramics and figurines from the historical period.	Christian ossuary from Jerusalem [V] ; idols [VI].
Mesopotamia	16	Ceramics; figurines; tablets; jewellery; weights; cylindrical seals; furniture ornaments; reconstruction of the Ur ziggurat.	**Votive terracotta from Gilgamesh** (c2250-1900 BC) [XIII]; development of writing [XV], relief from Khorsabad Palace (721-705 BC) [wall on right]; ivories from Nimrud [XXVI]

Mesopotamia was a highly developed civilisation situated between the Tigris and the Euphrates. Not only did it give us urban civilisation and writing, but also magnificent palaces decorated with expressive reliefs. Iran was the seat of various cultures, such as the one in Luristan which was characterised by fantastic and naturalistic figures, in the Kingdom of Achemides (550-330 BC) whose capital was Persepolis, and in the Seleucid, Parthian and Sassanian periods.

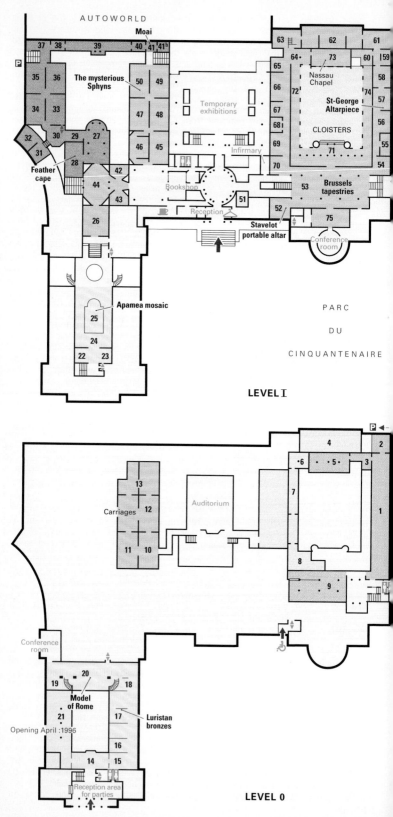

MUSÉES   ROYAUX

AUTOWORLD

Moai

The mysterious
Sphyns

Temporary
exhibitions

Nassau
Chapel

St-George
Altarpiece

CLOISTERS

Infirmary

Feather
cape

Bookshop

Brussels
tapestries

Reception

Stavelot
portable altar

Conference
room

Apamea mosaic

PARC

DU

CINQUANTENAIRE

LEVEL I

Carriages

Auditorium

Conference
room

Model
of Rome

Luristan
bronzes

Opening April : 1996

Reception area
for parties

LEVEL 0

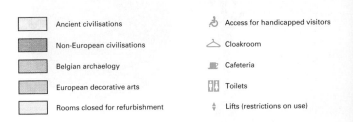

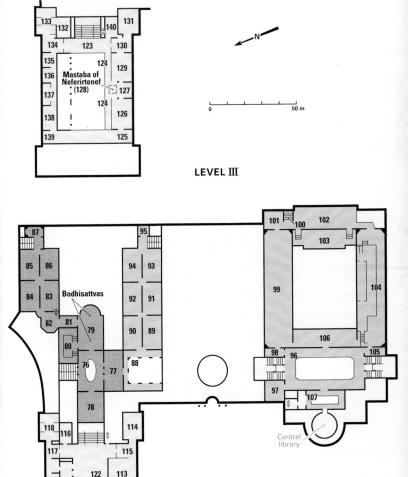

- Ancient civilisations
- Non-European civilisations
- Belgian archaelogy
- European decorative arts
- Rooms closed for refurbishment

- ♿ Access for handicapped visitors
- Cloakroom
- Cafeteria
- Toilets
- ↕ Lifts (restrictions on use)

N

0 _____ 50 m

LEVEL III

133 · 132 · 140 · 131
134 · 123 · 130
135 · 124 · 129
136 · Mastaba of Neferirtenef (128) · 127
137 · 124 · 126
138 ·
139 · 125

87
85 · 86 · 95 · 101 · 100 · 102
84 · 83 · 94 · 93 · 103
82 · 81 · 92 · 91 · 99 · 104
80 · 79 · 90 · 89
76 · 77 · 88 · 106
78 · 98 · 96 · 105
97 · 107

Bodhisattvas

118 · 116 · 114
117 · 115
119 · 122 · 113
121 · 112 · **Douris kantharos**
120 · 111
109 · 110
108

High dignitary

Central library

LEVEL II

Standard
from Luristan

Votive pin from Luristan

Musées Royaux d'Art et d'Histoire

Iran	17	Ceramics; seals; long-necked jugs; jewellery; weapons; silver plate	**Bronzes from Luristan** (13C-7C BC) [XXXIV, XXXV and XXXVI]
Near East	18	Mesopotamia: tour in braille (Gilgamesh Epic). Syria: ceramics. Arabian peninsula: reliefs.	Sabaean alabaster stele [LVII].
Syria Phoenicia, Petra (Jordan)	19	Syria: Palmyra, figurines, carved heads, idols. Phoenicia: divinities, vases. Petra: site and ceramics.	Palmyrene relief 1-3C [LXIX].
Rome	20	1/400th reconstruction (audio-visual presentation (French and Dutch): apply to guardian).	Scale model by the architect P Bigot, who lived at Villa Medicis from 1903 to 1908.
Islam		To be opened at the end of 1996.	

level I

Rome	22	Terracotta figurines;	
	23	Sculptures.	
Rome	24	Display cases presenting every-day objects; Syro-Phoenician glassware.	

level II

Greece	116	Technical room: manufacture and restoration of vases.	
Italy	117	Ceramics; lamps; bronzes; helmets.	Jewellery.
Pre-Roman Etruria	118	Ex-votoes; funerary urns; canopic vessels; balsam flasks; *bucchero* (black ceramic) vases.	Collection of **mirrors**; terracotta statue of Hercules as a youth (3C BC).
Rome	119	Gallery of busts (chronological); mosaics (4C).	Orators (3C); **high-ranking imperial civil servant** (c400); "Therapenides" mosaic (on the floor).
Rome	120	Relief room: sarcophagi and stelae.	
Rome	121	Apamea Room: large colonnade (c168);	Statue of Septimus Severus (modern head) **The "great hunt" mosaic** (5-6C). [level I]
	122	Mosaics	

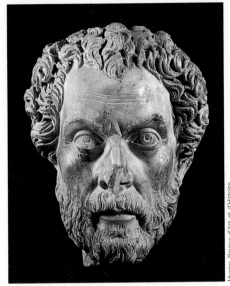

High-ranking imperial dignitary

Musées Royaux d'Art et d'Histoire

The large reconstructed column of Apamea is a result of the Belgian archaeological missions conducted in Syria since 1930. In the 5C, Apamea became the Roman capital of Second Syria; the large marble tessera mosaic was probably ordered from a studio in Constantinople.

Greece	108	Statues.	Panther satyr [4].
Greece	109	The Aegean world, Bronze Age: ceramics, Cycladic idols.	Mycaenean gold goblet (c1550-1450 BC).
Greece	110	Ceramics, geometric style, and 8-7C BC: Corinth and Cyprus.	Oriental-style Corinthian alabasters (7C BC) [II 4].
Greece	111	7-5C BC ceramics: Corinth, Boetia, Rhodes, Attica.	Boetian figurines [III 2] ; Attic amphorae [III 3]; Panathenaen jars [III 8]; Attic amphorae [III 13].

The narrative style led to the disappearance of the geometric style. In the 7C Corinth developed the so-called "black figure" style in which details are incised; mythological iconography with motifs reflecting trade with the East. In the 6C potters signed their elegantly shaped works and Athens developed the so-called "red figure" style in which details are painted – mythological, epic and everyday scenes. It reached its peak in the 5C with the so-called "severe", "free" and "floral" styles; this last style mainly depicted the feminine and mythological world.

Musées Royaux d'Art et d'Histoire

Kantharos by Douris

Greece	112	5C BC ceramics: Attica, archaic bronzes, glassware, terracotta.	Lekythi with white background [IV 5]; a kantharos by Douris (c490-480 BC) [IV 8]; red figure goblet [IV 9].
Greece	113	4C BC ceramics: Attica, Boetia, southern Italy. Sculptures, mirrors.	Fluted krater [VI 5]; rhytons [VI 3]; figurines from Tanagra [VI 4].
Greece	114	Sculptures.	Seated nymph (Roman replica).
Greece	115	3-1C BC Hellenistic ceramic. Figurines from Myrine. Jewellery.	Wooden table from Luxor.

level III

Egypt	123	Statuary.	The lion-headed goddess Sekhmet (*c*1300 BC).
Egypt	124	Writing material: stelae, cylindrical seals, papyrus.	Fragment of one of the most ancient *Books of the Dead* (*c*1700? BC).
Egypt	125	Technical display cases.	
Egypt	126	Prehistoric and archaic times: pottery, sculpture, reliefs, objects.	**Lady of Brussels** (*c*2600 BC); red terracotta vases (*c*3700 BC).

Old Kingdom (*c*2600-2130 BC): A highly organised State, with pyramids, mastabas and majestic statues. Middle Kingdom (*c*2040-1650 BC): A powerful State, with unbaked brick tombs and hypogea, skilfully executed sculpture. New Kingdom (*c*1550-945 BC): Golden age with the Eighteenth Dynasty, policy of expansion, gigantic temples, expressive, refined art, development of painting.

Egypt	127	Old Kingdom: reliefs and statuary	Head of King Mycerinus (*c*2500 B.C.).
Egypt	128	Mastaba of Neferirtenef (*c*2400 BC) from Saqqara.	**Low-reliefs** (painted limestone).
Egypt	129	Middle Kingdom: reliefs, stelae and funerary furnishings; figurines; statuary; vases; canopic vessels; ornaments.	Scale models of boats (*c*1900 BC); scenes from everyday life (*c*1900 BC); magic ivory knives; relief of the god Min; statue of a dignitary.
Egypt	130	New Kingdom: statuary, reliefs; art industry.	Relief of the god Osiris (*c*1550 BC).

Musées Royaux d'Art et d'Histoire

Relief of Queen Tiy

Egypt	131	New Kingdom: statuary; reliefs; ornaments; objects; ushabti (funerary statuettes); masks of mummies.	**Theban relief of Queen Tiy** (*c*1400 BC); the god Amon depicted as Tutankhamon; ushabti of Neferrenpet.
	140	Samples of antique marble.	
Egypt	132	Reconstruction of the tomb of Nakht (18C dynasty; *closed*).	
Egypt	133	Funerary cult: coffins and mummies.	Coffins of a Theban woman (*c*850 BC), the "embroideress" mummy (Roman era).
Egypt	134	New Kingdom: alabasters; terracottas. Funerary furnishings. Mummies of animals.	Ushabti figures and heart scarabs, Horkaoui's coffin (*c*200 BC).

The delicate Theban relief which was purchased in 1905 by the famous Belgian archeologist Jean Capart represents Queen Tiy, the wife of Amenhotep III. A beautiful copy of the Book of the Dead belonging to Neferrenpet recounts the vicissitudes of the journey of the soul to the abode of the blessed.

Close-up of the Neferrenpet papyrus

Egypt	135	New Kingdom: reliefs, ostraca; painted fragments.	**Papyrus of Neferrenpet** (*c*1200 BC); relief of Neferhotep.
Egypt	136	Art of the Ramses period: reliefs; statuary.	Memphite dignitary (*c*1250 BC); mica and ivory ornaments (Middle Kingdom); Meroitic ceramics.
Egypt	137	Nubia (now The Sudan): ceramics; ushabti figures; art industry.	Cube-statues; portrait of the priest Petamenope; bronze situla (funeral vase); divinity with a spatula-shaped head.
Egypt	138	Lower period (715 BC-395): statuary and reliefs; sacred bronze animals.	
Egypt	139	Later period: statuary; reliefs; terracottas; carved bones; Coptic capitals; glassware.	Portraits of mummies from Fayum (2C); head of King Ptolemy.

level IV *(not on map)*

| Egypt | | Saqqarah Room: moulds and reproductions. | Plaster model of the Djeser funeral complex in Saqqarah including the famous stepped pyramid. |

Go down to level I

level I

Precision and clock-making instruments	26	Geometry, measurement of time and matter.	Coronelli globes (late 17C); collection of clocks.
Vehicles	44	18C	Sedan chairs (18C)
America	27	North: ivory and terracotta objects. Meso-America: figurines, masks; figurative urns.	Seated divinity (Mexico, 600-900); funerary figurines, terracotta and bitumen head (Mexico, 600-900).
America	28	Textiles (Peru), feathers, wood, masks, sculpture.	**Feather cloak** (Brazil, *c*16C); Chimu statuette (1100-1450).
America	29	Maya: terracotta, carved panels, stelae.	Panel decorated with a warrior (*c*600); tetrapod vases (300-600).

The Maya era covers thousands of sites in Mexico (Yucatan, Tabasco, Chiapas), Guatemala, Belize, Salvador (East) and the Honduras (East). The zenith of this culture occurred around the year 700, followed by that of the Toltecs, from 950 to 1150. The conquering Aztecs had a uniting influence on Mexican art from 1350 to 1521, with religion as the main source of inspiration.

America	30	Precious materials: flint, shell, stone, alloys.	Mica silhouette of the claws of a bird of prey (USA *c*400); gold jewellery; ornaments in the shape of a double scroll (Columbia, 600-1500).
America	31	Feather ornaments; shrunken heads.	Shipibo vases (Amazonia, 20C).
America	32	Study.	Mummy from Rascar Capac (Peru).
America	33	Costa Rica and Panama: carved stone, polychrome ceramics.	"Axe-gods", four-figure metate.
America	34	Mexico: terracotta, carved stone, polychrome ceramics.	Effigy vases (900-1200); eagle's head (*c*1400).

In South America, the countries in the Pacific Basin underwent superior development to those on the Atlantic Coast. Among the pre-Hispanic civilisations, Peru dominated Columbia, Ecuador and Bolivia. Although its gold stirred the imagination of the Europeans, Peru knew various forms of expression, with the Mochicas in the north, the Nazcas in the south and, after 1480, the Incas.

America	35	South: terracottas, ceramics, figurines, pebbles.	Anthropomorphous incense holder (Ecuador), human figures (Columbia, 1200-1400).
America	36	Peru: terracottas, figurines.	Mochica portrait-vase (100 BC-600); Inca aryballos (1450-1533).
Polynesia	37	Tapas (fabric made of beaten bark) from the islands of Fidji, Hawaii and Samoa.	Replica of a colossal statue (Easter Island).
Polynesia	38	Navigation and migration.	
Polynesia	39	Tapas; everyday objects; fishing; ornaments.	Weapons and paddles (19C); Maori head (19C), fan-shaped festive headress (Raivavae Island).
Polynesia	40	Music, dance, games.	
Polynesia	41a		Colossal statue (Easter Island, 1100 to 1680).
Polynesia	41b	Evocation of the Franco-Belgian mission (1934-35).	
Art Nouveau and Art Deco	50	Decorative arts.	*The Mysterious Sphinx* (1897, Van der Stappen); ceramics.

The furniture in room 50 is a reconstruction of the display cases designed by Victor Horta in 1912 for Wolfers, the jewellers in Brussels. They were made of mahogany from the Honduras by the London firm Sage and contain mainly ivory sculptures from the 1897 World Fair.

Musées Royaux d'Art et d'Histoire

Outline of a bird of prey's talon

Musées Royaux d'Art et d'Histoire

The Mysterious Sphinx,
by Charles Van der Stappen

18-19C	49	Louis XVI, Directoire and Empire furniture, paintings on canvas.
Baroque and Rococco	48	Furniture from Liège.
17-18C	47	Brussels tapestries, after cartoons by J van Orley; Louis XV and XVI furniture, silverware, fans.
Regency	46	A Paris music salon; porcelain from Tournai; Gobelins tapestries, oak wainscoting.
16-18C	45	Furniture; tapestry; sculpture; silverware.
16-19C	42	Household silver.
16-19C	43	Household silver.

Gilt leather (probably Malines, 17C-18C).
Don Quichotte suspendu à la fenêtre (first half of 18C).

"Buffon bird" dinner service (*c*1790); snuff-boxes.

Pietà by M. van Beveren; Antwerp cabinets; Boulle "Mazarin" marquetry bureau.

Gold plate (Antwerp and Brugges).

level II

This section evokes several civilisations showing the cultural diversity of India and South East Asia (Hinduism, Buddhism and Jainism) as well as the astonishing continuity of China (the Shang, Chou, Han, T'ang, Sung, Ming and Ch'ing dynasties). This collection will provide useful chronological and topographical points of reference for Europeans.

Tibet and Nepal	77	Figurines of divinities; reliquaries; manuscript (Nepal, late 16C – early 17C).
India, Pakistan, Afghanistan, Sri Lanka	78	Figurines of the Indus; Gandhara art; statues of divinities; wooden pillars.
China	79	Neolithic; jade age; Bronze Age; Han archeology; T'ang (618-906), Sung (960-1279) and Ming (1368-1644) religious sculpture.

Collection of thang-ka (paintings on canvas rolls).

Bronze of the god Siva (Southern India, 13C).

Antique jade and bone objects (10-3C BC); 2 wooden **bodhisattvas** (*c*1200).

Bodhisattvas, which are expressions of Buddhist art, depict a magnificently moulded idealised face. Their very intense expression corresponds to a religious practice whose rite is aimed at "opening up to the light".

Bodhisattva

Musées Royaux d'Art et d'Histroire

China	80	Silk clothing; paintings and cal-ligraphy.	
China	81	Monochrome and "three co-lour" ceramics.	T'ang funerary figurines (618-906).
China, Korea	82	Large alcove bed (19C).	Korean pottery.
Vietnam	83	Collection of bronze drums.	Development of **ceramics** from neolithic times to the 17C.
Cambodia & Thailand	84	Khmer art. Paintings; statues of divinities.	Khmer sculptures (8-12C); window lintel (11C).
Indonesia	85	Weapons; carved wood; jewellery; basketwork.	Textiles.
Indonesia	86	Arts and crafts; statues, je-wellery, scale models of houses.	Grey stone statues.
	87	Gamelan orchestra; masks; marionnettes.	
Indonesia			
	88 to 95	*Extension of the Art Nouveau collections: opening in 1995 imminent.*	

From the circular entrance hall proceed to room 53 (tapestries) and down the stairs to level 0. On the way, between the circular entrance hall and room 53, note the Byzantine pieces and earthenware from Brussels.

level 0

National prehistory	1	A century of archeological research, from Paleolithic times (500 000 BC) to the end of the Iron Age: flint, tools, hunting, weapons, crafts, burials.	Lunula (neck ornament) from Fauvillers [31]; objects from the Eigenbilzen sepulture (c400 BC) [46]; Nervian cur-rency.
National prehistory	2	Audio-visual presentation: the main phases seen through the various sites *(30 mins).*	
Gallo-Roman Belgium	3	Blocks of pillars from funerary monuments.	Funerary mask.
Gallo-Roman Belgium	4	*Closed.*	
Gallo-Roman Belgium	5	Funerary objects and art	Votive sign (1C or 2C); phial in the form of a bunch of grapes (2C); glass kantharos (1C).

Gallo-Roman	6	*Closed.*	
Belgium	8	*Closed.*	
Merovingian	9	Funerary objects and art; architectural fragments.	8 tombs reconstructed on the ground (Harmignies, Hainaut); rings; fibulae; reconstruction of a bone-leaf casket [17];
Horse-drawn vehicles	10 13	Carriages, sledges, sedan chairs, saddles, spurs, stirrups, uniforms, models.	

level 1

| Byzantine art Roman and Mosan art (7-mid 13C) | 51 52 | *Closed.* Metal art: reliquaries, shrines, crooks, pyxides, Limoges enamels. Ivory sculpture. Statuary. | **Portable altar of Stavelot** (*c*1150-1160); reliquary of Pope Alexander I; ivory diptych from Genoels-Elderen; sedes sapientiae (*c*1070). |

Musées Royaux d'Art et d'Histoire

Portable altar of Stavelot

The altar from Stavelot Abbey, which is the finest piece in the Mosan art collection, draws its inspiration from Byzantine illuminations.
The quality of execution is equalled only by its iconographic design consisting of four Evangelists and the martyrdom of the eleven Apostles (on the perimeter) as well as Gospel and Biblical scenes.

Tapestries	53	Series of 8 tapestries, *The Triumph of the Virtues* (Brussels, *c*1550); sleds.	Flower-shaped sled (17C).
Cinema equipment	75	Projectors and cine cameras.	Animated plates (1980).
Middle Ages	54	Sculptures; ivories; reliquaries; altarpiece; tapestry.	Madonna and Child (France, 14C).
Middle Ages	55	Furniture; fresco; crockery; reliquaries; sculpture.	Alabasters from Nottingham (14C).
Middle Ages	56	Tapestries from Tournai (15C); sculpture (late15C-early 16C); Italian textiles.	*(tapestries exhibited alternately).*
Middle Ages	57	Sculpture.	**Passion Altarpiece** (Brussels, 1470-1480) and **St George Altarpiece** (Jean Borreman, Brussels, 1493).
Middle Ages	58	Sculpture; fragments of altar pieces; Brussels tapestries; stained-glass windows.	Altarpiece of the family of Sainte Anne (Brussels, *c*1500-1510).

Musées Royaux d'Art et d'Histoire

Passion Altarpiece - Close-up

Absolutely remarkable with regard to both quantity and quality, the altarpiece and tapestry collections alone make the museum worth visiting. A recent acquisition, the Brussels Passion Altarpiece retraces the Passion of Christ. This high quality work, whose panels (missing) were only opened on feast days, bears the stamp of Van der Weyden's art.

Middle Ages	59	German sculpture	Saint George (Swabia, late 15C).
Middle Ages	60	Technical room: the making of an altarpiece	
Renaissance	61	Sculpture and furniture.	**Passion Altarpiece** (Antwerp, c1525-1530) and the **Middelburg antependium** (southern Netherlands, c1518).
Renaissance	62	Religious furniture; sculpture; fragments of altarpieces; cradle said to be that of Charles V (of Spain); caskets; altarpiece.	La Légende de Notre-Dame de Sablon, tapestry (Brussels, 1516-1518); **L'Histoire de Jacob,** tapestry (Brussels, c1530).
Renaissance	63	Italian furniture; Majolica sculpture; ornate pavement.	L'Histoire d'Hercule, tapestry (Brussels, c1570).
Renaissance	64	Technical room; tapestry.	
Renaissance	65	Furniture; Majolica.	Pavement (Antwerp, 1532); Majolica jug (Antwerp, 1562).
Renaissance and Baroque	66	Furniture and wood sculpture; silverware; ceramics; tapestries; altarpiece.	Limoges enamel work (16C); **Malines alabasters** (late 16C).
Baroque	67	Furniture; leaded glass windows; Brussels tapestries.	Wardrobe (1680); Delft ware.
Baroque	68	Furniture; leaded glass windows; stove.	Terracotta sculptures; cabinet (Antwerp, mid 17C).
Baroque	69	Sculptures; tapestries; furniture; silverware; English embroidery.	Travelling Crucifix (c1700); Guild chain of office (17C).

Baroque	70	Brussels tapestries (*c*1650). Antwerp cabinets (17C).
Cloisters	71	Memorial stones; fragments and furniture from churches; leaded glass windows.

The cloisters gardens are open to the public in the summer. The cloisters are a partial copy of those at La Cambre Abbey; St George's Chapel, also called the Nassau Chapel, is a replica of the one in the Royal Library buildings.

Musées Royaux d'Art et d'Histoire

The Story of Jacob - Close-up

Cloisters	72	Pewter and stained glass.	Temperance plate (late 16C); leaded glass window by B van Orley (1540).
Nassau chapel	73	Brassware	Liturgical furniture; baptismal font (cast brass, 1149).
Cloisters	74	Glassware: from its origins to 18C.	Flask (Venice, early 16C); glasses engraved using a grinding wheel (Nuremberg, Hessen, Saxony).

level 2

Glassware and leaded glass	96	20C	101 pieces by M. Marinot.
Coptic textiles	97	Furnishings and clothing (linen and wool).	Child's slipper (5C?).
Cinema equipment	107	Projectors and cine cameras.	
Lace	106	16-19C; Italy, France and Belgium.	**Albert and Isabelle's bed cover** (1599); benediction veils.

An exceptional piece (lace did not exist before the 16C), the bobbin lace bed cover of the Archduke Albert and Archduchess Isabel was made for their wedding and their arrival on the ducal throne. The iconography consists of 120 scenes, while the border depicts the kings and emperors of Rome together with various Sibyls. The collection of Delftware, one of the most prestigious in the world, offers a unique panorama of the industry – from the famous blue to pieces with black, brown, olive green, yellow, or turquoise blue backgrounds.

Costumes and textiles	105	18C to the present day.
	104	Modern furniture.

Ceramics	102	Delft: development; Arnhem ware (1759-1773).	**Violin** (early 18C); landscapes attributed to Frédéric van Frijtom; tulip vases, some of which are shaped like obelisks; bird cage (1st half of 18C).
	100	Staircase from Hôtel de Hornes.	
Ceramics	101	Dutch tiles: Delft, Gouda, Rotterdam, Frisland.	Technical display case
Ceramics	103	Contemporary production.	
Precious Objects	98	Watches, jewellery, fans, miniatures, accessories	
European ceramics	99	Faïences and porcelain by major European manufacturers.	Bust of an old man (white faïence), Brussels, 1743.

★★ **Autoworld** (HS M[23]) ☉ – Since 1986 some 450 vehicles, mainly motorcars, have been on show under the high glass roof of the southern hall of Jubilee Palace (Palais du Cinquantenaire). Although the exhibition includes prize pieces from the De Pauw collection, formerly the Manhattan Center Museum, and cars owned by members of the Royal Veteran Car Club, most of the vehicles presented come from the prestigious **Ghislain Mahy collection.**

Born in Ghent in 1901, Mahy collected 800 motor, steam, electric and petrol vehicles over a period of forty years. Although the cars were often in a pitiful state when he bought them, he did his utmost to bring them back to life in his repair shop; today, nearly 300 cars are in perfect working order.

In chronological order, the ground floor tour shows the technical and aesthetic developments of European and American manufacturers. The collection, of which a fairly detailed selection is given below, begins with the first motor vehicle i.e. a horseless carriage, developed by the German Carl Benz.

Germany – A 1911 Hansa, with its very modern body; a 1911 Opel, which was the largest German production of the time; a 1915 Wanderer, a very popular two-seater, with one seat behind the other; a 1922 Mercedes, whose engine was derived from a plane engine; a 1925 Hanomag; a 1928 Dixi, ancestor of the BMW; a 1931 Brennabor; a 1936 Horch, the Auto-Union's top model – the 930V was often used as a staff vehicle during the Second World War; a 1940 BMW; a 1950 Volkswagen II, the biggest success in the world of the automobile, popularly called the "Beetle"; Mercedes-Benz C111, an experimental vehicle which could go at 403 km/hr – 252 mph, etc.

Belgium – Belga Rise, FN, Fondu, Hermes, Imperia, Miesse, Nagant and Vivinus are all represented, but the most famous is Minerva. Originally a bicycle, then a moped maker, the Antwerp manufacturer Sylvain de Jong presented his first prototype **Minerva** in 1902. The range, which initially included 3 models (2, 3 and 4 cylinders) increased steadily until the 1930s. The factory had 1600 workers on its payroll in 1911; it offered electric lighting as an option in 1912, followed by electric ignition in 1914, then in 1922, all four wheels were equipped with brakes. The firm acquired an excellent reputation for the high level of comfort offered by its superb automobiles with their silent engines. In 1930, Minerva had a range of 12 to 40 continental horsepower. But the golden age of the luxury automobile was coming to an end; the clientele turned to less expensive makes and, in 1934, Minerva went bankrupt.

The museum has about fifteen Minervas. The oldest dates back to 1910 and belonged to the Belgian Court. The 1921 30 cont.hp. model, with bodywork by Vanden Plas, was owned by King Albert. The most luxurious was the 1930 40 cont.hp., whose American bodywork is made of aluminium; it could go up to 140 km/hr – 87 mph. Other vehicles include a 1901 FN; a 1910 Nagant (D'leteran Room), a 6-seater made in Liège; two FN sports cars (1925 and 1930), built to compete in the 24-hour Francorchamps Grand Prix, and an astonishing 1930 FN 1400, whose body was custom-built for the Shah of Persia; a 1934 Belga Rise, sometimes called the Belgian Rolls, and a 1948 Imperia, the last Belgian car.

Minerva radiator cap

Ph. Cajic/MICHELIN

United States – A 1904 Oldsmobile; a 1911 Model T Ford, of which more than 15 000 000 were made between 1908 and 1927 – the 1921 Model T Ford just opposite is the first car bought by Mahy in 1944; a 1916 Detroit, an electric car; a 1917 Cadillac, a pioneer make in the field of electric lighting and ignition; a 1917 Hudson, a model used in France by General Pershing's staff to move along the front; a 1924 Ford TT, one of the first Mobile Homes in the world, shown here with Belgian bodywork; a 1925 Chrysler topping 100 km/hr – 62.5 mph; a 1930 De Soto roadster; a 1931 Pierce-Arrow, a very luxurious interwar make; a 1937 Cord with its 4 retractable headlights; a 1938 Cadillac, one of the official White House cars, of which only two exist; a 1956 Cadillac, used by J F Kennedy when he visited Berlin in 1963; a 1961 Studebaker, a version of the famous coupé designed by the Franco-American designer Raymond Loewy; a 1957 Lincoln Continental coupé, the most expensive American car of the time, etc.

France – An 1899 Aster tricycle; a 1901 de Dion-Bouton "vis-a-vis", owned by Albert De Dion; a 1906 Populaire, famous for its often-copied "crocodile-style" bonnet; a 1905 Clément-Bayard double phaeton; a 1906 Lacroix-De Laville with a tiller steering; a 1908 Renault, a master vehicle with a "chapeau de gendarme" bonnet; a 1910 Sizaire-Naudin with independent front wheels; a 1911 Darracq, taken over by Talbot at the beginning of the twenties; a 1911 Le Zèbe, a little two-seater which cost 3 000 gold francs; a 1913 Peugeot minicar designed according to drawings by E. Bugatti; a 1913 Alva and 1914 Panhard-Levassor; a 1914 Grégoire with one door at the front left and the other at the back right; a 1920 Bellanger, made in Paris with American parts, with the American left-hand drive of the time; a 1920 Delage, a luxury model from the 20s; a 1924 Renault whose body was fitted in Liège by Gamette; a 1925 Citroën 5 CV or "Cloverleaf"; a 1925 Ravel, a nautical style wooden sports car; a 1927 Darmont, a 3-wheeled sports car; a 1928 Bugatti type 44; a 1929 Omega-Six, an underslung racing car; a 1929 Voisin and its famous radiator cap mascot; a 1934 Citroën 7A with its so-called "front-wheel drive", a favourite with gangsters; a 1935 30 CV Hispano-Suiza with its body fitted out by Chapron as a "driver coupé"; a 1938 Delahaye; a 1941 Peugeot, with an electric motor; a 1951 Renault 4 CV, designed by Ferdinand Porsche, etc.

Great Britain – A 1921 Rolls-Royce Silver Ghost; a 1922 Daimler, with its snakeskin upholstery; a 1926 Rolls-Royce and its radiator mascot, the famous Spirit of Ecstasy; a 1928 Bentley; a 1936 Daimler, used as a ceremonial vehicle with enough headroom for a top hat; a 1938 Rolls-Royce Phantom in a model whose body was fitted in Belgium.

Italy – A 1931 Fiat; a 1933 Lancia Astura with a body fitted by Farina; a 1948 Alfa-Romeo, one of the most expensive automobiles of the time.

Salle d'Ieteren – Exhibition of horse-drawn vehicles, from the sleigh to the gala berlin (1852) whose body was fitted by Ehrler in Paris and used on the occasion of Napoleon III's marriage to Eugénie de Montijo. Note the "spider" (late 19C), a very light model on high wheels, nicknamed for its spindly silhouette.

Here and there are motocycles and minicars i.e. small-engined cars halfway between a toy and a classical automobile: Rovin (F-1950); Vespa (I-1959); Messerschmidt (1955); BMW Isetta (1962); the Porquerolle tricycle (F-1973). The Mahy workshop on the first floor contains less prestigious and more recent vehicles. A few models are worth noting, such as a vehicle decorated by the Belgian artist Folon and an amphibious vehicle.

Musée royal de l'Armée et de l'Histoire militaire (HS M⁸) ⊘ – The Royal Museum of the Army and Military History was created in 1910 in La Cambre Abbey at the initiative of Louis Leconte a carabineer officer who was its first extremely dynamic curator. The present museum was set up in 1923 for the Golden Jubilee. Potentially, it is the richest in the world, extending far beyond national military history and containing a number of extremely diversified collections owing to the very fruitful acquisition policy adopted by Louis Leconte. Unfortunately, a large number of pieces are in reserve (such as the unique collection relating to the Balkan States and the Ukraine). The museum is currently being completely reorganised which means the visitor may find a few surprises or changes with respect to the description below.

A library with a total of 450 000 volumes is open to the public.

★ **Salle d'armes et d'armure** – A splendid display of 11-18C weapons and late 15C-17C armour from former arsenals. A display case protects the armour of the Archduke Albert (worn during his "Joyous Entrance" in July 1599) and his horse, which he had stuffed after it saved him during the siege of Ostend, together with that of his wife, the Archduchess Isabelle; an astonishing child's armour (16C) which belonged to Joseph-Ferdinand of Bavaria, the son of the governor of the Netherlands.

Collection Titeca – Scheduled for re-opening in 1997. Housed under the quadriga of the archways in a long room ressembling a vaulted cellar, this varied collection consists of some 300 items of **military headgear** (Pre-Revolutionary France, England,

Germany, Russia, Netherlands, French Second Empire and Restoration), six hundred sabres and swords, as well as First Empire uniforms and musical instruments. The two terraces afford a magnificent **panoramic view** of the capital and the trunk road created by Leopold II, Avenue de Tervuren.

Salle de la Révolution brabançonne et de l'Empire (1750-1815) – Two sections or more exactly, two small displays are devoted to the two eventful periods which preceded independance. Numerous paintings (mid 19C) by Jules van Imschoot commemorate the episode of the Belgian "United States" Army. Opposite, various souvenirs evoke the French period, particularly the Battle of Waterloo. A portrait of Napoleon is attributed to David.

Salle technique – *To be re-opened*. The pieces, mainly portable firearms, come from the Herstal National Factory. The room is very interesting from a museological point of view (the oldest in this respect in Belgium, along with the Historical Room).

Salle historique (1830-1914) – This room contains the essence of the museum's collections; its display is very heterogeneous with *(right)* the development of the Belgian army's uniform, *(left)* the Civil Guard, the Belgian Royal Navy, long-distance expeditions, and the Belgian voluntary overseas service, from Congo to Peking and Mexico, *(back)* headgear and equipment from the war of 1870. The room also contains the personal effects (clothing and decorations) of Belgium's first two kings, Leopold I and Leopold II.

Salle de la Première Guerre mondiale et de l'entre-deux-guerres – *Closed*. Equipment used by the Allies and Germany during the 1914-1918 war, mainly heavy artillery.

Halle Bordiau (1939-1945 and Post-War Years) – *Scheduled for re-opening in 1997*.

★ **Section Air et Espace** – This section, which has been built up through an exchange system and is housed in a huge hall, includes some 150 aircraft (70 on display), mainly fighter aircraft, dominated by a Sabena Caravelle.

On the ground floor are fighter-bombers, and propeller and supersonic aircraft including the following: a British Spitfire (1943 – the most famous), a 1945 De Havilland Mosquito and a 1951 Meteor; an American Douglas DC3 "Dakota" (1935 – more than 13 000 constructed), a Fairchild C119 (1950 – used in Korea and Vietnam), a 1950 Sabre, and a 1958 Phantom; a 1945 Belgian Stampe (a biplane of worldwide renown), a Soviet Mig (1958 and 1975), a French Dassault Ouragan (1949 – the first mass-produced French jet aircraft), and a Fouga Magister (1951 – the first trainer jet in the world). Three subsections present engines from 1898 to today, Belgian military aviation in Africa and Belgian expeditions to Antarctica.

Musée de l'Armée, Air and Space Section

Apart from a small section devoted to ballooning, the gallery mainly features a particularly fine collection of First World War aircraft – a copy of Baron Manfred van Richthofen's German Fokker, a British Bristol, a Caudron, a Maurane-Saulnier, a Schreck, a Span, a French Voisin, etc.

Section des Blindés – *In the open air; access via Avenue des Gaulois which runs along the small park on the residential side.* This collection, in the open air, contains both Belgian vehicles (from 1935 onwards) and models from other countries (United States, France, Great Britain, Czechoslovakia, USSR). The most historical piece is a 1917 Mark IV tank with its original paintwork.

★ **Maison Cauchie** (HS W) ⊘ – *5 Rue des Francs.* This house was the residence (1905) of the architect and decorator Paul Cauchie. The astonishing façade is almost entirely decorated with graffiti. The graceful, delicately-coloured figures around the circular window show the influence of the Pre-Raphaelites. They depict the eight artistic disciplines.

The mezzanine and piano mobile have recently been opened to the public. They include some magnificent sgraffitti *(qv)*, furnishings inspired by the work of Charles Rennie Mackintosh and an exhibition of the work of Paul and Lina Cauchie (paintings, documents, etc.)

Everyone's dream avenue (HS) – Avenue de Tervuren was built to connect the World Fair organised in 1897 on the site of the Jubilee celebrations to the colonial exhibition presented in Tervuren. This major road, which was extremely modern for the times, begins almost at the foot of the arcades, cuts through the western suburbs, passes through Soignes Forest and ends up opposite the present-day Château de Tervuren built in 1896. A project for a "World City", designed by P Otlet, was envisaged without ever being built. The width of the avenue as it approaches Tervuren gives some idea of the scope of the dream entertained by the sovereign builder, Leopold II.

Options from Porte de Tervuren:

▶▶ Underground to the city centre (Quartiers de la Bourse, du Parlement, and du Palais Royal).

Quartier des Institutions Européennes by skirting the Cinquantenaire via Avenue de l'Yser and Avenue de la Renaissance then turning left into Avenue de Cortenberg and on to Rond-point Schuman.

Woluwe-Saint-Pierre and Woluwe-Saint-Lambert via Avenue de Tervuren.

Pol De Prins

Cauchie House

The "marvel" admired by Victor Hugo and the "rich backdrop" praised by Jean Cocteau is absolutely unique. Grand-Place is constantly in effervescence, with crowds of visitors converging on the square, and the atmosphere is quite unlike anything felt elsewhere.

It is beautiful at any time of day but is at its very best in the morning during the flower market in the summer, or at night when the floodlighting picks out its gilded features, modelling it into a surprising sort of high and low relief. Every two years, for just a few days during the month of August *(see Calendar of Events)*, a carpet of flowers covers the cobblestones of a Grand-Place lined with café terraces. During the festive season, Grand-Place is decorated with a Christmas tree and a crib with live animals.

Its Origins – A town cannot exist without a marketplace, which is why Ancient Athens had its *agora* and Ancient Rome its *forum*. In about 977 AD, Charles of France set up his *castrum*, or hillfort, overlooking the River Senne. This soon led to economic expansion resulting in the drainage of the marshes near the island of Saint-Géry with a view to the setting up of a *Nedermerckt*, or Lower Market.

The first market was totally unplanned. It spread as and when buildings were erected along irregularly-laid streets.

Even today, the names of most of the streets in the dip at the lower end of the city recall the many different trades and crafts that developed in this part of the urban community, with references to butter (Beurre), herring (Harengs), brewers (Brasseurs), coal (Charbon), cheese (Fromage), herbs (Herbes), skins (Peaux) etc. The houses were kept separate in order to minimise the fire risk and were built mainly of timber, seldom of stone. Then, in the 14C, the first covered markets began to appear (Bread Market, Linen Market, Meat Market, etc.), each of them an expression of the textile industry's prosperity and the subsequent fame enjoyed by Brussels.

From Market to Grand-Place – The marketplace was not only the centre of the city's economic life; it was also the setting for political meetings, the publication of police regulations, revolts, the declaration of privileges, the rendering of justice, and public celebrations. Gradually, the town ordered houses to be built further apart, creating a square. The council even expropriated a few residences in order to align the buildings and, after the construction of the Town Hall in the 15C, a square was opened up in the labyrinth of streets. In 1421, Philippe de Saint-Pol, who was appointed Regent by the States of Brabant, caused a revolt of tradesmen and craftsmen and had the Amtman (Mayor) beheaded. He then ensured that they were closely involved in the government of the city. This privilege was acknowledged by Duke John IV and the guilds, realising that the

Burgundian Court was visiting the town with increasing frequency, began to build their halls round the prestigious Town Hall. The Count of Charolais, the future Charles the Bold, laid the foundation-stone of its right wing in 1444. Depending on the century during which they were erected, these mainly stone-built houses reflected the vernacular architecture of their day and this gave the square a varied appearance. There were crow-stepped gables next to trefoiled windows or pinnacled gables (16C) and the superposition of architectural Orders next to triangular gables or rustication in the Italianate-Flemish style (17C). Flemish speakers have always called this spot *Grote Markt*, ie Main Market but in the eyes of the world as a whole Grand-Place (Main Square) was born.

The Bombardment of 1695 – The League of Augsburg which marked the alliance of

Grand-Place

the United Provinces, Great Britain, Germany and Spain against Louis XIV, ordered the bombardment of the coastal towns in the north of France and laid siege to Namur.

In reprisal, the Sun King ordered Maréchal de Villeroy to bombard Brussels which was weakened by the absence of Dutch and English troops (they were massed around the citadel in Namur).

So it was that, on 13 August, a French army of 70 000 men entrenched on the heights of Molenbeek pointed their cannons and mortars down at the town below and sent down a storm of incandescent cannon balls and mortar shells. This pitiless attack caused a terrible fire lasting two days and two nights. It ravaged Grand-Place and the streets round about.

Only the tower of the Town Hall was left standing, with the walls of the King's House and three house fronts. Not only was there a high cost in human lives but countless priceless treasures were also lost including, for example, the paintings representing the meting out of Justice by Rogier van der Weyden (also known as Roger de la Pasture), masterpieces that had been the pride of the Town Hall.

M. De Vigny, who was in charge of the French artillery, declared on 15 August, "I have never yet seen such a great fire nor so much desolation as that which I have seen in this town".

A Jewel beneath the Ashes – Shortly after the bombardment, the town's leaders received support from several other urban communities (Antwerp, Malines, Louvain, and Nivelles), as well as from Brabant, Holland and even Bavaria whose Prince-Elector, Maximilian-Emmanuel, was Governor of Brussels on behalf of the King of Spain. The town councillors immediately decided to require that designs for new buildings fronting Grand-Place be submitted to the authorities for their approval.

This type of regulation was an innovation in its day and the council even went so far as to threaten to impose a fine on anybody who failed to comply with it. It was given further impetus by the Governor's ambitions in the field of town planning. He wanted to give the hallmarks of princely power to a city centre that was decidedly middle-class. Faced with the rejection of the trades and crafts guilds who were traditionally very independent, only the building erected for the Dukes of Brabant reflected the Governor's ideas.

However, the most amazing aspect of this reconstruction is the architectural harmony despite the combination of Gothic, Italianate-Flemish Baroque and Louis XIV styles.

The extraordinary strength of this amalgam of buildings is the respect, within the same limited space and using the same concept of verticality, for the individualism of each of the guilds. This gives a soul to a gem which Victor Hugo described in 1837 when he said, "I am dazzled by Brussels".

E. Baret

THE TOWN HALL

With Henry III (1248-1261) at its head, Brussels had shaken off the hold of Louvain; with John I (1261-1294), the town enjoyed a major boom in international trade and it was time to build a Town Hall which would express the city's power and might. The foundation stone was laid in 1401 and the belfry and left wing were completed c1421. They were extended by a right wing on which building work lasted from 1444 to 1459. The design was based partly on fortified residences (rectangular with corner turrets) and partly on covered markets with an external staircase beneath a portico.

Whether Audenarde and Louvain like to admit it or not, the size and tower of the Town Hall in Brussels make it the finest such construction in the country. Described by Théophile Gautier as "a miraculous building" and by Victor Hugo as a "jewel comparable to the spire on Chartres Cathedral", the monument owes its partial survival to the fact that, in 1695, the French used the tower as a line-of-sight! The façades were raised from the ruins and the building as a whole is subject to regular restoration work.

The Tower – In 1449, the Town Council commissioned **Jan van Ruysbroeck** (early 15C-1485) to build a tower with spire in place of the belfry that no longer corresponded to the scale of the extensions being undertaken. The lower section has a square design, with four storeys of two windows; from the cornice upwards the windows are traceried. The second section is octagonal with three storeys and is flanked by bellcotes. Above them are pinnacles which draw the eye upwards to the pyramid-shaped spire. This elegant piece of lacework in stone is a marvel of architectural daring rising to a height of 96m - 312ft.

The famous statue of St Michael the Archangel made of copper plates by Martin van Rode, which had stood on top of the tower since 1465, was removed in 1995 so that it could be restored. And last but not least, if the doorway of the Town Hall is not absolutely in line, this is not because of a mistake in the architect's calculations (a long-lasting legend has it that he killed himself in a fit of despair) but because he retained the belfry porch and strengthened it so that he could add on the weight of his outstanding design.

The Wings – The original wing was designed by **Jacques van Thienen** but nobody knows who designed the right wing. Forty years passed between the building of the two sections. Yet the few visible differences in style do not interrupt the overall harmony. The ground floor consists of two galleries lined with arcades supported by jambs *(left)* and alternating jambs and columns *(right)*. To the left is the Lion Staircase (the lions were placed there in 1770) forming the main entrance to the original Town Hall. Above the two upper storeys is a crenelated balustrade reminiscent of medieval fortified mansions. This horizontal line has been skilfully integrated into the verticality of the building as whole, using full panels placed in line with the piers. The huge, sloping roof has four rows of dormer windows.

The Sculptures – The original sculptures are stored in the town's municipal museum *(see Maison du Roi)*. In the 19C, the frontage, side walls, tower and galleries were decorated with more than 150 statues. The ones on the frieze separating the two storeys on the left wing and beneath the canopy in the right wing represent the province's dukes and duchesses. The layout of the galleries is a particularly fine example of the work of the Brussels School which reached its heyday c1450.

To the left are some interesting brackets depicting an amazing variety of sacred and profane themes. The sculptures *(right)* are quite outstanding; they serve as reminders of the names of the three houses whose owners were expropriated in order to leave way for the building of the new wing. Capitals, corbels, brackets and keystones bear ornamentation that is designed to whet the curiosity. On the capitals, for example, there are people piling up chairs (a reminder of the *Scupstoel* House, the Flemish for shovel and chair), monks drinking and eating as a reminder of the *Papenkelder* (literally, "monks' cellar"), and scenes of a harem reminding visitors of the *Moor*. The coving round the portal beneath the tower is decorated with 8 prophets. The soft draped clothing indicates that they were carved in the late 14C. Again, these sculptures are striking for their realism and for a long time they were attributed to Claus Sluter who carved Philip of Burgundy's tomb in Dijon. At present, there is a tendency to attribute them to the Master of the Hakendover Reredos.

Tour ⊘ – The Town Hall contains a fine collection of tapestries, paintings, sculptures and furniture. Two fountains, the Scheldt (Pierre-Denis Plumier) and the Meuse (Jean de Kinder), decorate the inner courtyard. It is in the Council Chamber where the States of Brabant used to sit that the burgomaster, aldermen and city councillors have their meetings. The ceiling was painted by V Janssens and represents a meeting of the gods. The tapestries in the Maximilian Chamber, which were made in Van der Borght's workshop in Brussels, depict scenes from the life of Clovis. The paintings by Van Moer, an artist from Brussels (antechamber to the Burgomaster's Office), illustrate the city before the River Senne was closed over, in a

De Gulden Boot

range of warm colours. The paintings in the main staircase are a Glorification of Communal Power. The Gothic chamber used for official receptions has neo-Gothic wainscoting. The tapestries made to sketches by Guillaume Geefs represent the various guilds in Brussels. The registry office, which used to be called the Court, was once the meeting-place of delegates from the various trades and crafts represented in the town. Note the coats of arms of the guilds and the seven leading Brussels families decorating the wainscoting.

The Guildhalls

For further information on the general characteristics of the Italianate-Flemish style of architecture, see the chapter entitled Architecture in the Introduction.

1-2 Le Roi d'Espagne – The King of Spain's Hall belonged to the Guild of Bakers (1696-1697, rebuilt 1902). The style is more Classical than in the neighbouring halls and the design is attributed to Jean Cosyn, an architect and sculptor. Its general layout, balustrade and octagonal dome give it an Italian look but the brackets, trophy and torcheres decorating the dome give added dynamism to the design. Flanking the balusters on the first floor are medallions depicting emperors Marcus Aurelius and Nerva (A de Tombay), Dece and Trajan (A Desenfants). On the upper storey, in the middle of the trophy carved by J Lagae is a bust of King Charles II of Spain who was on the throne when the house was built. The six statues overlooking the balustrade are not original. They symbolise Strength, Wheat, Wind, Fire, Water and Foresight. At the top is a gilded weather vane representing Fame (P Dubois). *Le Roi d'Espagne* is now a café.

3 La Brouette – The Tallow Merchants' Hall (1644-1645 and 1697). Much of this house survived the bombardment and the Italianate-Flemish façade was finished by the same Jean Cosyn who designed the gable. The many reliefs accompanying the superposition of architectural orders are a delight to the eye. Two cartridges are decorated with a wheelbarrow (hence the name of the hall), and a statue of St Giles, the patron saint of tallow merchants (J van Hamme), occupies a niche in the gable. *La Brouette* is now a café.

Guildhalls

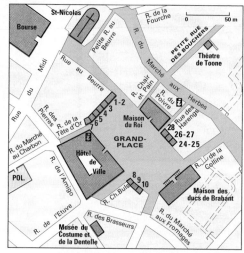

4 Le Sac – The Cabinetmakers and Coopers' Hall (1645-1646 and 1697). This hall was built in the Italianate-Flemish style and partially rebuilt by Antoine Pastorana who added the excessive ornamentation on the upper storeys. Above the front door is a strange sign which gave the hall its name. It shows a figure plunging his hands into a bag or sack held by another man. The third storey and gable are very ornate. They include a frieze consisting of cartridges, caryatids, twisted balusters, oval dormer windows, garlands, torcheres and vases. At the very top is a globe bearing a compass, an instrument commonly used by cabinetmakers.

5 La Louve – The Archers' Hall (1690 and 1696). This hall was mentioned as far back as the 14C but was replaced by a stone house after a fire in 1690. It was again destroyed in the terrible bombardment of 1695 and these two events led to the inclusion of a phoenix rising from its ashes among the decorative features. The well-balanced façade was designed by a painter Pierre Herbosch who sought inspiration in the early period of Italianate-Flemish architecture. The main entrance on the ground floor is topped by a group sculpture by M de Vos representing Romulus and Remus being suckled by the she-wolf (this gave the hall its name). With its four fluted pilasters supporting a cornice, the first floor is markedly Renaissance in style. Between the triglyphs on the frieze are narrative metopes bearing the guild's emblems. The pilasters on the second floor are concealed by statues symbolising Truth, Deceit, Peace and Discord. Above four medallions of Roman emperors (Trajan, Tiberius, Augustus and Caesar) is a pediment that was rebuilt in 1892 and decorated with a low relief illustrating the pursuit of the serpent, Python, by Phoebus Apollo. It was Apollo who invented the lyre, seen here on the balcony of the first floor.

6 Le Cornet – Boatmen's Guildhall (1697). This is a superb building representing the epitome of all that is best in the Italianate-Flemish style. The frontage was designed by Antoine Pastorana but he has given free rein to his imagination and refused to be restricted by the traditional superposition of architectural orders. It is a delightful construction topped by a gable which is obviously shaped like the bow of a 17C frigate, in homage to the trade that paid for the building work. Just below it are two seahorses with their riders flanking a triton catching a fish (G Devreese). The bulls' eye windows on the second floor are particularly elegant; they look down on ornamental features inspired by the boatman's craft. The upper pediment is decorated with a medallion containing a carving of King Charles II of Spain.

7 Le Renard – Haberdashers' Hall (1699). This façade is equally unusual and highly allegorical, with features typical of the Louis XIV style. In the low reliefs on the mezzanine (by Mr de Vos whose name, meaning "The Fox", has been given to the Hall itself) are cherubs undertaking the work of haberdashers. On the first floor, there are five statues symbolising Justice blindfolded and the four continents known at that time (Africa, Europe, Asia and America). The second floor is decorated with caryatids bearing a number of attributes (Golden Fleece, ears of corn, grapes, and flowers). The gable is topped by a statue of St Nicholas, the patron saint of the Haberdashers' Guild.

8 L'Etoile – A privately-owned house. The smallest house on the square was mentioned in documents dating back to the 13C and was demolished in 1852 to leave way for road widening (Rue Charles Buls named after a burgomaster of Brussels who was the driving force behind the reconstruction of the Etoile, or Star, Hall in 1897). The ground floor has been replaced by arcades.
In the passageway is a sculpture by Julien Dillens in memory of **Everard 't Serclaes.** In 1356, the patrician leader chased out Flemish troops under the command of Count Louis de Male. Later, in 1388, he was fatally wounded by the Lord de Gaasbeek's men during a confrontation aimed at defending the rights of his town in the face of unfair demands. Placing a hand on the highly-burnished bronze arm of the statue of the famous citizen-martyr is said to bring good luck. One of the brackets on the Lion Staircase in the left wing of the Town Hall is carved with an illustration of the 't Serclaes murder.

9 Le Cygne – The Butchers' Hall (1698). Before becoming a guild hall in 1720, The Swan was rebuilt for a private owner, Pierre Fariseau (his monogram can be seen in the centre of the façade), probably by Corneille van Nerven, the architect who designed the rear of the Town Hall. It is unusual in that it represents a frank move away from the decorative exuberance of the Italianate-Flemish style towards the Louis XIV style. Karl Marx and Friedrich Engels, who wrote *The Communist Manifesto* in Brussels in 1848, held two weekly meetings here when they lived in the city. *Le Cygne* is now a restaurant.

10 L'Arbre d'Or – Now the Brewers' Hall after being the Tanners' then the Tapestrymakers' Hall (1698). Architect Guillaume de Bruyn used the colossal order in the layout of a façade which he wanted to be as lavish and majestic as possible. Supported by dolphins and volutes, the top bears an equestrian statue of Charles de Lorraine (J Lagae, 1901). This anachronism can be explained by the fact that the original statue, representing the governor, Maximilian-Emmanuel of Bavaria, fell to pieces and was replaced by the effigy (1752) of a governor who administered the town some forty years later. This statue was replaced in its turn by the one we see today. At present, part of the building is used by the *Confédération des brasseries de Belgique*, the Belgian brewers' association; another section houses the **Musée de la brasserie** (Brewery Museum) ⊙. Old equipment used in beer-making is displayed in a reconstruction of an 18C public house. A newly-opened room contains information on the very latest brewing techniques (cylindrical-conical vats to allow the beer to ferment and age, a centrifuge to clarify it etc.). An audio-visual presentation and interactive terminals provide information about the origins of beer, the breweries in Belgium and other related topics. At the end of the tour, visitors can enjoy a glass of good Belgian beer.

11-12 La Rose et le Mont Thabor – Privately-owned houses (1702 and 1699).

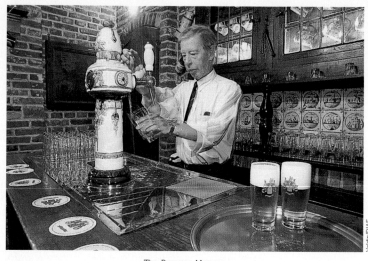

The Brewery Museum

13-19 Maison des ducs de Brabant – The House of the Dukes of Brabant got its name from the nineteen busts decorating the bases of the pilasters on the first floor. Its impressive façade (1698) is topped by a superb rounded pediment on which the tympanum was decorated by P Ollivier with an allegory of Abundance (1770). Here, as in L'Arbre d'Or, Guillaume de Bruyn applied the colossal order and produced two tiers of pilasters. Three flights of steps lead up to the houses concealed by this group of buildings. From right to left they are **La Renommée** (13, Fame) in which a single span leads to a house at the rear that is easy to see because of the statue-cum-sign above the entrance, **L'Ermitage** (14) which has a sign above the door, **La Fortune** (15) which is the Tanners' Hall, **Le Moulin à vent** (16, the millers' hall appropriately named the Windmill, with a sign in the centre of the façade), **Le Pot d'étain** (17, the Carpenters' and Wheelwrights' Hall known as the Pewter Pot, with a sign above the door), **La Colline** (18, the Sculptors', Stone-masons' and Stonecutters' Hall with a sign above the door), and **La Bourse** (19, the Stock Exchange with a sign in the centre of the façade).

20-21-22-23 Le cerf, Joseph et Anne, l'Ange – Privately-owned houses (1710, c1700 and 1697).

24-25 La Chaloupe d'Or – Tailors' Hall (1697). Again seeking inspiration in L'Arbre d'Or, Guillaume de Bruyn designed two orders beneath a triangular pediment. The influence of the Italian Baroque and Flemish-style decoration is quite obvious and the combination of the two is one of the main characteristics of the houses round the Grand-Place. The windows on the mezzanine, above some fine masks, are separated by the bust of St Barbara, the patron saint of tailors. The gable is topped by a statue of St Boniface, Bishop of Lausanne, who sought refuge in the Abbey of the Bois de la Cambre. *La Chaloupe d'Or* (the Golden Sloop) is now a café.

26-27 Le Pigeon – Painters' Hall (1697). Victor Hugo stayed here when he first arrived in Belgium in December 1851, after crossing the border disguised as a workman and bearing a false passport, some say in order to pander to his taste for play-acting. He wrote *L'Histoire d'un crime* and *Napoléon-le-Petit* here. His landlady, whose admiration for her tenant was tantamount to idolatry, is said to have dressed in mourning clothes throughout the reign of Napoleon III. The façade designed by Pierre Simon, the architect of this house, is austere with a superposition of Doric, Ionic and Corinthian orders. There are two particularly interesting features – the basket-handle arch above the window on the second floor and the picturesque masks on the same storey. They give The Pigeon its own very special charm.

28 La chambrette d'Amman – The "Mayor's Chamber" is also known as "Le Marchand d'Or" (the Gold Merchant) or "Aux Armes de Brabant" (At the Brabant Arms) because of the coat of arms visible on the façade (1709). It is said to indicate the premises used by the Amman, the magistrate who rep-resented the Duke of Brabant and, as mayor, was responsible for administering the town. However, it was from the top of the house known as L'Etoile (8) almost opposite that the mayor, having meted out justice, watched public execu-tions.

29-33 Maison du Roi – This large building, the "King's House", stands on the site of the former Bread Market which was replaced in the 15C by the Duke's House which accommodated the tax offices and the Law Courts. The house then passed to the Dukes of Burgundy and more particularly to King Charles V of Spain. It changed name in the same way as it changed owner. In 1515, the monarch decided to have a new house built and he commissioned **Antoine Keldermans the Younger** from Malines with the task. After the death of the first architect, Louis van Bodeghem, Rombaud Keldermans, Dominique de Wagemaker and Henri van Pede, who built the splendid Town Hall in Audenarde, took over the work and it was completed in 1536. Three centuries later, the burgomaster Charles Buls asked **Pierre-Victor Jamaer**, an admirer of Viollet-le-Duc, to rebuild the house which had by then become old-fashioned. In 1873, the architect redesigned the earlier building, retaining the Late Gothic style but adding a tower and arcades on the ground floor and first storey.

Musée de la Ville de Bruxelles ⊘ – The house contains a museum that boasts a collection of works of art and other items retracing the city's history. There are also numerous reminders of local industry and crafts.

The ground floor is undeniably the most comprehensive part of the museum. The "Gothic Sculpture" Room contains a number of unique items, in particular fragments from the Church of Notre-Dame-de-la-Chapelle *(see Quartier des Marolles)* and from the King's House itself. There are also the statues of the eight prophets from the entrance to the Town Hall *(see above)* on which traces of the original colouring can still be seen and a drawing attributed to Rogier van der Weyden (the original is in the Metropolitan Museum of New York) which suggests that he took part in the sculpture project for the Town Hall. In this respect, the three fragments of capitals are interesting. The "Renaissance and Baroque" Room contains two admirable alabaster figures of Apostles attributed to the sculptor from Metz, Jean Mone (*c.*1490-1549), Master Sculptor to Charles V, and the oldest example of Mannekin Pis by Jérôme Duquesnoy the Elder (*c*1570-1641). Also worthy of note are the terracotta pieces by Laurent Delvaux, G-L Godecharle and Jacques Bergé. The display cabinets in the "Faïence and Pewter" Room contain a superb collection of ceramics made in Brussels, with a large multi-coloured plaque signed Méry and based on a work by Pietro da Cortone illustrating the meeting of Aeneas and Venus in Carthage. The "Paintings and Altarpieces" Room contains two masterpieces – **Le cortège de noces** attributed to Pieter Brueghel the Elder (*c*1527-1569) in which the most outstanding feature is the separation of men and women, and the **Saluces Altarpiece** (early 16C) in which the seven niches illustrate scenes from the Life of the Virgin Mary and the Childhood of Christ. The "Tapestry" Room serves as a reminder of the craft that brought Brussels such fame from the 15C to 17C and contains several samples of very high-quality work including *La cérémonie funèbre de Decius Mus* to sketches by Rubens, *L'Épisode de l'histoire de Tristan et Yseult*, the *Légende de Notre-Dame de Sablon* based on sketches attributed to Bernard Van Orley and *Scène de chasse à l'épieu*. Finally, the "Porcelain" Room shows the value and quality of the 19C Brussels ware produced in the factories in Montplaisir and Etterbeek. All the ceramics are fairly similar because the painters tended to move from one factory to another. Before going upstairs, note the plaster low relief of the *Chasse de Méléagre* created by the famous Frenchman François Rude for the Prince of Orange's pavilion in Tervuren. The stained-glass windows decorated with the coats of arms of Charles V's States are also worth a closer look.

The first floor contains an exhibition retracing the development of the city and its changing face over the course of the centuries. There are plans, maps and paintings *(see L'infante Isabelle à la chasse au héron à proximité du Rouge-Cloître)* and educational models of Brussels from 13C to 17C (the 17C model shows the old tower on the church dedicated to St Nicholas).

Faience in Brussels

Following on from tapestry and altarpieces, Brussels ware enjoyed great success during the 18C, one hundred years after the launch of the famous Delft pottery. The items manufactured in Brussels were rarely signed and dated but are no less remarkable for their anonymity.

Corneille Mombaers, working with the Dutchman Witsemberg, created motifs in varying shades of blue. His successor, Philippe Mombaers, learnt his trade in Rouen and Sinceny and gave Brussels faïence the feature that was to distinguish it from its competitors, the "shaped pieces" representing animals or vegetables and the Toby jugs. The products created by Jacques Artoisenet are more usually associated with copper green decoration. The city had a number of workshops until the mid 19C (Ghobert de Saint-Martin, Bertholeyns, Van Bellinghen etc.) by which time porcelain had begun to replace glazed earthenware.

The second floor tells the story of the townspeople from the first settlement to the present time. A painting dating from the mid 16C gives a precise idea of the former ducal palace on the Coudenberg and the Nassau Residence, both of which have now disappeared. Numerous original documents illustrate the political, economic, social and artistic life. The final room contains the wardrobe of Mannekin Pis. The oldest costume on show is the one gifted to the town by Louis XV in 1747. Most of them are 20C.

34-35-36-37-38-39 Le Heaume, Le Paon, Le Petit Renard et le Chêne, Sainte-Barbe, L'Ane – The characteristics of the three architectural orders can be seen in this group of six houses which form the plainest group on the square.

ADDITIONAL SIGHTS

Grand-Place lies in the very heart of the city and, in order to soak up the incomparable atmosphere of this district, visitors should take time to stroll at a leisurely pace through the streets surrounding this superb world-famous square. As a meeting-place or point of convergence, Grand-Place and its café terraces act like magnets, drawing in any pedestrian or passer-by within hailing distance. The streets lining the square are constantly full of people, by day and at night. At dusk, the old district is full of young people because many of the old guildhalls contain bars and discos playing all types of music.

If you go for a walk, you will soon find yourself outside the boundaries of this particular district and we advise you to use the two detailed plans of the city centre in order to visit all the sights mentioned in the guide *(the districts are known as Bourse, Monnaie, Mont des Arts, Marolles, Vieux Centre)*.

At the north-east corner of Grand-Place is Rue de la Colline.

La Balance *(no 24)* has a magnificent frontage including a cartridge bearing the date 1704. The street contains one of the entrances to the Agora Gallery *(marked out on the plan in dotted lines)* which is full of inexpensive clothes shops.

Cross Grand-Place diagonally and turn into Rue de la Tête d'Or.

Le Corbeau *(no 3)* dates from 1696. At the corner of Rue du Marché au Charbon and Rue des Pierres, note the amusing fountain known as "The Spitter".

Go up Rue de l'Amigo. Turn right into Rue de l'Etuve and cross over immediately into Rue de la Violette.

Musée du Costume et de la Dentelle ⊘ – *6 Rue de la Violette*. The museum is small but it contains some remarkable exhibits that will be much admired by those with a love of the delicate craft of lace making. It should be remembered that, during the 17C and 18C, the southern area of the Netherlands was particularly productive as regards trimmings and lace, both of them sectors in which style and technique are closely connected.

The collection presented here includes some striking examples of the dexterity of the lacemakers.

The room on the ground floor is often used for temporary exhibitions and it includes a section devoted to costume (from 18C to the present day) which is regularly changed. Among the lace, note the series of Flemish and Brussels frills dating from the second half of the 17C and a superb Benedictine veil (early 18C) representing the consecration of the chapel in Laeken. The room on the first floor is given over to costume and liturgical vestments (superb late 18C stole that once belonged to Lady Hamilton, the mistress of Lord Nelson who won the Battle of Trafalgar). There is also a section dealing with modern-day lace.

The most interesting section is the room on the second floor containing four cupboards with drawers full of a whole range of antique pieces of lace from different schools named after the places in which they were set up – Italy, Brabant, Flanders, Alençon, Argentan, Chantilly, Lille, Paris etc. The schools differ in the techniques used so it was not unusual to produce Malines lace in Brussels or Valenciennes lace in Antwerp. Until the end of the 17C, the name "Flanders lace" referred to the lace produced in the southern area of the Netherlands ie Antwerp, Brussels *(see Introduction)*, Ghent, Liège, Malines, and Valenciennes. An information panel describes the various production processes in a clear, concise manner. It is interesting to note that, from the 18C onwards, the motifs followed changes in French style. During the reign of Louis XIV the motifs were set one above the other and laid out around a vertical axis. During the Regency, lace became very ornate with an abundance of different forms. The Louis XV style demanded flowers and birds in the midst of a decoration full of swirls and curves. A display cabinet contains a superb Lierre lace veil (*c*1815) and a Brussels lace tabernacle canopy (Regency period).

Take Rue de l'Etuve, cross Rue du Lombard and continue along Rue de l'Etuve on the other side.

★★ **Manneken Pis** (**JZ**) – *At the corner of Rue du Chêne and Rue de l'Etuve.* Yes, it really is that small! The little man (mannekin) has been regarded with much popular affection since 1619. The symbol of the city, shown accomplishing a natural gesture with such charm and grace, is an excellent reflection of the mockery and lack of prudery of Brabant. In order to spare his blushes, maintain decency or, to be more precise, honour the most famous and "oldest citizen in Brussels", it is usual to present him with a suit of clothes. This habit dates back to Maximilian-Emmanuel of Bavaria, Governor in the name of King Charles II of Spain, who was the first celebrity to give him such a gift in 1698. Since then, the rather cheeky little cherub has acquired an extensive wardrobe that occupies an entire room in the town's museum. Maurice Chevalier gave him a straw boater and several foreign heads of state have dressed him in the most representative costume of their respective countries.

E. Baret

Manneken Pis

Mannekin Pis is the most symbolic sight in Brussels and it has been stolen on several occasions. The first time was in the mid 18C, by English soldiers who were intercepted by the inhabitants of Grammant (East Flanders). The worthy citizens received a replica of the statue in gratitude for the return of the incontinent lad. The behaviour of the French solders was little better when Louis XV captured the town in 1747. The king made reparation for the attempted theft by giving the beloved little man a brocade suit embroidered with gold thread and decorating him with the Cross of Louis XIV. The last theft dates from the beginning of the 1960's when students stole him in order to draw attention to problems relating to educational policies.

The bronze original of the statue was made by Jérôme Duquesnoy the Elder (*c*1570-1641) to supply the district with water. At the time, the statue supplied drinking water and the sculpture was called "Little Julian" in memory of a fountain of the same type which already existed in the 15C. In 1770, it was flanked by a Louis XV style niche. Another theft perpetrated in 1817 by one Antoine Licas dealt a death blow to Duquesnoy's bronze – the former convict smashed it shortly after stealing it. The fragments were collected up and a mould was made so that the little man could be brought back into service again that same year. What visitors see today is, therefore, a replica, the first of a long line of little "lads relieving themselves" that the shops in Rue de l'Etuve sell in all sorts of forms, sometimes for unexpected uses.

From Grand-Place, you can travel in any direction to visit any district in Brussels that takes your fancy.

Quartier des INSTITUTIONS EUROPÉENNES

Julius Caesar tells how, before the Nervii were annihilated, they had gathered in an area of marshland that was difficult to penetrate. This was very probably the spot (wooded in those days) now occupied by the town of **Etterbeek**. The village, first mentioned in a diploma in 966AD, was long reputed for its stone mill "which could be seen from far away in every direction", and for its royal hunts on an estate reserved for the monarch and the Governor General.

Urban expansion removed the natural beauty of this once lush green suburb. The district now plays host to the many infrastructures of the European Community and is, therefore, the setting for the many special events in the European calendar (there is one every six days according to the statistics supplied by the *gendarmerie*). This is the most cosmopolitan part of the city. It is also a permanent building site, an area of office blocks that will, without doubt, be the most prosperous district in the city of the future.

Le rond-point Schuman – In 1950, Robert Schuman (1866-1963) took up an idea first mooted by the spiritual father of Europe, Jean Monnet, and suggested "placing all the production of coal and steel under the leadership of one common authority in an organisation that would be open to other European countries". In 1951, the Treaty of Paris set up the ECSC. The roundabout named after Robert Schuman lies between the Parc du Cinquantenaire and Rue de la Loi going up towards the city centre, in the midst of the first European offices to be established in the Belgian capital.

Why Brussels?

When, in 1951, the Treaty of Paris instituted the European Coal and Steel Community (ECSC), Brussels could have become the capital of the entire Community immediately. The Belgian Ministry of Foreign Affairs, however, opposed this move because the Belgian parliament had promised Liège that its application alone would be supported. Unfortunately for the town that had a history linked with Prince-Bishops, it had no infrastructure to its credit and the city of Luxembourg was selected in its place, rather by default it has to be said. When it was time to make the choice permanent, in 1954, the Grand-ducal Court vetoed it. The Belgian government took advantage of the situation and put forward the name of its own capital city. The six Member States accepted and asked Brussels to provide accommodation for the EEC and Euratom as of 1 January 1958, both bodies having been set up by the Treaty of Rome one year earlier.

Just next to it is the famous **Cité Berlaymont** (**GR**), built on the site of a convent founded by the Countess de Berlaymont in 1624. The office block was built in 1967 to designs by the architect Lucien de Vestel and is an enormous building covering an area of 169 000sq m – 1 818 400sq ft in the shape of an "X" supported by four wings of prestressed metal beams, an innovatory technique in its day. The building had to be abandoned at the end of 1991 for safety reasons because asbestos had been used in the structural work. However, it still symbolises the creation of Europe, as is evident in the demonstrations that take crowds of people past its empty windows. At present, the Commission employs some 10 000 civil servants in Brussels and, since the offices in Berlaymont were closed, they have been deployed in twenty or more office blocks in the immediate vicinity of the roundabout. The largest of them all is the **Breydel** on Avenue d'Auderghem. The Council for its part meets in the **Charlemagne** downhill from Cité Berlaymont at the corner of Rue de la Loi and Boulevard Charlemagne. This institution employs approximately 2 000 people and plays host to increasing numbers of national delegations. Since 1995, the delegations have been accommodated across the road in the **Consilium**, a large development including 215 000sq m – 2 313 400sq ft of offices catering for almost 2 500 civil servants and a press room for up to 1 000 journalists. This building may, though, prove insufficient if the European Union is extended to include the EFTA countries (European Free Trade Association). At 155 Rue de la Loi almost opposite the Charlemagne is the **Résidence Palace**, designed by the architect Michel Polak between 1923 and 1926. The luxury of this apartment block was unique in those days. It had a lift up to the eleven floors, a singularly beautiful Art Deco swimming pool (privately-owned) and a theatre (still functioning today). Unfortunately, other less attractive buildings were erected next to it by the architect's sons. Nowadays, the apartments have been turned into offices, in particular for the Council of Europe whose head offices are in Strasbourg.

Continue along Rue de la Loi and turn left into Rue de Trèves which crosses Rue Belliard. Go down the right-hand side of Rue Belliard.

L'Espace Léopold – Although the MEPs sit in Strasbourg, they, like their assistants, are supposed to be in Brussels three weeks out of every four for committee meetings or meetings of political groups. The Parliament buildings (**GS**) lie to each side of Avenue Belliard and are linked by a footbridge. They cover a total area of 114 000sq m – 1 226 640sq ft at the present time but the nearby architectural complex known as l'Espace Léopold (it includes the Gare de Luxembourg) will soon provide an additional 400 000sq m – 4 304 000sq ft and will be the largest administrative complex ever built in Belgium. It is a gigantic property development project creating a veritable European district and already the International Conference Centre (ICC) has emerged, funded by private entrepreneurs and financiers who, in 1992, rented it out to the European Union. The curved glass roof proudly juts up above the city skyline, rising to a height of 70m – 228ft. Since 1992, the building has been known as the **Hémicycle européen.** As to the citizens of Brussels, who are very quick to cut things and people down to size, they have taken advantage of its resemblance to a well-known cheese box and have nicknamed it *Caprice des Dieux*. Inside, a stainless steel structure designed by Olivier Stribelle flanks the huge staircase in the central foyer.

Parc Léopold (**GS**) ⊘ – *Main entrance Rue Belliard just beyond the Parliament buildings*. Set on the edge of the new European Union infrastructures and following on from the Maelbeek Valley which stretches from the woods at La Cambre and the lakes in Ixelles to Square Marie-Louise *(see "A Tour of the Squares" below)*, this public park is a haven of peace and tranquillity in the midst of the bustle of the urban thoroughfare that is Rue Belliard. The district is currently under-

Ch. Bastin et J. Évrard

Solvay Library

going a total transformation as is obvious from the impressive mass of the Hémicycle européen nearby but it has retained a number of buildings steeped in old-fashioned charm which serve as reminders of the Science Centre project dear to the heart of industrialist Ernest Solvay. The park was originally designed to be used as a zoo, hence the inscriptions visible to each side of the main entrance. It now includes the Fondation Eastman (Michel Polak, 1933-1935), the former Institut de physiologie that is now the Lycée Jacqmain (Jules-Jacques van Ysendijck, 1892-1893), the Ecole de Commerce (Constant Bosmans and Henri Vandeveld, 1902), the Institut de sociologie (C Bosmans and H Vandeveld, 1901-1902) which contains the wonderful **Solvay library** with mahogany wainscoting, the Institut d'anatomie (J-J van Ysendeck, 1893) and the Eggevoort Tower that is said to have been part of the medieval estate of the same name (15C, restored in 1914).

The park was opened in the middle of the 19C and given the name it has today to celebrate the fiftieth anniversary of Independence. This is a peaceful spot with a picturesque layout including a lake on which it is not unusual to see a heron standing immobile, apparently insensitive to the background noise of car horns, then flying nonchalantly off when a dog bounds towards it. The park lies on a steep slope and is overlooked by the rear of the two wings of the Muséum des Sciences naturelles. The left wing was designed by architect Emile Janiet (1839-1918) in collaboration with Edouard Dupont the paleontologist. The right wing corresponds to the former Convent belonging to the Congregation of the Most Holy Redeemer and was designed by Henry Beyaert c1860 in a neo-Romanesque style tinged with a certain eclecticism.

On the west side of the park *(172 Chaussée d'Etterbeek)* you can see the house that was the birthplace of sculptor Constantin Meunier (1831-1905).

★★ **Muséum des Sciences naturelles** (GS **M⁹**) (Institut Royal) ⊘ – *29 Rue Vautier*. The museum was set up in 1842 and, since 1891, has been housed in the buildings that were once the Convent of the Congregation of the Most Holy Redeemer within Parc Léopold *(see above)*. The official name of the museum has been Institut royal des Sciences naturelles de Belgique since 1948. It has undergone extensive development since it was first founded and is now a research centre specialising in the study of the living and fossilised world.

MUSÉUM DES SCIENCES NATURELLES

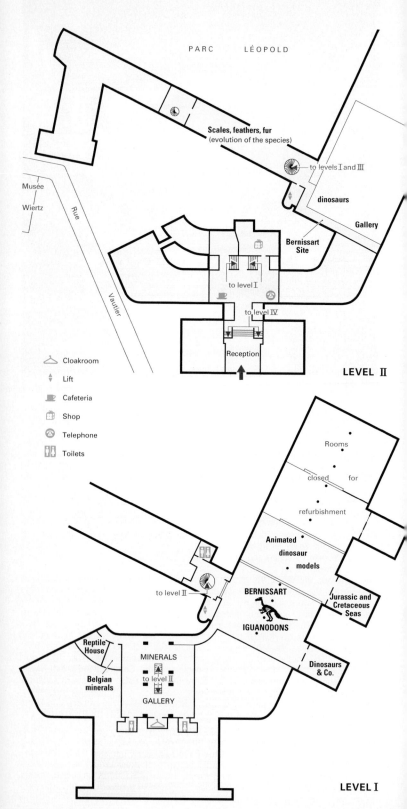

PARC   LÉOPOLD

Scales, feathers, fur
(evolution of the species)

to levels I and III

dinosaurs

Gallery

Musée
Wiertz

Rue

Vautier

Bernissart
Site

to level I

to level IV

Reception

LEVEL II

Cloakroom

Lift

Cafeteria

Shop

Telephone

Toilets

Rooms

closed   for

refurbishment

Animated

dinosaur

models

to level II

BERNISSART

IGUANODONS

Jurassic and
Cretaceous
Seas

Reptile
House

MINERALS

Belgian
minerals

to level II

GALLERY

Dinosaurs
& Co.

LEVEL I

116

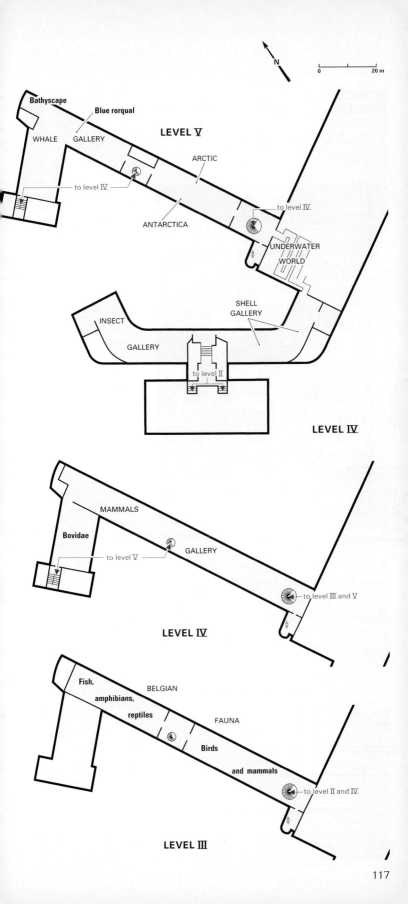

N

0   20 m

LEVEL V

Bathyscape

Blue rorqual

WHALE   GALLERY

to level IV

ARCTIC

ANTARCTICA

to level IV

UNDERWATER
WORLD

SHELL
GALLERY

INSECT

GALLERY

to level II

LEVEL IV

LEVEL IV

MAMMALS

Bovidae

to level V   GALLERY

to level III and V

LEVEL IV

Fish,   BELGIAN

amphibians,

reptiles   FAUNA

Birds

and mammals   to level II and IV

LEVEL III

The wide-ranging collections quickly required an extension of the buildings, initially in 1905 then in 1930 when the city's first tower block was erected, although it was not completed until fifty years later. The most interesting architecture can be seen on the side overlooking Parc Léopold.

Mineralogy – Display cabinets and explanatory panels describe and illustrate minerals and crystals, using magnificent aggregates. There is also an explanation of the composition of meteorites and terrestrial and lunar rocks. A small room illustrating the fluorescence of minerals always fascinates visitors. Another room contains a collection of Belgian minerals taken from the most famous deposits.

Reptile House – It contains mygalomorph spiders and scorpions.

J.-J. Rousseau/GLOBAL PICTURES

Muséum des Sciences Naturelles - The iguanodons

Dinosaurs – The wing built in 1905 to designs by the architect Emile Janiet houses the astonishing collection of iguanodon skeletons discovered in 1878 in a mine in Bernissart (a province in Hainault). The species died out 65 million years ago. Iguanodons (their name means "iguana tooth") were herbivorous animals which lived in herds during the Cretaceaous Period. These authentic specimens (5m - 16ft high and 10m – 32ft long) are shown in an upright position in the first display case and, in the second, in the position in which they were found in the natural well in Hainault. Next to them are the animated reconstructions of the "Dinosaurs & Co." exhibition including a tyrannosaurus, triceratops, allosaurus etc. Upstairs are moulds of iguanodons in movement, an extensive collection of fossils (crocodile, tortoise, fish, plants) and skeletons of crocodiles discovered in Bernissart.

Interactive terminals provide information about the various species of dinosaur on display.

The Seas in the Jurassic and Cretaceous Periods – Fossils, skeletons, moulds and models are used to depict the maritime environment during the Secondary Era.

Scales, Feathers and Fur – Using moulds of skeletons and a series of information boards, the museum shows the evolution of fish, amphibians, reptiles and mammals.

Belgian Fauna – An interactive terminal dealing with the migration of birds is followed by a number of dioramas. There is a superb collection of naturalised animals set out in thematic displays (fields, hedgerows, woodland, beaches and sand dunes, lakes, rivers, the sea).

Mammal Gallery – Eighty of the current one hundred and seven existing families of terrestrial mammals are displayed in new particularly well-designed dioramas. The gallery leads to a magnificent room dealing solely with bovidae.

Whale Room / Arctic and Antarctic Section – The room is impressive for its eighteen whale skeletons, especially the one of the largest mammal of all time – the blue whale. A bathyscaphe simulator will amuse older visitors and delight the younger ones.

The two Poles have been combined through their animal life, with displays including polar bears, seals, narwhal, and walruses representing the Arctic; penguins, seals, sea leopard and hump-backed whale representing the Antarctic. It is worth emphasising that Antarctica is officially a nature reserve given over to peace and scientific research.

The Underwater Environment – Huge photographs illustrate the wide variety of underwater life.

Shell Collection – This superb collection contains 1 000 species. There is an audiovisual presentation of coral reefs and a tropical aquarium with some magnificent fish on show.

Insect Collection – This room provides a general overview of insects (evolution reproduction and development, anatomy, camouflage, mimicry etc.).

When you leave the museum, turn right into Rue Vautier. The entrance to the Musée Wiertz is almost opposite the new Hémicycle européen.

Musée Wiertz (**GS M**[19]) ⊘ – *62 Rue Vautier.* This museum is only a few steps away from the Muséum des Sciences naturelles. It is housed in the former studio and home of Antoine Wiertz (1806-1865), a precursor of Symbolism and Surrealism in Belgium.

Some see him as a visionary artist; others claim that he was driven by ambition. Baudelaire described him, in his biting pages on Belgium, as an exponent of "philosophical painting". Despite the diversity of opinions, they are not incompatible. This was a man labelled as a Romantic and, at the same time, referred to as the "despair of the critics".

The huge compositions contained in the studio itself include *La Révolte des Enfers contre le Ciel* which is impressive for its sheer size (11m – 37ft high) but the most striking exhibit is the unusual *Belle Rosine* (1847). The works in the three adjoining rooms are indicative of Wiertz' sometimes tormented mind, especially his macabre *Inhumation précipitée* (1854). The artist invented a matt paint which was to replace oils. Unfortu-

Wiertz Museum

Ch. Bastin et J. Évrard

nately, the new medium has not withstood the passage of time.

One of the curators of this museum in times gone by was the Dutch-speaking novelist Henri Conscience.

Return to Chaussée de Wavre. Go down the street then turn left into Chaussée d'Etterbeek, skirting Parc Léopold. Continue along Chaussée d'Etterbeek which extends into Avenue Livingstone beyond the underpass beneath Rue de la Loi. Go on to Square Gutenberg, situated just beyond the pond in Square Marie-Louise.

A Tour of the Squares – A short distance from the Cité Berlaymont is a district which was planned from 1875 onwards by Gédéon Bordiau (1832-1904) an architect who had worked with Joseph Poelaert, the designer of the Law Courts. In the 19C, the expansion of the suburbs and the planning projects instigated by Leopold II resulted in the drainage and development of the marshy areas to the north-east of the town. This unhealthy stretch of land consisted, in those days, of a string of ponds which frequently burst their banks when the river was in spate. The planner skilfully took advantage of the specific characteristics of the Maelbeek Valley and decreased the size of the lake in Saint-Josse where Philip the Good is said to have once gone swimming. By doing so, he created enough space to lay out Square Marie-Louise (**GR 171**), the first of a series of squares dotted across the hills and dales of this area. However, it was not until the end of the century that the district acquired luxury housing, some of it eclectic, some built in a style that was resolutely new in its day (now known as "Art Nouveau") with a garden in front. This example of modern town planning, which for once ignored the concept of streets set out in a checkerboard pattern, is worth a visit on foot and it is particularly pleasant on a sunny day.

From the centre of **Square Gutenberg**, there is a good view of two painted façades *(nos 5 and 8)* by Armand van Waesberghe. The doors and windows are very ornate. There is also a white stone house (1901) which was Victor Taelemans' home designed in a geometric style **(70 Rue Philippe le Bon)**. From there, stroll along the left side of Square Marie-Louise to **Rue du Cardinal** and at no 46 (built 1900) note the allegory of Architecture and the superb front door. These early examples show the extent to which the decorative elements of the Art Nouveau style drew inspiration from Nature, particularly flowers and plants.

Turn back to the lake which G Bordiau rendered even more picturesque by building an artificial grotto there. Then head for the right side of the square beyond *La Cigale* (1900), a cricket carved by sculptor Emile Namur. Here the variety of styles and building materials in the block of eleven houses shows the architectural diversity that was rife at the end of last century. The first four houses *(nos 79 to 76)* are variations on the neo-Renaissance style. The first two are Flemish in design and the next two are French in style. At **34 Rue du Taciturne**, there is an eclectic construction designed by Paul Saintenoy *(see Old England)* which stands on the very edge of the district given a whole new look by the extension of the European buildings.

Return to the square and **Avenue Palmerston**. At the start of the avenue, there are three outstanding mansions designed by Victor Horta. The **Hôtel Deprez-Van de Velde** (1896, *no 3*) has an austere façade with an alternation of white and blue stone which gradually fades towards the uppermost sections of the wall. The windbreaks and slight undulations carved into the stonework, especially beneath the bow window, give this wide, almost Classical building a very real charm. The delightful side entrance (in Rue Boduognat) has lines that are typical of Art Nouveau. The elegant corner house (1898, *no 2*) is of a type dear to the architect's heart. In this instance, he produced a more sensual design that gives greater flexibility to the layout of the rooms. Finally, the **Hôtel van Eetvelde★** (1895-1898, *no 4*) is a brilliant piece of work in which Victor Horta, made use of a metal structure in a private mansion for the very first time. Technical progress achieved in the late 18C and early 19C reduced the cost of iron and led to an increase in its use (railway bridges and Crystal Palace in England, Baltard's covered markets and the Eiffel Tower in Paris, greenhouses in Laeken etc.) although it was still used fairly parcimoniously, and usually for utilitarian constructions. Victor Horta dared to use it in frontages and in the interiors of a number of luxury homes in the city. The façade here has, as its main features, metal uprights with two projecting storeys supported by symbolical brackets above a ground floor set back from the main line of the building. The rigidity of design is softened by the arched lintels above the windows on the first floor, and by the sections of wall decorated with mosaics full of arabesques which become increasingly complex towards the top of the house. The balustrade on the third floor is in line with the other houses in the avenue. This rigorous layout totally conceals the interior and its two sections of building linked by a luxurious octagonal hall on a mezzanine. The house has its original fittings and fixtures and decoration and a stained-glass roof that now reflects electric lighting. Vast rooms lead off this light-filled hall. They include the dining room and adjacent drawing room reached by a covered passageway. The decoration makes use of a wide range of different materials.

Just before **Square Ambiorix** (**GR**), the Villa Germaine (1897, *no 24*) has eyecatching glazed earthenware and coloured bricks, and a small bow window.

At no 11 on the square, set in a block of houses with austere frontages, is the house that once belonged to **Georges de Saint-Cyr** the painter (1900). It stands out from the others because of its narrow façade and unusual Baroque design. It was the work of one of Victor Horta's pupils, Gustave Strauven (another of his designs can be seen at 87 Boulevard Clovis) who gave many of his houses exuberant wrought ironwork, emphasising a mannerism that was in the end to stifle this very innovatory style. Unlike his teacher, however, who made use of craftsmen, Gustave Strauven used manufactured materials.

St-Cyr House - Close-up

Ch. Bastin et J. Evrard

120

In **Rue Campenhout** the house *(no 63)* overlooking Square Marguerite has a façade decorated with sgraffiti medallions *(see Introduction, Art in Brussels)*. The technique is similar to fresco-work and has been used in this instance to represent masonic emblems. In **Rue Le Corrège** there is a red brick house (1899, *no 35*) with stylised stained-glass windows and a blend of Art Nouveau and neo-Gothic architecture which arouses the curiosity of passers-by. It belonged to E Ramaekers the architect. Note the sgraffiti below the bow window; they represent two swans and a sunset.

Options from Rond-Point Schuman:

▶▶ City Centre (Quartier Louise, du Botanique, de Brouckère etc.).

Le Cinquantenaire by crossing the park of the same name on the east side of the roundabout.

Ixelles by going up Rue de la Loi to the inner ring road (Avenue des Arts) and turning left towards Porte de Namur.

Quartier LOUISE ★

Ever since it was first inhabited, the upper town has been a luxurious residential area whereas the lower end of the town, which in the past was often an unhealthy place, was full of breweries, mills and tanneries driven by the water of the Senne. Over the past few decades Place Louise and Avenue Louise, which were originally laid out as walks, have been turned into shopping streets.

There is no need for a map or signpost to direct people to this district as the gigantic Law Courts project vertically above the working-class Marolles District.

Palais de Justice (ES J) ⊙ – *Place Poelaert*. Work began on this quite outstanding colossal building designed by Joseph Poelaert (1817-1879) in 1866 and was completed in 1883, although not to everybody's liking. The huge building has very unusual dimensions (area 26 000 sq m – 279 760sq ft, sides 150m – 158yds and 160m – 168yds long; entrance porch 42m – 151ft high; dome 97.5m – 317ft high) and is undoubtedly one of the largest buildings in Europe. It was erected on the Galgenberg Hill on the site once occupied by the town gallows. Camille Lemonnier the writer described this impressive, austere mass as "a titanesque entablature surmounted by pilasters, penetrated by porticoes and articulated by flights of steps, a piece of architecture such as might be glimpsed through the clouds of an apotheosis".

The palace is inspired by the buildings of ancient Greece and Rome and is capped by a dome supported on gryphons. J Poelaert intended to include a pyramid, a form that had been little used since the days of the ancient Egyptians but he died before the work was finished. The dome was designed by an architect named Benoît and rebuilt after it had been set ablaze by the Germans in 1944. The main entrance to the palace is a vast peristyle opening into the grandiose **lobby** which is roofed with an impressive dome. Around it is a gallery reached by monumental flights of steps. The building originally had 27 court rooms and 245 secondary rooms.

From the balustrade overlooking Place Poelaert, there is a superb **view** of the west end and lower part of the city. In the centre of the square is the monument carved by Vereycken in 1935 to commemorate the infantrymen who fell during the First World War.

At the corner of the square and Rue de la Régence is the work commemorating British gratitude (1923) by the British sculptor C S Jagger. It pays homage to the fraternity of the men fighting under the flags of various nations during the 1914-1918 war.

Take Rue Aux Laines on the left of the courthouse to reach Place Jean Jacobs.

Place Jean Jacobs (ES) – The small gardens in the middle of the square are decorated with a group sculpture by Charles Samuel (1912) recalling the shipwreck of the *De Smet de Noeyer*, the first Belgian training ship, which sank in 1906. More interesting, however, is the elegant cartouche by the architect Jules Brunfaut decorating the left-hand corner of the square. It was erected in memory of Jean Jacobs (1575-1650), a native of Brussels who founded the grants system at the University of Bologna. It is surmounted by St Michael, the city's patron saint. On the odd-numbered side of the street, note the superb eclectic and Art Nouveau townhouses.

Return up Boulevard de Waterloo beyond Place Louise.

Parc d'Egmont (KZ) – *3 gates: between 10 and 12 Rue du Grand-Cerf, at 31 Boulevard de Waterloo and by a passageway behind the Hilton Hotel*. This park forms an oasis of peace and tranquillity in the heart of a very busy urban district. It contains

Peristyle on the Law Courts

two bronzes, *The Prince de Ligne* by John Cluysenaar (1935) and a reproduction of Sir George Frampton's *Peter Pan* (1924) (the original representing the "little boy who wouldn't grow up" is in Kensington Gardens in London). The *Groote Pollepel* is the last of the wells which used to provide the city's water. Between the main wing of the Egmont Palace *(see Sablon District)* and the riding school is the so-called "Wild Boar's Lawn" that was probably laid out by Servandoni.

Boulevard de Waterloo (**KZ 255**) **and Avenue de la Toison d'Or** (**KZ 238**) – In 1810, when Brussels was the "county town" of the *département* of Dyle, Napoleon decided to open out the pentagon formed by the city by ordering the demolition of the 14C walls and replacing them with a boulevard that would circumscribe the city.

This "inner ring road" has one unusual feature – its left and right sides do not have the same name.

Boulevard de Waterloo and Avenue de la Toison d'Or are, then, part of the same main thoroughfare which runs from Place Louise to Porte de Namur. It is famous for its luxury shops and cinemas, especially on Avenue de la Toison d'Or where the lateral avenue is for pedestrians only. In it, indeed almost concealed by it, is the **Église des Carmes déchaussés** ⊙ designed by the architect Appelmans in 1861 in the neo-Byzantine style.

The Galerie Louise (1964) is an updated version of the Saint-Hubert Arcade; it links Avenue de la Toison d'Or to Avenue Louise.

Avenue Louise (**FST**) – This avenue which is named after the elder daughter of Leopold II was laid out in 1864 to connect the city centre to Ixelles *(qv)*. In fact, it replaced the prestigious Allée Verte de Laeken, the most decidedly aristocratic promenade in pre-Revolutionary Brussels which is now of no interest. Avenue Louise was altered for the 1910 World Fair and gradually lost its charm as a wooded avenue as it attracted more and more traffic until, at the end of the 1950's, a number of underpasses were built.

The approach from Place Louise or the approach from the arcade of the same name arrive in Place Stéphanie which is named after Leopold II's second-eldest daughter. Avenue Louise is long and it is worth combining a visit to this street with a look at La Cambre Abbey *(see Ixelles)*. The **Solvay Residence** *(no 224, privately-owned)* was built in 1894 for Armand Solvay, the son of Ernest Solvay. He was the head of an industrial firm with a history closely linked to the development of chemistry. Indeed, he was so influential that in 1911 he succeeded in bringing to Brussels scientists such as Curie, Planck, De Broglie, and Einstein to discuss the experiments he had carried out.

The upper storeys of the symmetrical façade, which is a fine example of Art Nouveau, were built of stone from Euville, forming a stark contrast to the blue stone used for the ground floor. Note the superbly elegant doorway, the balcony on the first floor, the slender metal columns in the bow windows, and the craftsmanship evident in the cornice.

To the right of the crossroads with Rue du Bailli is the frontage of **Holy Trinity Church** *(église de la Trinité)* designed by Jacques Francart *(see Saint-Gilles).*

For the remainder of the visit, see Ixelles, the lake walk, the Max Hallet Residence and the King's Garden.

Options available from Place Louise:

▶▶ Sablon District via Rue de la Régence opposite the Law Courts.
Marolles District via Boulevard de Waterloo to Porte de Hal then turning right into the top end of the street.
Saint-Gilles via Boulevard de Waterloo to Porte de Hal.
Ixelles via Avenue de la Toison d'Or to Porte de Namur.

Every year
the **Michelin Red Guide Benelux**
revises its selection of hotels and restaurants which
– are pleasant, quiet, secluded;
– offer an exceptional, interesting or extensive view;
– have a tennis court, swimming pool or private beach;
– have a private garden...
It is worth buying the current edition.

Quartier des MAROLLES

The Marolles District, which lies between Porte de Hal, Notre-Dame-de-la-Chapelle and the Law Courts, has traditionally been an area of working-class and socially-deprived people. During the Middle Ages it was the home of weavers, fullers and prostitutes; later, it became a hotbed of many a social upheaval. From the 1860's onwards the expropriations caused by the building of the Law Courts removed many of the people who lived on the Galgenberg Hill where the gallows once stood. Les Marolles, as it is known locally, has remained essentially working-class. Real "locals" however are becoming increasingly rare and its picturesque dialect, which is something of a legend in Brussels, has almost totally died out in the district's streets and cafés.

The strange name Marolles comes from the former convent of the Apostolines of the Community of Mariann Colentes, a charitable institution which was opened here in the 17C but which moved to a site near Rue de Laeken in 1715.

The best place to begin the tour is Porte de Hal (see Saint-Gilles). From there, follow Rue Haute.

Rue Haute (JZ) – This is the longest and undoubtedly the oldest street in the city centre, running along the line once followed by a path laid out by the Romans at the beginning of the Christian era. With Rue Blaes, it forms the backbone of the Marolles District. St Peter's Hospital *(no 322)*, which was rebuilt in 1935 to designs by Dewin, stands on the site of St Peter's Hospital for Lepers first opened in the early 13C. The street has been full of shops since the mid 19C but has lost most of its bars. A museum (⊘ *no 298A; third floor*) in the **Centre Public d'Aide sociale** (CPAS) (Public Social Welfare Centre) ⊘ exhibits a small collection of paintings, sculptures, furniture, silver plate, and tapestries, including a painting by Josse Momper, a triptych attributed to B Van Orley and a *Vierge de Douleur* (1522) said to have been carved by P Borreman. For some time, Auguste Rodin had his studio *(no 224)* in this street. The so-called "Spanish House" *(no 164)* is an elegant brick building topped by a crowstepped gable. The delightful red brick house *(no 132)* was once the residence of **Pieter Brueghel the Elder** and his great-grandson, David Teniers III.

Take the second street on the left and walk down to Place du Jeu de Balle.

Place du Jeu de Balle (ES **139**) – The square gets its name from the ball game *(balle pelote)* that used to be popular throughout Belgium.

A flea market is held here every morning, the largest being on Sundays. This "old market" has existed since 1640 but before 1873 it used to be held on the site of what is now known as Place Anneessens. The buildings along the shorter sides of the square are older than the square itself which was only laid out in the middle of last century.

The old fire station, built in 1861-1863 to designs by the architect Poclaert *(see Quartier Louise, Law Courts)* was turned into flats and shops in the late 1980's.

Ch. Bastin-J. Évrard

Flea Market, Place du Jeu de Balle

Return to Rue Haute;
turn right into Rue Christine to reach the Church of the Order of Minim Brothers.

Église Sts-Jean-et-Etienne-aux-Minimes (JZ **N¹**) – *Rue des Minimes.* This church belongs to the Order of Minim Brothers and is dedicated to St John and St Stephen. It dates from 1700-1715 and is typical of the transitional period between Flemish Baroque and neo-Classicism. It is all that remains of the former monastery (17C) of the same name which was built on the site of the house belonging to André Vésale the famous anatomist (1514-1564). The church backs onto the foundations of the Law Courts *(see Quartier Louise)* and is famous for its concerts of classical music.

Return to Rue Haute at the north end of which is Place de la Chapelle.

★ **Notre-Dame-de-la-Chapelle** (JZ) – *Place de la Chapelle. Chancel closed for restoration.* In 1134, Godefroi I, Duke of Brabant, decided to build a chapel outside the town walls. It became a parish church in 1210 and was very soon popular as a place in which to worship the Blessed Virgin Mary. The statue of Our Lady of Grace (13C-14C) had a reliquary on its bust accompanied by an inscription in Dutch which read, "Here is enclosed a relic of the arm of St John, from the tomb of Our Lady, in the place where Mary was born and in the place where Mary rose up into Heaven." In 1250 Duke Henry III gave five pieces of the True Cross to the church which began to attract pious and influential people and became a place of devotion. It was also here that Pieter Brueghel married Mayken Coecke in 1563. The church was originally Romanesque but the nave was rebuilt in 1421 after a fire in 1405. The Bishop of Cambrai came to consecrate it in 1434. The transept was built in a transitional style midway between Romanesque and Gothic (post-1210) and was completed only shortly before the chancel (built after 1250-1275) which contains features indicative of the Brabant Gothic style that can be seen in various places in the church.

Exterior – The building has been the subject of a long, meticulous restoration programme. Although it is mainly Gothic, the most striking feature of its outline is its somewhat disconcerting Baroque belltower. The reason for this addition was a bombardment in 1695 which also destroyed the tower above the transept. Beneath the belltower set up here by Antoine Pastorana the architect who also designed the Le Sac Residence in Grand-Place, is the main tower dating from the early 16C. Along the sides are lines of gables marking the side chapels. The gables are decorated with crockets and topped with finials; they are typical of Brabant architecture. On the east side, on a level with the south arm of the transept, are traces of the original Romanesque chapel, a very rare sight in Brussels.

The carved decoration in the Romanesque-Gothic part of the chapel (chevet and transept) consists of a frieze round the cornice and a large number of modillions and gargoyles with very realistic monsters' heads, probably carved by foreign stonecutters because there was no local school of art when they were made in the early 13C. These illustrations of Evil have a natural place on the outside of the church, as Good was reserved for the interior. The west door has a reconstructed tympanum decorated with a carving of *The Holy Trinity* by Constantin Meunier (1892).

Interior – The well-proportioned nave is six bays long and two storeys high. Light enters the church through the Flamboyant style clerestory; the tracery dates from restoration work in the 19C. The gallery beneath has a delightfully-traceried balustrade (15C). The statues of the Apostles placed on the columns date from the 17C and some of them were carved by Luc Fayd'herbe or Jérôme Duquesnoy the Younger. The columns are a typical feature of Brabant-style architecture. They consist of a tall base, a thick column and a surbased capital with curled cabbage leaves. The aisles, built between 1436 and 1475, are lined with chapels including three engaged columns in the corners. The unusually tall bases indicate that the walls are actually buttresses.

The decorative features include a few interesting works of arts, the best-known being the **memorial** to Pieter Brueghel the Elder (d 1569) and his wife, made by his son Jan Brueghel and renovated by his great-grandson David Teniers III (north aisle, 4th chapel). *Christ remettant les clefs à Saint Pierre* is a copy of the Rubens original that was sold in 1765 and is now in an art gallery in Berlin. The tomb of the painter Lens (d 1822) *(left of the entrance)* is by Gilles-Lambert Godecharle. In the south aisle, note the *Adoration des Mages* by Henri de Clerck (1599) and the reliquary of St Boniface, Bishop of Lausanne, who sought refuge in the abbey of La Cambre (5th chapel), a fine wooden statue of St Margaret of Antioch made c1520 (4th chapel), a statue of *the Descente de Croix* (16C) attributed to Martin de Vos' studio (3rd chapel), and a **statue** of Our Lady of Solitude, fully clothed in accordance with the custom introduced by the Spaniards and said to have been gifted by the Infanta Isabella c1570 (2nd chapel). Finally, the pulpit by P Plumier (1721) is an amazing piece of work representing the prophet Eli in the desert receiving manna from an angel.

On leaving the church, take Rue de la Chapelle (right) down the hill.

Église des Brigittines (JZ) – *3 Petite Rue des Brigittines.* This chapel, which has a nave but no aisles, dates from 1665. It used to be the chapel for the Brigittines convent but the remainder of the community has now totally disappeared. The Italianate-Flemish façade is reminiscent of contemporary urban housing in the Netherlands, particularly in the doorway and windows. The orders of architecture are set one above the other as they are on certain houses in Grand-Place. This building has been used for a variety of purposes. In particular, it was a butcher's shop and a dance hall during last century. Nowadays it is only open for concerts.

Turn back up Rue de la Chapelle and go past the church as far as Boulevard de l'Empereur.

Tour Anneessens (JZ C[1]) – *Boulevard de l'Empereur.* This corner tower was rediscovered in 1957 and restored in 1967; it is a remnant of the first town wall (late 11C – 13C). An octagonal staircase turret is clearly visible against the circular tower and, on the top of a stretch of wall beside it, is a section of parapet walkway lined with merlons. This is part of a two-storey curtain wall with semi-circular arching. The tower itself stands above two storeys with ribbed barrel vaulting. Nearby used to be the *Steen poort* (demolished in 1760) where François Anneessens (1660-1719) is said to have been imprisoned. He was the local martyr who went to the scaffold in Grand-Place for his part in defending the community's freedoms. A sculpture (1889, by Thomas Vinçotte) decorates a square named after him, in the city centre.

On the other side of the boulevard is a café *(53-55 Rue des Alexions)* with a variety of decorative features, *La Fleur en papier doré.* It was here that the Belgian Surrealists liked to meet; monthly poetry meetings are now held in the café.

Walk a few yards down Rue des Alexions to the Dutch-speaking St Joris School built of brown brick. From here, there is a view of the Villers Tower through a panel including a large number of openings.

Tour de Villers (JZ A) – This other remnant (tower and curtain walls) of the first town walls was uncovered in 1947 when the old working-class houses backing onto it were demolished. There are traces of slit windows and staircases, as well as of stone corbels and merlons.

Options from Notre-Dame-de-la-Chapelle:

▶▶ Quartier du Mont des Arts by going up Boulevard de l'Empereur.
Quartier du Sablon by taking Rue J Stevens leading off Place de la Chapelle at the corner of Rue Haute.
Quartier du Grand-Place by walking down Rue de l'Escalier opposite the Anneessens Tower and going along Rue du Chêne beyond it.
Saint-Gilles by Rue Blaes leading off Place de la Chapelle.

Michelin Green Guides are revised regularly.
Use the most recent edition to ensure a successful holiday.

This district lies between Place de Brouckère and the Stock Exchange. It is bordered on the other two sides by Église Sainte-Catherine and the cathedral dedicated to St Michael and St Gudule. It gets its name from the minting workshop where, from the early 15C onwards, ducats and other coins of the Duchy of Brabant were minted. Place de la Monnaie is pedestrianised and is situated at the point where two main shopping streets converge, Rue des Fripiers and Rue Neuve. This is a delightful place to stop for a rest. When the stifling heat of a Brussels summer prevents even the smallest and lightest of leaves from moving on the trees (the town, after all, is built in a dip that was once marshland), the fountains on the square provide a much-appreciated note of freshness.

★ **Théâtre royal de la Monnaie** (JY) ◷ – *Place de la Monnaie*. The "Monnaie" was built on the site of the Ostrevant Residence where coins were minted in the 15C. A historically-important event took place there on the eve of the Belgian Revolution. On 25 August 1830, there was a performance of *The Mute Girl of Portici*, an opera in five acts by Frenchman Daniel Auber with libretto by Scribe and Delavigne. The duet was to become famous:

« Amour sacré de la Patrie,	(Sacred Love of my Fatherland,
Rends-nous l'audace et la fierté !	Return to us our daring and our pride!
A mon pays je dois la vie,	I owe my life to my country,
Il me devra la Liberté ! »	It shall owe me my freedom!)

As soon as the tenor sang the opening bars of this patriotic piece, the audience began a rebellion by leaving the theatre to join a rowdy crowd that had already been stirred by news of the July Revolution in Paris. This was the prelude to the "September Uprising" *(see Introduction)*.

Architecture and Decoration – All that remains of the neo-Classical building designed by the Parisian architect Damesme between 1817 and 1819 is the peristyle consisting of eight Ionic columns and the pediment on which *L'Harmonie des passions humaines* by Eugène Simonis the sculptor was unveiled in 1854. After a fire in 1855, the theatre was rebuilt to designs by the architect Poelaert. From Place de la Monnaie, it is easy to see that the height of the auditorium was raised by 4m – 13ft during the major renovation project of 1985-1986, for reasons relating to security and in order to adapt the theatre to the latest technical developments in stage sets.

This addition, which is often quoted as an example and is described as post-Modernist, has not altered the harmony of the façade and it proves that ancient and modern can sometimes be happily combined.

From the entrance, visitors enter the foyer and its grand staircases designed by Joseph Poelaert. The floor and ceiling were decorated by two leading contemporary American artists, **Sol LeWitt** and **Sam Francis**. The royal drawing room has been turned into the green room. It was decorated by Charles Vandenhove, jointly with

The Foyer, La Monnaie

Ch. Bastin-J. Evrard

Daniel Buren and Giulio Paolini, other internationally-famous artists. The auditorium is luxurious and has been renovated throughout; it was designed by J Poelaert in the middle of last century in the Louis XIV style with tiers of balconies and boxes. The dome is decorated with an allegory of Belgium protecting the Arts.

The National Opera – The Théâtre royal de la Monnaie is world-famous for the artistic quality of its performances and its programmes; it is also known as the Opéra National. It has had a particularly eventful history. In 1860, Richard Wagner conducted two performances of his work here. World premieres have been staged here among them *The African Woman* by Giacomo Meyerbeer and Jules Massenet's *L'Hérodiade*. A number of French adaptations were performed here for the first time including *The Ring Cycle* and *The Flying Dutchman* by Richard Wagner, Giuseppe Verdi's *Aida*, Richard Strauss' *Salomé*, Giacomo Puccini's *Turandot*, and *The Rake's Progress* by Igor Stravinski, to name but the best-known. The greatest voices have rung out across the auditorium, from La Malibran to Maria Callas and Elisabeth Schwarzkopf, Enrico Caruso to Mario del Monaco and José van Dam, the famous Belgian baritone. Sarah Bernhardt performed here, as did Jacques Brel in *The Man of La Mancha* (1968). It is obvious that an all-inclusive list would be too long; nor would it be effective in showing the immense artistic value of this theatre. The famous choreographer **Maurice Béjart** and his fabulous Ballet du XXᵉ siècle, which he created in 1960, have also contributed to the reputation for excellence enjoyed by the Théâtre de la Monnaie. Indeed, the man from Marseilles enjoyed fame and glory in the Belgian capital before moving to Lausanne. He was a difficult man to follow but **Anne Teresa De Keersmaeker** (1960), whose style is resolutely contemporary, has succeeded in confirming a personality and a creativity that give the theatre all the prestige it deserves. In short, the Opéra National is a mandatory stop for anybody who is fond of ballet and/or the lyric arts.

There is an excellent record and book shop, selling specialist works as one might expect, in Rue des Princes. The booking office is in Rue de la Reine.

Historium (JY M[20]) ⊘ – *In the Anspach Center, 1st Floor, Place de la Monnaie.* A series of waxworks tableaux tell the history of Belgium from Caesar and the Conquest of the Gauls to the present day.

Return to Rue de l'Ecuyer, cross over and go down Rue de la Fourche a short distance to the right. Then turn left into Rue des Bouchers.

Rue des Bouchers (JY 25) – This is the most international street in a city with a strongly cosmopolitan air because it attracts the largest number of visitors. It is one of the pedestrian precincts in the "Ilot Sacré" *(see box)* and it draws in the tourists both for its unique atmosphere and because of the never-ending bustle (especially in the evening). Its name dates back to the days when there was still a butcher's shop there; now the street has a plethora of restaurants with tables and counters spilling out onto the narrow pavement. Many of the houses have crow stepped gables and there is a row of superb decorated doors dating from the 17C. It is pleasant to be carried along in the warm, friendly atmosphere of Rue des Bouchers but it would be a pity not to take a closer look at these fine witnesses of days gone by.

The famous **Galeries St-Hubert** are divided into the Galerie du Roi, the Galerie de la Reine and the Galerie des Princes *(see below)* and they divide the street into two sections. In the part towards the top of the street, opposite no 58, there is a vaulted passageway leading to a small square adorned with a delightful fountain. In summer, visitors appreciate the tranquillity and freshness of this spot *(on weekdays, the square is open from 0830 to 1700. Also accessible from 52 Rue de la Montagne).* In the lower part of the street, at the end of the Impasse de la Fidélité, the small fountain known as "Jeanneke Pis" is reminiscent of its famous malecounterpart, Manneken Pis *(see Quartier de la Grand-Place).* It is a bronze figure by Debouvrie unveiled in 1987. A coin thrown into the basin is said to ensure the virtue that has given the cul-de-sac its name (Faithfulness).

L'îlot sacré

The central part of the old town was nicknamed the "Ilot Sacré" (Sacred Islet) by the journalist Louis Quiévreux who fought against a number of property development schemes from 1958 onwards. "We must protect an islet that is intangible and sacred!" he wrote. In 1960, the City Council voted in an urban improvement plan which aimed to restore all the house fronts within the area around Grand-Place. The plan also prohibited the construction of any building which did not fit in with the traditional architecture.

Several of the streets have been fully pedestrianised, such as Rue des Bouchers; some of them, like Rue des Brasseurs, have been partially given back to the pedestrians. They are lined with shops and cafés and form the most picturesque and busiest district in the capital. The Ilot Sacré is also known as "the Belly of Brussels" because of the wide range of restaurants within its perimeter.

Petite Rue des Bouchers

★**Petite Rue des Bouchers** (**JY 24**) – This street lies at right angles to the previous one and links it to Rue du Marché aux Herbes near Grand-Place. The narrow street is as full of restaurants as its sister and it boasts a number of fine 17C and 18C houses.

Impasse Schuddeveld cuts through the line of buildings beside no 23. In it is the **Théâtre de marionnettes de Toone** (**JY T²**) ⊘. It is a pub during the day but, in the evening, this pillar of Brussels folklore opens its famous puppet theatre. Puppets are, by nature, never contented with their lot and they have found here a setting that gives them ample opportunity to weave their spell. The puppets, though, are not here by chance, for Toone VII (his real name is José Géal) is perpetuating the tradition of a long line of actors and performers who worked under this name and made it famous throughout the working-class Quartier des Marolles. Toone VII has preserved the mocking, fun-loving spirit of the district and has instilled it into the wooden figurines which, since 1963, have been delighting audiences of adults who have never lost their childlike souls. The cheeky *peochenellen* perform, with an ease that is quite astonishing, all the great classics such as *The Three Musketeers* or *Lucrecia Borgia*. People, however, do not come here for Dumas or Hugo; they come for the actors. They come to see *Woltje*, Brussels' version of Mr. Punch, play Hamlet, and *Boumpa* breathe life back into Charlemagne. They watch *Poupa* change into Pardaillan or *Schuun Mokske* become the most beautiful princess of our dreams. During the interval, the audience can visit a small museum. *Phone in advance to find out about the shows (there are performances in dialect, French, Dutch, English and German).*

The Petite Rue des Bouchers leads into Rue du Marché aux Herbes.

Impasse des Cadeaux lies between 6 and 8 of Rue du Marché aux Herbes. At the end of the cul-de-sac is an old pub called *A l'Imaige Nostre-Dame.*

Go back up Rue du Marché aux Herbes.

★★**Galeries Saint-Hubert** (**JKY**) – The arcade was inaugurated by King Leopold I in June 1847 and beyond the peristyle opening onto Rue des Bouchers it includes the Galeries du Roi and de la Reine. The Galerie des Princes was added at a later date. These arcades were built before the famous Victor-Emmanuel Gallery in Milan despite the fact that the Italian arcade is reputed to be the oldest in Europe. After the examples set in Paris and London, cities such as Brussels, Hamburg, Nantes and Trieste all followed the fashion for these streets sheltered from the elements but the Galeries Saint-Hubert were the finest and most elegant of them all. The covered passages appeared in the days of the Industrial Revolution, usually built by private entrepreneurs, and they were the shop windows of a whole new social order. There are those who consider them to be the successors to the galleries in the Palais-Royal in the days of Philippe d'Orléans; others who believe that they were, more simply, pedestrian precincts designed to protect passers-by from the mud thrown up by carriage wheels. Still others see them as a modern form of the Roman marketplaces and bazaars of the Orient.

In Rue de la Montagne, the architect Jean-Pierre Cluysenaar (1811-1880) built an elegant Classical façade decorated with pilasters. The central section has a number of sculptures and the motto *Omnibus omnia* (Everything for Everybody). The arcade is 213m – 231yds long and lined with luxury shops, a superb bookshop (Tropismes), a theatre (Théâtre royal des Galeries), a cinema (Arenberg-Galeries), elegant tea shops and several restaurants including the Taverne du Passage which has an Art Déco interior and l'Ogenblick where the atmosphere is typical of Brussels. There are three storeys and the arcades as a whole are roofed with glass barrel vaulting (except in the Galerie des Princes) across a slender metal framework. The decorative features were by Joseph Jaquet.

It is said that the Galeries Saint-Hubert, having become a very fashionable meeting-place shortly after the official opening, attracted the *Cercle Artistique et Littéraire*, an artistic and literary circle frequented by Victor Hugo, Alexandre Dumas and Edgar Quinet who came here to listen to lectures given by Deschanel.

The Galerie du Roi leads into Rue de l'Ecuyer. Almost opposite is Rue Montagne aux Herbes Potagères.

A la mort subite (Sudden Death) *(no 7)* is one of Brussels' veritable institutions. The unusual name of this typical Brussels café even provided the inspiration for the title of a ballet choreographed by Maurice Béjart. It is said to come from the name given to the loser in a game of *pitchesbak*, which we now know as 421, a game which used to be popular with the many journalists who frequented the district.

Continue along Rue Montagne aux Herbes Potagères and turn left into Rue Fossé aux Loups.

At 47 Rue Fossé aux Loups is the Hôtel S.A.S. in which the foyer contains a stretch of the original town walls. Some say it has been excessively restored; others believe that its preservation is extremely fortunate.

Options from Rue du Marché aux Herbes:

▶▶ Grand-Place and its district via Rue Chair et Pain opposite Petite Rue des Bouchers.

Quartier de la Bourse by going down the street then turning left into Rue de Tabora.

Quartier du Béguinage by going down the street and continuing straight along Rue Marché aux Poulets. Then turn right into Rue de la Vierge Noire to get to Tour Noire.

Quartier de la Place de Brouckère by going down the street and turning right into Rue des Fripiers. Beyond the Théâtre de la Monnaie, turn left into Rue Fossé aux Loups.

Cathédrale des Saints-Michel-et-Gudule by going up the street and turning left into Rue de la Montagne.

Quartier du Mont des Arts by going up the street then going along Rue de la Madeleine on the right.

Quartier du MONT DES ARTS ★

This district was founded by King Leopold II who gave it its name because he wanted to concentrate one of the finest art collections in the world within this area. The Mont des Arts overlooks the old town around Grand-Place and stretches from Boulevard de l'Empereur to Rue Montagne de la Cour, its main feature being the equestrian statue of King Albert I (A Courtens) opposite the statue of his wife, Queen Elizabeth, on Place de l'Albertine.

It was *c*1880 that Leopold II decided to have the ill-famed Saint-Roch District razed to the ground and to replace its insalubrious alleyways and streets with a wide boulevard flanked by a temple in honour of the Fine arts. Once however the district had been demolished, hesitation and indecision led the king to have gardens laid out for the 1910 World Fair instead. He entrusted the commission to a Frenchman named Vacherot and paid for the work out of the privy purse. The terraced gardens were bulldozed in 1955 to make way for the architectural complex that exists today.

BIBLIOTHEQUE ROYALE DE BELGIQUE (KZ M⁴)

The royal library was set up by the government in 1837 and is also unofficially known as the Albert I Library and, more simply, as Albertine because its present premises were erected in memory of the "king-knight". Its distant ancestor was the 15C Burgundy Library that contained some 900 illuminated manuscripts. In 1559 Philip II brought the works in the ducal palace together under the name of "Royal Library". Most of the works survived the fire that raged through the Coudenberg in 1731 and the library was opened to the public in 1772.

The present buildings were inaugurated in February 1969. They were designed by M Houyoux, R Delers and J Bellemans. The multi-storey structure (67 000sq m – 720 920sq ft) includes the library tower (17 floors and some 100km – 62 miles of shelving). The library purchases, catalogues and stores all books, manuscripts or printed works produced within the kingdom of Belgium. All Belgian publishers and all Belgian authors published abroad and resident in Belgium are required to deposit one copy of their work here. The library also has the main international publications and constitutes a centre of scientific research.

Collections – *Reserved for the bearers of an admission card, except for the chalcography section.*

Prints department: *1 place du Musée (see Quartier des Musées des Beaux-Arts*, Charles of Lorraine's apartments).

The printed works department contains four million works that can be consulted on the spot.

The special sections contain documents considered as particularly valuable. The legal reserve *(floor 4)* stores Belgian works published since 1 January 1966. The valuable-document reserve *(level -2)* contains more than 35 000 printed works including 3 000 incunabula (works printed before 1501) and a large number of bindings from the 15C to the present day. The library contains 140 000 maps and plans *(level -2)* but this figure includes atlases, terrestrial and celestial globes and aerial photographs. The music section *(level 4)* contains sheet music and works on musicology, records and recordings and has a 150-seat chamber music auditorium. The etchings room *(1 Place du Musée, see Lorraine Palace)* contains 700 000 items from the 15C to the present day, including a collection of modern drawings. The manuscripts room *(level -2)* contains a number of collections, in particular the **manuscripts of the Dukes of Burgundy.** The medals and coins room *(ground floor)* has a number of series of coins spanning the period between the 7C BC and the present day, as well as several personal collections that are absolutely outstanding.

The documentation centres combine several specialist departments designed to assist researchers in very specific fields.

The research centres include the archives and literature museum *(level 3)* which stores manuscripts, autographs, and documents relating to French works published in Belgium (the Dutch equivalent is in Antwerp), the Center for American Studies *(level 2)* and the African documentation centre *(level 3)*.

The library also houses the **chalcography** section ⊙ *(1 Place du Musée, see Lorraine Palace)* which has more than 5 000 historic and modern engravings which it prints or reprints on request.

Chapelle de Nassau ⊙ – *Ground floor; temporary exhibitions.* This chapel dedicated to St George stands on the site of a private chapel of the same name. The building was completed *c*1520. It was commissioned by Engelbert II of Nassau, Governor General of the Netherlands during the reign of Philip the Fair (1493-1506).

The Flamboyant Gothic building has a number of unusual features such as fan vaulting and windows of varying heights which echo the fact that Rue Montagne de la Cour slopes down from the Coudenberg towards Grand-Place. The chapel was integrated into the new buildings but traces of the street are still visible along the exterior stonework. Note the ogival arching and the delicately-carved roodscreen, the modern stained-glass window by Sem Hartz (1969) bearing the coat of arms of the House of Orange-Nassau and the statue of St George in a niche outside.

There is a replica of the chapel *(see Cinquantenaire)*, created when it was decided to demolish the original. Like many other places of worship, it was used for quite another purpose after the outbreak of the Revolution. A brewer even used it as a warehouse. It was restored in 1839 before Bernissart's iguanodons were assembled in it *(see Natural History Museum)*. Its name brings to mind the Nassau Palace (depicted in a low relief (1969) on the outside to the left of the entrance to the Library), the most ornate of the palaces after the ducal palace which used to stand on the Coudenberg. The building, which was greatly admired by Albrecht Dürer, had a number of illustrious visitors including William of Orange, the Duke of Marlborough, and Prince Eugène of Savoy. It was finally rebuilt by Charles of Lorraine.

Musée du livre et cabinets de donations ⊙ – *Level -2.* Six studies pay homage to the generosity of a number of donors. The study of Emile Verhaeren (1855-1916) *(left of the wrought-iron grille)* is an exact replica of his study in Saint-Cloud near Paris. Everything in it is authentic. Note two portraits by Theo van Rysselberghe and James Ensor of the great poet born in Saint-Nicolas in Flanders, *La Bacchante* by Bourdelle, *Venice* by Paul Signac and *Aux Folies-Bergère* by Kees van Dongen. In the corridor, the first two studies *(right)* serve as a reminder of the outstanding quality of the donation from Mrs Louis Solvay. Opposite is the study of Max Elskamp (1862-1931) and Henry van de Velde (1863-1957). It combines memories of the poet and the architect who were childhood friends. The furniture was designed by H van de Velde; the works of art are by Edward Munch, T van Rysselberghe, Emile Claus and Auguste Rodin. The study *(also left side)* of dramatist Michel de Ghelderode (1898-1962) recreates the atmosphere of his flat in Schaerbeek. The collection *(right)* of Voltaire's works that belonged to the Count of Laumoit contains the famous edition of his complete works published in Kehl near Strasbourg in 1781-1790 by Beaumarchais.

The history of books in the Western world from the 8C to the present day is illustrated in the room at the end of the corridor. The lighting is intentionally dim owing to the fragility of the works on display. The exhibits consist of a choice of manuscripts *(left)* and printed works *(right)* selected according to four criteria –

the media used and the form of the work, the illustrations, changes in writing and type faces, and bindings. The selection is changed every six months. The books are taken from the store of valuable works or from the manuscripts room *(see Collections)*, the only exception being the papyrus scrolls which are on permanent display (they date from 1 000 BC). The exhibition is particularly well set out and it gives visitors an excellent insight into the way in which knowledge has been passed on down the centuries. On display are manuscript rolls, codices, parchments as thin as velum, the minute Carolingian script that was fashionable in the reign of Charlemagne and replaced the capital letters used by the Romans, Romanesque illuminations, Gothic miniatures or works by famous printers.

Musée de l'Imprimerie ☉ – *Corridors on levels -2 and -3. Reserves accessible to guided tours only.* The discovery of printing (1440) was attributed to Johann Gutenberg, a goldsmith in Mainz; it marked the beginning of a whole new era in the history of thought ie the unlimited reproduction of texts using separate mobile letters. In fact, it was the Chinese who developed this technique (7C) but the difficulties of adapting their alphabet to printing had greatly restricted its development. Several processes have revolutionised the printing world since then, in particular the metal presses with a system of counterbalances designed by Lord Stanhope in 1795, lithography developed by Alois Senefelder in 1796, and the hand, cylinder or pedal-operated presses dating from the early 19C.

The collection, one of the largest in Europe consisting of almost 300 machines, is scheduled to move to more adequate premises. The presses date from the period between the late 18C and the 20C and there are several examples illustrating the history of printing (typography, etching, lithography, screen-printing, and offset), binding or gilding. There are Belgian "lion" presses and platen presses, British Albion presses, engine-driven machinery, and even automatic presses. Also on display are various fonts – letter, algebraic, and music – type face drawers, a bed, the press used by Félicien Rops, trimmers, guillotines, sizing machines, typewriters and linotypes used to make line-blocks etc.

Garden – The garden, which replaced the one laid out by Jules Vacherot at the request of Leopold, was the work of René Pechère, a lecturer at the La Cambre College of Architecture and the Decorative Arts from 1939 to 1978. The outstanding feature of this design is that it is, in fact, a hanging garden suspended above the car park.

Palais de la Dynastie (**KZ G**) – On the other side of the Mont des Arts Garden is the palace. One wing is used as the **Conference Centre** (*Palais des Congrès*, **KZ G¹**) and hosts an international film festival every year. Above the rear of the arcade is a timepiece with Jack-o'-the-clock figures representing characters from history and folklore.

Place de l'Albertine at the foot of the Mont des Arts district lies on the edge of the Sacred Islet (see Quartier de la Monnaie) which explains why the fairly recent houses that line the square between Rue Saint-Jean and Rue de la Madeleine have the Flemish façades that were characteristic of the 17C.

Go down Rue de la Madeleine.

Galerie Bortier (**JKZ 23**) – *Entrances at 55 Rue de la Madeleine and 17 Rue Saint-Jean.* Like the famous Saint-Hubert Arcade *(see Quartier de la Monnaie)*, this one was designed by architect Jean-Pierre Cluysenaar. The arcade was inaugurated in 1848 and named after Pierre-Louis-Antoine Bortier, the owner of the land who commissioned the building of this pedestrian precinct. The

Ch. Bastin-J. Evrard

Bortier Arcade

narrow passage (65m – 70yds long) is naturally lit by the sun overhead. It is lined with shops and was once an integral part of the Madeleine market which was demolished in 1958; the blue stone frontage can still be seen in Rue Duquesnoy. The decoration, restored in 1977, was inspired by the Renaissance – scrolls, vases, twisted bases etc.

Although the arcade was traditionally famous for its booksellers, it also contained the shop belonging to Jean-Baptiste Moens who, in the early 1850's, sold the low-cost revenue bands which later led most philatelists the world over to consider him as a pioneering spirit.

Cluysenaar kept the delightful frontage (late 17C – early 18C, probably altered in 1763) of a middle-class house overlooking Rue de la Madeleine, at Bortier's request. A triangular pediment containing gods of the seas tops Ionic pilasters and two rusticated columns. In fact, this was the old coaching entrance used by stage-coaches.

Chapelle de la Madeleine ⊘ (**JKY**) – This small church was rebuilt in the Gothic style two years after the bombardment of 1695 and restored in 1957 – 1958. The Baroque-style St Anne's Chapel (1661) backing onto it used to stand at the corner of Rue de la Montagne. Inside, St Rita's Chapel dates from the restoration; the frescoes are by A Blanck.

Carrefour de l'Europe (**KY 90**) – This is both the name of the square situated at the entrance to the main station (V Horta followed by M Brunfaut, 1910 – 1952) and the name of the wide triangle flanked by Boulevard de l'Impératrice, Rue de la Madeleine and Rue de la Montagne. In the eyes of many of the locals, this area illustrates the failure of a property development policy that was implemented rather too often in the capital, to the detriment of an exceptionally rich architectural heritage. Although the conservation orders protecting the Sacred Islet *(see Quartier de la Monnaie)* have ensured that no more traces of the city's past have been lost here since 1960, the Carrefour de l'Europe is an example of the many clumsy attempts at urban development. Old gabled houses can be seen sandwiched between higher apartment blocks and the recent central buildings are an unfortunate copy of the traditional style which gave the old city centre such grace and elegance.

Options from Carrefour de l'Europe:

▶▶ Grand-Place via Rue de la Colline.

Quartier de la Monnaie by going through the Saint-Hubert Arcade then turning left into Rue de l'Ecuyer.

Cathedral at the end of Boulevard de l'Impératrice.

Quartier du Palais Royal by going up the Mont des Arts and Rue Montagne de la Cour to Place Royale.

Quartier des Musées des Beaux-Arts de Belgique by going up the Mont des Arts and turning right at the top of the flights of steps towards Place du Musée.

Quartier du Sablon by going along Boulevard de l'Empereur then down the flight of steps leading to Rue J Lebeau and on up to Place du Grand Sablon.

Quartier du PALAIS ROYAL★

The rise overlooking Mont des Arts and the Quartier de la Grand-Place used to be known as *Frigidus Mons* or *Coudenberg* (ie the "Cold Hill"). It has been the site of Place Royale since the end of the 18C and the residence of the Dukes since the 13C. The building of the royal palace at the back of the square in the 19C confirmed the vital role of the Coudenberg in the history of Brussels and its people, or arguably in the history of the nation as a whole.

Owing to the proximity of the royal art galleries *(see Musées royaux des Beaux-Arts)* and the central position of this district between the old town and the shopping areas of the Porte de Namur *(see Ixelles)* and Place Louise *(see Quartier Louise)*, it has become a very popular tourist venue that is as inevitable as it is attractive.

A Capital like Vienna – When, early in the 18C, Austria took possession of what was later to become Belgium, the people could not help feeling a certain sense of mistrust, fearing that they would be integrated into the hereditary States of the House of Austria. This, though, was not the case. When Maria Theresa married Duke François of Lorraine in 1736, he ceded his duchy to France. François then mounted the imperial throne and his younger brother, Charles, became Governor of the Low Countries. He exercised very real government as is obvious from the number of accredited diplomats but he did not enjoy total autonomy for the plenipotentiary minister Cobenzl ensured that imperial opinions and wishes were respected.

Brussels underwent a period of urban improvement during the popular period of government of Charles of Lorraine *(see Quartier des Musées des Beaux-Arts,* Charles of Lorraine's apartments) who was determined to set his capital on a par with Vienna. His aim was to given the new Coudenberg District a "general unity of style" and a number of squares that would be an integral part of predefined plans. Place Royale, the Palais de la Nation *(see Quartier du Parlement)* and the streets flanking the Parc de Bruxelles are outstanding examples of this neo-Classical style in which the main features are the use of Classical columns, pilasters and pediments, an emphasis on symmetry and the limewashing of many of the house fronts.

★ **Place Royale** (KZ) – The uniform square that visitors see today was laid out by French architects Nicolas Barré and Barnabé Guimard who took inspiration from Place Stanislas in Nancy and Place Royale in Rheims. It was known successively as Place de la Cour, Place de Lorraine, and Place Impériale, but it was eventually downgraded to Place Royale even though no monarch ever resided there (Albert I was born there on 8 April 1875: *see the plaque on the wall of the Cour des Comptes overlooking Place Royale*). The square is perfectly symmetrical with eight Louis XVI style pavilions that have gradually been restored over the past few years and a church which replaced the older Gothic church in the Coudenberg monastery. The west front of the **church of St-Jacques-sur-Coudenberg** ⊙ (consecrated in 1787) was also designed by architects Barré and Guimard. The building was erected by Louis-Joseph Montoyer then Tilman-François Suys gave it a new attic and campanile in 1849. Originally, the church was dedicated to St James the Great. It may have escaped damage by fire in 1731 *(see Palais Ducal, below)* but it was unable to withstand the onslaught of Charles of Lorraine and his urban planning project. It was demolished and the new church was sited in line with Rue Montagne de la Cour. It was turned into a Temple of Reason during the French Revolution. The biblical statues of Moses and David were merely renamed Solon and Lycurgus but the low relief of *Le Sacrifice du Messie* on the tympanum of the pediment was removed. The fresco entitled *La Vierge consolant les Affligés* is a late work by Jean Portaels (1852); it is topped with three sculptures (St Andrew, St James and St John) carved by Egide Mélot.

The interior is plain but solemn. Note the Stations of the Cross by J Geefs, and two large paintings by J Portaels at each end of the transept. They represent the *Crucifixion* and *La Croix consolatrice*. In the chancel *(left)* is the royal pew linked by a gallery to the palace gardens.

On 21 July 1831, Prince Leopold of Saxe-Coburg-Gotha took the oath that made him the first King of the Belgians, on the steps leading up to the peristyle of the church.

In the centre of the square is an equestrian statue of Godefroid de Bouillon, King of Jerusalem, made by Eugène Simonis in 1848 to replace a statue of Charles of Lorraine that had been demolished during the French Revolution. From this central position, there is a superb **view** of the tower on the Town Hall *(east side)* and the Law Courts *(south side)*.

Since 1995, archeological digs have been undertaken to clear the *Aula Magna*, the large state chamber built during the reign of Philip the Good at the expense of the town (it was completed in 1460). This remarkable building used to contain the famous ducal throne which was richly decorated with pearls and cloth of gold. Nearby is Rue Isabelle by which the Infanta used to go to the cathedral; it is now an underground passageway. The remains of the old ducal chapel (1524-1553) are also visible.

Hôtel Bellevue (**KZ M³**) – *Entrance on Place du Palais*. This neo-Classical mansion was built between 1776 and 1777 as a luxury hotel. At the beginning of the 20C, the building underwent extensive alterations in line with plans drawn up by the architect, Maquet, and it was incorporated into the royal palace. Princess Clémentine, Leopold II's daughter, lived there, as did the future Leopold III and Princess Astrid. The first and second floors house the **Musée de la Dynastie** ⊙ containing an extensive set of documents (paintings, lithographs, sculptures, memorabilia, photos etc.) relating to the Belgian royal family from 1831 to the present day. A memorial to King Baudouin will soon be open to the public.

FROM FORTRESS TO ROYAL PALACE

Palais Ducal du Coudenberg – *For the corresponding dates, see the Introduction: Reigns of successive royal families*. Towards the second half of the 11C, Count Lambert II of Louvain had a castle built on the Coudenberg hill to provide back-up for the fortress on the island of Saint-Géry erected by the town's founder, Charles of France. At the end of the 13C, Jean I abandoned the damp banks of the island of Saint-Géry and moved, instead, to a ducal castle overlooking the town. The island then fell out of favour with the dukes. After the building of the second town wall during the second half of the 14C, the castle was turned into a palace and lost its military purpose. The work was a long-term project and was not completed until the end of the reign of Duchess Jeanne. Coudenberg then became the almost permanent seat of the Court.

During the days of the Dukes of Burgundy, the ducal palace *(see the various paintings in the Musée communal)* met the requirements of the Grand Duke of the Western World, Philip the Good. With each reign that passed, however, the palace was refurbished and improved until the word "luxury", when applied to this building, was something of an understatement. Unfortunately, on the night of 3 to 4 February 1731, it was totally destroyed by fire and a plethora of works of art were reduced to ashes.

Royal Palace

Palais royal (KZ) ⊘ – In March 1815, Napoleon's return from the Island of Elba immediately caused William of Orange to proclaim himself King of the Netherlands. On 30 March, he formally entered Brussels. On 9 June, the Congress of Vienna confirmed the reunification of Belgium and the Netherlands. William I of Orange-Nassau, though, was an accomplished diplomat and he decided that Brussels and The Hague would share the function of capital city. From then on, the building of a royal palace became a necessity.

Exterior – The original plans for the royal palace were drawn up by an architect from Dinant named Ghislain-Joseph Henry who died while the building work was in progress. Charles van der Straeten succeeded him and was later replaced by Tilman-François Suys who added a monumental entrance between the two pavilions (Belgiojoso and Bender) built during work on Place Royale. He gave the frontages uniformity and linked them to the Walckiers Residence *(left)* and Belle-Vue Residence *(right)*. The work was completed in 1829 then taken up again in 1862 when the Duke of Brabant, the future Leopold II, commissioned Alphonse Balat (1819-1895), who was his regular architect for some forty years, to alter and extend the building. Alphonse Balat also altered several of the rooms inside the palace, turning them into Louis XIV style chambers. In 1902, the King asked Henri Maquet to redesign the frontage. It is built of Euville stone and has a monumental portico in the centre decorated with Corinthian columns topped by a pediment bearing sculptures by Thomas Vinçotte. The small pavilions at the end of the curved galleries have small domes which Leopold II called "the covers of Mr. Maquet's coffin".
If the national flag is flying above the palace, it means that the King of Belgium is in residence.

Interior – The foyer (busts by Geefs, Courtens, Samuel, and Rousseau) and grand staircase lead to the grand antechamber. The staircase is undoubtedly A Balat's finest piece of work. The marble steps and white stone walls have a majestic austerity. *Peace* carved by C-A Fraikin is represented by Minerva. The Empire Chamber (paintings include *King Leopold I* by C-A Fraikin and *Prince Philip* by Thomas Vinçotte), which dates from the days of the Dutch monarchy, leads into the two white chambers (furniture by Jacob Desmalter). The Secretaries' Staircase (the tapestry was made in Madrid to designs by Francesco de Goya), vestibule to the royal apartments and Venice Staircase (Venitian works by Jean-Baptiste van Moor) lead to the Goya Chamber (tapestries made in Madrid and chairs made for Napoleon by P-B Marcion), the Leopold I Chamber and the Louis XVI Chamber (*Princess Charlotte* by G Geefs). The Blue Room still contains the "Buffon birds" plates and the dazzling scallop-shell dinner service that was made in London. The Marshals' Chamber contains a portrait of Leopold I (a copy of the original by Franz Winterhalter).
Visitors then enter the great reception rooms designed by A Balat. The grandiose **Throne Room★** is divided into three sections. The doors into the wings are topped by low reliefs by Thomas Vinçotte. The two side rooms are separated from the central section by three arches supported on pilastered pillars. Auguste Rodin worked on the decoration of one of the four low reliefs at the ends of the central section of the room. Note the musicians' gallery. The Marble Chamber leads into the great gallery which is 40m – 130ft long. The Thinker's Chamber is used for lying-in-state ceremonies after the death of a member of the royal family. It opens onto the Hall of Mirrors which is used solely for State occasions.

★ Parc de Bruxelles (KYZ) – In the 14C, Duke Jean III purchased land which he then walled in to create a private park. During the following century, Philip the Good brought in game. The park was extended during the 16C by Charles V and was famous throughout Europe for its fountains and grottoes, and for the valley where guests could hunt stags and wild boars. During the summer, jousting tournaments were staged here.

The Park – After the fire that raged through the nearby ducal palace in 1731, the park was left to its fate until 1776 when Empress Maria Theresa commissioned Barnabé Guimard and an Austrian named Joachim Zimmer to lay out a formal, French-style park resembling the public esplanades that had been created in all the great European capital cities. The park was opened in 1780 and decorated with statues from the former labyrinth in the ducal park, from Tervuren Castle and from the Thurn und Taxis Residence in the Quartier du Sablon. In 1830, the Dutch army retreated to the park during the September Uprising but was forced to leave its re-entrenchments in the face of attack from courageous Belgians patriots.
The park was altered as a result of the extensions to Place du Palais in 1904 and now covers an area of 13 hectares. There are some delightful views punctuated by the fountains in the park and statues abound. Opposite the palace are three gates decorated with groups created by Gilles-Lambert Godecharle (*Hunting Trophies, left and right*), Victor Poelaert (*Spring, centre*), and Egide Mélot (*Summer, centre*). Inside the park (it is said to have been laid out in accordance with masonic symbols), there are a number of outstanding sculptures. *The Lion* (1895) with its paw resting on a ball was created by Alphonse de Tombay, an artist from Liège who

Brussels Park

worked in Rome. Near the small octagonal basin is a graceful *Fillette à la coquille* (1901), again by A de Tombay; it is actually a bronze fountain but there is no longer any water supply to it. In days gone by, it provided drinking water for children playing in the park. The memorial to Gilles-Lambert Godecharle beside Rue Ducale was erected by Thomas Vinçotte; his main works are summarized in the medallion. There are also a few buildings including a bandstand, the Royal Theatre (1782) designed by Montoyer, and the Vauxhall (1776) behind it designed by the same architects as the park itself. This building has recently been restored. Originally designed for a variety of leisure activities, it still has a very rare type of stage. Just opposite the royal palace are two ravines flanking the side entrance. They are very unusual in that their retaining walls bear the letters V.I.T.R.I.O.L. along their entire length. This is a Latin formula much-beloved of alchemists, meaning "Go down into the bowels of the Earth and, through distillation, you will find the stone which is not a stone". Some people believe that Charles of Lorraine, who was Grand Master of the Teutonic Order, carried out extensive research into the mysteries of the philosopher's stone. This discreet lettering may be proof of their claim.

The surrounding area – B Guimard, a French architect who lived in Brussels and had already been involved in the design of Place Royale (little else is known about him), drew up the plans for the private Louis XVI style townhouses bordering the park. In order to build them, an appeal for funds was sent out to all the great abbeys in Brabant which bought the plots of land and paid for the building work. It has to be said that, in those days, or to be more precise in 1777, the area including Place Royale and the streets beside the park was designed as a closed urban district which would hide from the Prince's view the irregular thoroughfares in the old-fashioned districts adjacent to these wide avenues which left plenty of space for pomp and ceremonial.

Rue Belle-Vue was turned into Place du Palais at the beginning of this century. Rue Royale is undoubtedly the most aristocratic of the avenues. Opposite the east gate into the park is the side entrance of the art gallery *(Palais des Beaux-Arts, see Quartier des Musées des Beaux-Arts)*. At the junction with Rue Baron Horta is a statue of the French General Augustin-Daniel Belliard (1769-1832). As soon as Belgian Independence had been declared, the high-ranking officer was sent to Brussels to protect the nation from the return of Dutch forces. The statue is a fine piece of work by Guillaume Geefs and the army is said to have given up one day's pay to cover the costs. Rue de la Loi also includes a row of fine, austere, Louis XVI house fronts. In the centre is the Palais de la Nation *(see Quartier du Parlement)*. Rue Ducale was treated with greater simplicity. Its mansions used to back onto the second town wall. Lord Byron stayed at 51 Rue Ducale in 1816 *(see Introduction, Brussels and Foreign Celebrities)*. Walthère Frère-Orban (1812-1896), the great liberal politician *(see Quartier du Parlement)*, died at 23. The furnishings in the British Ambassador's residence *(no 17)* are all museum pieces.

Palais des Académies (KZ) – *Rue Ducale*. This former palace in the neo-Classical style was the residence of the Prince of Orange (William I's son) until 1830. Building work, to designs by Charles van der Straeten, had begun in 1823 and was completed by Tilman-François Suys in 1825. The ground floor is used as a foundation level supporting two upper storeys bordered by Ionic pilasters, in a style reminiscent of an Italian *palazzo*. The palace has been State property since 1842 and it was used for several different purposes until, in 1876, it became the Palais des Académies. It is the seat of the Royal Academy of Sciences, Letters and Fine Arts of Belgium, an institution founded by Empress Maria Theresa in 1772. Seve-ral other Academies have joined it over the years.

The garden is decorated with a few statues. Opposite Place des Palais is a statue of Alphonse Quetelet (1796-1874), an astronomer, statistician, mathematician, sociologist, and founder of the Brussels Observatory. On the side flanking Boulevard du Régent, there are three bronzes – *Caïn maudit* by Jehotte, *Le Vainqueur à la course du stade* by Geefs and *Le Lanceur de disques* by Kessels.

Equestrian statue of Leopold II – *Place du Trône*. This work by Thomas Vinçotte (1850-1925), a talented sculptor whose most outstanding works were arguably the low reliefs decorating the pediment of the royal palace, is a fine homage to the particularly strong personality of the King-Builder.

Opposite is Rue du Luxembourg with the Gare du Quartier-Léopold at the end (the railway station was designed by Gustave Saintenoy, 1855). It has recently found itself overshadowed by the new European Parliament building. Also opposite, but slightly to the right, at 24 Avenue Marnix, are the head offices of the Banque Bruxelles-Lambert designed by an American architect, Gordon Bunshaft, in 1959. The esplanade is decorated with a bronze sculpture by the great British artist, Henry Moore.

Options from Place du Trône:

▶▶ Quartier des Musées royaux des Beaux-Arts by returning to Place Royale and going down Rue de la Régence.

Quartier du Mont des Arts by returning to Place Royale and going down Rue Montagne de la Cour.

Quartier du Parlement by taking Rue de la Loi on the other side of the Park.

Quartier des Institutions européennes by crossing the "inner ring road" and going along Avenue des Arts then right into Rue Belliard. Do not take the underpasses if you are in your car. Instead, take the side-avenue then turn left into Rue Froissart.

Ixelles by following Boulevard du Régent to Porte de Namur.

MICHELIN GREEN GUIDES

Art and Architecture
History
Geography
Ancient monuments
Scenic routes
Touring programmes
Plans of towns and buildings

A selection of guides for holidays at home and abroad.

Quartier du PARLEMENT

This district, which includes the Parliament and several government offices, lies to the northeast of the town centre and is bounded by Rue de la Loi, Rue Royale, Boulevard Bischoffsheim and Boulevard du Régent.

Most of the streets to the north of the Palais de la Nation were designed by an architect named Mennessier shortly before 1880, on the site of the former Notre-Dame-aux-Neiges area that was popularly nicknamed the "Lacemakers' District" because so many of them lived and worked there. The fact that Brussels Park and the seat of the Parliament (since 1831) were nearby encouraged the Town Council to build a residential district in place of the network of mainly working-class narrow streets and cul-de-sacs. Since then, the district has boasted a very homogeneous set of fine middle-class houses and huge mansions.

Palais de la Nation (KY) ⊘ – *1 and 2 place de la Nation, rue de la Loi.* The foundation stone was laid in 1779. This palace was designed in the neo-Classical style by the French architect Barnabé Guimard and built to house the Council of Brabant, the High Court of Justice. In those days, counsellors had to speak and read French, Dutch.... and Latin. The building work was completed in 1784. The palace has a superb façade set attractively in line with the central avenue in Brussels Park *(see Quartier du Palais Royal).* Eight Ionic columns bear a pediment decorated by low reliefs by Gilles-Lambert Godecharle (1750-1835).

The building, which was restored after a fire in 1883, is the seat of the Chamber of Representatives and the Senate, the two houses in the Belgian Parliament. On 17 February 1994, Belgium became "a federal State consisting of communities and regions" in line with Article 1 of its Constitution. This alteration changed the composition of the parliament. It now has 150 M.P.'s in the lower house and 71 senators in addition to HRH Prince Philippe, Duke of Brabant, who has a hereditary right to sit in the upper house as a member of the royal family likely to accede to the throne.

Two flights of steps lead off the inner peristyle; the one with the green carpet leads to the Chamber of Representatives; the red carpet to the Senate. Several statues decorate the foyer including one of Duke John I by Charles Geerts, another of Philip the Good by Jean-Baptiste de Cuyper, and Charles V by Jean-Baptiste de Bay. A number of rooms and drawing rooms are open to view. The public can also sit in on sessions in the Chamber and Senate. The **Senate Session Room★** is decorated in a particularly refined manner. The style is a combination of Louis XVI and Louis-Philippe and the room is lit by a dome decorated with the coats-of-arms of the 9 provinces (since 1 January 1995, Belgium has had 10 provinces). The portrait gallery immortalises the leading lords and sovereigns from the Middle Ages to the end of the 18C. The panels on the end wall illustrate a few of the most outstanding episodes in Belgian history – the Flemish people resisting foreign aggression (Charles the Bold forcing Louis XI to witness the punishment of his allies from Liège – *left;* the Duke d'Albe resisting the Count of Egmont and William the Taciturn – Louis XIV besieging Brussels – *centre;* revolutionary uprisings against Emperor Joseph II – Napoleon's defeat at Waterloo – *right.*)

Walk along Rue de la Loi towards the city centre and turn right into Rue Royale.

Rue Royale – This street (2km – 1 mile long) runs straight from Place Royale *(see Quartier du Palais Royal)* to St Mary's Church *(église Sainte-Marie, see Quartier du Botanique).* Opposite the offices of the daily newspaper, *Le Soir,* first published in 1887 by Emile Rossel, is a Classical building *(no 13)* with a shop window on the

Palais de la Nation

ground floor decorated with the graceful swirls characteristic of the Art Nouveau style. The window★ (**KY F¹**) was the last one to be designed by architect Paul Hankar (1896) who was famous for this type of work. Almost directly opposite the Congress Column, the chocolate maker, Mary (*no 73*), will delight those with a sweet tooth anxious to taste the "pralines" that are a Belgian speciality. The Hôtel Astoria *(no 101-103)* was built for the 1910 World Fair; its luxurious past is remembered in its neo-Victorian foyer with glass roof. The Pullman bar is a reconstitution of a 1920's sleeping carriage. The hotel is the traditional haunt of the rich and famous. History has it that the Aga Khan's wife once took a bath of she ass's milk here.

Ch. Bastin - J. Evrard

Shop-front by Paul Hankar in Rue Royale

Colonne du Congrès (**KY K**) – *Place du Congrès*. This monument which was designed and inaugurated in 1859 by Joseph Poelaert (1816-1879) who also designed the Law Courts, commemorates the national congress which drew up the Belgian Constitution just after the revolution in 1830. The column (47m – 153ft high) contains a flight of 193 steps *(closed to the public)* leading up to the statue of Leopold I carved by Willem Geefs (1805-1883). The corners of the pedestal bear the names of the 237 members of the Congress and the main articles of the Constitution; they are decorated with seated female statues (by J Geefs, B Simonis, C-A Fraikin). These allegorical figures symbolise the nation's four main freedoms – freedom of worship, freedom of association, freedom of the press and freedom of education. To each side of the entrance is a lion carved by Eugène Simonis, standing guard over the tomb of the unknown soldier placed here on 11 November 1922. Like the tombs in Great Britain, France, Portugal, Italy and the United States, a flame burns here night and day, perpetuating the memory of the soldiers who died during the First World War.

The square was designed by Cluysenaar. The architect Poelaert designed the private residences that surround the square, built in the style of Italian palaces. From the nearby esplanade between local government office buildings (1958-1984), there is an interesting general view of the city.

Turn into Rue du Congrès opposite the Column.

Four streets radiate out from Place de la Liberté (the statue of minister Charles Rogier is by De Groot, 1897); they bear the names of the freedoms guaranteed by the Constitution. Rue de l'Enseignement includes the **royal circus**, *a very popular theatre and concert hall. The building (1877) was named after its famous Parisian counterpart.*

From the square, go down Rue de l'Association and turn right into Rue de la Révolution.

Place des Barricades (**KY**) – The only circular "square" in the city centre commemorates, through its name, the fighting that occurred during the 1830 revolution. The square, though, was laid out during the days of Dutch control to plans by the architect Vifquain (*c*1828) who designed its neo-Classical houses in a particularly austere style. In the centre of the square is a statue of André Vésale (1514-1564), an anatomist from Brussels. It was carved by Joseph Geefs in 1846. Andries van Wesele (his name has since been Frenchified) who was physician to Charles V later Philip II was the first person to describe muscular function, the role of the nervous system and the way in which the voice is produced.

Victor Hugo was living at no 4 when he was expelled from Belgium *(see Introduction, Brussels and Foreign Celebrities)*. Adèle Hugo died here on 27 August 1868.

Walk along Boulevard Bischoffsheim, cross the "inner boulevards" in Place Madou and turn right into Avenue des Arts.

★ **Musée Charlier** (FR M²¹) ⊘ – *16 Avenue des Arts*. Henri van Cutsem was a wealthy art lover who, in 1890, purchased two adjacent houses on the Avenue des Arts in the town of Saint-Josse. After combining the two, he commissioned his friend, Victor Horta, to design glass roofs that would let in light onto his collections of works of art. Then he asked the artist Guillaume Charlier (1854-1925) to move into the residence. The latter was sole heir to his patron's estate after his death in 1904. Charlier inherited the mansion and had a museum built in Tournai, designed by Victor Horta, to house the collections of Impressionist paintings that had belonged to H van Cutsem.

The Charlier Museum contains a large number of paintings and sculptures by different artists; it also has interesting collections of furniture, tapestries and objets d'art. A few of the exhibits are worth particular attention either because they are the works of famous artists or because they are steeped in the charm inherent to works produced by people with talent but no genius or again because they reveal a little-known aspect of the artistic past of the capital city. The concerts organised in the museum on the first Thursday of the month are an excellent initiative.

Ground Floor – Charlier Room: among the pieces of porcelain in a Louis-Philippe mahogany bookcase, note the late 18C Chineseware produced by the Montplaisir porcelain works in Brussels. The beautiful floral spirals in two glass **cabinets** (silverware and crystal) are said to be the work of Victor Horta. Drawing room: The award-winning *Prix de Rome* in 1882 was a sculpture named *Idylle* made by G. Charlier; it can now be seen on a Louis-XVI style sideboard that is a copy of a Riesener piece kept in the Château de Chantilly. *Lucy Kufferath* is a delightful portrait by Jean Gouweloos and the two plaster casts by Emile Namur are representative of the eclectic tastes of the 19C. Concert room: this room contains a wonderful *Marine* by Marguerite Verbockhoven, a painting entitled *Fleurs et papillons* by **James Ensor** and *L'Homme à la pipe* by Ramali, all of which naturally draw the eye. Another interesting work is *Floréal* by Louis Plon, a perfect example of grisaille, exhibiting a realism inspired by the new craft of photography. Chinese Drawing Room: it contains examples of the excessively-ornate European Orientalist style which the Chinese, who preferred simplicity, produced especially for Western customers. Staircase: pastoral painting by Constantin Meunier.

First Floor – Reception Room: note the three decorative paintings above the doors and the Audenarde tapestry (mid 17C) with its mythological subject matter. Louis XVI Room: the drop-leaf desk is typical of the Louis XVI style; the clock on the mantelpiece is representative of the Empire style. On the wall is an Impressionist painting, *Vase de fleurs*, by Anna Boch who was a member of the Circle of XX. Empire Drawing Room: superb set of furniture bearing the stamp of Jean-Joseph Chapuis, a cabinetmaker from Brussels who trained in Paris where he obtained his craftsman's qualifications. Louis XV Drawing Room: the Rococo clock on the mantelpiece was made by Le Noir a Parisian clockmaker. Tapestry Drawing Room: there is Delft porcelain in a niche. The Brussels tapestry (c1500, *left*) which is still Gothic in composition, illustrates one of the articles of the Nicene Creed. Christ's Drawing Room: flanked by soft-coloured *verdures* (late 17C Aubusson and late 16C Brussels tapestries) is *Le Pilote*, a bronze draft by G Charlier of a monument that can be seen in Blankenberge, a resort on the North Sea coast.

Second Floor – Empire Bedchamber: the mahogany bed bears the stamp of J-J Chapuis. Folklore Room: a reminder of the history of Saint-Josse.

Continue along Avenue des Arts and turn left into Rue de la Loi. Take the 3rd turning on the right into Rue de l'Industrie.

Square Frère-Orban (FR 104) – This oasis of greenery in the midst of office blocks bears the name of the Liberal, Walthère Frère-Orban (1812-1896) who served several terms as Prime Minister. The square was laid out in 1860 to plans by Tilman-François Suys.

The two huge buildings flanking **St Joseph's Church** are eclectic in style. The church itself (1842-1849) is built of blue stone and was also designed by Suys. The Italian neo-Renaissance façade includes a high relief above the central doorway depicting the *Triumph of Faith*.

On the left is the mansion *(33 Rue des Sciences)* that belonged to the Marquis d'Assche. It was designed by Balat the architect in 1858 and now houses the Council of State.

Options from the Palais de la Nation:

▶▶ Quartier du Palais Royal via Brussels Park.
    Cathedral via Rue Royale, turn into Rue des Colonies, then turn right into Rue de la Chancellerie.
    Quartier du Botanique via Rue Royale.
    Quartier des Institutions européennes by skirting the park and turning into Rue Belliard. Do not take the underpasses but follow the lateral avenue then turn left into Rue Froissart.

Quartier du SABLON★★

This district with its aristocratic past is closely linked to the history of the church of the guild of crossbowmen. At the turn of the century, it was decidedly working-class. Over the past thirty years, however, almost the entire population has moved out and its shops have been bought by dealers in bric-à-brac or antiques or been turned into art galleries. It is true that Place du Grand Sablon, having now become "chic", has an undeniable charm to which the illuminated windows of its church add the finishing touch after nightfall.

This district of Brussels is a busy place at any time of the day or evening, acting as a sort of "lynch-pin" between the "upper" and "lower" towns. It has numerous cafés and restaurants.

Place du Grand Sablon (KZ 112) – The people of Brussels refer to the square quite simply as "Sablon". Its name has an ancient origin. In 1374, the archives of St Gudule's Church (now the cathedral) mentioned a "sandy lake". The cross-bowmen used to train there and they built a chapel on the site in honour of their patron saint, the Virgin Mary. Numerous festivities and processions were held here. Houses were built nearby and, in the 16C, wealthy aristocrats (among them Egmont, Bréderode, Mansfeld, Thurn and Taxis) had luxurious mansions built in the upper part of the district with the result that, by the following century, this had become the most expensive district in the town. Time and fashions came and went, and high society deserted the Sablon District which was gradually taken over by a large number of modest little shops. For many years, the district hosted the finals of the "Balle Pelote" competition, otherwise known as the "Little White Queen". This was a popular sport but its popularity waned with the increase in the number of cars.

At the beginning of the 17C, the Sablon Marshes (Zavelpoel) were filled in. Jacques Bargé's Fountain of Minerva was built on the site in 1751, paid for by Lord Thomas Bruce, Count of Aylesbury, in gratitude for the welcome he had received in Brussels where he spent 40 years in exile for his political opinions. Minerva is shown seated, holding a medallion decorated with effigies of François I and the Empress, Maria Theresa.

The top end of the square has traditionally been used for markets since the 15C. Every Saturday afternoon and Sunday morning, there is an antiques and bric-à-brac market housed in green and red marquees (the colours of the city). As soon as spring brings warmth to the air, the terraces of the Sablon's cafés are filled with the city's wealthy young people. The *Wittamer* cake shop *(no 12-13)* is something of an institution, despite being rather expensive.

Musée des postes et des télécommunications (JKZ M²²) ⊘ – *40 Place du Grand Sablon. Entrance: 2 Rue des Minimes*. The Postal and Telecom Museum traces the history of the post office through documents (licences, letters etc.) and old-fashioned equipment (dies, postmarks, cornets, uniforms, letter boxes, and a reconstitution of a 1900 post office). There is also a small room that will be of particular interest to philatelists. The Telecommunications section describes the development of the telegraph (needle and dial, Morse system) and telephone (replica of Bell's first phone, switchboards, candlestick and keypad phones). There is an interactive terminal at the entrance.

★ **Église Notre-Dame-du-Sablon** (KZ) ⊘ – This church is one of the finest Flamboyant buildings in Belgium. It replaced the chapel commissioned by the guild of crossbowmen in 1304. Legend has it that in 1348 the pious Béatrice Sodkens had a dream. The Virgin Mary wanted to thank the town of Brussels, and in particular the Guild of Crossbowmen, for having erected a chapel in Her honour. Béatrice was told to go to Antwerp and steal the statue of the Virgin Mary which worked miracles. She gave it to the crossbowmen of Brussels who were the forerunners of the present-day *gendarmerie*. After the 1421 uprising, the crossbowmen decided to enlarge their church which had become a place of pilgrimage. It was completed *c*1550 and marked the final stage in the development of ogival architecture. The architects are unknown. From the end of the 19C to the beginning of the 20C, the church underwent total restoration and was given a "new exterior casing". The architects J-J and M van Ysendijck, followers of Viollet-le-Duc, added turrets, bellcotes, pinnacles, balustrades and statues.

This church is the starting point of the annual Ommegang procession to Grand-Place *(see Calendar of Events)*.

Exterior – The church was built in the following order – chancel (1435), transept (1450), nave (second half of the 15C) and main door (*c*1530). The most interesting features are the sacrarium (1549) in the chevet of the chancel, the South door on which the coving bears illustrations of the Resurrection beneath a splendid rose window consisting of 12 four-leafed clovers, and the aisles with the row of gables that is so typical of Brabant-style architecture.

Stained-glass window, Notre-Dame-du-Sablon

Interior – *Enter by the doorway in Rue de la Régence. For details of the stained-glass windows and numerous works of decorative or commemorative art, ask for a plan to the right of the entrance.* The nave has five bays. This is unusual in Brussels where most of the chapels are separated by walls acting as buttresses. The capitals in the nave, surmounted by statues of the Twelve Apostles (mid 17C), are decorated with curly kale leaves, a form of ornamentation that was specific to the Brabant Gothic style. Above the triforium and its traceried gallery is the clerestory in which the windows have Flamboyant tracery. They admit light onto the vaulted roof where the keystones are decorated with coats of arms. Near the pulpit of truth (1697, Marc de Vos) is a plaque commemorating Paul Claudel who often came here to pray when he was French Ambassador to the Belgian capital.

In the north transept is the tomb of French poet Jean-Baptiste Rousseau (left of the entrance). Above the entrance is a statue of the Virgin Mary in a boat.

The chancel is particularly tall and lit by eleven lancet windows. It is decorated with carved squinches which are difficult to see because of the lack of light, depicting the massacre of the Holy Innocents (above the sacristy door) and the four Evangelists (at the entrance to the sacrarium). This polygonal construction, although not very large, has a lantern turret with small but attractively-carved keystones.

The delightful **funeral chapel of the Thurn and Taxis** is dedicated to St Ursula. It was built in the 17C by L Fayd'herbe and V Anthony. The black marble Baroque chapel is decorated with white marble sculptures. The statue of St Ursula in the chapel was made by Jérôme Duquesnoy the Younger. Allegorical figures such as Fidelity are a reminder of the reliability of the post office set up by this famous family.

The second chapel, which is dedicated to St Marcou, was also commissioned by the Thurn and Taxis.

★★ **Musée instrumental** (KZ M²) – *Scheduled to move shortly to 94 Rue Montagne de la Cour (see Quartier des Musées des Beaux-Arts de Belgique).*

The musical instrument museum has a prestigious collection of 6 000 instruments representing numerous countries and periods ranging from the Bronze Age to the present day. The display is slightly cramped but will have room to expand in its new premises, the splendid Old England building.

The ground floor houses wind instruments including numerous oboes, flutes, clarinets, bassoons, bombards, trumpets and cornets produced by makers in Brussels, Mons, Tournai or other countries between the 16C and 18C. There are also more unusual items such as a set of 16C crumhorns (Praetorius Room) or the elegant walking stick-flutes made by a Belgian named Joseph Dupré (19C) for those who enjoyed a romantic stroll. One room is filled with exhibits relating to Charles-Joseph Sax from Dinant who settled in the capital city in 1815, and his son, **Adolphe Sax** (1814-1894), who settled in Paris in 1843 and revolutionised the production of brass wind instruments by creating saxhorns, saxotrombones, saxtubas and, more particularly, saxophones which became popular through their use by brass bands before becoming an essential part of jazz bands, attracting the attention of Berlioz and Folklore is represented in hurdy-gurdies, diatonic accordions, dulcimers, balalaikas, bagpipes, water whistles etc. There is also a "Gamelan" band from Java (Indonesia).

The first floor displays keyboard instruments. Virginals and spinets, which were very fashionable from the 17C onwards, stand next to a keyboard-harp made in Brussels in the 19C and a few harpsichords including one made in Germany in 1734 and decorated with paintings by Van der Meulen. The vertical harpsichord or "clavicytherium" (Tournai, 1751) is unusual for its vertical casing which had the double advantage of being space-saving and sending the sound directly out towards the audience. The female figure in the lead rose carries a harp and is surrounded by the initials of the instrument-maker, Albert Delin. The pianoforte was invented in Italy in the late 17C and perfected in Germany, England and, later, in France where it was most notably popularised by Pleyel and Erard in the 19C, one hundred years after first being introduced into the country. In those days, pianos were more varied in shape than they are today. There was the piano-table, the grand piano, the square piano, the upright piano or the astonishing piano-closet made in Brussels in 1835 which resembles a cupboard with curtains hiding the mechanism. The organ, which was invented by Clesibios of Alexandria in the late 3C BC, completes this prestigious collection.

The entrance to the second floor displays eight particularly fine harps with admirable carvings. The display focuses on string instruments. The room also has 3 tympanons (17C) and a trumpet marine (Namur, 1680), a single-stringed instrument designed mainly to accompany hymns in convents. The adjective "marine" is said to have come from an incorrect translation of the German "*Marientrompete*" meaning "trumpet (of the daughters) of Mary". The guitar was popular during the Baroque period (one of the exhibits was made in Venice in 1630), as were the sistrum and mandolin (fashionable in the 18C). The viola da gamba was a cousin of the violin. It first appeared in the late 15C. Note the painted decoration on the bass viola "with the map of Paris" (17C) and the superb viola made by Joachim Tielke from Hamburg (1701) with its wonderful ivory inlay. The workshop of the Bernard family, instrument-makers in Liège, has been reconstructed to show the different stages in the craft. A glass cabinet contains a leather case made by Pietro Mircoli (Perugia, 1780). After 1600, the violin became very important in Italy owing to the first operas. In addition to the small number of instruments manufactured in the southern part of the Netherlands, note the 5 "pocket violins". They were used solely by dancing masters to give the rhythm of the dance.

★ **Place du Petit Sablon** (**KZ 195**) – This square occupies the site of the former graveyard of St John's Hospital and was given its present layout by architect Henri Beyaert in 1890. The delightful little public garden is closed off by a magnificent wrought-iron gate and surrounded by neo-Gothic colonnettes which are all different. On top are 48 charming bronze statuettes, one of which has disappeared, representing the arts and crafts of Brussels. They were made by almost 20 sculptors. The crafts are identified by their emblems, a fairly difficult exercise given that most of the crafts have now died out. They include arquebusiers (an arquebuse and an anvil), linen croppers (scissors), belt-makers and pin-makers (belts) or tallowmakers (a dead goose and a bottle) etc.

Arts and Crafts, Place du Petit Sablon

Inside the gardens, where the atmosphere is peaceful and calm, are statues of the Counts of Egmont and Hornes by C-A Fraikin (1817-1893), symbolising resistance to Spanish tyranny. The sculptures, which date from 1864, used to stand on the Grand-Place opposite the King's House *(see Quartier de la Grand-Place)*. Other statues represent politicians and leading 16C Belgian Humanists ie William the Taciturn (C van der Stappen) who fomented a country-wide revolt against the Spaniards, Louis van Bodegham (J Cuypers) who designed the King's House, Henri de Bréderode (A van Rasbourgh) who also resisted tyranny, Corneille de Vriendt also known as Floris (J Pécher) a sculptor and architect, Rombaud Dodonée (A de Tombay) an eminent botanist, Gérard Mercator (L van Biesbroeck) the famous geographer, Jean de Locquenghien (G van den Kerckhove) the town's amman, Bernard van Orley (J Dillens) the great Renaissance painter, Abraham Ortelius (J Lambeaux) author of the first geographical atlas, and Philippe de Marnix de Sainte-Aldegonde (P de Vigne) diplomat and philosopher. The gardens are flanked by houses dating from the beginning of the century with the exception of the King of Spain's House *(no 9)* which is said to date from 1601 or 1610. The square is a historical digest and a homage to the country's past lyrically represented by late 19C thinking. Karl Marx lived here in February 1845.

Counts of Egmont and Hornes – Lamoral, **Count of Egmont**, (1522-1568), was born near Ath and married Sabine of Bavaria, daughter of the Count Palatine. He covered himself in glory on the battlefield and was appointed Commander of the Spanish Armies in the Netherlands by King Philip II. He demanded the abolition of the Inquisition. When the king's policies contradicted the promises that had been made to him in Spain, he approached William of Nassau, Prince of Orange, although he remained faithful to the Roman Catholic Church.

Philippe de Montmorency, **Count of Hornes** (*c*1518-1568), was a supporter of the House of Orange and the Count of Egmont and, as such, contested the measures implemented by Cardinal Granvelle who had taken action against the Calvinists since 1539. All three men sought a pardon for the confederate noblemen but the city was shaken by severe unrest from 1566 onwards and Philip II reacted by despatching the Duke d'Albe to Brussels the following year. The Duke soon instigated a policy of repression. The Prince of Orange fled and the emissary was left with the brave Egmont and Hornes on whom to express Spanish displeasure. The "Council of Disorder" sentenced them to death and they went to the block on 5 June 1568 in front of the King's House.

Palais d'Egmont (**KZ**) – *Annex of the Ministry of Foreign Affairs (International Conference Centre)*. The building dates from 1533 to 1534 and was commissioned by the Princess of Gavre, mother of the famous Lamoral of Egmont who continued the work. The design of the Renaissance section of the building at the end of the main courtyard was based on the Granvelle Palace which no longer exists. It has nine arches separated by Doric pilasters on the ground floor and Ionic columns on the first floor. At the top is a continuous cornice and dormer windows. The gallery with colonnettes was added in 1832. In 1759 the Duke of Aremberg commissioned the Florentine architect Giovanni Nicolo Servandoni to add several features including a Classical wing which was rebuilt after a fire in 1892, overlooking the park. From 1830 to 1839, the architect Tilman-François Suys *(see Quartier du Palais Royal)* extended the buildings and constructed the left wing, as well as a riding school. In 1905 Flanneau added a wing jutting out in the direction of the park, maintaining the Renaissance order of the older façade as he did so. The palace was restored in 1971 and is a very homogeneous piece of architecture despite its extent (almost 100m – 108 yds long). Wool used to be dried in **Rue aux Laines** *(right)*. On the even-numbered side, note the fine group of early 20C houses. The superb neo-gothic mansion (no 56) was built in 1901 to designs by the architect M van Ysendijck.

Parc d'Egmont – *See Quartier Louise.*

ADDITIONAL SIGHTS

To the north of Place du Petit Sablon, in **Rue des Six-Jeunes-Hommes** (**KZ 268**) which was laid out in the 17C, there are a number of delightful old houses with so-called "Spanish"-style brick bonding. The sign at no 14 is a reminder of the story of the six young men (there are only four of them left on the sign) who were hung for having thrown soot in the face of a man named Vargas, an agent of the much-feared Duke d'Albe. The date 1503 carved on the frontage of no 12 is pure imagination but the door is attractively decorated.

Rue de la Régence (**JKZ**) contains the seat *(no 4)* of the Western European Union (W.E.U) and the Musées royaux des Beaux-Arts de Belgique *(no 3)*. On the other side of Place du Petit Sablon is the **Royal Academy of Music** (**KZ**) (Conservatoire royal de musique, *no 30*) (1872-1876) built in the neo-Renaissance style by Cluysenaar and the **synagogue** (**JKZ**) *(no 32)* designed by the architect De Keyser in the Romanesque-Byzantine style in 1875.

Rue de Ruysbroeck (**KZ 219**) lower down the square, dates approximately from the same period as the first town walls. It was named after the stream that used to flow alongside it. The street has suffered badly over the 20C but still has a few attractive houses. The ones at 55 and 53 date from the 17C; the frontage on 35 has a delightful rounded bay and the gabled house at 29 dates from the early 18C. Set at right angles to this street is the narrow Rue Sainte-Anne, a pedestrian precinct which, like Place du Grand Sablon, boasts a large number of antique shops.

The picturesque **Rue de Rollebeek** (**JZ 217**) at the bottom of Place du Grand Sablon includes a superb 17C entrance *(no 7)*. Next door *(no 9)* there is a charming crow-stepped gable.

Options from Sablon:

▶▶ Quartier des Musées Royaux des Beaux-Arts de Belgique by turning left up Rue de la Régence (the Museum of Ancient Art is at no 3).

Quartier du Palais Royal by turning left up Rue de la Régence to Place Royale.

Quartier Louise by turning right up Rue de la Régence.

Quartier Marolles by going down Rue J Stevens to the left of Rue de Rollebeek.

Quartier du Mont des Arts by walking down Rue J Lebeau then going down the steps beside the bridge and turning right onto Boulevard de l'Empereur.

Cathédrale
des SAINTS-MICHEL-ET-GUDULE★★

The old **collegiate church of Saints-Michel-et-Gudule** (**KY**) shares with Malines the title of cathedral for the archdiocese of Malines-Brussels. This "ship anchored in the heart of Brussels" is a superb building which is unusual for the combination of several different architectural styles, ranging from the Romanesque to the full splendour of 16C Gothic.

The cathedral has been used for all major ceremonial events since 1912 when Duke John II was buried there. In 1993, the funeral of King Baudouin I was held in this church and it was here that he married Dona Fabiola de Mora y Aragon on 15 December 1960.

The Name – In 1047, Count Lambert II founded a church on the Treurenberg Hill and dedicated it to Michael the Archangel *(see box)*, who is not a local saint. Veneration for the archangel came originally from the Orient and spread northwards via Italy. It was prevalent in Flanders in the mid 8C.

As to Gudule, she is a Carolingian saint who was born in Moortsel in Flanders. Her relics lay in the chapel dedicated to St Géry *(Quartier de la Ville Ancienne)* near the *castrum* built by Charles of France, Duke of Lower Lotharingia. Lambert II had the relics transferred to the Church of St Michael because, as Count of Louvain, he was hoping to retake the title of Duke of Lotharingia. In the end, it was Godefroid who acquired the title, in the early 12C.

The West Front – Visitors coming from the Grand-Place or Quartier de la Monnaie, ie emerging from a labyrinth of narrow streets and alleyways, are always amazed to find

---

The Brussels coat of arms

The coat of arms consists of a golden figure of St Michael slaying a black dragon on a red background. The shield is supported by two yellow lions, one of which is holding a banner bearing the coat of arms of Brabant and the other the city's coat of arms. Brussels dates back some one thousand years but its coat of arms was not designed until 25 March 1844 in accordance with a decree from King Leopold I. A statue of St Michael the archangel has however been on the top of the tower of the Town Hall since 1455 (it was removed a short time ago for restoration purposes). The saint has also featured on the town's seal since 1229.

Legend has it that Lambert II, Count of Louvain and Governor of Brussels (1041-1063), was sentenced to death by his father, Henry I, for having kidnapped the paternal fiancée. In order to escape his fate, Lambert II prayed to St Michael who enabled him to escape, altogether miraculously. The Count is then said to have proclaimed the archangel patron saint of the town.

themselves confronted by this huge stone construction which has regained its original whiteness as a result of recent restoration. A superb monumental flight of steps (1860) leads up to the entrance to the building. Together they form a delightful parvis.

The presence of two towers, like the ones seen on French churches is an exception because in Brabant architectural custom required a single tower placed to one side, in theory at least. Supported by powerful piers, the towers here date from the 15C. **Jan van Ruysbroeck** (early 15C-1485) who designed the wonderful tower on the Town Hall was undoubtedly involved in this building and was probably commissioned to design the spires but he died before his task could be completed. At the foot of the towers are three doorways with ribbed arches. At gable height, there is a delicately trac-

Cathedral - Close-up of the West Front

eried balustrade resembling fenestration. Topped by a tall window with Flamboyant Gothic tracery, the 15C central doorway is elegantly decorated with the Three Magi (Melchior, Gaspard and Balthazar) on the central pillar while the tympanum contains six statues of Apostles (19C). The remainder of the series can be seen to each side of the central doorway. This decoration undoubtedly has a great deal in common with the altarpieces, consisting of a central panel flanked by side panels.

The Interior ⊘ – *Entrance by the right door.* Clearly-designed explanatory panels have been placed in the north aisle so that visitors can distinguish the different periods of construction easily in chronological order.

Visitors are immediately struck, walking towards the nave, by the austerity of the decoration despite the fact that the cathedral dates mainly from the Baroque period. The nave was completed in the 14C up to window level. Its enormous columns, topped with capitals decorated with crockets, are backed by statues of the Twelve Apostles carved in the 17C. These sculptures were the work of Luc Fayd'Herbe, Jérôme Duquesnoy the Younger, J van Meldert and Tobie de Lelis known as Tobias, some of the most brilliant artists of the century and all of them natives of Brussels. To the left are Simon the Zealot, Bartholomew, James the Less, John the Evangelist, Andrew and Peter; to the right, Thaddeus, Matthew, Philip, Thomas, James the Great, and Paul. The **pulpit** (1699) is a masterpiece by Henri-François Verbruggen (1655-1724) a sculptor from Antwerp. It depicts Adam and Eve being chased out of the Garden of Eden and, on the top, the promise of Redemption illustrated by the Virgin Mary of the Immaculate Conception on her crescent moon stamping on the head of the serpent. This piece of furniture is so audaciously decorated that it is an unfailing source of surprise; it was brought here from the church in the Jesuit convent of Saint-Michel in Louvain. The triforium and clerestory date from the 15C. The vaulting, which was completed in the early 16C, has some fine keystones, still with their original paintwork. On the west side, the **stained-glass window** depicting the last judgment (1528, J de Vriendt) is particularly outstanding for its dazzling colours. The greens and blues are particularly deep and intense. The south aisle (14C) was built in the radiating style. The ribs in the vaulting are supported on engaged columns while the Flamboyant Gothic north aisle (2nd half of the 15C) is unusual for its clusters of colonettes. The aisle leads to the **Romanesque remains** uncovered during archeological digs beneath the nave in the 1980's. The visit below ground level gives an excellent idea of the original Early Romanesque church (10C) with its two round towers (c1200) flanking a massive projecting fore-part (c1200). The remainder of the west front is thought to date from the 11C.

The chancel is flanked by an ambulatory and is the oldest part of the present building. It was completed in 1280 in the Early Gothic style. The stained-glass windows by Nicolas Rombouts, a master glass-painter to the Court of Margaret of Austria, date from the 16C. The hexagonal Maes Chapel (17C) which was built in line with the chancel was once used as the burial crypt for the family after which it is named.

Above the north side of the ambulatory is the Flamboyant Gothic Chapel of the Holy Sacrament (16C), embellished with Renaissance windows designed by J Haeck to sketches by Bernard Van Orley. Others are by Michel Coxie the painter and the central window above the altar, representing the *Glorification du Saint-Sacrement*, was the work of J-B Caponnier. To the right of the ambulatory is the chapel of Notre-Dame de la Délivrance, built at the request of the Infanta Isabella in 1649. It too has magnificent stained-glass windows, this time by J Labaer to sketches by Théodore Van Thulden, one of Rubens' pupils; they depict the main episodes in the life of the Virgin Mary. At the back of the chapel is a black and white marble altar with an Assumption of the Virgin Mary in the centre. The work was by J-B de Champaigne, Philippe de Champaigne's nephew.

The vast cathedral restoration programme has not yet been completed and access to the chancel has been closed off by a temporary partition. On it hangs a fine *Crucifixion* by an artist from Brussels, Michel Coxie (1499-1592).

Options from the cathedral:

▶▶ Quartier de la Grand-Place by going down Rue de la Montagne then Rue du Marché aux Herbes. Turn left immediately into Rue de la Colline.
Quartier de la Monnaie by going down Rue de l'Ecuyer.
Quartier du Mont des Arts by going along Boulevard de l'Impératrice to Place de l'Albertine.
Quartier du Parlement by going round the chevet of the cathedral. Go back up the Treurenberg and along Rue Royale.
Quartier du Palais Royal by taking the same route then turning right along Rue Royale to the square of the same name.

Quartier de la VILLE ANCIENNE

This district is the historical centre of the town, the place where Duke Charles of Lower Lotharingia set up his *castrum c*979 AD on the island of Saint-Géry. Few traces of its medieval past, however, have survived to the present day. When the weather is good, there is a delightful atmosphere in Rue du Marché au Charbon and in the streets round about. Notre-Dame-de-Bon-Secours is an interesting church. The proximity of the Stock Exchange and, more especially, of Grand-Place goes some way to explaining the crowds of mainly young people. Finally, the nearby Rue du Midi is a heaven for philatelists.

Covering the Senne – The future monarch, Leopold II, was greatly impressed by the grand boulevards laid out in Paris during the Second Empire when Baron Haussmann took responsibility for urban planning and, while he was still Duke of Brabant, Leopold decided that work should be undertaken to give the centre of Brussels a facelift and make it a healthier place to live. After the terrible cholera epidemic that killed 3 467 people in 1866, the authorities decided to cover over the River Senne since its waters had become polluted. The work was completed between 1867 and 1871, at the request of the burgomaster Jules Anspach.

According to Louis Quiévreux, initiator of the Ilot Sacré *(see Quartier de la Monnaie)*, "the gigantic project totally isolated the river, and changed the centre of Brussels more radically than any air raid could have done". It is true that the work radically changed the face of the oldest part of Brussels which, as chroniclers of times past liked to emphasise, previously bore a resemblance to Bruges. The project was managed by Léon Suys the architect, who could be described as the Haussmann of Brussels, and resulted in wide boulevards in the city centre (Boulevards Le Monnier, Anspach, Max, Jacqmain), the opening of squares (Fontainas, Bourse and de Brouckère), and changes in the layout of winding narrow streets dating from the Middle Ages. This major project resulted in personal success for burgomaster Jules Anspach, who overcame all the political and financial obstacles put in his way by the government of the day.

The direct consequence of the covering over of the Senne was a change in the concept of urban housing in Belgium *(see Quartier de la Place de Brouckère, A Touch of Paris)* and a rapid increase in Brussels' population, taking it up to the million.

For sixty years, the River Senne flowed from the Gare du Midi to the other railway station, the Gare du Nord. Then its course was deviated so that excess water could drain off into the Brussels-Charleroi Canal.

The following sights lie to each side of Boulevard Anspach linking Place de la Bourse and Place Fontainas. The second of the squares marks the start of Rue du Marché au Charbon.

Notre-Dame-de-Bon-Secours (JZ) ⊘ – *Rue du Marché au Charbon*. The architect Jean Cortvrindt (?-1681) drew his inspiration from Italy when designing the layout for this church. He combined the traditional line of the nave and aisles with a hexagon opening onto semi-circular apsidal chapels. The central chapel contains the chancel. This design was probably inspired by Notre-Dame-des-Consolations in Vilvorde (1665), since the church in Brussels was not completed until twenty-nine years later. The skilful combination has produced a very interesting Italianate-Flemish church that differs greatly from the traditional Flemish style as seen in buildings such as Saint-Jean-Baptiste-au-Béguinage *(see Quartier du Béguinage)*, a prime example of conventional design. The west front is attractively proportioned and contains bulls' eye windows beneath a triangular pediment. In the middle is a statue of the Madonna and Child in a shell-shaped niche. The most outstanding elements of ornamentation are Governor Charles of Lorraine's coat of arms above the door (Cross of the Teutonic Order of which he was the Grand Master), and the hat and shell (door) that traditionally represent the route taken by pilgrims heading for Santiago de Compostela.

The interior is particularly elegant. The dome was originally topped by a lantern turret. Three very short aisles are overlooked by balustraded galleries. This layout, which is unusual in the southern part of the Netherlands, produces a markedly Renaissance atmosphere. The decorative features underline the tribute paid to 17C Italy, for example in the corner pillars on which the composite pilasters support a huge entablature. In the chancel, which is divided by pilasters topped by an architrave, the marble and painted wooden high altar dates from the early 18C. The oak statue of Notre-Dame-de-Bon-Secours (Our Lady of Assistance) dates from the 14C. The name is said to have been granted because of the statue's miraculous virtues which were acknowledged by none other than the Infanta Isabella herself.

Take Rue du Jardin des Olives to Boulevard Anspach then turn right and left into Rue des Riches-Claires.

Église Notre-Dame-des-Riches-Claires (ER) – *Rue des Riches-Claires. Closed to the public.* The church is attributed to Lucas Fayd'herbe (1617-1697) the architect from Malines; it was commissioned by a community of nuns in 1665. It was extended in the 19C and seriously damaged by fire in 1989. The restoration work is still not complete. The gable with scrolls above the rounded sections of the building is typical of the Italianate-Flemish style.

The layout of the church met a twofold purpose. Part of it was designed for use by the general congregation; the other part, adjacent to the cloisters, was reserved for the nuns. The extension work did away with this distinction by adding side aisles. The dome has been rebuilt.

Part of the former Convent of Riches-Claires has been turned into private flats.

Rue de la Grande Ile leads to Place Saint-Géry.

Halles St-Géry (ER) – *Place Saint-Géry.* The first settlement grew up on the island known as Saint-Géry and its historical importance as a central marketplace was underlined by the construction of a covered market in 1881 (see the straps on the façades) on the site of the church that had been razed to the ground in the late 18C by French revolutionaries. The building is a combination of Flemish neo-Renaissance style and materials that were fairly innovatory in their day, such as glass and iron. Inside, the building has a pyramid-shaped fountain brought here from the former abbey in Grimbergen.

The renovation work carried out in the late 1980's preserved the wrought-iron work.

In the St-Géry covered market

The shops have recently re-opened and are designed in a style reminiscent of Covent Garden in London.

Opposite the covered market is the former coaching inn, *Le Lion d'Or*, said to date from 1622. From the inner courtyard next door beyond a carriage entrance, there is a superb **view** of the River Senne and the Église des Riches-Claires.

From Place Saint-Géry, cross Rue Van Artevelde and go into Rue R. Pletinckx which leads onto Place du Jardin aux Fleurs.

Not far from Place Saint-Géry is *In't Spinnekopke (1 Place du Jardin aux Fleurs)*. The name of this old pub, which is a listed building and is said to be the oldest pub in Belgium, means "At the Little Spider". Real Belgian beer is served here, with typical Brussels food (the menu is printed in French and in the Brussels dialect).

Options from Boulevard Anspach:

► ► Quartier de la Bourse by going along the boulevard to Place de la Bourse.

Quartier du Béguinage by going along the boulevard to Place de la Bourse then turning left into Rue A Orts which extends into Rue A. Dansaert (**ER**). Turn right into Rue du Vieux Marché aux Grains which leads to Place Sainte-Catherine.

Quartier de la Grand-Place by going along the boulevard to Place de la Bourse then turning into Rue au Beurre behind the Stock Exchange.

The Suburbs

Although the origins of this town are lost in the mists of time (traces of Iron Age housing, remains of a 4C Roman villa, Merovingian graveyard), the name appears for the first time in a document dating from 1046 when it was the place of residence of a chapter of canons; they stayed until 1796.

Anderlecht has been very famous over the past decade because of its football team but it is a mainly industrial town, with numerous workshops and factories strung out along the Charleroi and Senne Canal not far from the abattoirs built at the end of last century. The town has a working-class reputation but it also has quiet, residential districts around the Parc Astrid. The streets round Place de la Vaillance are filled with small shops; the ones around Place Bara flank the Gare du Midi and its new high-speed train line. This is also a bustling district, full of wholesale fashion houses.

From Boulevard Poincaré in the "inner ring road", turn into Chaussée de Mons then right into Rue Wayez just beyond the canal. Stop at Place de la Vaillance.

★ **Église Saints-Pierre-et-Guidon** (**AM Y**) ⊘ – *Place de la Vaillance. Work in progress.* The very respectable size of this fine 14C-15C Gothic collegiate church (it is second only to the cathedral) serves as a reminder of the erstwhile importance of the chapter of Saint-Pierre, set up *c*1078 by Reinilde of Aa whose family was, for many years, one of the most influential in the duchy.

The most interesting feature outside is the South porch dating from about 1350. It underwent major alteration during restoration work last century and the statues were placed in the niches in 1908. The fact that the church door faces in this direction was the result of the geographical situation of the village. Originally, the porch stood on its own; the adjacent chapels were added in later years. The row of gables along the side wall is a superb example of one of the most outstanding features of Gothic architecture in Brabant – the line of roofs set perpendicular to the nave. The square tower dates from 1517. The octagonal spire was erected in 1898 and is not, therefore, visible on the delightful pen-and-ink drawing (1612) done by the Florentine artist, Remigio Cantagalina (1582-*c*1630) on display in the Maison d'Erasme (Rhetoric Chamber).

Tradition has it that, in days gone by, the winner of the horse race which consisted of riding five times round the church was then allowed to enter the building on horseback.

The interior contains a few fine surprises. The nave dates back to the late 14C. The four bays are not very high and the ogival vaulting is supported directly on capitals decorated with crockets, another characteristic feature of Brabant-style architecture. Murals (15C-16C) can be seen in several chapels but the most outstanding ones are in **Chapelle Notre-Dame-de-Grâce**. The vault includes angels that are the precursors of the ones seen in Jacques Cœur's palace in Bourges. On the walls are illustrations of the life of St Guidon who died in 1012 and is greatly venerated as the patron saint of peasants and protector of horses. The south transept contains the tomb of Albert Ditmar, physician to Philip the Good, who died in 1438. The wood carving is particularly attractive for its realism. The north transept includes a few Romanesque features which are visible in the semi-circular window in the east wall. The chancel (*c*1460) is deep and fitted with choirstalls for the canons. It was designed by Jan van Ruysbroeck, architect of the tower on Brussels City Hall. The most eyecatching stained-glass windows are in the first bay to the left (late 15C) and the first bay to the right (16C). Also in the chancel is the recumbent statue of Jean Walcourt (d 1362), Lord of Aa opposite the tomb of Arnoul de Hornes (1505) and his wife, Marguerite de Montmorency.

The crypt (late 11C) beneath the chancel is one of the very few examples of Romanesque architecture in the city. Two corridors lead to three aisles subdivided by six central columns. The eleven windows are narrow and semi-circular, splayed and devoid of any ornamentation. The type of stone used, and its pinkish tinge, would seem to lend cogency to the legend stating that the pillars came from the Roman villa uncovered within the town's boundaries. The central pavement is said to be the gravestone of St Guidon.

Square J Dillen at the chevet of the church leads into Rue du Chapitre.

★★ **Maison d'Erasme** (**AM**) ⊘ – *31 Rue du Chapitre.*
This brick house was built in 1468 and extended in 1515 (see the date worked in the wrought iron to the right-hand side of the frontage). It was one of the houses belonging to the chapter of Saint-Pierre and was used by the canons to accommodate their most illustrious guests such as the geographer Gérard Mercator or the Humanist Juste Lips. Pierre Wijchman, schoolman of the chapter, corresponded regularly with Erasmus Desiderius Roterodamus, better-known as Erasmus (1469-1536). He was a genius, born in Rotterdam, and he wanted to reform the Roman Catholic Church. In doing so, he denounced the abusive prac-

tices of certain Faculties of Theology and the rivalries between certain Orders. His writings were full of irony and he remained ever-faithful to his motto, *"I yield to no man"*. He was a contemporary of Martin Luther and a close friend of Thomas More. He travelled extensively in an attempt to quench his thirst for knowledge and guarantee his independence. Before stopping here for five months (end of May to end of October 1521) between a period in Louvain and a final move to Basel where he settled permanently, he had been a canon in Gouda, a student in Paris, a lecturer in Oxford, Cambridge and Bologna, and tutor to Prince Alexander of Scotland. He was an erudite scholar, and the most widely-published and widely-read author of his day, with admirers among the highest-ranking members of society. The house was purchased in 1931 and has recently been restored. It now houses a local museum which was inaugurated in 1932 by the future King Leopold III. In addition to an extensive collection of portraits and works relating to the "Prince of Humanists", the rooms (which are absolutely magnificent if flooded with sunlight) contain a few choice works and an outstanding collection of **furniture**.

Chambre de rhétorique – The so-called Rhetoric Chamber was once a meeting-room. It contains a statue of St Erasmus made of Lombardy stone (late 15C), a painting entitled *Le Dernier Séjour d'Érasme à Bâle* by Félix Cogen (1838-1907), an oak chest (1500-1550), the oldest **Charter of Brabant** (1078) and a collection of Erasmus' letters (published in Paris in 1525).

Cabinet de travail – The study contains not only **portraits** of Erasmus by Quentin Massys, Albrecht Dürer and Hans Holbein the Younger (copy) but also an oak credenza with fenestration and an effigy of St Catherine (late 15C-early 16C), the 16C oak writing-desk, and a wash highlighted in white chalk by Albrecht Dürer representing St John the Evangelist, an *Étude de chauves-souris* by Hans Holbein and, in the glass case, a mould of the great humanist's skull.

Erasmus' study in Anderlecht

Ph. Gajic/MICHELIN

Corridor – Note the mirror in the Renaissance polychrome oak frame (16C), the gilded marble statuette (early 16C) and, at the foot of the staircase, a piece of furniture with parchment ornamentation (16C).

Salle du Chapitre or **Salle Renaissance** – The chapter house is undoubtedly the most beautiful room in the house and its very cosy atmosphere seems to extend an invitation to take a long look at the furniture and paintings which it contains. The walls are covered with turquoise Malines leather with gilded motifs (16C) that sets off the superb furniture including an oak cupboard with parchment ornamentation and a heart-shaped lock (late 16C), an oak credenza with two doors (early 16C) and two late 15C credenzas flanking the fireplace. The **paintings** are amazing for their variety. They include *Saint Jérôme se fustigeant avec une pierre* by Joos van Cleve (early 16C), *Saint Jean-Baptiste* and *Saint Jean l'Évangéliste* from the School of Rogier van der Weyden (late 15C), *L'Adoration des Mages* by Hieronymus Bosch (late 15C), *La Fuite en Égypte* by Cornelis Massys (mid 16C), *Mater Dolorosa* from the studio of Dirck Bouts (late 15C), a *Pietà* from the studio of Hugo van der Goes (late 15C), and *La Tentation de Saint Antoine* by Pieter Huys (mid 16C). In the glass cases, note the first edition of *The Praise of Folly* (Strasbourg, 1511), the letters signed by François I and Charles V of Spain (Carolus) and two delightful miniatures by Hans Holbein's pupils set in frames decorated with Tudor roses (16C).

Staircase – The statue is said to represent Erasmus as a pilgrim (16C). On the landing is a two-door credenza with, in the centre, St Georges slaying the dragon (early 16C).

Salle Blanche – The former dormitory, now known as the "White Room", houses some priceless first editions. The most interesting glass case is the one containing the works by Erasmus that were subject to ecclesiastical censorship. The last display cabinet contains a collection of wonderful bindings. There is a series of letters bound half in leather and half in wood with brass clasps, a piece of work typical of the German tradition and dating from 1531. Another fascinating exhibit is the guild chest made of moulded oak and inlaid with ebony and citron wood; there is also a four-door chest with parchment ornamentation and decorative roses. The straps are mounted on pieces of leather (late 16C).

Library – This small room, which contains various editions of works by the Humanist, is of anecdotal interest. In this respect, it is probably Erasmus' own caricature of himself that is most worthy of note (no 556). The 16C oak cupboard has some wonderful Flamboyant Gothic fenestration.

Behind the house is a delightful garden of medicinal herbs relaid by René Pechère a few years ago.

Return to Square J Dillon and head northwards into Rue Delcourt. Turn left straight away into a narrow tree-lined passage leading to the Beguine Convent.

Beguinage (AM) ⊘ – *8 Rue du Chapelain.* The convent was founded in 1252 and was unusual because of its rural setting. It was partially rebuilt after a fire in 1756 and was given a secular purpose during the French Revolution. Only 8 sisters lived in it at that time. They were very popular with the local people because they were relatively free to come and go as they chose and they therefore took part in local life, helping those who were sick or providing free lessons for poor children.

The convent is a very modest affair consisting of two houses opening onto an inner courtyard. The buildings now house a **museum** dealing with local history, art and folklore. Note the small chapel with its eight prayer stools.

On Place de la Vaillance, turn right into Rue P Janson and continue to Rond-point du Meir.

Parc Astrid (AM) – The park contains the Constant Vanden Stock Stadium, home ground to the very famous **Royal Sporting Club d'Anderlecht** which has existed since 1908. The "Mauves and Whites" have been Champions of Belgium more than twenty times, as well as the winners of the Cup Winners Cup, the UEFA Cup and the UEFA Supercup.

Royal Sporting Club d'Anderlecht

From Rond-pont du Meir, take Rue du Limbourg then turn left into Rue de Veeweyde and continue to Place de la Vaillance. Turn back into Rue Wayez and Chaussée du Mons and take the Boulevard Poincaré direction. Park the car beyond the junction with Avenue Clemenceau and walk down the third road on the right (Rue Gheude) which is a one-way street.

★ **Musée de la gueuze (ES M[14])** ⊘ – *56 Rue Gheude.* The last family brewery left in Brussels set up this museum in 1978 within the buildings where it still makes the traditional *lambic, kriek, gueuze* and *faro.* Before the First World War, the capital had almost fifty family breweries.

From the brewing room where the beer is made in vats to the keg store with its oak or chestnut casks, visitors are shown all the stages in beer production. The amazing huge copper vat known as the "cooling tank" placed under the roof not only cools the wort but also brings it into contact with the ambient Brussels air so that it ferments with *brettonomyces bruxellensis* and *lambicus*, micro-organisms that are only found in the Senne Valley. Without them, it would be impossible to make *lambic* (beer about 2 years old).

The brewery is open to the public right through the year but only produces beer from the end of October to the end of April. Twice a year, a "public brewing" day gives visitors a chance to watch *lambic* being made, from the mixing at 0600 to the pumping out of the wort in the middle of the afternoon (*please phone for information*).

Options from Porte d'Anderlecht:

▶▶ City centre by going down Boulevard Poincaré along the inner ring road and turning left at the traffic lights into Boulevard M. Lemonnier (Quartiers de la Bourse, de la Ville ancienne, de Brouckère).

Saint-Gilles by going down Boulevard Poincaré and Avenue de la Porte de Hal and the inner ring road to Porte de Hal.

Forest by going down Boulevard Poincaré along the inner ring road and turning right beyond the railway bridge into Avenue Fonsny which extends into Avenue Van Volxem. Turn right into Chaussée de Bruxelles to Place Saint-Denis.

AUDERGHEM

This town lies on the edge of the vast Soignes Forest to the west of the city. Its name literally means "old dwelling" and its history begins in the second half of the 13C when the Val-Duchesse Convent or *'s Hertoghinnedael* was founded and a hamlet grew up around the roads linking Brussels to Tervuren and Wavre.

These days, Auderghem is a quiet, residential town which has attracted most of the Japanese nationals who work in the European capital. Boulevard du Souverain, which was laid out during the reign of Leopold II, is the best point from which to begin a tour.

Val-Duchesse (**DN**) – *259 Boulevard du Souverain. Not open to the public.* This Dominican convent (1262) was closed by the Austrian government in 1784. It was one of the oldest in Belgium and was named after its founder, Duchess Aleyde of Burgundy, widow of Henri III. Before reconstruction work in the 18C, the buildings were ranged round a square. The castle, one of the two remaining buildings, is government property, used for international meetings; it was the scene of the drafting of the Treaty of Rome.

The old **Chapelle St Anne** is concealed by the vegetation. The oldest part of this small building is its tower (11C or 12C). The nave was rebuilt, as is obvious from the bricks on the upper sections, and is lit by only three windows. The reredos that once decorated the chapel is now in the Royal Museums of Art and History (room 58). Women hoping to become pregnant used to come to pray to the patron saint of the chapel.

Hôtel communal – *175 Boulevard du Souverain.* This building stands at the junction of Chaussée de Wavre and Boulevard du Souverain and forms part of the "outer ring road". It was inaugurated in 1970 and includes an arts centre and a theatre.

On the outskirts of the town, take Chaussée de Wavre and turn left onto Chaussée de Tervuren (direction Tervuren). After 400m – 408yds turn right into Rue du Rouge Cloître, a surfaced road at the corner of the junction. Drive on for 600m – 608yds.

The Rouge-Cloître (**DN**) – *Car park in the enclosure.* This monastery set in the Soignes Forest (*qv*) was originally a hermitage, founded in 1368. There is some controversy as to the origin of the name. Either it comes from the nickname *Rood Clooster* (meaning Red Cloisters) because the walls were covered with red-coloured

Lakes, Le Rouge-Cloître

cement made from crushed tiles or it is an incorrect translation of the Dutch word *roo* meaning a clearing indicating that the monastery was built in a place where the trees had been felled. The priory of Austin canons enjoyed a period of prestige when it was protected by Charles V. Hugo van der Goes the painter retired to the monastery where he died in 1482. The suppression of the community by Joseph II in 1784 led to the monastery itself being sold during the Revolution. The church was destroyed by fire in 1834.

The outbuildings, which are close to the entrance, include the gatekeeper's house *(right)* and the farmhouse *(opposite)*. Flanking the latter is a delightful, more recent building that has been very well restored and houses an Arts Centre. The **Soignes Forest Information Centre** ⊘ *(top floor)* contains a permanent exhibition of educational panels, photos and models presenting scientific information for the general public through a description of various aspects of the forest environment overall and the surrounding forest in particular.

Savoy House *(left)*, once the prior's lodgings and the chapter house, is now a restaurant and tavern.

Beyond the nearby watermill, the banks of the two lakes lined with aspen and lime trees have footpaths that penetrate right into the heart of the forest. There is one path with signposts and information panels describing ecological aspects of the woodland.

At the end of the only road leading out of Le Rouge-Cloître, turn sharp left into Chaussée de Tervuren. Turn left into Chaussée de Wavre and left a third time again beyond the A4-E411 motorway bridge. Do not join the motorway but take the road which runs parallel to it.

Château forestier de Trois-Fontaines (DN) – *Park by the Soignes Forest Sports Centre (a rectangular dark glass building) on the edge of the Soignes Forest and take the Trois-Fontaines path below the motorway flyover.* The castle was also known as *Drif borren* and its keep served as a prison for the brigands captured in the Soignes Forest; they were shut into iron-bound trunks. The castle which was originally a ducal hunting lodge and totally surrounded by a moat, is thought to date from the 14C. All that remains is a small, red-brick building *(not open to the public)* with ribbed arching that reflects its medieval history.

A visit to the ruins of this old castle is more particularly an excuse for a walk in the Soignes Forest *(qv)*. Three **jogging paths** have been signposted from the Sports Centre waymarked in green (5km – 3 miles), blue (10km – 6 miles) and red (20km – 12 miles).

EXCURSION

Pass under the motorway and turn left to pass under it a second time and join the A4-E411 motorway. Take the first exit and turn left across the bridge.

Jezus-Eik – This village, known in French as Notre-Dame-au-Bois, attracts walkers who come here for a meal and a chance to taste one of the famous onion and radish cheesecakes that are a speciality of the Brussels area.

The **église Notre-Dame** (late 17C) ⊘ was probably built to plans by architect Jacques Francart. The original frontage was rebuilt during restoration work in 1970. The interior is decorated with fake marble and contains numerous portraits brought here as votive offerings.

Options from the Town Hall in Auderghem:

►► City centre along Boulevard du Souverain and via Woluwe Park. Turn left into Avenue de Tervuren extending beyond two underpasses into Rue de la Loi (Quartiers du Parlement and de la Cathédrale des Saints-Michel-et-Gudule).
Woluwe along Boulevard du Souverain and via Woluwe Park. Turn left into the lateral avenue beside Avenue de Tervuren and continue to Square Leopold II which is easy to see because of its white obelisk.
Watermael-Boitsfort by taking Boulevard du Souverain south.
Tervuren via Chaussée de Wavre which leads towards the outskirts of the city, then turn left onto Chaussée de Tervuren (direction Tervuren) which becomes Avenue de Tervuren.
Soignes Forest *(qv)*.

Forest may date back to the 7C. Legend has it that St Amand came here to convert the village to Christianity. He dedicated the parish church to St Dionysius the Areopagite. From 1354 to 1795, Forest was part of the Brussels dip; two years later, the village gained its independance.

The top end of Forest centres on the Forest and Duden Parks and the Altitude Cent. The lower end of the village grew up around Place Saint-Denis near the church of the same name and Forest Abbey.

The huge **Forest National** (1969) (**BN**) hall, which has recently been refurbished, is used for pop and rock concerts, various types of show and sports events.

Parc de Forest (**BN**) – In 1875, King Leopold II decided to have a vast park (13 hectares – 32 acres) laid out within the boundaries of Forest. A few years later, the layout was slightly modified by the architect and landscape gardener, Laîné *(see Woluwe, Parc de Woluwe)*. All round the park, wide avenues were built, lined with attractive private houses dating from the early years of the century. The Art Nouveau building *(5 Avenue du Mont Kemmel)* is a real eye-catcher. It is a superb house (1905), with a first floor shaped like the arc of a circle, and it belonged to an architect named Arthur Nelissen. The house at no 6 combines traditional and innovatory features. Its roof gives it a rustic look. Go down Avenue Besme opposite. This Art Nouveau house (no 103) was built in 1901. It combines a piano nobile shaped like the arc of a circle with an elegant porch, and has woodwork and wrought-iron work carved and shaped into curves.

Go downhill to Square de la Délivrance, Avenue Besme, Avenue Reine Marie-Henrietta and on to Square Laîné which was laid out in 1949. It forms the link between the Forest and Duden Parks.

Parc Duden (**BN**) – This picturesque park (23 hectares – 57 acres) is full of very steep hills. In days gone by, the park was part of the Soignes Forest. Its last owner, Wilhelm Duden, was a German businessman who bequeathed the park to Leopold II in 1895. The town of Forest purchased it in 1911 and, one year later, the park was opened to the public. The former Château Duden, built in the neo-Classical style, houses a film school. From the park, there is a superb view of the dome on the Law Courts.

From Parc Duden, go along Avenue Victor Rousseau to Place de l'Altitude Cent.

Place de l'Altitude Cent (**BN 7**) is one of the highest points in Brussels. In 1936, it was chosen as the site for one of the few Art Déco churches in the city. Église Saint-Augustin was built of reinforced concrete to designs by architects Léon Guianotte and André Watteyne. The building is in a deplorable state and renovation is due to begin very shortly.

Go back along the same streets, skirt Parc Duden via Avenue V Rousseau and Rue du Mystère. Go down Chaussée de Bruxelles to Place Saint-Denis.

★ **Église St-Denis** (**ABN**) – The original church dated from the 13C but it has been subject to alteration on several occasions since then. It lies at the foot of the hill, not far from Forest National *(see above)*. The nave and chancel are Early Gothic in style (c1300). The huge square tower, in which the lower section dates from the 15C, resembles a keep. The upper brick section was added three centuries later. The church contains a number of chapels. **Chapelle Ste-Alène** which projects far beyond the line of the chancel can be divided into two parts. The older 12C section is all that remains of the original church and still includes a few traces of Romanesque windows. The chapel contains the black stone tomb of St Alène (12C). All round the walls are paintings illustrating the legend of the saint. Note, too, the wrought-iron grille (1769) in the Louis XV style and the carved keystones. A semi-circular arch links the original chapel to the more recent section, built in the 15C. The 16C polyptych telling the story of the Annunciation, the Nativity and the Adoration of the Magi is attributed to Jan Van Coninxlo. The chapel dedicated to St Joseph and the Lady Chapel were both added in the 16C. The chancel has an attractive early 13C Crucifix.

Abbaye de Forest (**ABN**) – Fulgence, Abbot of Affligem, founded a Benedictine abbey near the church dedicated to St Denis *c*1105. The abbey was destroyed by fire and rebuilt in 1764-1765 to drawings by Laurent-Benoît Dewez *(see Jette)*. The buildings are ranged round a vast inner courtyard and now house an arts centre. On the side overlooking Place Saint-Denis, there is a superb Louis XVI style entrance.

*The annual **Michelin Red Guide Benelux***
offers comprehensive up-to-date information in a compact form.
An ideal companion on holidays, business trips or weekends away.
It is well worth buying the current edition.

HEYSEL

Heysel is not the name of a town or village within the Greater Brussels area; it is the name of a plateau to the north-west of the city centre near the royal residences in Laeken and Le Belvédère (Laeken Park). Leopold II, who was keenly interested in large-scale town planning projects, had a 200-hectare estate laid out there then bequeathed it to the State on his death in 1909 and, for many years, it remained untended. In order to bring new life to this part of the capital, it was decided that the site would be used for international exhibitions, beginning with the one celebrating the centenary of national independence. However, the project did not really come to life until 1935 because the centenary was celebrated solely in Liège and Antwerp.

★ **Atomium** (**BK**) ⊘ – This spectacular symbol of the atomic age is a survivor of the 1958 World Fair; it represents an iron crystal molecule expanded 165 billion times. Its steel structure is coated with aluminium and it consists of 9 spheres, each measuring 18m – 59ft in diameter, representing the Belgian provinces (since 1 January 1995, Belgium has actually had 10 provinces). The spheres are interlinked by tubes 29m – 94ft long and 3m – 10ft in diameter and the Atomium has an overall weight of 2 400 tonnes. It was its designer, an engineer named André Waterkeyn, who found the name for the molecule that had taken 18 months to design and as many months to build. It is almost a piece of sculpture (it was restored in 1993), rising to a height of 102m – 332ft, and it illustrates the hopes of an entire generation which had just signed the Treaty of Rome and dreamed of seeing the first sputnik in orbit. It also summarised the perspectives for progress based on the splitting of the atom.

Each sphere has two storeys. Four of them contain the **Biogenium** exhibition dealing with current scientific knowledge, particularly in the field of medicine. The main topics are illustrated in the form of models, photographs, information panels, and interactive terminals. In the bottom sphere is an exhibition relating to major advances in medicine and microscopics. Take the escalator up to the first of the lower spheres (genetics and the human cell). The second escalator leads up to the central sphere (virology). Then come back down to the second of the lower spheres (immunology).

A lift in the central tube takes visitors up to the topmost sphere in just 23 seconds, providing a **panoramic view** of Brussels and the surrounding area. On a clear day, it is even possible to see the belltower of St Rombaut's Church in Malines. The structure of the Atomium is flexible and it moves in the wind for safety reasons – the structure would snap if it was totally static. The upper sphere, for example, moves almost half-a-metre (18 in) but this movement is imperceptible to visitors.

Parc des Expositions (**BK**) – The park is used for fairs, exhibitions and conferences and has kept the layout and a few buildings from the days of the World Fairs held in 1935 and 1958. Of the 125 000sq m – 1 345 000sq ft of area overall, the **Grand Palais** (Van Neck, 1935) also known as the Centenary Palace, covers 14 000sq m – 150 640sq ft in itself. The main characteristics of its screen-like façade are four pillars and eighteen allegorical figures which echo the rather stiff, colossal style common to the period. The concrete arches inside have a span of 86m – 280ft.

The foundation stone for the former Heysel Stadium *(left)*, now known as Stade Roi Baudouin, was laid in 1930. Its name has become synonymous with the tragic events that took place there on 29 May 1985 but

The Grand Palais

158

it has undergone alterations since then. Opposite the entrance, on the lawns, are two decorative bronzes – *Le Serment olympique* by P de Soete and *Les Lutteurs* by J Lambeaux.

At the foot of the Atomium is the **Bruparck**, a vast recreation ground with Mini-Europe (*see below*), the Kinepolis with almost 30 cinemas including one cinema-in-the-round in which the screen covers an area of 600sq m – 6 456sq ft, l'Océade laid out for water-based sports and leisure, and The Village with its cafes and restaurants.

Mini-Europe (BK) ⊙ – All the countries in the European Union are represented here in 1:25 scale models of buildings of socio-cultural, historic and symbolic interest. The 2.5 hectare park includes the Acropolis of Athens, Danish houses from the days of the Vikings, Louvain Town Hall (15C), the austere monastery in l'Escurial (16C) commissioned by Philip II to the north-west of Madrid, houses lining Amsterdam's canals (17C), the English city of Bath which is a masterpiece of 18C town planning, the Pompidou Centre in Paris etc.

Among the more up-to-date displays in the park are an offshore oil rig, the Ariane rocket, a high-speed train (TGV) and a jumbo-ferry.

Options from Heysel:

▶▶ City centre via Avenue J Sobieski then Boulevard E Bockstael extending into Boulevard du Jubilé. Turn left into Boulevard Léopold II and on along Boulevard d'Anvers before turning right into Boulevard Emile Jacqmain (Quartiers du Béguinage, de Brouckère and du Botanique).

Laeken via Avenue J Sobieski. From there, turn left into Avenue des Robiniers. Koekelberg via Avenue Houba de Strooper then turn right into Boulevard de Smet de Naeyer extending into Avenue J Sermon.

Jette via Avenue Houba de Strooper then right into Boulevard de Smet de Naeyer extending into Avenue J Sermon. Turn right into Avenue D Poplimont extending into Avenue de l'Exposition universelle.

Meise via Chaussée Romaine then right onto N276 (follow signs to Plantentuin).

IXELLES ★

In 1210, *Elsele* (from the Dutch *els* meaning alder or the alder domain) included two seignories – Haut-Ixelles and Ixelles-sous-le-châtelain also known as Boendaal. It was highly reputed for its agriculture and stone quarries. At the beginning of the 19C Ixelles was only a village with a population of about 1 500 people, but, following the demolition of the curtain wall round Brussels, it soon grew and today it is one of the largest towns making up the modern conurbation.

A lively district – The boundary between Ixelles and the centre of Brussels, in particular the Royal Palace district, is the Porte de Namur (Namur Gate) from which Chaussée d'Ixelles leads to Place Flagey. The district is well-known on more than one count. This part of the upper town is an important traffic interchange for the underground, tramways, buses and cars which carry commuters and shoppers to the offices and stores which extend as far as Avenue de la Toison d'Or (*see Quartier Louise*). Some of the shops specialise in products from Central Africa and are concentrated in and around the Ixelles Gallery (between Chaussée d'Ixelles and Chaussée de Wavre) which is also known as Matongué.

Ixelles is well-known not only for its attractive lakes – the remains of the Maelbeek Valley which used to extend as far as Marie-Louise Square in Etterbeek – but also for its bustling cafés, restaurants and shops and its lively student population.

Ixelles is mainly home to students and artists and those who like a relaxed lifestyle.

From Porte de Namur take Chaussée de Wavre.

Maison des écrivains belges de langue française (FS M²⁴) ⊙ – *150, Chaussée de Wavre.* The association of French-speaking Belgian writers, founded in 1902, has its offices in an attractive house built in 1889. It also houses the **Musée Camille Lemonnier** (*see The Arts in Brussels in the Introduction*). Although rather antiquated, it does contain a few interesting works and memorabilia as well as the faithful reconstruction of a writer's study.

Continue along Chaussée de Wavre and immediately turn left into Rue de la Tulipe which leads to Place Fernand Cocq.

★ **Maison communale (FS H¹)** – *Place Fernand Cocq.* Belle Campagne was the home of La Malibran (1808-1836), the famous opera singer of Spanish origin who was said to have "gold in her mouth". In 1836, she married Charles de Bériot the Belgian violinist whom she met in 1830. She died in London after falling from a horse and is buried in Laeken cemetery. The building was constructed in 1833 in the neo-Classical style by the architect Van der Straeten; it was bought by the town of Ixelles in 1849. The garden was given up to make room for Place Fernand Cocq.

Nearby are the birthplace *(no 57 Rue Keyenveld)* of Auguste Perret, the famous French architect who worked in reinforced-concrete, the birthplace *(73 Rue de l'Arbre-Bénit)* of Michel de Ghelderode, the playwright, and the last home *(55 Rue Mercelis)* of Charles de Coster the novelist.

Take Rue du Conseil, then turn right into Rue Van Aa which comes to an end opposite the museum.

★★ **Musée communal d'Ixelles** (GT **M**[11]) ⊘ – *71 Rue J van Volsem.* The municipal museum was inaugurated in 1892 in the buildings of a former slaughter-house, enlarged in 1973 and partially restructured in 1994. It frequently holds high-quality exhibitions (two rooms in the basement and the first room on the ground floor) and presents a permanent collection containing several outstanding works.

The collection, which is mainly devoted to the 19C and 20C, is divided into three parallel wings and a new perpendicular wing *(the third gallery is closed).*

The first wing is divided into several rooms containing works from 16 to 19C, particularly *La Cigogne*, a sketch by Albrecht Dürer, *Tête d'homme* attributed to Bartolomeo Passerotti from Bologna, *Tobie et l'Ange* by Rembrandt, *Réunion villageoise* by Isaac van Ostade, *Nature morte* by Willem Heda, *Peter Paul Rubens* by the Antwerp sculptor Michael Rysbrack, a terracotta (1743) (its bronze replica is in the Victoria and Albert Museum in London), a portrait of Sir John Raede by the Scotsman Allan Ramsay, a red chalk drawing by Jean-Honoré Fragonard (1732-1806), studies by Théodore Géricault (1791-1824) and Eugène Delacroix (1798-1863) and *L'Homme à la corde* by Jacques-Louis David. A large **collection of posters** introduces the 19C and 20C. The museum owns nearly all the posters designed by Henri-Toulouse Lautrec, as well as others by Jules Chéret, and by Alphonse Mucha a Czech, and one by René Magritte, etc.

The next two wings have excellent natural lighting. The collection is varied and highly interesting: Theo van Rysselberghe, one of the founders of Les XX (1883) and The Free Aesthetic (1894), Berthe Morisot, Maurice Denis, Jean van Eeckhoundt, Rik Wouters, a very endearing artist who died before being recognised, Edgar Tytgat, Georges Creten, Auguste Oleffe, Émile Claus, Maurice de Vlaminck, Gustave de Smet, Constant Permeke, who belonged to the second group of Laethem-Saint-Martin, Xavier Mellery, Gustave van de Woestyne, Jean Brusselmans, etc.

The **sculptures** are remarkable: a marble *Idylle* and two terracottas, *La Lorraine* and *J B Willems* by Auguste Rodin; the superb *Vierge folle* by Rik Wouters; *Maternité* and *Fuga* by Oscar Jespers; *L'Agenouillée de la fontaine* by Georg Minne.

The new wing is divided into three galleries, one above the other, featuring both internationally-famous and lesser-known artists. On the ground floor, *L'Heureux donateur* and *Le Visage du génie* by René Magritte, *Femmes nues* by Paul Delvaux, *Opus 53* by Victor Servranckx, *Rumeurs* by Jo Delahaut, *Cobra de transmission* by Pierre Alechinsky, *Obscurité illuminée* by Asger Jorn, together with paintings by Pierre-Louis Flouquet, Felix de Boeck, Marcel-Louis Baugniet, Louis van Lint, Marc Mendelson, Anne Bonnet, René Guiette, Jean Milo, Pol Mara, Félix Roulin, Roberto Matta and Wifredo Lam, rub shoulders with works by Michel Frère, Walter Swennen, Alan Green, Francis Dusépulchre, Xiao-Xia, a Chinese artist living in Brussels, Pal Horvath, Jacques Charlier, Patrick Corillon, Maurice Wyckaert, Roger Raveel and Adami.

On the first floor a set of works from the first third of the century features several Belgian artists of repute including Jan Toorop, Theo van Rysselberghe, Max Liebermann, Leon Spilliaert, Fernand Khnopff, Paul Dubois, Victor Rousseau and Edgard Tytgat; see in particular *La Glèbe* by Constantin Meunier, *Saint-Tropez* by Paul Signac, *La Saltimbanque* by Félicien Rops, *Paysage, Effet de nuit* by William Degouve de Nuncques, *Mélancolie du soir* by Rik Wouters, and *Palace-Cannes* by Raoul Dufy. There is also a famous *Casserole de moules* by Marcel Broodthaers, several paintings by Gaston Bertrand, a few works by Ferdinand Schirren, and secondary works by French and Belgian artists (De la Fresnaye, Lhote, Picabia, Picasso, Poliakoff; Pompe, Vantongerloo, Guiette, Van den Berghe, De Smet, Mesens, Mariën, Cordier) and a small photographic display.

On leaving the museum, turn right and right again into Rue Sans-Souci. This was the street where François Raspail the politician lived in 1848 before residing in Uccle in 1855, and where Rodin had a studio. Turn right into Rue Malibran and continue to Place Flagey.

Place Flagey (BN **93**) – One side of the square is occupied by a building which once housed the National Broadcasting Institute (INR); it was constructed between 1935 and 1937 and its yellow bricks and horizontal lines were used as a model for other buildings in the square. It was designed by Joseph Diongre (1868-1963) to look like an ocean liner and illustrates the Belgian modernistic postwar architectural movement. It contains one of the finest concert halls in Europe. Although the building is partially listed, its future is uncertain, as the INR has moved to Boulevard Reyers.

The monument (1894) to Charles de Coster the writer next to the lake is the work of Charles Samuel the sculptor. De Coster is mainly known for his masterly epic of Thyl Ulenspiegel (*see The Arts in Brussels in the Introduction*) depicted here in the company of his fiancée, Nele; the author is shown in the centre.

A closer look shows amusing details relating to the story, such as the

Institut National de Radiodiffusion (INR), Place Flagey

A. Schroeder/GLOBAL PICTURES

owl and mirror on the façade of the monument – "uil en spiegel" in Flemish.

Proceed to nearby Place Sainte-Croix and the church of the same name.

Promenade des Etangs – From Place Sainte-Croix, take Avenue des Eperons d'Or along the eastern bank of the first lake. Nos 3 to 14 (except for two modern buildings), designed by four architects (including three brothers) called Delune, feature elegantly eclectic façades. The corner building known as "The Tower" on the left of the intersection with Avenue Guillaume Macau was built for Baron Snoy by Caluwaers. On the other side of the street are two very eclectic houses *(nos 3 and 5)* designed by Edmond Delune.

Cross Square du Souvenir which separates the two lakes and turn right into Avenue du Général De Gaulle.

Ch. Bastin – J. Évrard

A private house in Rue du Lac

The façade *(no 41)* inspired by Classical architecture contrasts strongly with the modernistic shell of The Cascade *(no 36)* designed by R Ajoux in 1940. It is worth pausing a moment to look at Ernest Blérot's twin houses (1902, *nos 38 and 39*), whose **wrought ironwork** is a veritable hymn to beginning-of-the-century aesthetics.

A little further on, turn left just after the corner house designed by Ernest Delune (1903-1905) and continue on to Rue du Lac (the second street) where his cousin, Léon Delune, created a rather original house *(no 6)* containing an artist's studio; the stairwell is decorated with a magnificent stained-glass window with a floral motif.

Go back to Rue de la Vallée (the first street).

Like most of the buildings on the even-numbered side (1903-1905), no 32 was designed by Ernest Delune. At the intersection with Rue Vilain XIIII, the corner building *(no 22)* by Ernest Blérot (1901), has an attractive wrought-iron corner balcony discretely illustrating the scrolls and curves of Art Nouveau (the same architect also built the house at no 40).

Continue along Rue de la Vallée to the top of Jardin du Roi.

King's Garden is one of the numerous creations of King Leopold II. He bought the land when Avenue Louise was being built *(see Quartier Louise)* and vowed never to build on it. The district, very much sought after by real estate promoters, is still embellished by this little sloping park connecting Avenue Louise to the Ixelles lakes. *Le Tombeau des lutteurs* by Charles van der Stappen stands at the top opposite a sculpture inaugurated in 1994 – *Phénix 44* by Olivier Strebelle symbolising the V for Victory of 1944 and commemorating the entry of British tanks into the Belgian capital.

Turn right into Avenue Louise.

Hôtel Max Hallet (1903, *no 346*) by Victor Horta presents a superb façade designed in 1904; it has a certain classicism which the master of Art Nouveau invigorated by highlighting his composition with very elegant light mouldings.

The mansion is next to a very attractive house which is now a café-restaurant called *Le Rick's* with a mainly American clientele; from the terrace can be seen the rear façade of Hôtel Max Hallet, particularly three glass roofs which are in sharp contrast with the severity of the front façade.

Turn right into Rue du Lac.

The yellow tower of the old Broadcasting Institute in Place Flagey *(see above)* can be seen clearly.

Turn right again into Rue Vilain XIIII and cross Rue de la Vallée.

Note the corner building *(no 17)* by Ernest Delune. In the lower part of the street are two houses *(nos 11 and 9)* by Ernest Blérot (1902). The bow-window *(no 7)* was designed by the architect Franz Tilley (1902).

Take Avenue du Général de Gaulle again, but to the right this time.

In direct line with King's Garden, there is a sculpture by De Tombay depicting the mineralogist Alphonse Renard (1906), and, in the distance, a sculpture of King Leopold II.

One of the corners *(no 51)* is occupied by "Le Tonneau", built in 1939 by Jean-Florian Collin and Stanislas Jasinski, an excellent example of successful pre-war modernistic architecture.

Walk around the lake.

Note the bronze by Jules Herbays, *La Danse*. Admirers of Auguste Rodin will be interested to learn that, in 1910, the *Burghers of Calais* was placed here for the Brussels World Fair. In Avenue des Klauwaerts there are two other twin houses *(nos 15 and 16)* by Ernest Blérot (1907).

In a little hollow, just after the second lake, is La Cambre Abbey.

★★ Abbaye de La Cambre (CN S)

A stormy past – In 1201, Duke Henry I and his wife Mathilda gave the Cistercian Sisters a small valley watered by the Maelbeek River, so charming that it was nicknamed Little Switzerland. Sister Gisela founded a monastery there. The future Saint Boniface, then Bishop of Lausanne, although originally from Brussels, went to live in the abbey in 1242 to flee the Emperor Frederick II who had just been excommunicated by Pope Gregory IX. The abbey prospered, grew rich and attained the peak of its glory in the late 13C.

But after the rise came the fall. The following lines will give an idea of the realities of monastic life in past centuries. The abbey suffered from the Wars of Religion in the 16C. In 1581, the nuns left the abbey which was devastated by Spanish troops who set fire to the building to prevent the army of the States from seeking refuge there. Ever tenacious, the nuns returned in 1599, until Henri de Nassau

The gardens

caused the ruin of Brabant in 1622. A short time after in 1635 the sisters evacuated the abbey to leave way for French and Dutch troops. They returned just in time to see Louis XIV on his way to besiege the town of Maastricht. Unfortunately, in the words of Vicount Terlinden, "this dazzling apparition of war in lace collars soon disappeared, leaving in its wake only the sad reality of pillaging, extorsion, ruin and death".

The Abbey of Notre-Dame-de-la-Cambre was suppressed in 1796 by the French Republic and now houses the services of the National Geographic Institute and several sections of the National School of Architecture and Decorative Arts, known as "La Cambre".

La Cambre is a translation of the Latin *camera* (chamber) which lost its "h" under the influence of the Dutch *Ter Kameren.*

The setting – The attractive **main courtyard**, with its abbey lodgings flanked by corner pavilons and outbuildings arranged along a semi-circular plan, forms a very harmonious 18C ensemble, born of the desire of the abbesses to recreate the atmosphere of their family châteaux.

The community usually consisted of about a hundred women, many from the noblest families in the duchy.

Avenue De Mot which overlooks the abbey provides the best view of the French-style terraced **gardens.** They were designed in about 1720 and restored in 1930. They are very restful, particularly on summer evenings when the illuminations are very attractive.

The church ⊙ – The original 14C building was destroyed during the 1581 fire *(see above).* When rebuilt at the end of the 16C, under the auspices of Philippe II, it was incorporated into the surrounding buildings. The graceful Gothic façade is decorated with several sculptures.

The Classical blue stone portal conceals a much more sobre Gothic style porch which is partially concealed. The chevet and its beautiful buttresses are visible from the courtyard.

The entrance is in the northern transept which is, in fact, a false transept formed by two chapels. On the east wall is the shrine of Saint Boniface (rebuilt in the 17C). The single nave exemplifies Cistercian simplicity. It is ceiled with wooden barrel vaulting (partially polychrome) and lit by eight high tracery windows, it is decorated with Stations of the Cross by Anto Carte (1886-1954).

The chancel has stained-glass windows by the same artist but has lost its original vaulting which was replaced in the 17C.

The most interesting features are a *Christ aux outrages*★ by Aelbrecht Bouts (c1452/1460-1549) on the north wall of the nave; the Chapel of the Holy Sacrament, parallel to the nave, is dedicated to St Philip Neri; the south transept which is also the Lady Chapel (see the consoles carved with figures and symbolic animals) communicates with the chancel via a small opening.

A. Schroeder/GLOBAL PICTURES

A door in the west wall of this arm of the south transept leads into the cloisters which date from 1610 (40m – 131ft by 37m – 121ft) but were restored from 1932 to 1934. The coats of arms and devices of the abbesses decorate the windows overlooking the inner courtyard. The stone portal with its mouldings opening onto the nave was restored in the 17C.

Turn left into Rue du Monastère and take the 2nd street on the left, Rue de Belle-Vue. Cross Avenue Louise and take Rue de l'Abbaye.

★ **Musée Constantin Meunier** (BN M¹²) ⊙ – *59, Rue de l'Abbaye*. After residing in Louvain where he also taught, the sculptor of social realism lived in this house with its rather modest façade during the last few years of his life. He was born in the neighbouring town of Etterbeek on 12 April 1831 and died in Ixelles on 4 April 1905. The beautiful first floor and studio of this great artist, too little known beyond the borders of his native country, are open to the public.

Numerous sculptures are on display, as well as a large number of paintings and drawings, which indicate just how much the work of Constantin Meunier was inspired by the world of labour and more especially the "black landscape" of the coal mines.

The highlight of the tour is his bronzes – *Le Débardeur, Le Puddleur, Hiercheuse à la pelle, Pêcheur de crevettes à cheval, Le Laboureur*. Certain very evocative paintings, however, are also worthy of attention, such as *Charbonnage sous la neige* and a series of small, very well executed oils on wood, together with several attractive pastels. The display cases in the corridor contain several photographic documents as well as a mould of the artist's hand, his tools and two palettes. The pieces in the studio form a remarkable ensemble – **bronzes** such as *Le Hâleur de Katwijck, Le Moissonneur, Vieux Cheval de Mine* and the superb *Émile Zola; l*arge, somewhat rigid plasters *(Débardeur, Faucheur au repos, Semeur, Faucheur, Marteleur, Maternité)*, to which some may prefer the model for *Monument à Émile Zola* (never completed) from which *Fécondité* executed just before his death was taken.

It is possible to either proceed to the Bois de la Cambre at the end of Avenue Louise, or return to Rue du Monastère and down Avenue G. Bernier, which leads up to Rue du Bourgmestre and the Children's Museum.

★ **Bois de la Cambre** (CN) – In 1852 Napoleon III sold Bois de Boulogne, the woods on the western side of Paris, to the City of Paris. Eight years later, the Belgian government, also desirious of providing its capital with a public park, sold the 123 hectares – 304 acres of La Cambre Woods which occupy the part of Soignes Forest closest to the conurbation.

The woods owe their name to the Abbey Notre-Dame de la Cambre which owned several woods under the Old Regime. They were landscaped by Keilig, a German architect born in Saxony in 1827, who designed two oval-shaped meadows in the landscape also known as the English style, so-called because of its origin, which aimed at imitating nature; the woods therefore include an artificial lake and a bridge over a gully, as well as a wide variety of trees. They were an immediate success and soon became the city's favourite aristocratic promenade. Queen Marie-Henriette, the wife of Leopold II, was often to be seen driving her own horse and carriage; she also participated in the Longchamp Fête, a revival of the Parisian tradition which was a pretext for the ladies to display their latest finery.

The two neo-Classical pavilions which mark the entrance to the woods were erected in 1835 at Namur Gate to collect the city toll; the tax was abolished in 1860 and the buildings transferred to the end of Avenue Louise because of their somewhat faded beauty. None of the four buildings originally constructed in the park are still standing (the last, Robinson Chalet, was burnt down in the early 1990s). The Bois de la Cambre is still very popular with the people of Brussels who like to come here for weekend strolls or on summer evenings when the atmosphere in the city is close.

Musée des enfants (CN M²⁵) ⊙ – *15 Rue du Bourgmestre*. The Children's Museum is an excellent initiative for younger children (4 to 12 years). The thematic itinerary, which is renewed every 3 years, aims to assist children in getting to know themselves better through entertainment. Children can wander at will and touch all the displays. The cooking, colour, handyman and drama workshops are permanent. When the weather permits, the aromatic plant garden is also open to the public.

Go back down Avenue G. Bernier. Turn left into Avenue E Duray which overlooks the Abbey. Take the very wide Avenue F. Roosevelt.

Université Libre de Bruxelles – U.L.B. (CN U) – *50 Avenue Franklin Roosevelt*. The Free University of Brussels (ULB) was founded in 1834. Until 1923 it occupied the extraordinary Granvelle Palace which unfortunately had to be demolished to make way for the Nord-Midi railway junction. The land to the east of La Cambre Woods was donated by the municipality; a financial project was developed and chosen by the Commission for Relief in Belgium Educational Foundation, and in particular by the future US president Herbert Hoover who organised food supplies to Belgium during the First World War. The project by the architect Alexis Dumont was finally selected – red brick buildings (1924-1930) ressembling the late 17C Netherlands style. In front is a statue of the founder, P-T Verhaegen, by G Geefs (1865). The Solbosch campus includes seven faculties, together with various institutes and research centres, designed to accommodate some 20 000 students.

There is another campus, known as La Plaine – physics, chemistry, pharmacy and student residence – on the other side of Ixelles Cemetary, between Boulevard de la Plaine and Boulevard du Triomphe. Lower down, towards Boulevard Général Jacques, are the buildings of the Vrije Universiteit Bruseel, the Dutch-speaking wing of the U.L.B.

The "chic" avenue of West Brussels (CN) – Avenue F Roosevelt (formerly Avenue des Nations) was built on the site of the 1910 World Fair and soon attracted a rich clientele who commissioned some of the best Belgian architects of the time to design villas, private mansions and luxury apartment buildings which will no doubt be of interest to amateurs of pre-war architecture: no 27-29, Henry van de Velde (1931-1932, an annex of La Cambre School); no 39-41, Adrien Blomme (1937); no 52, Adrien Blomme (c1928, currently the U.L.B. Administrative Office); no 60, Henry van de Velde (1927); no 74, Victor Bourgeois (1928); and no 67, Michel Polak (1931, for Baron Empain).

At the corner of the university campus, take Avenue A Depage, turn left into Rue A Buyl and right into Avenue de l'Université. Continue to the roundabout.

Ixelles Cemetery (CN) ⊘ – Several well-known figures are buried here, such as C De Coster and C Lemonnier the writers, E Ysaye the violinist, C Meunier the sculptor, V Horta the architect and M Broodthaers the artist whose stele (Avenue 1) has an intriguing rebus on its tip.

At the end of Avenue 3 is a tomb with a truncated column bearing the names Marguerite and Georges, but no family name. It is the burial place of General Boulanger and his mistress Madame de Bonnemain. The famous officer fled with her to Brussels in April 1889 after his attempted coup d'état on 27 January. Marguerite died on 16 July 1891. On 30 September the same year the general committed suicide on the tomb of his mistress. Beneath her name is written "A bientôt" (See you soon) and beneath his, "Ai-je bien pu vivre deux mois sans toi" (Did I really live two months without you").

Options from Ixelles Cemetery:

►► City centre on bus 71 (Quartiers de la Monnaie, de la Bourse, and de Brouckère).

Auderghem and the Rouge Cloître lakes via Chaussée de Wavre (follow the signs).

Watermael-Boitsfort, taking Avenue Franklin Roosevelt, then Chaussée de La Hulpe and Boulevard du Souverain.

Go to Uccle by walking through La Cambre Woods then taking Avenue W. Churchill to the roundabout; turn left into Avenue Errera and go to Van Buuren Museum.

JETTE

The town gets its name from a stream known as the Gette which used to flow past the spot where the town first developed.

For centuries, white stone quarries stood on the sites now occupied by three woods (Laerbeekbos, Poelbos and Dieleghembos). They were worked by the monks from the abbey who provided stone for their own needs and for the building of constructions such as the Cathédrale Sts-Michel-et-Gudule.

Rue Bonaventure leads to Hôpital Brugmann which was built thanks to the generosity of the famous banker, Georges Brugmann (1829-1900). At the entrance to the building, which was designed by Victor Horta, is a monument symbolising Suffering and Gratitude (the sketches were by J Dillens). The hospital was built between 1911 and 1926.

The busiest shopping streets are to be found around Place Reine Astrid or the Quartier du Miroir. In Rue Léopold, the old inn (1636) known as the "Pannenhuis" (i.e. "house with tiled roof") used to be the meeting-place of traders on their way to the markets in Brussels. It is now a grill room.

Demeure abbatiale de Dieleghem (BL M¹⁵) ⊘ – The abbot's palace stands on the Dieleghem plateau and is all that remains of an abbey founded in 1095 by the Canons of St Augustine who joined the Premonstratensian Order as early as 1140. The abbey was damaged and set on fire on several occasions (1488 and 1580) and, in 1796, the Revolutionaries finally expelled the monks. The abbot's palace is a superb Classical construction dating from 1775 and built of Diegelhem stone to designs by Laurent-Benoît Dewez. The outer façades are preceded by a slightly-projecting fore-part and are notable for their sobriety and austerity which contrasts with the Louis XVI interior. The main wooden staircase leads to the **drawing room** in which the doors are decorated with stucco low reliefs of putti carrying attributes representing the Seasons, Farming and Hunting. The same decorative cherubs can be seen in the dome where the work represents the four elements. The palace now houses the **Musée national de la Figurine historique** ⊙ and contains an extensive collection of figurines illustrating historical scenes, many of them with a military slant, from Classical times to the present day. Note the Seven Gates of Brussels, and a chess set in which the pieces serve as reminders of the Battle of Waterloo (on one side are the French troops; on the other, the Allies). Other outstanding exhibits include a display cabinet containing very old wooden figurines (1900-1910), a copy of a painting by Jordaens *(The "King" Drinks – see Musées des Beaux-Arts, Musée d'Art Ancien)*, Louis XIV's standards and trophies of war, and the helmets of cuirassiers displayed in the superb room on the first floor. The second floor houses the **Musée communal du Comté de Jette** ⊙, a museum which retraces the history of the town since prehistoric times.

KOEKELBERG

To the west of the city centre right at the end of Boulevard Léopold II is the small town of Koekelberg, extending beyond Molenbeek Saint-Jean. Its name is closely linked to the vast basilica church of which the impressive outline can be clearly seen from the various hills in and around the capital.

★ **Basilique du Sacré-Cœur** (**ABL**) ⊙ – King Leopold II's first idea was to commission a national pantheon; he then decided, in 1902, to build a basilica church dedicated to the Sacred Heart, like the one in Montmartre in Paris which he had just visited. The foundation stone was laid in 1905. However, the church was not finally completed until 1970 and, in the meantime, the neo-Gothic design drawn up by Pierre Langerock had been replaced (1920) by the design drawn by Albert van Huffel (1877-1935) from Ghent for reasons relating to cost.

Basilique du Sacré-Cœur

Ch. Bastin - J. Evrard

The focal point of the huge brick and reinforced concrete church is the dome, rising to a height of 90m – 293ft above the esplanade on Koekelberg Hill. In front of the 3 porches in the atrium is a wide narthex. The view along the nave (141m – 458ft in length) is particularly eyecatching and the sheer size of the church is a source of amazement. Unusually it is not built along an east-west line. The combination of brick, yellow terracotta, sandstone and concrete adds to the impression of grandeur that permeates the nave. In the centre of the church built in the shape of a Latin Cross is the chancel beneath a cupola 31m – 101ft in diameter. The chancel forms a square at the top of two flights of steps. The transept from which visitors can descend to the crypt is 108m – 351ft long, and the great apse containing the chancel of the parish church measures 45m – 146ft in length.

All these figures underline the extent to which the building, which was consecrated in 1951, was designed first and foremost as a place for major religious services attracting huge congregations. This is very well catered for by the layout which centres on the altar and the design of the aisles enabling the congregation to move around the church as required by the new liturgy used by the Benedictines. The design and building materials are such that the church, though often criticised, is an example of functionalist architecture. There are those, however, who claim to see the influence of the Viennese Secession which totally banished ornamentation; others, on the contrary, claim that the church contains a plethora of Art Deco features.

The **ciborium** above the high altar is topped by a Cross and four bronze angels in a kneeling position, cast by the Danish sculptor Harry Elstrom. Numerous **stained-glass windows** depicting the story of Christ's love for mankind let a warm light into the building. Most of the very modern windows were by Anto Carte (*Jugement dernier* above the entrance) and Michel Maertens.

Outside, beside the chevet, is a huge statue of the Crucified Christ by Georg Minne.

Visitors can climb up to the **gallery** and to the top of the **dome**, for a panoramic **view** of Brussels.

Options from the basilica church:

► ► City centre by going down Boulevard Léopold II to Place Sainctelette then taking Boulevard d'Anvers along the inner ring road to Place Rogier and turning right into Boulevard Emile Jacqmain (Quartiers du Botanique, de Brouckère etc).

Heysel by taking Avenue J Sermon extending into Avenue de Laeken and Boulevard de Smet de Naeyer. Turn left into Avenue Houba de Strooper and follow the signs to Bruparck.

Laeken by following the same route to Boulevard de Smet de Naeyer then continuing along Avenue des Robiniers. The avenue brings you out near the royal palace.

Jette by taking Avenue J Sermon then turning left into Avenue D Poplimont extending into Avenue de l'Exposition universelle.

LAEKEN

To the Belgians, Laeken is synonymous with the monarchy as the royal residence was built here to the north of the capital, in a district that lay within the boundaries of Brussels.

Little is known about the history of the village of Laeken. It is said that the local church was already a place of pilgrimage in the early 9C. From the 11C onwards, large crowds of pilgrims came here to pray to the Virgin Mary in a shrine where miracles occurred. In the 14C, the village was attached to the town of Brussels. In the 18C, the Austrian Governor-General, the Duke of Saxony-Teschen and the Archduchess Marie-Christine bought a vast plot of land here and had a castle built. This was the distant ancestor of the present royal palace.

Laeken was annexed to the capital in 1921 so that Brussels could extend its very large harbour installations.

Laeken is now a very quiet, mainly residential district.

Église Notre-Dame de Laeken (BL Z) ⊘ – *Avenue de la Reine*. The church was built in memory of the first Queen of the Belgians, Louise-Marie, daughter of Louis-Philippe. Work began in 1854 to designs by Joseph Poelaert *(see Quartier Louise, the Law Courts)* but the church was never completed. It was consecrated in 1872. It was built in the neo-Gothic style but was not aligned like most Gothic churches along a west-east axis because the front had to be in line with Avenue de la Reine, part of the royal route linking the palace in Laeken to the city centre.

Behind the monumental and, perhaps, rather heavy exterior is an amazingly rich interior. Once beyond the porch, visitors see a nave and two side aisles of equal height separated by pillars with engaged colonnettes. The perfect smoothness of the columns comes from the building materials used. They are not built of stone but of bricks faced with cement.

Cardinal J Cardijn (1882-1967), founder of the Young Christian Workers movement *(Jeunesse Ouvrière Chrétienne)*, is buried in the east arm of the false transept. Among the most outstanding items of church furnishings are a statue of the *Virgin Mary* (13C) which was painted at the end of last century (right of the high altar), a statue of *St Roch* (17C) (left of the high altar), and the font (1745) from the church that previously stood on this site (end of the left side aisle).

Behind the high altar is the entrance to the **royal crypt** ⊙. The pavement, which is visible from both flights of steps, is decorated with the coats of arms of the kingdom's nine provinces (in fact, since 1 January 1995, Belgium has had ten provinces). The crypt is the last resting-place of Leopold I and Louise-Marie (in the centre), Leopold II, Marie-Henriette and Baudouin I (to the right), Albert I and Elisabeth, Leopold III and Astrid (to the left). Also buried here are Louis-Philippe and Charlotte, Marie, Philippe, the princes Baudouin, Charles and Leopold, and Princess Josephine.

To the left of the square in front of the church are two monuments. The first one was erected in memory of Maréchal Foch; the second is the tomb of the unknown French soldier, placed here in honour of the French soldiers who fell on Belgian soil during the First World War.

Laeken cemetery

Cimetière de Laeken (BL) – Laeken Cemetery contains the graves of numerous well-known Belgians and people of other nationalities. Near the cenotaph, which commemorates the French General, Augustin-Daniel Belliard *(see Quartier du Palais Royal, Parc de Bruxelles)* are the graves of three painters – François-Joseph Navez, Xavier Mellery, and Jef Dillen whose tomb is marked by Auguste Rodin's **The Thinker,** Joseph Poelaert and Tilman-François Suys the architects, and Maria Felicia Garcia (1808-1836) the famous Spanish soprano better-known as La Malibran.

Standing alone in the midst of the graves and the now anonymous mausoleums is the **chancel** of the former church which was demolished at the beginning of the century. It is a fine example of the Early Gothic style that was introduced into Brabant *c*1260. The remains of the church consist of two bays and a five-span apse. The gargoyles will be of interest to those who have already visited the Church of Notre-Dame-de-la-Chapelle *(see Quartier de Marolles)*. The usual squat early 13C gargoyle is replaced here with a gargoyle on which the gaping mouth spews out rainwater some distance from the walls. The Flamboyant Gothic entrance and delightful garland of flowers are additions dating from the restoration work undertaken in 1905.

At the entrance to the graveyard is **Ernest Salu's studio** where three generations of sculptors have devoted themselves to funeral art. A museum is scheduled to open here soon.

Parc de Laeken (BK) – This park of attractive valleys dotted with thickets of jasmine and rhododendron conceals two buildings that are heavily protected. Stuyvenbergh Castle was once the residence of Emperor Charles V's architect,

Louis van Bodeghem; it underwent alteration on the orders of Leopold II and is used to accommodate high-ranking foreign visitors. The Belvedere is Crown property. It dates from the late 18C and was extended by Leopold II in the style of the Italian villas. Opposite the royal castle stands a neo-Gothic monument in memory of Leopold I (1880). The cenotaph, designed by architect L de Curte, includes a statue of the monarch by G Geefs.

Château royal (BL) – *Avenue du Parc royal. Not open to the public.* At the eastern end of Laeken Park is the royal estate (160 hectares – 395 acres), the usual residence of the sovereigns of Belgium although King Albert II preferred the nearby Belvedere (*see above*) where he lived as Prince of Liège.

The castle was originally designed by architects Payen and Montoyer at the request of Archduchess Marie-Christine and her husband, Duke Albert-Casimir of Saxony-Teschen, governors (1781-1790) during the Austrian rule of Joseph II. It was restored in 1804 by Ghislain-Joseph Henry from Dinant, on the orders of Napoleon who stayed here on numerous occasions and signed the declaration of war on Russia here in 1812. Leopold I died in the castle on 16 December 1865. Leopold II commissioned an architect named Balat to rebuild the castle after a fire on 1 January 1890. The Louis XVI-style building is screened by wrought-iron gates. It was extended in 1902 by Charles Girault (1851-1932), a Frenchman who also designed the Petit Palais in Paris, the royal museum of Central Africa in Tervuren and the arcade in the Cinquantenaire.

★★**Serres royales** (BK S¹) ⊙ – *Entrance in Avenue du Prince Royal, between the castle gates and the Neptune Fountain.* The new 19C technique of combining metal and glass and the success of the Crystal Palace, designed in London by Joseph Paxton, meant that the architectural version of the glasshouse could scarcely escape the notice of a man such as Leopold II. The king-builder was always quick to appreciate progress and make use of the latest inventions. He therefore commissioned his architect, Alphonse Balat (1819-1895), to build the royal glasshouses in 1873. They were designed not only to house collections of plants from tropical countries but also to be used for receptions given in honour of high-ranking figures and could, therefore, be altered to suit the occasion.

The main building in this "ideal glass palace" is the **Jardin d'hiver** (1870, 651 533 kilos of iron), a rotunda with a magnificent lantern tower. The outline is reminiscent of the Palm House at Kew on the banks of the Thames in south-west London. The central dome (diameter of 41m – 133ft) is supported by a Doric colonnade consisting of thirty-six columns and a glazed circular gallery. This splendid glass gallery is linked by the adjacent glasshouses to the Congo Glasshouse and the Orangery built in 1817 during the Dutch period. A number of other glasshouses complete the complex ie the Dining Room, Embarkation Platform (a railway station was to be built here), Landing Stage, Diana, Congo, Palm Tree, Rhododendron, Azalea and small Fern Cross glasshouses, not forgetting the "iron church" which was built in 1895 but abandoned five years later after a chapel was built within the castle. After the death of A Balat, other architects continued the work. The Maquet Glasshouse (1902) was named after its architect. The Theatre Glasshouse (1905) was designed by C Girault *(see Château Royal, above)* and six more glasshouses were built during the reign of Albert I.

The area currently covered by this vast, majestic group of buildings is 1.5 hectares – almost 4 acres ; the glass roof measures 2.5 hectares – 3.6 acres. Those with a love of flowers and plants are sure to enjoy the various collections inside them. The main collections include the orange trees, one of the finest collections in the world dating back to the Tervuren Orangery erected by the Archduke Albert and his wife, Isabel, the palm trees from the Duke of Arenberg's Castle in Enghien, and the camelias which were Leopold II's passion (the glasshouses containing the collections of these plants, immortalised in the work by Alexandre Dumas the Younger, are not open to the public but a number of specimens are placed in the orangery during visiting hours).

The tour (approximately 1km – 1/2mile), which includes only those glasshouses open to the public, begins at the Landing Stage (it contains a copy of Donatello's *David*) and the Palm Tree Glasshouse which provides an ideal opportunity to admire ferns, banana palms and orchids. Then comes the Azalea Glasshouse and the great gallery 200m – 217yds long (geraniums, fuchsias and flowering maples in the colours of the Belgian flag) leading through the Diana Glasshouse (tree ferns) to the Mirror Glasshouse and its wonderful staircase. The underground gallery takes visitors to the Embarkation Platform Glasshouse (mediullas) and the Congo Glasshouse (rubber plants, palm trees and ferns) on which the roof is topped with the star symbolising the Congo. Finally, there is the Winter Garden with its wide range of trees and flowers, and the Orangery with its outstanding collection of plants.

The only disadvantage to this delightful visit apart from having to queue at the entrance is the whitewashing of the glasshouses in summer in order to reduce the intensity of the light, which partially conceals the beauty of the aerial structure of the royal glasshouses when they are open to the public.

The "Tour du Monde" de Laeken – After visiting the *World Tour* designed by Alexandre Marcel (1860-1928), the Parisian architect, for the 1900 World Fair in Paris, King Leopold II, who was full of ideas and wanted to give his people a sort of open-air museum, decided to find a site near his castle in Laeken in which people could see replicas of famous buildings. Although the imaginary tour had not been completed by the time the king died in 1909 (far from it, indeed) owing to the problems of cost and allocation of land, three sections of the project were nevertheless finished – the Neptune Fountain, the Chinese pavilion and the Japanese tower, all of them outstanding for the superb quality of the craftmanship.

Fontaine de Neptune – *Avenue J. van Praet (Carrefour du Gros Tilleul)*. The original of this splendid fountain, designed by Giambologna (1529-1608) who was a native of Douai, can be seen in Piazza del Nettuno in Bologna. The replica in Carrefour du Gros Tilleul was made by Romain Sangiorgi. The king bequeathed it to the nation in his will.

Pavillon chinois (BK) ⊘ – *44 Avenue J. van Praet*. The Chinese pavilion, a reminder of the Edwardian love of all things exotic, was designed by Alexandre Marcel. Work began in 1901 and was completed in 1909. The pavilion was originally designed as a restaurant but it is more than a mere example of *chinoiserie;* all the external woodwork and the kiosk were made in Shanghai. The finishing touches were given to it by interior decorators from Paris, most of them anonymous. Painters, stucco artists, bronze sculptors, sculptors and cabinetmakers were asked to add a touch of fantasy, one might even say eccentricity, that should be immediately visible from the entrance.

Although the pavilion looks authentic and oriental owing to the size of the roof and the decoration along the ridge, it contains a few unusual features. The multi-coloured fascia panels in glass paste by Jacques Galland and the superb flamed earthenware by Emile Müller added a "Western" touch which was completed by an amusing detail included in the façade opening onto the kiosk – the small portrait to the left of the central French window which is said to depict Leopold II; the one on the far right is said to represent Ferdinand Verbiest the Jesuit who became astronomer royal to the Emperor of China.

The museum is an annex of the Royal Museums of Art and History *(see Cinquantenaire)* and contains an outstanding collection of Chinese and Japanese porcelain made for the export market. The items are placed on display in rotation. They illustrate the history of the porcelain trade between the Far East and Europe, which was particularly active from the 17C to the 19C, in particular owing to the various East India Companies. The large room on the ground floor is flanked by the Delft and Saxony rooms containing porcelain made especially for the pavilion. The Delft Room is decorated with drawings illustrating the Fables of La Fontaine. The ceiling in the Saxony Room includes a "caricature" that was probably inspired by the Monkey Study in the Rohan residence in Paris and that was a vital part of any *chinoiserie* art in the 18C. The small reception rooms on the first floor have been laid out like private studies, decorated with paintings by the Dutch School and Chinese furniture (late 19C – early 20C).

A subterranean passageway running under the Avenue J. van Praet links the two buildings.

Tour japonaise (BK) ⊘ – *44 Avenue J. van Praet*. The Japanese tower is the common name of this Buddhist pagoda (1901-1904) which consists of three sections. The entrance pavilion is the porch of the *World Tour* organised in Paris for the 1900 World Fair by Alexandre Marcel; it was bought when the Fair came

J.-C. Getmeyer/GLOBAL PICTURES

Japanese Tower

to an end. The tower and wing contain the great staircase and were built in Brussels to designs by the same architect, whom Leopold II had invited to Brussels from the French capital.

One of the interesting features of the pagoda is A Marcel's compliance with the building methods used in the land of the rising sun which require that no iron be included in the assembly of a timber construction. The attempt to ensure utter authenticity included commissions for craftsmen in Yokohama for the decorative carvings on the doors, woodpanelling and ceilings and for the many copper plates. The only part of the work lacking in authenticity is the central heating and the lift, both of which were more appropriate to European ideas of comfort. Like the Chinese pavilion, the pagoda was decorated by interior designers from Paris who produced work that is recognised as being very coherent. The thirty-four stained-glass windows on the **grand staircase** illustrating the epics described in the 19C Japanese etchings of heroic legends were produced by Jacques Galland. The master glass-painter created a very attractive range of harmonising colours here, mainly in blue-green tones, and drew scenes that captured and exalted the dramatic tension of the warlike tales of the country across the seas. The "camellia" wall lights and "water lily" chandeliers in the grand staircase were made by Eugène Soleau. The result of this combination is magnificent and the climb up to the fourth, and last, room in the exhibition gives an impression of grandeur that is as surprising as it is unexpected.

The items on display in the Japanese Tower are all connected with the Far East but it is impossible to describe particular exhibits as they are drawn on rotation from the extensive reserves of the Royal Museums of Art and History.

Europe on a single sheet: **Michelin Map** *no 970.*

SAINT-GILLES

The town, which lies between Anderlecht, Forest and Ixelles, was formerly known as *Obbrussel* before taking the name of the patron saint of its parish church. St-Gilles is divided into two distinct parts – the upper town which is famous for its Art Nouveau and eclectic style houses and the lower town around Porte de Hal (gate) and the recently-redeveloped square in front of the church. In addition to the private houses, there are two public buildings of particular note – the remarkable Tudor-style prison and the Town Hall in which the local registry office has a ceiling decorated by Fernand Khnopff.

★ **Porte de Hal** ⊘ – *At the junction of Boulevard de Midi and Boulevard de Waterloo; entrance from the town.* This huge medieval construction was spared when the second town walls were dismantled, because it was used as a prison. It is the only surviving gate from the old town walls out of an original total of seven. However, even if it is the only gate to have survived, the restoration work undertaken by the architect Henri Beyaert in 1870 *(see Quartier du Sablon, Place du Petit Sablon and Cité Fontainas below)* radically altered the original gate dating from the second half of the 14C. Medieval buildings enjoyed such enormous popularity in the late 19C that nobody had any scruples in altering the appearance of an existing building to make it look more authentic than the real thing.

The gate situated right in the middle of the inner ring-road is seen at its most interesting from within Saint-Gilles itself. The two sturdy buttresses stand out quite clearly, and between them is the former cart track which led into the walled town. The building is topped by machicolations, bartizans and a sloping roof that is quite different to the original flat roof.

Interior – The Porte de Hal, which has recently re-opened after extensive refurbishment, houses a **musée de Folklore.** The ground floor contains a burial plaque from the abbey in Villers-la-Ville (French-speaking Brabant) and 18C torcheres representing various guilds. This floor offers a good vantage point from which to view the cart track already seen outside. There is also the portcullis-slot in the splendid pointed barrel vaulting of the passageway, that used to be closed off by a drawbridge.

Before going up to the next floor, stand in the newel of the spiral staircase for an unusual view upwards. The thirteen historic statues were based on drawings by the talented painter Xavier Mellery (1845-1921). He showed his works at the Salon des XX *(qv)*. The statues were executed by several artists such as V de Haen, É Namur and AJ van Rasbourgh.

The **room** on the first floor is quite magnificent, with its six massive columns supporting pointed vaulting. A thick glass slab set in the floor provides a safe view of the portcullis-slot. The baroque oak door *(right)* was brought here from the so-called Maison des Poissonniers (Fishmongers' House) (note the low-relief carvings on the sides). The fine Malines fireplace *(left)* dates from the early 16C.

The second floor is devoted to old toys, often referred to as popular crafts. However, most of the exhibits were once the playthings of children from relatively wealthy families. The collection of dolls is interesting for its variety. There are dolls made of porcelain, leather, wood, crushed stone, wood pulp, cardboard, oilcloth, celluloid and vinyl. The dolls' houses are typical of the 19C and give an instructive insight into middle-class interiors of the period. Before leaving the room, note the machicolation in an alcove. Its overhang allowed projectiles to be dropped down onto assailants.

The loft has magnificent rafters. The parapet walk provides a fine panoramic view of Brussels. Both are open to the public on request (ask at reception on the ground floor).

Downhill along the inner ring-road is the Cité Fontainas (left).

Cité Fontainas (**ES**) – *Rue De Paepe, Rue Fontainas.* The palatial appearance of this district should not be allowed to hide the fact that it is actually an area of low-income housing built in 1867. This monumental construction of neo-Classical and eclectic design is something of a paradox, for it conceals small semi-detached houses built round a semicircle. They have recently regained their original purpose. The central section houses the Fondation pour l'Art belge contemporain (Belgian Contemporary Art Foundation) which organises temporary exhibitions. The triangular pediment above the central fore-part is decorated with a medallion flanked by two angels each holding a child. André Fontainas was not the architect (the estate was designed by Antoine Trappeniers and Henri Beyaert); he was the city burgomaster and a strong advocate of state education. The district that bears his name used to house retired primary teachers.

THE ART NOUVEAU TRAIL

A drive through the streets of Saint-Gilles between Rue Vanderschrick and Rue Américaine gives an insight into a number of trends in the Art Nouveau style which was particularly popular in Brussels at the turn of the century. The following examples give a good general view of the use of the style in private houses.

Start at the Porte de Hal and drive along Avenue Jean Volders.

Avenue Jean Volders was built at the turn of the century. It is interesting for the uniformity of its architecture. Uncommonly for Brussels, the row of buildings has remained intact. At the corner of Rue Volders and Rue Vanderschrick is the Porteuse d'Eau grill-room which has a neo-Art-Nouveau interior.

Take the first street on the left.

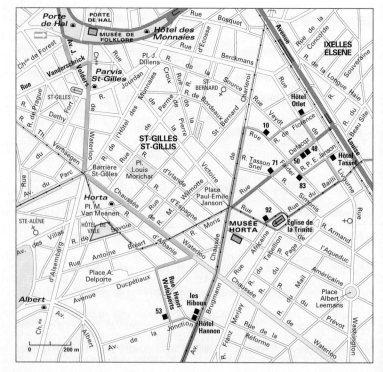

Rue Vanderschrick – Note the fine row of private houses (1900-1902) on the odd-numbered side designed by the architect Ernest Blérot. He has skilfully broken up the line of façades by embellishing them with sgraffiti, bow windows, gables, wrought-ironwork and balconies. No two houses are identical. The one at no 19 has a stained-glass peacock on the piano nobile; the house at no 21 includes a delightfully-shaped oriel window. Both were built in 1902.

Turn right into Chaussée de Waterloo. In the centre of the roundabout in Saint-Gilles is a charming statuette known as The Water Carrier (Julien Dillens). Continue along Chaussée de Waterloo (5th street on the right), then take the 4th street on the right, Avenue Ducpétiaux and turn left immediately into Rue H. Wafelaerts.

No 53 **Rue Henri Wafelaerts** was built by Antoine Pompe for his friend, Doctor Van Neck. There is nothing particularly striking about the architecture of this former orthopaedic hospital nowadays but when it was first built (1910) it was considered as very avant-garde.

Turn left into Rue de la Jonction and continue until reaching the intersection with Avenue Brugmann.

Hôtel Hannon ⊘ –
1 Avenue de la Jonction.
This Art Nouveau residence was built in 1903 by the architect Jules Brunfaut (1852-1942) and decorated by the French artists Louis Majorelle and Emile Gallé, founder of the Nancy School. It was neglected for many years and most of the furniture was lost. The building was restored in 1985 and is currently occupied by a photographic gallery named after the industrialist Edouard Hannon who was also a talented photographer. The frontage is attractive; the interior beautiful and spacious. Note the low-relief sculpture (depicting a woman spinning) by Victor Rousseau (1865-1958), the winter garden window and its Tiffany stained glass by Evaldre, the fresco on the staircase and the decoration of the smoking room. The art work was undertaken by the Rouen-born artist Paul-Albert Baudouin, a pupil of Puvis de Chavannes.

Ch. Bastin-J. Evrard

The Owls House - Close-up of the façade

Nearby (*no 55* Avenue Brugmann) is the so-called **Owls' House** built by Edouard Pelseneer in 1899. It gets its name from the ornamentation at the top and the sgraffiti above the front door.

Go along Avenue Brugmann towards Avenue Louise. Beyond Chaussée de Waterloo, the road is called Chaussée de Charleroi. Take the first street on the right (Rue Américaine). Park the car and walk the rest of the way.

★★ **Musée Horta** ⊘ – *23 & 25 Rue Américaine.* The museum is housed in the two narrow-fronted residences designed by architect Victor Horta (1861-1947) between 1898 and 1900 as his home and studio. These may not be the most spectacular house fronts designed by the Father of Art Nouveau in Belgium but once visitors open the front door, they are confronted with a world where harmony and elegance are the order of the day, where glass and iron are the main building materials and where curves and counter-curves blend gracefully into each other.

In his *Memoirs*, V Horta wrote, "I was by no means the first architect of my day to design furniture but my style of design reflected my architectural preferences". Or again, "If only people would realise that, in each house, I designed

Musée Horta - Museum staircase

and created the models for every piece of furniture, for every door hinge and handle, for all the carpets and wall coverings..." The interior design here, centring on a magnificent **staircase**, shows a quite outstanding degree of unity.

In the hall, the column-like ribbed radiator indicates that everything has been looked at in far greater detail than is usually the case. The first flight of steps leads up to the dining room, in which the white enamelled brick walls come as something of a surprise. Beyond it are the music room, the waiting room and the office, all of them accessible with an ease that very few functional buildings succeed in achieving. The rooms are all on different levels, which brings a delightful sense of fluidity to a house of generally modest proportions. The staircase (note the lines of the handrail) leads to a bedroom with an adjacent dressing-room and another drawing room with a small winter garden and patio. The Hortas' daughter's bedroom overlooks the street. At this level in the staircase, there are two mirrors set in the wall, a skilful artifice which, along with the curved glass roof, increases the flow of light into the house.

The architectural and decorative effects are particularly ornate and sophisticated. Take a close look at the ceilings of the dining and music rooms. In the first of these two adjacent rooms, Victor Horta used the metal structure as a form of ornamentation, underlining the contrast between matter and colour. In the second room, on the other hand, he sought inspiration in Gothic vaulting which is more reminiscent of an alcove. Horta was an architectural genius and he, more than any other Art Nouveau designer, succeeded in creating buildings in which even the tiniest detail reflected the building as a whole, through the material used and its decorative function.

Return to Chaussée de Charleroi and continue to Avenue Louise. Beyond Place Paul Janson, take the second turning on the right (Rue Faider).

The frontage on 10 **Rue Faider** is eye-catching for its academic rigour. Octave van Rysselberghe (1855-1929) designed it in 1882 for Senator Goblet d'Alviella. Above the medallion of Minerva in profile is a string-course decorated with a frieze representing water as one of the four Elements. It was based on a drawing by Julien Dillens who worked on the sculptures for the Stock Exchange. A young woman is shown seated, holding a plumb line in her hand. She represents the Accuracy of Architecture.

Turn left into Rue de Florence.

Hôtel Otlet – *13 Rue de Florence. Not open to the public.* This private mansion, which belonged to Paul Otlet, the eminent Belgian sociologist, was also designed by Octave van Rysselberghe but its frontage is quite different. Twelve years separate the two buildings. In the meantime, the architect had abandoned his academic rigour and begun to make use of the curved lines of the Art Nouveau style. Volume then became more important than decoration (in this particular instance, there is virtually no ornamentation at all). The famous Henry van de Velde was commissioned to carry out the interior design work including the stained glass.

Go down Rue de Livourne opposite the corner of the Hôtel Otlet and turn right into Rue Defacqz.

The house (1897) which belonged to Albert Ciamberlani, an artist from Bologna, stands at 48 **Rue Defacqz.** Paul Hankar (1859-1901), the architect, created a surprising frontage revealing the geometric trends of Art Nouveau. Yet its concept and decoration make this is very much an Art Nouveau house.

The pictorial work was carried out by the owner. The sgraffiti round the large windows symbolise the Three Ages of Man. The medallions on the frieze beneath the cornice should depict several of the labours of Hercules but unfortunately there is very little left to see. The admirable balcony is typical of the work of Paul Hankar.

The house next door *(50 Rue Defacqz)* belonged to the artist René Janssens and was also designed by Hankar.

Like the Tassel Residence *(see below)*, Paul Hankar's own home (1893) *(71 Rue Defacqz)* was a precursor of Art Nouveau architecture in Brussels. The façade gives a clear indication that the architect's training had concentrated on the neo-Gothic and neo-Renaissance. It is interesting to note the use of colour on the façade, the bow window and its brackets, and the four sgraffiti beneath the cornice representing Morning, Day, Evening and Night, in the form of a bird. This was a highly innovatory construction in its day. The Parisian architect, Guimard, even came to Brussels especially to draw it.

Go down Rue Faider from the even-numbered side of Rue Defacqz.

Opposite Rue P-E Janson (*no 80* **Rue Faider**) is a work (1900) by Albert Roosenboom, a pupil of V Horta whose influence is quite obvious. The architect, who usually favoured the neo-Rococo style, gave free rein to his imagination in the wrought ironwork on the balcony. A splendid sgraffiti flanks the upstairs window. Note, too, the wonderful curved shoescraper on the ground floor.

Go down Rue Paul-Emile Janson opposite.

At 6 **Rue P-É Janson** is the Hôtel Tassel (1893), the first Art Nouveau building designed by the master of the genre, Victor Horta. In its day, the residence aroused as much admiration as dislike but the architect nevertheless succeeded, through this work, in acquiring a reputation that was never to wane. The innovatory features are scarcely visible from the outside and are very few in number. They include mainly the curves and counter-curves on the façade, the different-sized windows, and the entire layout and design of the interior. Only a visit to the Horta Museum *(see above)* can give any real idea of the interiors designed by this architect.

Shoe-scraper at the door
of a private house in Rue Faider

Ch. Bastin-J. Évrard

Before leaving Saint-Gilles, walk just a few yards back the way you came and turn left into Rue de Livourne then first right into Rue du Bailli.

Église de la Trinité – *Rue du Bailli.* This building is particularly interesting for the west front which was brought here from the Eglise des Augustins designed by Jacques Francart (1583-1652) between 1620 and 1641 and demolished c1895 to leave way for the Place de Brouckère in the town centre. The façade was entirely reconstructed here. It is outstanding for its strong relief work (facing, pilasters, columns and pointed pediments) which were unheard of in Brabant until that time. The swirls are rather too slender for such a massive building but they were designed to accentuate the sense of verticality in the construction as a whole.

Go along the right-hand side of the church.

At 92 **Rue Africaine** is a privately-owned house in the Art Nouveau style built in 1905 to plans by the architect Benjamin De Lestré-De Fabrlbeckers. The well-balanced frontage includes a large number of geometric details.

Options from Avenue Louise at the end of Rue de Bailli:

▶▶ City centre by tram via the following districts: Quartiers du Palais Royal, du Mont des Arts, and du Botanique.

Ixelles by driving up Avenue Louise to Porte Louise then turning right into Boulevard de Waterloo and heading for Porte de Namur.

Uccle by travelling down Avenue Louise to the Bois de la Cambre and going through the woods to Avenue W Churchill and the roundabout. Then turn left into Avenue Errera (Musée Van Buuren).

UCCLE

Uccle is one of the largest towns in the Brussels conurbation. Most of its streets date only from the end of last century. Many of them are tree-lined and the architectural unity is of a kind rarely seen in Brussels. This is particularly obvious in Avenue Brugmann and Avenue Molière, both of which have a number of outstanding frontages showing eclectic taste or a liking for Art Nouveau.

Uccle is a residential and much sought-after area with a well-justifed reputation for peace and quiet. The houses here belong to the wealthier members of society and they are carrying on a long tradition that first began when the aristocracy took up residence here as soon as Brussels came into being. Uccle is mentioned in a document dating back to 1098. This explains the large number of mansions hidden away in the town, well-concealed from indiscreet eyes by the thick vegetation in their grounds.

★ **Musée David et Alice van Buuren** (BN M[13]) ⊘ – *41 Avenue Léo Errera.*

This red brick house with no particularly outstanding architectural features was built in 1928. It now contains the amazing collection of Dutch financier and enlightened patron of the arts, D van Buuren. The magnificent staircase (the handrail decorated with geometrical motifs was designed by David van Buuren himself) is made of Brazilian rose-wood. The Art Deco interior (most of the furniture was made by Parisian decorator Dominique and the carpets are reminiscent of De Stijl) still retains the cosy atmosphere created by the art lover for both modern and older works.

Among the numerous paintings, one of the most eye-catching is a version of *The Fall of Icarus* by **P Brueghel the Elder** in the library. On the walls of the dining room hang works by **G van de Woestijne,** a family friend and member of the first school of

Musée Van Buuren - The Garden of the Heart

Ch. Bastin-J. Evrard

Laethem-Saint-Martin. In the rooms open to the public are landscapes by J Patenier (16C) and H Seghers (17C), a *Madonna* by J van Cleve (16C), the interior of a church in Saenredam (17C), a seascape by F Guardi (18C), still lives by H Fantin-Latour, sketches by P Brueghel the Younger and V van Gogh, and works by C Permeke, E Tytgat, R Wouters, K van Dongen, J Ensor, L Thévenet, and T Foujita. There are also sculptures by G Minne and J Martel, items of Delftware, and lights attributed to R Lalique. The collections are remarkably well-preserved. Note the piano in the music room with its Art Deco cover. It once belonged to Erik Satie.

The garden has its own special charm, with the Picturesque Garden, the Garden of the Heart, and the Labyrinth laid out by R Pechère *(see Quartier du Mont des Arts, the hanging garden)*. The various areas recall the verses in the *Song of Solomon*.

Return to the roundabout and take the first exit on the right (Rue Montjoie) then turn right again into Rue E Cavell. Cross Avenue De Fré and go down Avenue Houzeau, opposite. Note the Van de Velde House (1933-1934) (no 99) designed by architect Adrien Blomme.

Observatoire Royal (BN) ⊘ – *3 Avenue Circulaire*. This building was constructed between 1883 and 1890 in a circular park covering an area of 12 hectares. The shape of the park was designed to echo the planets which the institution studies. The architect of the scientific complex was Octave van Rijsselberghe who took symmetry as his over-riding concept. As years pass, other buildings have been added but they have not concealed the original constructions with their movable domes designed especially for telescopes.

Go left along Avenue Circulaire.

There is a villa (no 70) built by V Horta in 1899 and a villa (no 146) designed by Victor Dirickx dating from 1925.

Turn into Dieweg and continue beyond Avenue Wolvendael.

At no 292 Dieweg is a house designed by Henry van de Velde (1933). The pure lines and white frontage are reminiscent of the International Style.

Cimetière du Dieweg (BN) ⊘ – *95 Dieweg*. This graveyard has not been used since 1958 except for a special waiver granted in 1983 so that Georges Rémi alias Hergé, the creator of the famous character Tintin could be buried here. It is an unexpected combination of gravestones and luxuriant undergrowth, especially in the Jewish section which was laid out according to age-old ideas on Jewish cemeteries. Although most of the names engraved here for all eternity are meaningless to anybody who has not been born and brought up in Brussels (with the exception of architects Hankar and Cluysenaar), the paths are steeped in a form of romanticism that is reflected in the multitude of sculptures, each one more lyrical or anecdotal than the next.

Return to Dieweg and turn left into Avenue Kamerdelle. Turn left into Avenue du Manoir and go down to Avenue De Fré.

Russian Orthodox Church (BN X) – *19 Avenue De Fré*. This onion-domed church is only a few yards from the Embassy of the Russian Federation. It was designed by Iselenov the architect in 1936 and its shape is reminiscent of the churches in Novgorod.

Turn right along Avenue De Fré then left into Avenue de l'Echevinage.

Avenue de l'Echevinage – The house of Dotremont the collector and industrialist (*no 3*) was built in 1931 to plans by Louis-Herman De Koninck (1896-1984) the architect. The frontage, a fine example of geometric volumes, is built of reinforced concrete shells which was considered a very audacious technique at that time. On the other side of the street (*no 16*) is a house built in 1930 to designs by R Delville.

Le Cornet (BN V) – *At the corner of Avenue De Fré and Chemin du Crabbegat*. This charming inn is said to have received a visit from **Till Ulenspiegel**, the hero of the epic novel written in 1867 by Charles de Coster. He was portrayed on the silver screen by French actor Gérard Philipe and it was here that he "met blind people, women archers from Uccle and fellow imbibers". The old manor (1570 but with 18C extensions) was a café much-frequented by artists until the beginning of the century. Turn into **Chemin du Crabbegat**, one of the last sunken paths in the Brussels conurbation. It is a very picturesque pathway, lined with thick vegetation in the shade of tall beech trees.

Go back the way you came then go down Avenue De Fré to Square des Héros.

Parc de Wolvendael (BN) – *Main entrance on Square des Héros. There are a number of side gates*. This 18-hectare estate, which is mentioned in documents dating back to 1209, has been a public park since 1921. The small white stone castle was built c1763. In 1877, it was the setting for the wedding of Queen Paola's grandparents. A short distance away is a low relief by R Huygelen. The Louis XV pavilion alongside Avenue Wolvendael is now a restaurant. The square, blue stone building that once stood in Amsterdam was brought to Uccle in 1909. It is a pity that it is flanked by wooden fencing but its carvings are still visible (shells, leaves, vases and scrolls) and they are obviously a foretaste of the Louis XVI style. Slightly to one side is a Louis XVI style well, decorated with a low relief of three naked cherubs.

The park's hills and dales are reminiscent of the ducal forest which covered the area before the park was opened. The trees are mainly beech, with some maples, sweet chestnuts etc.

Take Avenue Brugmann and Avenue de Stalle beyond it.

Chapelle Notre-Dame-des-Affligés (**BN R**) ⊘ – *50 Rue de Stalle.* This small chapel built of brick and sandstone from Lède probably dates from the end of the 15C. The stucco ceiling and the pavement are late 17C. The statue of Our Lady of Succour above the entrance is 18C.

Almost opposite the chapel is the tiny **Parc Raspail** *(at the corner of Rue de Stalle and Rue Victor Gambier)* which has only very recently been designated as a listed monument. It was named after the French chemist and politician François Raspail (1794-1878), once MP for Marseilles. He lived on the estate during his period of exile (1855-1859) but the "Raspail House" was demolished in 1972.

Go back up Rue de Stalle and Avenue Brugmann where there is an amazing Art Deco townhouse (no 384) built in 1928 to designs by Courtens the architect.

Options from the crossroads of Rue de Stalle and Chaussée d'Alsemberg:

▶▶ Forest. From Rue de Stalle, turn right into Chaussée de Neerstalle. Continue along this street to Place Saint-Denis.

Saint-Gilles by going up Chaussée d'Alsemberg to the roundabout known as Barrière de Saint-Gilles then turning into Chaussée de Waterloo and continuing down to the Porte de Hal.

Quartier Louise by going along Avenue Brugmann then Chaussée de Charleroi to Place Stéphanie which is close to the Porte Louise.

Ixelles by taking the same route and continuing on to Porte de Namur.

WATERMAEL-BOITSFORT

Until the beginning of the 20C, the old ducal hunting grounds of Watermael and Boitsfort (Watermael is mentioned in documents dating back to 914 AD) were two distinct villages and were totally unaffected by the hustle and bustle of the capital city. The construction of Avenue de Tervuren and Avenue Franklin Roosevelt which were linked by Chaussée de la Hulpe and Boulevard du Souverain, and the building of the railroad to Luxembourg, all contrived to disrupt the peace and quiet of the two localities that were then merged to form a single town.

Watermael-Boitsfort, however, has remained essentially a residential town, primarily because it was never integrated into the urban planning of the capital. This explains why the local housing is so varied and why the maze of little streets is as complex as a labyrinth. Eclectic picturesque architecture rubs shoulders with small modest houses. This is an indication of the two faces of this quiet little town which could whimsically be said to fulfil the wish expressed by Alphonse Allais for a city in the country. Perhaps it is this special atmosphere which attracted so many artists, notably Paul Delvaux and Rik Wouters.

Train du soir, by Paul Delvaux

Watermael-Boitsfort - Flowering cherries in blossom

Église Saint-Clément (CN) – *Rue du Loutrier.* The church dedicated to St Clement stands in a tree-lined grove and this setting, along with its sturdy, thousand-year-old **tower**, give it a rustic appearance which is not without charm. The door in the tower is not original. A few gravestones from the old cemetery lean against the church walls. The church dates from the end of the 12C and was built in the shape of a Latin cross. It was extended in the 18C but the Romanesque nave retained its sober lack of ornementation and its wooden roof, both features dating from the 12C.

There is an interesting Renaissance pulpit and a 16C painting of the *Holy Trinity.* The pavement is decorated with hunting emblems.

Go down Rue Loutrier (left) and Avenue des Princes Brabançons which leads to Square des Archiducs.

Garden-Cities of "Le Logis" and "Floréal" (CN) – *They are built in the tiny streets between the square and Boulevard du Souverain.* Built between 1921 and 1927 by and for tenant co-operatives, these garden-cities became a point of reference for low-cost housing policy in Belgium. ("Le Logis" differs from "Floréal" by the green house frames). The architects J-J Eggericks (1884-1963) and L-M van der Swaelmen (1883-1929) based their designs on similar projects seen in England and the Netherlands, especially as regards the use of traditional materials such as brick masonry and wooden frames.

At the end of April or the beginning of May there is a marvellous display of pink ornamental cherry blossom.

Go back up Boulevard du Souverain and Avenue Delleur. The sculpture representing "Domestic Chores" (1913) by Rik Wouters between the avenue and Chaussée de la Hulpe marks the entrance to the Parc Tournay-Solvay.

Parc Tournay-Solvay (CN) ⊘ – *Entrance in Chaussée de la Hulpe next to the Boitsfort railway station.*
This park (7 hectares – 17.5 acres) once belonged to the famous Solvay family. Its hills and dales include an informal English-style garden, a number of tropical trees and plants, an orchard, a vegetable garden and a recently laid-out rose garden. The château (1878) was damaged by fire and is now a ruin; it was originally built in a Flemish neo-Renaissance style.

Go back up Chaussée de la Hulpe and turn left at the first traffic lights into Drève du Comte.

Promenade dite des "Enfants noyés" – *For map, see Forêt de Soignes. Car park 400m – 435yds.* It takes about an hour to walk through Soignes Forest and it is particularly pleasant because of the wide range of plants growing there.

Having parked the car, go down Drève du Comte to the shores of Etang du Fer-à-Cheval. From the lake, follow the surfaced path *(left)* known as the Chemin des Tumuli. From the hillside there is a fine view to the left over the Etang des Enfants Noyés. The path cuts through a mixed forest of oaks, maples, beech and hazel trees. After the junction with the Chemin des Deux Montagnes, there is a vast beech grove *(right)* preceded by old elderberry trees and Scots pines *(left)* beside towering fir trees and a clump of larches. Take the gravelled Chemin de Vuylbeek *(left)* at the bottom of the incline beyond the dry pond. It runs between the trees alongside marshy terrain. To the right of this little valley is a splendid forest of

179

Corsican pines bordered by bracken. The path continues between the two Etangs de l'Ermite then goes uphill and crosses the Chemin des Deux Montagnes. The plateau is covered with beech trees planted at the beginning of the 19C. Some 100m – 110yd further on, the road turns sharply to the right and goes down to the Nouvel Etang where there are often red squirrels. Go round the left-hand side of the lake and on to the Etang des Enfants Noyés. The name, meaning Lake of the Drowned Children, is a literal translation of the Flemish name of the owner of an old mill *Verd(r)oncken* (= "drowned"). His children later took over the running of the mill hence the name of the lake (the Drowned Children). These two lakes form the natural habitat for frogs, coots, ducks, grebes and even tortoises and are also full of young fish (carp, perch, bream and pike) which are used to stock other ponds. The path runs between oaks and beeches, then rejoins the Etang du Fer-à-Cheval and Drève du Comte.

Options from Chaussée de la Hulpe:

▶▶ Auderghem via Chaussée de la Hulpe and Boulevard du Souverain before turning left into Chaussée de Tervuren and heading for the Etangs de Rouge-Cloître (lakes, signposted).
Quartier Louise via the other side of Chaussée de la Hulpe and Avenue Franklin Roosevelt. Then go up Avenue Louise to Porte Louise.
Ixelles by the same route then go on to Porte de Namur via Avenue de la Toison d'Or.

WOLUWE

It was in the 12C that the towns and villages in Woluwe (pronounced "Voluvey") began to add their patron saint's name to their own.
Until the middle of last century, the valley crossed by the Woluwe stream that rises in the Soignes Forest had preserved its old, picturesque appearance. Gradually, however, the trees were chopped down and it became part of Greater Brussels although it retained its rural character until the years between the two world wars. It was then subjected to the major urban development that had already spread its tentacles across the upper section of the two Woluwes since the work carried out in nearby Cinquantenaire.
The two towns are now well-known residential areas, the home of famous names of past and present including Jean Capart the archaeologist, Adrien de Gerlache the South Pole explorer, and Edgard Tytgat, Oscar Jespers and Constant Montald, artists.

WOLUWE-SAINT-PIERRE

Home of the Count of Paris – From 1926 to 1939, the heir apparent to the throne of France lived in Anjou Manor *(365b Rue de la Cambre; not open to the public)*. Originally known as Putdael Castle, the building had been purchased in 1913 by Philippe VIII, Duke of Orléans, and immediately renamed Anjou Manor in memory of Louis XIV's brother. When the Duke of Orléans died, his cousin, the Duke of Guise, was forced to leave French soil since he then became subject to the law of exile.
Count Henri's first five children were all born here. Inside, there is a fireplace bearing the motto "Montjoie-Saint-Denis".
The wide, wooded Avenue de Tervuren *(see Cinquantenaire)* is the best place from which to begin a tour of the sights listed here. You can also reach them via the Boulevard de la Woluwe set at right angles to it.

From Square Montgomery, go down the lateral avenue to Square Léopold II which is easy to spot because of its fine obelisk in memory of the cavalry.

★ **Palais Stoclet** (DM **P¹**) ⊙ – *279-281 Avenue de Tervuren*. This magnificent private residence *(not open to the public)* was commissioned from the Austrian **Josef Hoffmann** (1870-1956) by the engineer-businessman Adolphe Stoclet, uncle of the French architect Mallet-Stevens. J Hoffman was a pupil of Otto Wagner and a member of the Secession movement and, until then, had designed very few buildings. His reputation was based mainly on his work in interior decoration and furniture. He was able to give expression to the principles of the *Wiener Werkstätte* here. Like the *Arts and Crafts* movement in England in the second half of the 19C, its aim was to teach artists and craftsmen the techniques of mass production.
The palace took six years to complete (1905-1911) and among those who worked on it were the sculptors Powolny, Luksch and Metzner and the very famous artist, **Gustav Klimt**. Like the Horta Residence, the Stoclet Palace is one of Brussels' finest examples of a total work of art. J Hoffmann and his studios were responsible for every aspect of the work, from the door handles to the layout of the garden.

The exterior has become a traditional reference for early 20C art work and architects from all over the world have drawn inspiration from it. The perfection of the work and the modernity of the architectural volumes have withstood the test of time quite magnificently. From the wrought-iron gates, it is easy to see certain features such as the ledge-less windows and the quality of the decorative string-courses that gracefully bring life to the white marble surfaces and the bays in the only wall visible from the street. Note, too, the magnificent staircase tower decorated with four figures and a half-circle in bronze by the sculptor Metzner.

The residence, with its pure, abstract lines, is still lived in by the Stoclet family.

Go down the avenue to the traffic lights and turn right into Rue Jules César. When you reach the memorial to the Korean War, bear left into Avenue de l'Atlantique. Turn into the first street on the left.

Palais Stoclet

Ch. Bastin - J. Evrard

★ **Bibliotheca Wittockiana** (DM **B**[1]) ⓥ – *21 Rue du Bémel. Guided tour with the curator by appointment only, except during temporary exhibitions.* This private museum housed in modern, purpose-built premises contains the large collection of antique books belonging to industrialist Michel Wittock. From the great hall used for temporary exhibitions, visitors enter the store containing some one thousand one hundred volumes, many of them priceless. It is a small room, only open to small groups for reasons of security, and it contains rare bindings from the 16C to 20C and a 15C incunabulum. Among the works in this collection are 10 books printed in the 16C which were once the property of the "Prince of Libraries," Jean de Broglie, treasurer to François I, a work decorated with shells that belonged to Queen Margot, Mary Stuart's bedside book, a mosaic binding made for Henri of Lorraine, a book bound in Morocco-leather with an ex-libris written in Marie Antoinette's own handwriting etc. If there are too many visitors, a glass panel enables them to admire a few

P. Dijkmans/GLOGAL PICTURES

Bibliotheca Wittockiana - A binding

181

outstanding exhibits such as bindings embossed with the ciphers of Louis XIV, Louis XV, the Count of Arundel and Napoleon Bonaparte. In the room containing 20C works, the curator, wearing gloves to ensure that the acidity of his fingers does not attack the leather, shows visitors a few works that are representative of changes in style.

A collection of 500 baby rattles (the largest private collection in the world) covers forty centuries of history, beginning in the Hittite period. Some of the items are steeped in a symbolism designed to ward off illness and disease. They are made of terracotta, rock crystal, coral, mother-of-pearl, ivory, silver, silver-gilt or gold and have a wide range of different shapes eg animals, dumbbells or musical instruments.

At the end of the street is Parc de Woluwe.

Parc de Woluwe and Etangs Mellaerts (**DN**) – In order to improve the marshland that bordered "his" Avenue de Tervuren, King Leopold II asked a Frenchman named Laîné to create an English-style park in 1895. The valleys are popular in the summer months.

On the other side of Boulevard du Souverain are the Mellaerts Lakes, named after their former owner. In the summer months, they are used for boating.

Whether you come from the Woluwe Park or the Mellaerts Lakes, cross Avenue de Tervuren at the junction with Boulevard du Souverain and turn into the lateral avenue alongside Avenue de Tervuren in order to park in the first street to the right, Rue de Leybeek.

Musée du Transport urbain bruxellois (**DM M²⁶**) ⊙ – *364b Avenue de Tervuren. The admission fee includes a return trip (about 1 hour) to the Soignes Forest or Cinquantenaire on a 1930's tram.*

The **tramway** or "American railway" as it was known at the time, first appeared in the Belgian capital in May 1869. It was a horse-drawn tram linking Porte de Namur to Bois de la Cambre. In 1894, after the innovations introduced by the German, Siemens, and the Belgian, Van de Poele, who developed the pantograph, electricity replaced the horses and the steam engines that had such difficulty in climbing the steeply-sloping Boulevard de Waterloo and Boulevard du Jardin botanique. Thereafter, the engines and trailers became more powerful and more comfortable, as did the buses brought into service in 1907 and the trolley buses used from 1939 to 1964.

The museum is housed in a former depot of the Société des Transports intercommunaux de Bruxelles (S.T.I.B.) and it retells the story of the trams and buses with yellow and white paintwork that have been a characteristic sight in the city since the First World War. The horse-drawn trams popularly known as "dung engines", the horse-drawn double-decker that is the oldest exhibit, and the "shifting-track" tram all bring back, for just one brief instant, the flavour of more elegant times that are now long gone. They are followed by the all-electric engines developed in the 1950's which were the forerunners of the ultra-modern T2000 tram that has been running through the city since 1994.

A trip on an old tram

WOLUWE-SAINT-LAMBERT

From the Brussels Urban Transport Museum, turn right onto Boulevard de la Woluwe and left at the second set of traffic lights into Rue Voot.

Église Saint-Lambert (DM Z[1]) – *Place du Sacré-Cœur.* Although the basilica-style church was restored and extended in 1939, it has retained part of the nave and tower which would appear to date back to the 12C. The Romanesque belltower still looks like a fortified shelter. The contents of a glass cabinet come as something of a surprise – a charming sculpture on wood of the future king, Albert I, carved when he was only 12.

One of the arches in the north aisle contains a modern organ which was especially designed for 16C Spanish Baroque music.

Go back down Rue Voot via Place Saint-Lambert (bric-à-brac is sold here on the first Sunday of every month) and cross over Boulevard de la Woluwe. Turn left into Chaussée de Stockel.

Château Malou (DM) – *Chaussée de Stockel.* This building, standing at the entrance to a vast park overlooking a lake and regularly decorated with sculptures, belongs to the local authority. It was built in the late 18C and now houses a gallery in which the works of art are all on loan. It is also used for temporary exhibitions. The castle accommodated two statesmen in the past – Van Gobbelschroy, Minister of the Interior of the Kingdom of the Netherlands, and Jules Malou, former Minister of Finance to King Leopold II. He died here in 1886.

Go back down Chaussée de Stockel and Rue Veet then turn right into the lateral avenue alongside Boulevard de la Woluwe.

After fairly recent restoration, the waterwheel in the **Lindekemals Mill** (DL) again ploughs through the waters of the small Woluwe stream. The rate of flow has now been regularised by a collector. The building is said to date back to the 15C and it has two crow-stepped gables. It was originally a paper mill before becoming a flour mill. Nowadays, it is a restaurant. A few yards away, still on Boulevard de la Woluwe, is **"het Slot"**, the final remains of the early 16C mansion that used to belong to the Counts of Hinnisbael, lords of Woluwe and Krasinhem by marriage.

Retrace your steps and turn into Rue J-V Debecker then left into the small Avenue de la Chapelle.

Chapelle de Marie la Misérable (DM) – *Corner of Avenue de la Chapelle and Avenue E Vandervelde.* This delightful chapel was built c1360 in honour of a pious young girl who lived during the reign of John II. She had repulsed the advances of a knight and was then accused by him of having cast a spell on him and stolen a valuable chalice (he had, in fact, hidden it in the young girl's home). She was found guilty and buried alive. As for the dastardly knight, he became insane. Miracles occurred on the spot where the young girl had been tortured. At the entrance to the chapel is the superb tomb of Georgy Kieffel and his wife, Anna van Asseliers, dating from the 17C. A chancel screen from the same period separates the nave from the polygonal apse lit by Gothic windows. The chancel is decorated with a painting representing the seven pains of the Virgin Mary and episodes from the life of the chapel's patron saint. The timber roof is decorated with coats of arms.

Cross Avenue E Vandervelde and go down Rue Klakkedelle opposite. After crossing Avenue Chapelle-aux-Champs, turn off straight away onto a footpath.

The old 18C **Moulin à vent** (DL) known as the "burnt mill" comes from the Tournai area. It was restored in 1987.

A short distance away is the Catholic University of Louvain (*Université Catholique de Louvain*, U.C.L) which has a medical faculty around the teaching hospital. The Medical Centre is a student residence (1975) designed by architect Lucien Kroll.

To each side of Avenue E Vandervelde, almost adjacent to it, is the **Kapelleveld Garden City** (DM), which was planned between 1921 and 1926 at the request of a tenants' association and strongly influenced by a Dutch movement call "De Stijl". It was designed by five modernist architects including Antoine Pompe, Louis-Martin van der Swaelmen and Hujb Hoste. The two buildings, which so closely resemble each other despite the fact that half-a-century separates their completion, will be of interest to those with a love of functionalist architecture.

Options from the Kapelleveld Garden City:

▶▶ City centre by underground (Quartiers du Béguinage, Louise etc.).

Le Cinquantenaire by going down Rue E Vandervelde which extends into Avenue P Hymans and Avenue de Broqueville. Beyond Square Montgomery, follow Avenue de Tervuren.

Auderghem by going down Rue E Vandervelde then turning left onto Boulevard de la Woluwe. Turn left into Avenue de Tervuren and immediately right onto Boulevard du Souverain.

Tervuren by going down Rue E Vandervelde then turning left onto Boulevard de la Woluwe; turn left into Avenue de Tervuren to the end of the street.

Tervuren. Musée Royal de l'Afrique centrale

The Outlying Districts

Beersel belonged to the lords of Witthem who rose to fame at the end of the 15C by supporting Maximilian of Austria in his struggle against the rebellious towns in the Low Countries. In 1489, the people of Brussels revolted and laid siege to the castle which Philip, Maximilian's son, had come to help defend. The reinforcement by a French artillery corps ensured the success of the people of Brussels; however, they were soon defeated by Albert de Saxe who pacified the city. As a reward for his loyalty, Henri de Witthem, a powerful leader, was made a knight of the Golden Fleece before becoming chamberlain to Philip the Fair (his tomb, with recumbent figure, is in the formerly fortified Church of St Lambert).

The Dutch-speaking novelist Herman Teirlinck (1879-1967) lived in Beersel from 1936 onwards.

Fortress (AP) ⊙ – The brick fortress overlooking the Senne Valley was built between 1300 and 1310 and reconstructed at the end of the 15C. It has not been lived in since 1554. Restoration work based on an engraving by Harrewyn showing the fortress at the end of the 17C has restored it to its former splendour.

The castle consists of three round watch towers with crowstepped gables. The towers are connected by high curtain walls surrounding an elliptical enclosure. It is a very romantic-looking place encircled by a moat reflecting the machicolated parapet walkway and is the best-preserved fortress in Brabant even though the central buildings have disappeared. The walls are more than 2 m thick (*c*6ft 6in). The date 1617 visible on the cramp irons on one of the façades probably refers to a period of restoration.

Huizingen – Its **provincial recreation area** ⊙ covers 90 hectares – 225 acres. It is well maintained and is a veritable oasis of greenery (it includes some 1 200 species of plants) in the heart of an industrial region. There are three paths through the woods (55 hectares – 138 acres) of both broad-leaved trees and conifers. There is also a garden designed for the blind with explanatory audio terminals *(in French and Dutch)* enabling the visually-handicapped to enjoy a very pleasant walk. In summer, the outdoor swimming pool is open to the public.

Beersel Castle

Join us in our constant task of keeping up-to-date.
Please send us your comments and suggestions.

Michelin Tyre PLC
Tourism Department
The Edward Hyde Building
38 Clarendon Road
WATFORD – Herts WD1 1SX
Tel: 01923 415 000

GAASBEEK ★

The Payottenland – This gently rolling landscape lies to the southwest of the capital city. It is bordered to the north by the E40 motorway to Ostend, to the west by the Dendre Valley, to the south by the linguistic frontier, and to the east by the Senne Valley.

This is a very fertile region that was not named until the 19C. It is a charming venue for people on cycling holidays as the whole area is dotted with rich farms, windmills and watermills, and delightful villages on the valley floors.

The Payottenland produces barley, wheat and hops. Like the Senne Valley, it is also the home of several famous types of beer – *kriek, lambic, faro* and *gueuze.*

★★ **Château et parc de Gaasbeek** ⊙ – Godefroid de Louvain, the younger brother of Duke Henry II of Brabant, built a fortress on the plain at Gaasbeek *c*1240. At the time, Gaasbeek was no more than a hamlet of Lennik but from then on the entire area round about became part of the powerful feudal Gaasbeek Estate. It was much feared, both because of its strong geographical location and because of the wealth of the family who owned it. In the 14C, the barony passed into the hands of the Hornes family, and in 1565, the castle and seventeen villages within the Gaasbeek area were sold to the famous Lamoral d'Egmont, Governor and Captain General of Flanders and Artois, knight of the Golden Fleece, who was to die three years later. He was beheaded in Grand-Place in punishment for the crime of lèse-majesté.

The original fortress was elliptical in shape with huge curtain walls connecting four semi-circular towers and the guard room. This system of defence was unable, however, to withstand the fury of the people of Brussels who ransacked the castle in 1387 following the murder of Everard 't Serclaes *(see Quartier de la Grand-Place).* Philippe de Hornes had it rebuilt and the Marquis d'Arconati Visconti had it restored and embellished in the 19C. The embellishments complied, however, with the fashion of the day. In fact, they consist of rather fanciful decorative features.

The castle has belonged to the Flemish community since 1981 and it still seems to be watching over the welfare of Brabant. From the terrace of the main courtyard, there is a view over the countryside which brings to mind the works of Brueghel the Elder who came to paint this region, particularly St-Anna-Pede. Its church is easily recognisable in one of his paintings: *La Parabole des aveugles,* now in the Museum in Naples.

The park, where beech trees predominate, is magnificent.

The interior – The visit begins on the first floor. The room in the gatehouse is furnished in Flemish Renaissance style with a magnificent Tournai wool and silk tapestry (early 16C) depicting a gypsy camp; the walnut bath tub decorated with sea horses dates from the 18C. The room with the glass roof, similarly furnished, contains a charming French miniature (early 16C) and the Judgment Tapestry (Tournai, early 16C). In the room known as the Arrivabene Chamber because it was named after the count who stayed there occasionally from 1827 to 1859, note the biblical scenes with alabaster reliefs (Nottingham School, 15C) and the Russian processional cross (18C) given by the Grand Duchess Maria Feodorovna to Giammartino Arconati Visconti, whose family owned the estate in the 19C; the Limoges enamel (16 C) is of a beautiful blue but the workmanship is clumsy.

Beyond the medallion representing Emperor Charles V attributed to Leone Leoni (16C) is the Knights' Hall which has a polychrome neo-Gothic ceiling painted by Jean van Holder. The pictures are of minimal artistic interest, depicting several episodes from local history, such as the sack of Gaasbeek by the French in 1684, shortly before Maréchal de Villeroi demolished part of the castle with his cannonballs while on his way to bombard Brussels. Two gatehouses contain a sundial with the arms of the Medici family and an astronomical clock made in 1588 by Georg Kostenbader of Strasbourg.

In the library is a photograph of the Marquise Arconati Visconti who gave the castle to the Belgian state in 1922. The photograph is next to the portrait of her husband. The archives and Hornes staircase are decorated with a series of **Brussels tapestries** telling the story of Tobias (*c*1540). The perspectives in the landscapes and the floral and animal motifs in the borders are remarkable. The display cabinet contains the prenuptial contract of Peter Paul Rubens and Hélène Fourment, and the artist's will. In the next two rooms, there are some early 16C tapestries from Brussels and Tournai and a panel depicting Mary of Burgundy with a hunting bird on her hand (*c*1480).

The bedroom is hung with blue silk. It contains an **alabaster bust** (16C) of Emperor Charles V and Isabel of Portugal, probably made at the time of their marriage; the glazed earthenware tondo comes from the Florentine studio of della Robbia; the four Renaissance alabasters from a studio in Malines. On the ground floor, the Egmont Bedroom contains a 16C reredos from Antwerp, two statues of St Catherine (Germany, *c*1470; northern Netherlands, *c*1530), and a

Gaasbeek Castle - The inner courtyard

Ch. Bastin - J. Evrard

display cabinet with ivory objets d'art. The richly decorated gallery contains a late 15C silver bust of Isabel the Catholic, a Spanish work decorated with precious stones. The portrait of Eleanor of Austria, Charles I's elder sister, is attributed to Joas van Cleve who worked at the court of François Ier. Above the mantelpiece in the guardroom are portraits of Lamoral d'Egmont, William of Orange and Philippe de Hornes, the three main protagonists during Cardinal Granvelle's investigations. The ivory and *repoussé* copper hunting horn is thought to have belonged to Egmont.

Beyond the dining room and kitchen is the Rubens room dominated by *The Tower of Babel*, a picture full of anecdotal detail by Maarten van Valckenborch (a painter of the second half of the 16C). Next is the Infanta's bedroom with two paintings of the Infanta Isabel, the daughter of Philip II. One is a full-length portrait; the other showes her at the festival of crossbowmen in front of the church in the Quartier du Sablon in 1615. The two statues of winged angels are made of oak covered with a layer of plaster painted in a bronze colour. Over the door is a painting of the Holy Family from the studio of Jordaens.

GRIMBERGEN

This town lies not far from Meise to the north of Brussels *(take A12 to Meise then turn right)* and is famous for its huge Baroque church. The houses round the attractive church square date from the 18C.

Former Premonstratensian Minster – This is one of the most interesting pieces of architecture and Baroque decoration in Belgium. Building began in 1660 based on plans by Gilbert van Zinnick and the church was consecrated in 1725. It remained unfinished (the nave was supposed to have four spans rather than two) and has an elongated chancel extending into a square tower. The interior is majestic because of the height of the vaulting and the dome. The furnishings are particularly ornate. The four early 18C **confessionals**★ are attributed to Henri-François Verbruggen; they are decorated with allegories and figures from the Old and New Testaments. The 17C church choirstalls are exuberantly decorated (twisted columns, scrolls, cherubs, medallions etc.).

In the middle of the high altar (it is thought to be the work of Langhermans, a sculptor who learnt his craft from L Fayd'herbe) is a representation of the Assumption of the Virgin Mary. The lower section of the altar is made of black and white marble. The church contains several Baroque paintings including the *Élévation de la Croix* attributed to G Maes and sculptures such as *Les quatre évangélistes* thought to have been carved by J Quellin. The chancel contains the tomb of Philippe, Prince of Bergues and Lord of Grimbergen. It also includes the memorial to the abbots.

The **great sacristy** (1763) to the left of the chancel is decorated with some outstanding wainscoting. The fresco and *grisailles* on the ceiling illustrate episodes from the story of St Norbert, founder of the Order.

The small sacristy contains some wonderful 17C paintings.

Located north of the capital near the A12 motorway to Antwerp, the town, whose Gothic church boasts a set of 47 bells, is mainly known for the Bouchout Estate which contains the national botanical gardens.

★★ **Jardin Botanique** (Plantentuin) (BK) ⊙ – More than a half a century ago it was decided that the Belgian National Botanical Gardens would move from Rue Royale to the huge estate of Bouchout bought by the State in 1939. The transfer was delayed by the Second World War; a decade was needed to restore the park which had been extensively damaged by the occupation of various armies between May 1940 and January 1946. The park was opened to the public in 1958 but the plant collections were not accessible until 1965. The park has now completely absorbed the transfer of the Botanical Gardens; the greenhouses contain some 18 000 species of plants from all over the world and provide an opportunity to stroll through a very pleasant park (93 hectares – 230 acres). The park owes its appearance to its scientific plantations, its clumps of trees interspersed with lawns and ponds and its remarkable free-standing trees. A stroll through the park reveals collections of hydrangeas, magnolias, rhododendrons, oak and maple trees depending on the season.

Château de Bouchout – The fortress seems to date from Godefroid I, Duke of Brabant from 1095 to 1140. Although the square watch tower (22m – 72ft high) dates from the 12C, the castle's current appearance dates from 1832. The building has been highly restored and now houses temporary exhibitions. It was here that the Empress Charlotte, the sister of King Leopold II and widow of Maximilian, Emperor of Mexico, died on 21 January 1927.

Palais des plantes ⊙ – Twelve of the thirteen glasshouses are open to the public; there are also twenty-two small glasshouses only open to researchers. The tour includes tropical and subtropical plants divided into geographical regions, but the labelling is unfortunately somewhat sparse. "Victoria's" glasshouse with its water lilies, water hyacinths and brightly coloured orchids should not be missed. The water is kept at a temperature of about 30°C – 86°F.

Open air collections in the southern section ⊙ – These are at their most attractive from June to September and consist of four main areas: ligneous plants (Fruticetum), mainly shrubs; medicinal plants, classified according to their pharmacological use; herbaceous plants (Herbetum) from all 5 continents; and evergreen conifers (Coniferetum).
The Herbetum includes a delightful glasshouse built by Alphonse Balat *(see Serres Royales de Laeken)* in 1853 and formerly situated in Parc Léopold, and then in the Botanical Gardens in Rue Royale. The labelling is clear and sometimes gives interesting historical and anecdotal details.

Botanical gardens, Meise

The woods and valleys of the western part of Brabant, set between the Soignes Forest and the town of Wavre, provide a choice of destinations and itineraries. The towns and villages in the east of the capital are quiet, wooded areas with a markedly residential character.

A small number of international companies have set up their head offices here, in particular *Swift* in La Hulpe. The company commissioned Ricardo Boffill the Spanish architect to design a prestigious building.

Follow the signposts from the Rosière exit on the A4-E411 motorway.

Château ⊘ – *Entrance to the left of église Sainte-Croix.* The castle has belonged to the Mérode family since the late 17C. One of its members, Félix de Mérode, was a member of the provisional government in 1830 *(see the monument opposite the church)*. One of his daughters, Anne-Marie, married the famous French Catholic writer, Charles de Montalembert, who spent some time in the castle, writing part of his *Monks of the West.* The pink brick building was erected between 1631 and 1662, initially for Charles de Gavre and, later, for Philippe Spinola, Counsellor to Archduke Albert and Archduchess Isabel. The castle can only be visited with a guide. This being so, the following description, which is purposefully selective, aims simply to draw attention to its most interesting and most unusual aspects. Almost all the furniture comes from the castle in Ancy-le-Franc in Burgundy which was bequeathed to Françoise de Mérode, née de Clermont-Tonnerre.

Before beginning the guided tour, go into the main courtyard. Three of the sides have galleries with basket-handle arches; this is a fairly unusual design in Belgium. Overlooking the courtyard is a tower-porch topped by a spire. The north wing has attractive mullioned windows and a Baroque entrance with a pediment bearing Philippe Spinola's coat of arms which is also the emblem of the city.

The dining room is lined with **wainscoting** which was purchased in 1920 by the second Félix de Mérode and brought here from the manor house in Nérac (Lot-et-Garonne, France) that was the residence of the future King Henri IV (one of the two doors still contains a hole caused by a gunshot, traditionally said to be a reminder of an unsuccessful attempt on the future sovereign's life). The table is laid with a 17C Royal Copenhagen porcelain dinner service. On the landing, ask the guide to open the superb ebony cabinet carved with scenes from mythology so that you can see the marquetry inside, crafted with rare woods. The windows in the main drawing room overlook the formal gardens said to have been designed by Le Nôtre (only the basic design is now visible). The drawing room contains a gold and silver filigree jewel case from Toledo, a 17C cabinet made in Antwerp and two fine Gobelins **tapestries** representing *The Kidnapping of Europa* and *Diana the Huntress* (they are part of a series of four tapestries, the other two being in the Metropolitan Museum of New York). The bedchamber of Monseigneur Xavier de Mérode has remained as it was during his lifetime. He began his career in the army before becoming Pope Pius IX's secret Chamberlain during the capture of Rome in 1870. It was Xavier de Mérode who introduced the papal troops. The so-called Flower Chamber gets its name from the **painted motifs** on the wainscoting found in the castle in Ancy-le-Franc, the residence of the de Clermont-Tonnerre family whose initials can be seen on the ceiling, accompanied by the prince's crown denoting the Mérodes. The motifs are said to have been painted by Primaticcio, an Italian interior decorator brought to France by François I and appointed Superintendant of Royal Buildings by François II in 1559. Finally, the Weapons Gallery contains items collected by the French mathematician Gaspard Monge during Bonaparte's Egyptian campaign. Note the dromedary saddles, and the superb coral inlays on some of the rifle butts.

Outside the castle, if the weather is sunny, you can try and decipher the time on the sundial above the tower-porch overlooking the courtyard and outhouses. A conversion table hanging on the right-hand side of the carriage entrance is useful if you want to work out the current time of day.

EXCURSIONS

From Château de Rixensart, follow the signs to Lac de Genval.

Lac de Genval – This lake is the weekend haunt of many a local. It is a vast stretch of water covering an area of 18 hectares – 44 acres and ideal for water sports of all kinds. There is very little building along its wooded shores. At the "Château Schweppes" estate (the house is built in a vaguely Tudor style) there is a mineral spring; the water is sold to the public. There are also a number of cafés with terraces along the banks. Boating is authorised on the lake.

A short distance away is the **Musée de l'Eau et de la fontaine** ⊘ *(63 Avenue Hoover),* an attractive museum. Not only does it contain numerous specimens of drinking fountains; it also has photographs and educational panels illustrating their mechanisms, and explaining the distribution and quality of water.

Take the "Ring" direction to La Hulpe. The Solvay estate is signposted.

Domaine Solvay ⊘ – Large houses and manors are scattered throughout the wealthy town of La Hulpe. The Solvay estate (220 hectares – 544 acres) was once the property of industrialist Ernest Solvay and his family and was later bequeathed to the State. The park is magnificent, forming a sort of forest museum dotted with lakes and footpaths. It is dominated by a stately home (1840) refurbished by Victor Horta in 1894 (he had already been commissioned by the family to build a monument in the courtyard of the factory in Couillet near Charleroi, the grave in Ixelles cemetery and Armand Solvay's private residence on Avenue Louise in Brussels). The house was modernised in the early 1930's. It now belongs to the French Ministry of Culture and was used for many of the scenes in the film *Le Maître de musique.*

Forêt de SOIGNES★★

The Charcoal Forest and Ducal Hunting Grounds – The name of Soignes has connections with Senne, the name of the river which skirts the forest. Both have the same Celtic origin, *Sonia.* This area of woodland, which lies on the edge of the charcoal forest that used to stretch from the River Sambre to the River Scheldt, included prehistoric settlements and it was here that the Nervii under the leadership of Ambiorix were defeated by Caesar's Roman legions. This disaster marked the beginning of Belgian history.

The forest belonged to the dukes in the 12C and quickly gained a reputation for its excellent hunting among noblemen throughout the western world. Charles V enjoyed riding to hounds here; it provided an opportunity to hunt wild boar while remaining within easy reach of Brussels. However, the estate was also and most importantly a source of considerable revenue since the dukes were accustomed to mortgaging the woodland without ever actually selling off what they considered as "the finest jewel in their crown".

A Cathedral in Wood – As time passed, the forest became flanked on all sides by estates including land, farms and castles, each of them doing their best to outshine their neighbours. The most splendid of all the estates was Tervuren *(qv).* It was much larger than the area now known as Tervuren and included a large number of monasteries attracted here by surroundings that were ideal for meditation and penitance. Fourteen monastic communities were set up here in the days following the Crusades. They were Wezembeek, Tervuren, Val-Duchesse, Rouge-Cloître, Groenendael, La Cambre, Bootendael, Forest (Brussels), Sept-Fontaines, Ter Cluysen, Wauthier-Braine, Nizelle, Bois-Seigneur-Isaac, and Aywières (Hal). All of them disappeared at the end of the 18C. A few rare buildings survived including the enclosure at Le Rouge-Cloître (which still lies within the forest boundaries), and the chapel of Notre-Dame-de-Bonne-Odeur built in 1485 on the spot where a small statuette of the Virgin Mary had been fixed to a tree. The chapel was altered then moved, in the mid 19C, to the end of the drive which bears its name.

A Peasant Reigns – With the exception of the period of revolt against Spain, the forest was a place of unusual tranquillity. Marie de Medici, having escaped from Compiègne to which she had been exiled by her son, Louis XIII, used to enjoy strolling beneath the trees in the company of Duchess d'Ornano. However the War of the Augsburg Succession between Spain and Austria turned the forest into the scene of many a skirmish between the French soldiers who had occupied Charleroi in 1692 and the troops of "Fayctneans" raised by the Governor General in order to protect the woodland. For three years, this troop, under the command of a daring peasant named Jacques Pasture, who was even raised to the peerage by Maximilian of Bavaria, led the French a merry dance. Despite this, the French reached Brussels, after pillaging Waterloo on the way. They laid siege to the capital in 1695 *(see Quartier de la Grand-Place)* but the intrepid Jaco Pasture continued to spread terror in the forest where his men robbed anybody who ventured along its paths. A district in Uccle known as Fort Jaco keeps alive the memory of this astonishing commander-in-chief.

State Forest – The French Revolution put an end to the jurisdiction of the dukes. The Republicans divided up the land and shared it out between the surrounding towns and villages. The forest became State property in 1843 and was then managed by the equivalent of the Forestry Commission *(Office des Eaux et Forêts).* It used to cover three times as much ground as it does today (4 386 hectares – 10 838 acres) and it included a large number of streams and lakes, some of which

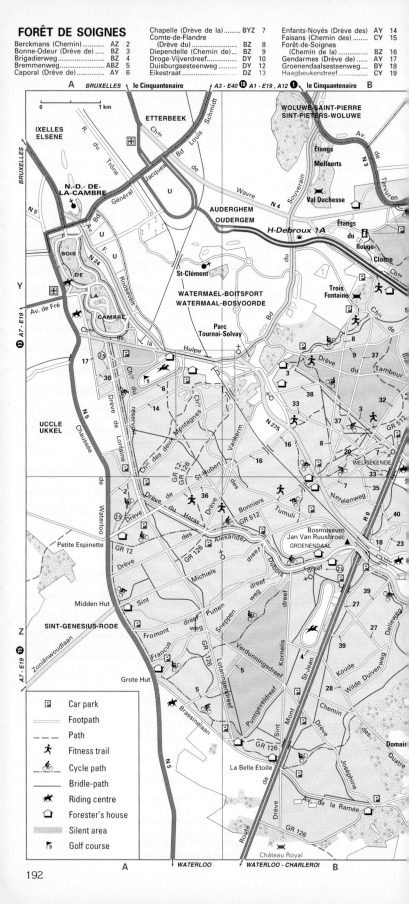

FORÊT DE SOIGNES

Legend

P	Car park
	Footpath
- - -	Path
🏃	Fitness trail
🚴	Cycle path
	Bridle-path
🐴	Riding centre
⌂	Forester's house
	Silent area
⛳	Golf course

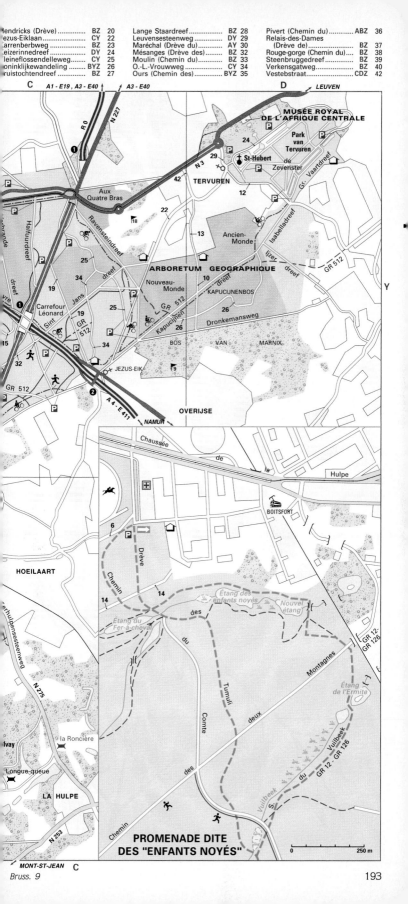

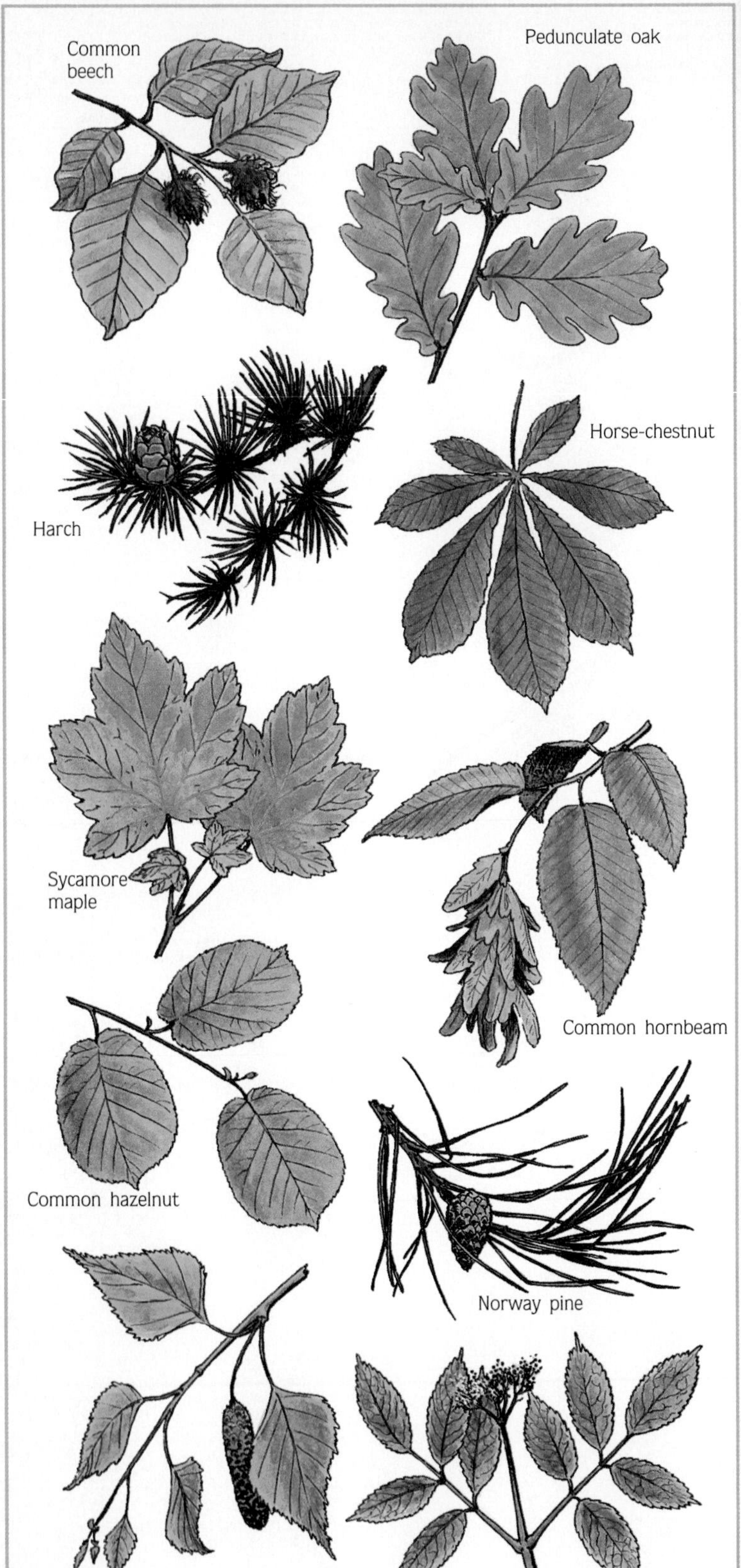

Common
beech

Pedunculate oak

Harch

Horse-chestnut

Sycamore
maple

Common hornbeam

Common hazelnut

Norway pine

Silver birch

Common elder

194

disappeared when work was undertaken by the city of Brussels in the mid 19C to improve the water supply. The area was subjected to extensive deforestation over the centuries and also suffered from the rise in the population. It now lies within the boundaries of eleven towns or villages.

Flora, Fauna and a Place for a Stroll – The woodland consists mainly of beech groves (80%), with oaks and conifers making up the remaining 20%. There are, though, other varieties of trees on the edge of the forest. The preponderance of beech trees dates from the days of the Austrians; the oaks are a reminder of French influence. In the undergrowth and clearings, walkers with some knowledge of botany will find a large number of different varieties of plants including heather and ling, primroses, hyacinths, ferns, creeping ivy, veronica etc.

In days gone by, the forest was the haunt of wolves and bears, wild boar and large wild animals; today, it boasts little more than foxes and deer. Many small rodents such as field mice cohabit with the native red squirrel which is tending to die out and another species of red squirrel, a fairly tame creature introduced by accident in the 1970's. There are many different species of bird in the trees but it takes discretion and patience to spot wrens, tits, cuckoos, green woodpeckers, tawny owls, buzzards etc.

In addition to the main roads, there are numerous footpaths, bridlepaths, and cycle paths running through some very attractive parts of the forest. Lakes provide a romantic setting especially at Groenendael where the famous mystic Jan van Ruysbroeck, nicknamed Jan the Admirable, lived in the 14C (for other sites, see Auderghem, Tervuren, and Watermael-Boitsfort).

TERVUREN ★

St Hubert, the patron saint of hunters, is said to have died here in 727AD in a building situated on the spot where, c1200, Duke Henri I had a castle built on the edge of the Soignes Forest. This magnificent austere building was flanked by massive round towers with slit windows. It was turned into a palace by Margaret of York, Duchess of Burgundy, the "gracious, debonair princess" who had the surrounding woodland laid out as parks and gardens. The Archduke Albert and Archduchess Isabel, who were very fond of this spot, commissioned Wenceslas Coberger (1560-1634) to restore the castle and build St Hubert's Chapel. They also had the park boundaries marked out with ten gates named after the localities in which they were situated (some of them are still used today). The castle, which is said to have been uniquely beautiful, was dismantled in 1782 on the orders of Joseph II.

Tervuren, nicknamed the Versailles of Belgium by writer Roger Martin du Gard, is an ideal spot for a very pleasant stroll.

Go to the town centre.

Église Saint-Jean-l'Evangéliste ⊘ – This 13C Gothic church (with 14C aisles and a west front built in 1779) contains the tombs of the Dukes of Brabant, Antoine of Burgundy (son of Philip the Bold) who was killed at Azincourt in 1415, John IV and Philippe de Saint-Pol who had been Captain General of Paris. In addition to the fine roodscreen made by the Keldermans brothers (1517) and later used as an organ loft, the most outstanding piece of furniture is the Renaissance high altar bearing the coat of arms of Charles of Lorraine and two Gothic confessionals. In the sacristy is an ivory hunting horn decorated with silver blades. It is carried in procession on the last Sunday in October and is said to have belonged to St Hubert himself. In fact, it dates from the 17C.

Main entrance from Klarastraat and Tervurendreef.

A French "Folly"

Olympe Mancini, Cardinal Mazarin's niece and the widow of Comte de Soissons, was a courtisan who was considered as one of the most beautiful women at the French Court. She moved to Brabant after being involved in the Voisin affair. An act signed in Madrid in March 1689 by King Charles II of Spain granted her the right to live in the ducal palace in Tervuren. She was a "merry widow" and is described in Saint-Simon's *Memoirs* as leading such a dissolute life, not to mention neglecting to pay the rental owing on the estate made available to her, that the Elector, Maximilian of Bavaria, had "Mademoiselle" shut away in a convent in 1698. She escaped and again lived life to the full in the ducal palace, refusing to change her attitude and ruining the building. She died in mysterious circumstances in 1708.

Parc domanial – Visitors approaching the park from the village enter by the *Warandepoort* built in 1897 for the Colonial Exhibition. To the right, opposite the former stud which has been turned into barracks, is **Chapelle St-Hubert** *(not open to the public)*, a red brick church designed by Cobergher in the Italianate-Flemish style. Riders, horses and hounds are blessed here on the day of the Hunting Horn Procession (*see above*). Near the chapel on the shores of the lake are the foundations of the former ducal palace. The park was extended to its present size between 1615 and 1635 and redesigned in the 19C with formal gardens set out in terraces opposite the Musée royal. Further on, between the lake known as the "Naval Battle" and the Etang de Vossem is the 17C Spanish House, which is in a very dilapidated condition. It is clearly visible because of its three crow-stepped gables. The central crossroads in the park is marked by three standing stones discovered in the nearby village of Duisburg. The north-west section of the park once contained the Prince of Orange's Hunting Lodge (built in 1817 and burnt down in 1879) that was superbly decorated by the famous sculptor François Rude whose reliefs adorn the Arc de Triomphe in Paris. In its place is the Palais des Colonies (1896) designed by an architect named Acker in the neo-Classical style. It faces Avenue de Tervuren and was used in 1897 for the very first Colonial Exhibition.

★★ **Musée royal de l'Afrique centrale (Koninklijk Museum voor Midden-Afrika)** ⊙ – *Car park on Leuvensesteenweg. Entrance beside the park.*

In 1897, King Leopold II, "sovereign founder of the Independant State of the Congo", organised a colonial exhibition in Tervuren *(see above)* as part of the World Fair being held in the Cinquantenaire. It was so successful that, the following year, the king set up a permanent museum which was also to serve as a scientific research centre. He commissioned the Frenchman Charles Girault (1851-1932), designer of the Petit Palais in Paris, to build the Musée du Congo as part of a larger complex including museums devoted to China and Japan, a World School and a conference centre. The project was never completed in its entirety.

Girault only succeeded in designing the central building, in the Louis XVI style, and the two side pavilions. The work began in 1904 and was totally funded by the income from Leopold II's private estate in the Congo. Work ceased in 1910 and the building was formally inaugurated by King Albert I.

Although the museum collections are a bit "dusty", they present a vast panoramic view of Africa and the storerooms contain some 250 000 items. The sculptures and other items are representative of various ethnic groups, particularly in Central Africa where pride of place is given to the ex-Belgian Congo (now Zaire) and West Africa. The museum also provides the resources for fundamental research into the African continent and has 13 specialist libraries containing in excess of 85 000 works.

Ask for a free plan of the museum at the ticket office and turn right from the foyer in the rotunda.

Room 2b – Arts and crafts of Central Africa presented on a tribal basis: Pygmies, Kongo, Tshokwe (Angola, hence the Portuguese influence), Zande and Mangbetu, Kuba (fabrics and masks), Ngbaka (Zaire), Kasai (masks), Luluwa, Kwango, Lega (initiation masks), Luba, Lengola (statues), Tabwa **(buffalo mask)**, and Songye (Zaire, **mask**).

Room 3 – *Closed.*

Room 4 – Sculpture. The exhibits in the display cabinets come mainly from the southern part of Central Africa where the designs are both varied and lavish (unlike the north where they are fewer in number, austere and geometric in design). Some of the sculptures have fluid shapes, especially the carvings of the **Luba** tribe (Zaire) which do not have the rigidity that is a usual characteristic of African art.

Room 7 – Developments in cartographic representation of the African continent and memorabilia relating to explorers such as Stanley, Livingstone etc. Extensive collection of crucifixes including some of specifically African shape (with people in prayer), and representations of the Europeans as seen by local artists.

Room 9 – Five dioramas (equatorial forest, mountainous forest, bamboo forest, heather forest, alpine level) explain the interrelation between the fauna, flora, and climate in the Ruwenzori, a mountainous region situated on the Equator.

Room 6 – *Closed.*

Room 5 – *Used for temporary exhibitions only.*

Room 10 – With more than 50 000 samples, of which only a few are on display, the museum has the second largest timber library in the world. Description of farming and forestry, and an indication of the various virtues of plants.

Room 8 – The Belgian presence, especially that of Leopold II, in Western, Central and Eastern Africa. The famous "anti-slave" campaign led in the Congo against the Arabs. The role of Stanley and Savorgnan de Brazza. The strange collection of mantelpieces inspired by symbolism or history bear witness to the influence of African art on the decorative arts in Belgium.

Room 11 – Naturalised mammals give a general view of the fauna in the savana and the equatorial forest.

Room 12 – Various families of naturalised birds including Congolese peacocks (Case 6), a very rare species.

Room 13 – Naturalised fish, reptiles and amphibians ie catfish, coelacanth, tilapia, python, cobra, adder, crocodile, tortoise, lizard, cameleon etc.

Room 16 – Mineralogy and geology. An instructive tour of the planet Earth, its situation within the solar system, its internal structure, its chemical composition and its physical properties. On the wall is an interesting painted map showing major explorations.

Room 14 – The largest collection in the world of Central African insects (cases 1-15), a region in which almost three-quarters of known animals are insects. Cases 16-25 contain invertebrates; cases 26-35 deal with the seasonal or sexual dimorphisms of insects. Cases 36-58 contains parasites and a selection of molluscs.

Room 17 – Prehistory and archeology. The evolution of life on Earth and a look at archeological techniques. Artefacts from the Stone Age to the Iron Age and recon-struction of a grave in the Shaba Region (Zaire). In the "Protohistory" display, note the superb bronzes from Nigeria and the Ivory Coast, especially the moulds of a royal head from Ifé (12C-13C) and a princess' head from Bénin (16C-17C).

Room 15 – Groups of naturalised animals from Central Africa including an elephant standing 3.4m – 11ft high at the shoulder.

Room 2a – Central African material culture in comparison with the cultures of Aus-tralasia and America (green cases). The dugout canoe of the Lengola tribe is 22.5m – 73ft long and can hold up to one hundred people.

In the vicinity – Punters may enjoy a trip to the Sterrebeek race track not far from the Musée royal de l'Afrique centrale *(Access: from the car park on Leuven-sesteenweg, take the Brussels direction and turn into the first road on the right (Grenstraat). Turn right again into Perkstraat then take the second on the right (Rue du Roy de Blicquylaan)*. The most interesting places in the immediate vicinity of Tervuren, however, are the Soignes Forest *(qv)* and the geographical arbore-tum.

★ **Arboretum géographique** ☉ – *Access from the town is fairly complicated. We therefore advise taking the Brussels direction along Tervurenlaan and turning left at the traffic lights into Vestenstraat. Turn right into Jezus Eiklaan which runs into the forest. At Carrefour Saint-Jean, the entrance to the arboretum is signposted.* This arboretum (100 hectares – 247 acres) was set up in 1902 in the Bois des Capucins. It is outstanding because it constitutes a botanical geography lesson with the trees planted according to their country of origin and not set out in systematic order according to species and varieties as is the case in traditional arboreta *(unfor-tunately, there are no explanatory signs)*.

The nursery, which has 460 ligneous species, is divided into two sections – the New and the Old Worlds. From Carrefour Saint-Jean, the royal path begins with the New World (gigantic trees such as Douglas firs, redwoods, tsugas, and pines, Southern pines, maples, ash, sweet chestnuts, walnut trees, tulip trees etc.). The Droge-Vijverdreef, which cuts across the Kapucijnendreef at right angles, marks the passage into the Old World section planted with larches, oaks, birches, Scots pines, Austrian pines, beeches, firs etc. The Asian section has an extensive collection of deciduous bushes and fairly rare conifers. The Japanese forest is represented by some sixty different species of tree.

"Waterloo! Waterloo! Waterloo! morne plaine!
Comme une onde qui bout dans une urne trop pleine,
Dans ton cirque de bois, de coteaux, de vallons,
La pâle mort mêlait les sombres bataillons..."

"*Waterloo! Waterloo! Waterloo! Desolate plain,*
Like a wave bubbling in an overfull urn,
In your circus of woodland, hills, and valleys,
Pale Death mixed the dark battalions..."

There can hardly be a Frenchman who does not know the first lines (from *Les Châti-ments*) that the ultra-famous Battle of Waterloo inspired in Victor Hugo – and he could scarcely be described as a Bonaparte supporter. It was on 18 June 1815 that the Anglo-Dutch allies under the command of Wellington and the Prussians led by Blücher finally put a stop to the Napoleonic epic.

The Duchess of Richmond's Ball

On 15 June 1815, the Duchess of Richmond gave a ball in Brussels and it has remained famous because it was during the evening that a letter arrived inform-ing the Commander-in-Chief of the Allied forces, the Duke of Wellington, that Napoleon was now only 14 miles from the capital. It is said that the ballroom emptied in a mere 20 minutes. Nobody knows exactly which of the private man-sions in the town hosted the ball.

"... Everything was joyous as a church bell pealing merrily after a wedding cere-mony. Then came silence! Listen! A sinister noise resounded, like the knell of the funeral bell! The fearsome sound can still be heard. It is as if the clouds were acting as echoes. It seems to be coming nearer and more distinct with each pass-ing minute. It is more and more terrifying. It is the brazen voice of battle begin-ning its clamour!... (Lord George Byron)

Preparations for Battle – When Napoleon returned to France after his exile on the Island of Elba and regained power during the period known as the One Hundred Days, it was hardly surprising that his former adversaries (Great Britain, Prussia, Russia and Austria) began to worry. France, on the other hand, was threatened with encirclement after the Treaty of Vienna that was signed on 25 March and danger seemed increasingly imminent, especially in the north where the Prussians and British had already begun to mass huge forces (to the south-east and in the centre of Belgium respectively).

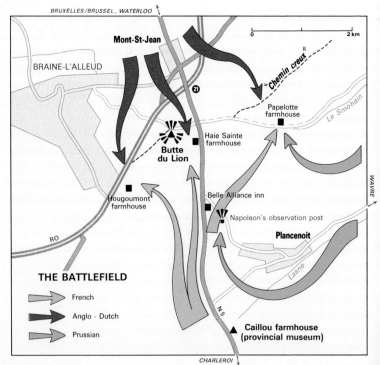

It was to dispel this threat that Napoleon rebuilt a vast army and, in an attempt to catch his enemies unawares, set off northwards to put his daring plan into effect. He would crush each opposing army separately. On 16 June, in Ligny to the north-east of Charleroi, the Emperor won what was to be his last victory, over Blücher's forces. Meanwhile, Maréchal Ney was advancing on Brussels where the British forces were concentrated. Then Napoleon ordered Maréchal Grouchy to pursue the Prussian army in its apparent retreat northwards. He, in turn, took control of Brussels while Ney tried unsuccessfully to defeat the British at Quatre-Bras. On 17 June, Napoleon pursued Wellington's troops and, at nightfall, reached the **Caillou** Farm. Wellington set up his headquarters in the village of **Waterloo**, while his troops dug in near Mont-Saint-Jean. Napoleon decided to attack the following morning.

The Strength of the Armies – The Anglo-Dutch army under the command of the Duke of Wellington (British and Dutch troops with contingents from Brunswick, Hanover and Nassau) included 99 000 men and 222 cannon. The Prussian army under Field-Marshal Prince Blücher von Wahlstatt had 117 000 men and 312 guns. The French forces consisted of 112 000 men and 366 cannon.

The Battle – On 18 June, battle did not commence until nearly noon, since bad weather on the previous day had delayed the arrival of some of the French troops. The first French guns were set up near the **Belle Alliance** coaching inn; the hostelry was also Napoleon's observation post. The Goumont Farm, better-known as **Hougoumont**, was the scene of particularly bloody fighting between the British and French, and it was to last until nightfall. The French then attacked the farms at La **Papelotte** and L**Haie-Sainte**. The second of the farms was under the control of the German legion with reinforcements of companies from Nassau. The fearsome counter-attack by the Britcavalry was repulsed but the action forced the enemy back. After repeated assaults the loss and recapture of certain positions, the French entered the famous "**sunken p**at about 4pm under a blazing sun. Here, the furious cavalry charges led by Ney Kellerman foundered.

Napoleon was waiting for reinforcements in the form of 30 000 men under the mand of Grouchy who were supposed to be arriving from Wavre to the east. Blücher, however, having regrouped his troops and avoided Grouchy, skirted the right flank of the French troops and met up with the British forces. The first waves of Prussian troops then captured **Plancenoit**.

By 7.30pm hours, Napoleon was surrounded and he sent the Old Guard out to face the British troops. The Frenchmen were massacred as they passed along the sunken path. By nightfall, the battlefield was carpeted with 49 000 dead and dying men and Napoleon's troops withdrew, routed despite Ney's heroic efforts. During the night, Napoleon disappeared in the direction of Genappe.

THE BATTLEFIELD

As soon as Napoleon had abdicated and been exiled to the Island of Saint Helena, British tourists began flocking to the continent and Waterloo became particularly popular. Lord George Byron the poet (the third song in his famous *Childe Harold* describes the battle), was, like the writers Robert Southey and Sir Walter Scott, one of the many tourists. Yet, despite the interest shown by the British and the victory won by the Allies, a visit to the battlefield also gives some idea of the sheer scope and tenacity of people's love and admiration for the Emperor.

In 1861, Victor Hugo came to stay at the Hôtel des Colonnes in Mont-Saint-Jean (the hotel no longer exists). While there, he wrote the chapter in *Les Misérables* describing the battle; it had already featured in the opening pages of Stendhal's *The Charterhouse of Parma* (1839).

Although the battlefield has changed tremendously since 1815 (it is now crossed by a motorway and main road), it is still dotted with historic buildings and memorials. Every five years, there is a historical re-enactment of the battle in which more than 2 000 people take part.

This is a very busy tourist venue but it has retained an old-fashioned atmosphere that is rather attractive thanks to the Lion Mound and Panorama.

La Butte du Lion ⊙ – *Not recommended for people suffering from heart problems.* The Lion Mound is 40.5m – 132ft high and was built in 1826 by the Netherlands on the spot where the Prince of Orange was wounded while fighting the Old Guard. The Mound is topped by an iron statue of a lion (4.45m – 14ft) weighing 28 tonnes. The plaster mould was created by Van Geel and the iron statue cast in Liege by Cockerill. Legend has it that the sculpture was cast using gunmetal picked up on the battlefield but this is totally incorrect.

From the summit, there is a good overall view of the site. At the foot of the mound on the south side is the famous sunken path, although it is now almost on a level with the remainder of the field since the surrounding area provided the earth used to build the Mound.

The Lion Mound

Centre du Visiteur ⊙ – The Visitors' Centre stands at the foot of the Lion Mound. Its audio-visual presentation carries the audience right into the heart of the events that occurred on 18 June 1815. A model (10sq m – 108 sq ft) with synchronised lighting and commentary picks out the most strategic spots on the battlefield and illustrates the major phases in the actual combat. The second part consists of a fairly pleasant film without much educational value.

Panorama de la Bataille ⊙ – At the foot of the mound is a circular building erected in 1912. It contains a canvas 110m – 358ft in circumference and 12m – 39ft high painted in 1913-1914 by Louis Dumoulin, a French naval artist, working with five other painters.

This panoramic work depicts a few of the most salient moments in the battle just as Ney sent the cavalry along the sunken path. Taking as the main marker the Emperor seated on his white horse in the background behind General Guyot's mounted grenadiers the work shows *(right to left)* the light cavalry and the farm at La Haie-Sainte, the fighting on the sunken path, the resistance put up by the troops from Nassau and the German legion, the Prince of Orange and the Duke of Wellington, the British infantry in square formation under attack from Ney, the cavalry charge by General Donop's troops (he is lying on the ground, wounded), the Hougoumont Farm in flames in the background with the Empress's dragoons in the foreground, and Ney (hatless) engaging the brigade of cuirassiers, followed by his staff.

On the ground floor is a permanent exhibition of uniforms, weaponry and documents.

Musée de Cires ⊙ – Near the Mound, almost opposite the Panorama, is a small somewhat old-fashioned waxworks museum containing an illustration of Napoleon's last council-of-war with his staff in Le Caillou Farm. There are also waxworks of the three commanders of the allied forces who took part in the battle – the Prince of Orange (1792-1849), the Duke of Wellington (1769-1852), and Blücher (1742-1819). The costumes are not originals *(see Musée royal de l'Armée et de l'Histoire militaire in the Cinquantenaire).*

Take the N5 Charleroi road to the Musée provincial du Caillou 4km – 2 miles away.

The Belgians' Monument at the crossroads is an indirect reminder of the strange situation of the "future Belgians". Although they had been a Dutch dependency since 1814, many of them chose to fight in the French ranks.

The next memorial is to Lieutenant-General Gordon, Wellington's aide-de-camp; the one beyond it commemorates the Hanoverian troops. On the right is La Haie-Sainte Farm. Further away on the left is a fairly rough-hewn column erected in memory of Victor Hugo. On the right is a sculpture by Gérôme called *The Wounded Eagle.*

Musée provincial du Caillou ⊙ – Le Caillou Farm, now the provincial museum, stood on the southern edge of the battlefield and was Napoleon's headquarters on the eve of the battle. He spent the night of June 17-18 with Prince Jérôme, Marshals Ney, Soult and Bertrand and his famous mameluke, Ali.

The Emperor's bedchamber still contains one of his camp beds (on loan from the Musée de l'Armée in Paris) and a few pieces of memorabilia (marble bust by Chaudet, a seal, and a Napoleonic Code dating from 1807). The other rooms contain works on the 1815 campaign by various French generals, along with maps, a bronze funeral mask of the Emperor on St Helena, and relics from the battlefield (including the skeleton of a hussar discovered on the site of the "last stand"). In the garden, there is an **ossuary** (1912) built up as a result of successive archaeological digs and bearing the Latin inscription "Often for the Emperor, always for the Country". The presence of the balconies from the Hôtel des Colonnes in Mont-Saint-Jean where Victor Hugo stayed in 1861 adds to the feeling of general veneration for this erstwhile French leader. The orchard includes a monument reminding those who look at it of the final evening spent by the Imperial Guard before the battle.

Continue on the N5 to Waterloo (9 km – 6 miles).

THE TOWN

From the 15C to the mid 17C, a hamlet gradually grew up along the Genappe-Brussels road. Waterloo was a staging post but was not marked on maps until the end of the 17C. It has been world-famous since the resounding victory won here by the allies and a multitude of similarly-named places can now be found across the globe, including more than forty in the United States alone.

Musée Wellington ⊙ – *147 Chaussée de Bruxelles (N5)*. The inn (built 1705, restored 1975) where Wellington set up his headquarters has been turned into a museum with three sections – the Duke's HQ, a section depicting the history of Waterloo, and a library *(if you wish to consult the books, please see the receptionist)*.

A succession of small rooms containing paintings, engravings, documents, weapons and memorabilia illustrates the political situation in the Europe of 1815 and the character of Arthur Wellesley, Duke of Wellington, Prince of Waterloo. Among the items on display, note the 18C handrail, the bedroom where Lieutenant-Colonel Alexander Gordon, Wellington's aide-de-camp, died on the night of 18 June, and the British pioneer's sabre with the rear edge shaped like a saw. The Duke of Wellington's bedroom suite is in the corridor and includes his campaign table and a number of personal effects (a Sèvres dinner service given to him by Louis XVIII, and a Meissen dinner service given to him by Frederick-Augustus of Saxony). There is also a painting of the Prince of Orange after he had been wounded (Dutch Room), a fine **engraving** depicting the meeting of Wellington and Blücher (Prussian Room), and an astonishing drawing of the French cavalry by James Thiriar (French Room). Finally, across the tiny garden containing the gravestones of three British officers, is the well-lit maps and charts room which retraces the various stages in the battle. The room also contains items of outstanding historic interest relating to the battle such as *"La Suffisante"*, a gun cast in Douai (1813) and captured at Waterloo, and other objects with rather more curiosity value such as the Duke's umbrella-sword.

Église Saint-Joseph ⊙ – Originally, the church opposite the museum was no more than a chapel in the forest. It is a delightful building that has withstood the passage of time and now marks the entrance to the new church containing a large number of tombstones in memory of the officers and soldiers who fell at Waterloo.

The chapel was built to a central layout (1685-1691) at the request of the Marquis de Castaffaga, Governor and representative of King Charles II of Spain, in the hope of seeing an heir to the throne born one day (see the inscription on the pediment above the peristyle). The dome is lit by six bulls' eye windows and a lantern turret. Two low reliefs decorate fake portals. The bronze door (Wiener) symbolises Victory holding a laurel branch in her right hand and a crown in her left; the other white marble entrance (Geefs) represents the coat of arms of Great Britain and is a memorial to British officers. Just in front of it is a bust of Wellington by C Adams (1855).

ZAVENTEM

This village to the east of Brussels *(take Chaussée de Louvain then turn left)* is best-known for its airport. It was opened in 1958 and has recently been extended, making it the largest airport in Belgium.

The parish church stands on the village square.

Église Saint-Martin – This Gothic-style church, which is thought to date back to the Romanesque period, has been extended on several occasions (16C, 17C, 19C). It has a nave (1602-1646) divided into three sections, a square tower, a transept and a chancel (1567). The church contains an interesting painting by Sir Anthony van Dyck, *Saint-Martin partageant son manteau*. Tradition has it that Van Dyck stayed in Zaventem in 1624 and fell in love with a young woman while he was there. The figure of St Martin is said to be a self-portrait of the artist.

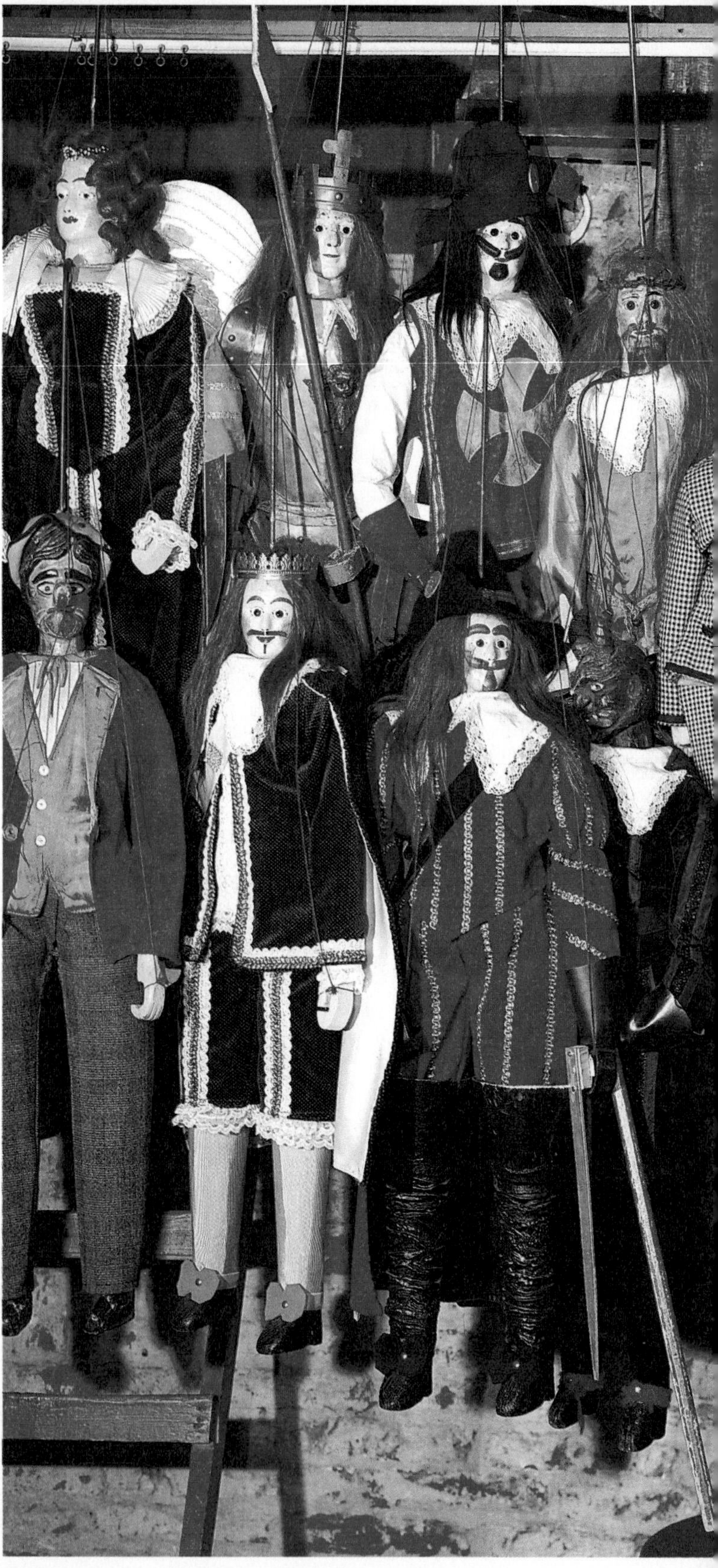

Théâtre royal de Toone, traditional marionettes

Practical
Information

Before You Leave

In order to organise your journey, collect the necessary literature or check out certain information, begin by contacting the nearest Belgian Tourist Office, Embassy or Consulate to your home.

BELGIAN TOURIST OFFICES:

Belgian Tourist Office
21 Princes Street
London W1R 7RG - United Kingdom
☎ 0171 629 19 88
Fax 0171 629 04 54

Belgian Tourist Office
780 Third Avenue Suite
New York NY 10017 - USA
☎ 212 758 81 30
Fax 212 355 76 75

SABENA AIRLINE OFFICES:

London
Sabena Ticket Office, Leicester Square
☎ 0171 494 26 29

Toronto
Swissair, 2 Bloor Street, West Suite 502
☎ 416 960 42 70

New York
Sabena Swiss Center, 608 Fifth Avenue, New York 10020 - ☎ 212 247 83 90

ADMINISTRATIVE FORMALITIES

Personal identity – All persons wishing to enter Belgium should hold a valid passport.

Health care – In case of accident or illness, visitors from European Union countries can claim free health care on presentation of an E111 form.

Drivers – Drivers of motor vehicles should be in possession of a valid driving licence.

Car papers – Please ensure that you carry your car log book and international insurance certificate with you.

TRAVELLING TO BRUSSELS

By air – Most airlines fly to Bruxelles-National Airport in Zaventem. Ask your travel agent about current terms and conditions including charter and low-cost flights.
Sabena, Bruxelles-National Airport, 1930 Zaventem. Bookings, ☎ 723 23 23. Departure times, ☎ 723 23 45. Luggage queries, ☎ 723 60 11.
Taxis and trains provide a service between the airport and the city centre. The Airport City Express stops at three stations – Bruxelles-Nord, Bruxelles-Centrale and Bruxelles-Midi.

By rail – Thanks to the **Eurostar** service, it takes only three-and-a-half hours to travel from London-Waterloo to Bruxelles-Midi.
There are six trains a day from Monday to Saturday, and five on Sundays.

By boat – There are numerous ferry links between England and Belgium ie Ramsgate-Ostend, Dover-Zeebrugge, Felixstowe-Zeebrugge, and Kingston-upon-Hull-Zeebrugge. To find out more about times and prices, contact your local travel agent.

By car – "Le shuttle" links Calais and Folkestone in just 35 minutes, The number of departures depends on the volume of traffic (there are two to four services every hour during the day and one every hour during the night).

Michelin maps – There is a Michelin map of Great Britain and Ireland (No. 986).

In Brussels, as in any large city, driving is not easy, especially during the rush hours, but the underpasses along the inner ring road *(Petite Ceinture)* make life a lot easier for drivers wishing to travel from one side of the city to the other or visit the towns and villages on the outskirts of the city. Tourists visiting the city centre should leave their car in one of the many car parks and continue on foot. This is the best way to see the sights in any town. Make sure you have 5 or 20 Belgian franc coins for the parking meters. Parking is often limited to a maximum of one or two hours.

TOURIST INFORMATION IN THE CITY

T.I.B. (Office de Tourisme et d'Information de Bruxelles), City Hall, Grand-Place, 1000 Brussels. ☎ 513 89 40. Fax 514 45 38. Every year the Tourist Office publishes a practical guide to Brussels called *"Bruxelles Guide and Map"*. The T.I.B. also provides a wide range of tourist products including a hotel and restaurant guide, a "Visit Brussels" pass that gives the holder numerous reductions and includes a one-day travel pass for use on public transport, a calendar of special events etc.

Maison du Tourisme (Belgian Tourist Office), 61 Rue du Marché-aux-Herbes, 1000 Brussels. ☎ 504 03 90. Fax 504 02 70. This office also provides visitors with literature about Brussels.

Accommodation

Michelin Red Guide to Benelux – This guide is updated every year and recommends a wide choice of hotels which have been visited and rated. For each hotel mentioned, the guide book indicates the amenities offered, the prices for the current year, the credit cards accepted and the telephone and fax numbers.

Bookings – You can book a room through the **T.I.B.** (Office de Tourisme et d'Information de Bruxelles), Grand-Place, 1000 Brussels. ☎ 513 89 40, Fax 514 45 38. The Tourist Office publishes its own hotel guide every year. The **Maison du Tourisme**, 61 Rue du Marché-aux-Herbes, 1000 Brussels, ☎ 504 03 90, Fax 504 02 70 and the **BTR** (Belgian Tourist Reservations), 111 Boulevard Anspach, 1000 Brussels, ☎ 513 74 84, Fax 513 92 77, also provide a hotel booking service.

Youth Hostels – There are three youth hostels in Brussels:
– Auberge de Jeunesse Jacques Brel, 30 Rue de la Sablonnière, 1000 Brussels, ☎ 218 01 87.
– Auberge de Jeunesse de la Fonderie Jean Nihon, 4 Rue de l'Eléphant, 1080 Brussels, ☎ 410 38 58.
– Jeugdherberg Bruegel IYHF, Heilige Geeststraat 2, 1000 Brussels, ☎ 511 04 36.

Accommodation for Young People – These places provide moderately-priced rooms.
– Sleepwell – Auberge du Marais, 23 Rue du Damier, 1000 Brussels, ☎ 218 50 50.
– Centre d'Hébergement de l'Agglomération de Bruxelles (C.H.A.B.), 8 Rue Traversière, 1030 Brussels, ☎ 217 01 58.
– Espace International, 205 Chaussée de Wavre, 1050 Brussels, ☎ 644 16 81.

Campsites – There are a number of campsites within a reasonable distance of Brussels city centre.
– Beersel, 75 Steenweg op Ukkel, 1650 Beersel, ☎ 331 05 61.
– Camp Paul Charles, 114 Avenue Albert Ier, 1332 Genval, ☎ 653 62 15.
– Camping de Renipont, 7a Route du Ry Beau Ry, 1380 Ohain, ☎ 654 06 70.
– Druivenland Leon Kumps, 80 Nijvelsebaan, 3090 Overijse, ☎ 687 93 68.
– Holiday Parks, 4 Park, 3040 Huldenberg, ☎ 687 34 16.
– La Cala, 17a Rue Cala, 1473 Glabais, ☎ 242 22 51.
– Paul Rosmant, 52 Warandeberg, 1970 Wezembeek-Oppem, ☎ 782 10 09.
– Provinciaal Domein, 6 Provinciaal Domein, 1654 Huizingen, ☎ 380 14 93.
– Spitsberg, 21 Spitsbergstraat, 3040 Huldenberg, ☎ 687 79 87.
– Veldkant, 64 Veldkantstraat, 1850 Grinbergen, ☎ 269 25 97.
– Welcome, 104 Kouterstraat, 3090 Overijse, ☎ 687 75 77.

Bed & Breakfast – Bed and breakfast accommodation is very reasonably-priced. For the B&B brochure, contact **Taxistop**, 28/1 Rue Fossé aux Loups, 1000 Brussels, ☎ 223 23 10, Fax 223 22 32 or the **T.I.B.**, Grand-Place, 1000 Brussels, ☎ 513 89 40, Fax 514 45 38.

Books to read

Art Deco, A Duncan *(Thames and Hudson)*
Civilisation (History/Flemish Primitives), K Clark *(Penguin)*
Medieval Flanders, D Nicholas *(Longman)*
Pieter Paul Rubens: Man and Artist, C White *(Yale University Press)*
Through the Dutch and Belgian Canals, P Bristow *(A & C Black)*
Niccolò Rising (fiction), D Dunnett *(Penguin)*
The Sorrow of Belgium (fiction) H Claus *(Penguin)*
Blue Guide Belgium and Luxembourg, J Tomes *(A & C Black)*
Access to the Channel Ports (Guide for the Disabled), available from Access Project, Pauline Hephaistos Survey Projects, 39 Bradley Gardens London W13 8HE
The 19C in Belgium - Architecture and Interior Design, Jos Vandenbreeden and Françoise Dierkens-Aubry *(Iannoo)*
Art-Nouveau in Belgium - Architecture and Interiors, Jos Vandenbreeden and Françoise Dierkens-Aubry *(Iannoo)*
Contemporary Architecture in Belgium, Geert Bekaert *(Iannoo)*
Politics of Belgium, John Fitzmaurice *(Hurst)*
From Revolt to Independance: The Netherlands 1550-1650, Martyn Rady *(Hodder & Soughton 1990)*.
The Dutch Revolt, Geofrey Parker *(Penguin 1977 and 1985)*
Spain and the Netherlands (1559-1659) (10 historical studies), Geoffrey Parker *(Fontana 1979)*.

Food and Drink

The people of Brussels enjoy their food. So much so, in fact, that their nickname is "*keekefretter*", which means "chicken eater". The area has many different specialities *(see also Introduction, Living in Brussels)* eg *stoemp* (hotpot), *choesels* (ox or veal offal), *bloedpans* (black pudding made with diced bacon and blood), rabbit cooked in beer, Brussel sprouts, chicory, *smoutebollen* (doughnuts), Greekstyle bread etc.

Two Traditional Recipes

Kassuul mossele, the well-known pan-cooked mussels – Chop a small stick of celery and an onion. Place in a saucepan with a good-sized knob of butter. Cover and cook for about ten minutes without allowing the vegetables to brown. Add one litre of cleaned mussels (change the water several times when washing them). Salt

A. Lorgnier/VISA

lightly, add a pinch of ground pepper and the juice of half a lemon. Cover and cook for about ten minutes. When all the mussels have opened, place in a large salad bowl, add some chopped parsley to the cooking stock and pour over the mussels. Serve with a plate of chips.

Brussels Waffles – Put 250 g flour in a mixing bowl with a spoonful of sugar, a large pinch of vanilla powder, a small pinch of salt, and eight egg yolks. Mix all the ingredients together then blend in half-a-litre of sweetened cream or fresh milk. Melt 250 g butter in a small pan. Whip the eight egg whites until very stiff. Add the melted butter to the mixture, followed by the whipped egg whites. Lightly grease a waffle iron and heat. Fill one side with a good spoonful of waffle mix, close the iron and cook the waffle until golden. To serve, dust generously with icing sugar.

A. Lorgnier/VISA

Brussels waffles

Beer

Lambic is a traditional drink in the Brussels area. It is made with a blend of wheat (30 to 35%) and malted barley. Hops are added to the must produced by this mixture and it is then cooked before being cooled in an open tank in the loft of the brewery. This open-air stage in the production process is designed to encourage the development of a natural micro-organism that is only found in the Senne Valley. Like other regional beers, *lambic* is unusual in that it ferments spontaneously and does not contain any yeast. The beer is then matured in kegs known as "*foudres*". It does not froth and has an alcohol content of approximately 5%. At the end of July or beginning of August, the breweries turn some of the *lambic* into **kriek** and **framboise** by adding local cherries and raspberries to it.

Gueuze is produced by blending several lambics from different years, thereby producing a second fermentation process as a result of the sugar content in the youngest *lambic*. The natural champagne-type process obtained by this method makes the beer slightly more frothy but retains the characteristic sharp taste.

A. Kouprianoff/EUREKA SLIDE

Calendar of Events

FESTIVALS

January
International Brussels Film Festival   Palais des Congrès

End of May - Beginning of June
Jazzin Brussels ....   Various locations in the city

July
**Klinkende Munt
(summer concerts)** ....   Place de la Monnaie and Beursschouwburg, Rue Orts
**Brosella Folk & Jazz
(2nd weekend)** ....   Théâtre de Verdure (open-air theatre), Heysel
**Les dimanches
du Bois de la Cambre** ....   Bois de la Cambre, Ixelles

August
**Boterhammen in het park
(summer concerts)** ....   Parc de Bruxelles

November
Jazz Festival ....   Various locations in the city

FAIRS AND EXHIBITIONS

January
Antiques Fair ....   Palais des Beaux-Arts
**Motor Exhibition
(even-numbered years)** ....   Parc des Expositions (Exhibition Centre), Heysel

March
Eurantica (Antiques) ....   Parc des Expositions (Exhibition Centre), Heysel
**Foire internationale du livre
(International Book Fair)** ....   Parc des Expositions (Exhibition Centre), Heysel
**Salon des Vacances, du Tourisme
et des Loisirs (Holiday, Tourism
and Leisure Exhibition)** ....   Parc des Expositions (Exhibition Centre), Heysel

December
**Cocoon (international interior
design exhibition)** ....   Parc des Expositions (Exhibition Centre), Heysel

Hudders/EUREKA SLIDE

The "Ommegang" Procession

SPORTS EVENTS AND COMPETITIONS

June

20 km de Bruxelles
12-mile race,............................ Parc du Cinquantenaire

August

Mémorial Ivo Van Damme
(end of month)......................... Ivo Van Damme Memorial, Stade Roi Baudouin, Heysel

September

Brussels marathon

SPECIAL EVENTS

July

Ciné Drive-In .... Esplanade du Cinquantenaire
Ommegang .... Historical pageant, Grand-Place
Concerts.................................. Grand-Place

Mid-July / Mid-August

Kermesse de Bruxelles .... Brussels Fête, Quartier du Midi

21st July

Military parade .... Place des Palais
Fireworks display .... Parc de Bruxelles

August

Planting of the "May Tree" .... City Centre
Ciné Drive-In .... Esplanade du Cinquantenaire
Concerts.................................. Grand-Place
Carpet of Flowers
(even-numbered years)............... Grand-Place

December

Christmas crib, Christmas market,
Christmas tree......................... Grand-Place

The Ommegang Procession

In days gone by, every major town in Flanders or Wallonia celebrated the anniversary of its founding by a procession symbolising its splendour, morals and enthusiasm. The civilian, religious and military authorities all did their utmost to outdo their rivals at the *Ommegang*, literally "doing the rounds". Although its origins were religious (a statue of the Virign Mary was carried in triumph), the austere procession which began in the 13C quickly gained a more secular character. Over the years, it became the main event in the capital of Brabant, as famous for its extravagance and strangeness as it was for the magnificence encouraged by the sovereigns. The custom enjoyed its heyday in the 16C and it was attented by Emperor Charles V in 1549. It was revived in 1930 and the procession of guilds and local magistrates is now held on an annual basis *(see Calendar of Events)*. The Albert and Isabel bedcover *(see Cinquantenaire, Musées royaux d'Art et d'Histoire, room 106)* is decorated with a series of scenes illustrating the celebrations.

Admission times and charges

Because of increases in the cost of living and the constant changes in the opening times of most of the places to visit, the information given below is intended only as a guideline.

The information applies to tourists travelling on their own and not entitled to any reductions. For parties, it is usually possible to obtain special rates and different opening times by prior arrangement.

Churches are not open to visitors during services. They are usually closed between noon and 1400. Admission times and/or charges are indicated if the interior is of particular interest.

Prices are given in Belgian francs.

In the descriptive section of the guide book, places to visit that are subject to specific admission times and charges are marked with the following symbol ⊙.

A

ANDERLECHT

Collégiale des Saints-Pierre-et-Guidon – Collegiate church, open weekdays 0900 to 1200 and 1430 to 1800 (1700 in winter). ☎ 521 84 15

Maison d'Érasme – Erasmus' House, open daily (except Tuesdays and Fridays) 1000 to 1200 and 1400 to 1700. Closed New Year's Day and Christmas Day. Admission: 50 F. ☎ 521 13 83.

Musée de la Gueuze – Beer Museum, open weekdays 0830 to 1630 and Saturdays 1000 to 1700 (1000 to 1300 early June to mid-October). Closed Sundays and public holidays. Admission: 70 F (including free drink). ☎ 521 49 28.

AUDERGHEM

Centre d'Information de la Forêt de Soignes – Soignes Forest Centre, open daily (except Mondays) 1400 to 1700 November to April and 1400 to 1800 during the remainder of the year. Closed Mondays, public holidays and during the week between Christmas and New Year. ☎ 629 34 11 or 660 64 17.

B

BEERSEL

Fortress – Open daily (except Mondays) 1000 to 1800 from beginning of March to mid-November and 1000 to 1800 during weekends February to December. Guided tours available – contact Mr. Cornelis, ☎ 331 00 24. Closed Mondays and throughout January. Admission: 100 F (Children: 40 F). ☎ 735 09 65.

BRUSSELS   🖪 Grand-Place – 1000 – ☎ (02) 513 89 40 – Fax (02) 514 45 38

Appartements de Charles de Lorraine – Towards the end of 1996, a new museum will open. Contact Bibliothèque Royale Albert Ier, Boulevard de l'Empereur 4, 1000 Brussels. ☎ 519 53 71.

Autoworld – Open daily 1000 to 1800 from beginning of April to end of September and 1000 to 1700 during the remainder of the year. Closed on New Year's Day and Christmas Day. Admission: 150 F (Children: 80 F). ☎ 736 41 65.

Bibliothèque Royale Albert Ier – Royal library. Guided tours only (2h) by prior arrangement with the Educational service, ☎ 519 53 57 or 519 53 71. Closed Sundays, also the last week of August, public holidays, November 2 and 15, and Boxing Day.

Le Botanique – Botanical gardens, open daily 1000 to 2200. During temporary exhibitions, open daily (except Mondays) 1100 to 1800. ☎ 226 12 11.

Cathédrale des Saints-Michel-et-Gudule – Cathedral church, open daily 0700 to 1900 (0730 on Saturdays and 0800 on Sundays) April to end of October. Closing time 1800 November to end of March. Guided tour by prior arrangement with Animation Chrétienne en Tourisme, Rue du Bois Sauvage 13, 1000 Brussels. ☎ 219 75 30 or 217 83 45. No admission charge for cathedral, 40 F for entry to crypt.

Centre belge de la Bande dessinée – Comic strip centre, open daily (except Mondays) 1000 to 1800. Closed Mondays, New Year's Day and Christmas Day. Admission: 180 F (Children under 12: 60 F). ☎ 219 19 80.

Chapelle de l'Hospice Pachéco – Chapel. Guided tours only, Mondays to Thursdays 1400 to 1600 by prior arrangement with Mr. Luc Witpas, 7 Rue du Grand Hospice, 1000 Bruxelles. ☎ 226 42 11.

Chapelle de la Madeleine – Chapel, open 0700 to 1930 Mondays to Fridays, 0900 to 2000 Saturdays and 0700 to 1200 and 1700 to 2000 Sundays. ☎ 511 28 45.

Église Notre-Dame-de-Bon-Secours – Church, open daily (except Sundays) 1000 to 1800. For information, contact Animation Chrétienne en Tourisme. ☎ 219 75 30.

Centre de la Bande Dessinée - Entrance hall

Église Notre-Dame-de-la-Chapelle – Church, open daily 1000 to 1700 June to October and 1300 to 1600 November to May. ☎ 229 17 44.

Église Notre-Dame-du-Sablon – Church, open daily 0900 to 1800. ☎ 511 57 41.

Église Sainte-Marie – Closed for repair.

Église Saint-Jacques-sur-Coudenberg – Church, open Tuesdays to Saturdays 1000 to 1800, Mondays 1500 to 1800. ☎ 511 78 36.

Église Saint-Jean-Baptiste-au-Béguinage – Church, open 1000 to 1700 Tuesdays, 0900 to 1700 Wednesdays to Fridays, and 1000 to 1700 on 1st, 3rd and 5th Saturdays of the month. On Sundays, the church is only open during services (1000 to 1100 and at 2000). ☎ 217 87 42.

Église Saint-Nicolas – Open daily 0800 to 1800. ☎ 511 27 15.

Église Saints-Jean-et-Étienne-aux-Minimes – Open daily 1000 to 1300. ☎ 511 93 84.

Grand-Place – Personal stereo hire at Tourist Office (T.I.B.), City Hall, Grand-Place, daily 0900 to 1800 without a break (except Sundays during winter, 1000 to 1400). ☎ 513 89 40.

Halles de Schaerbeek – Covered market. Closed for repair.

Historium – Open daily 1000 to 1800. Closed New Year's Day, July 21, and Christmas Day. Admission: 190 F. ☎ 217 60 23.

Hôtel de Ville – Town Hall. Guided tour only (in French). No advance booking required. Open 1045 to 1430 on Tuesdays, 1430 on Wednesdays, and 1045 on Sundays and public holidays (by appointment only on Thursdays and Fridays) from beginning of April to end of September. Same opening times (closed Sundays and public holidays) from beginning of October to end of March. Closed New Year's Day, November 1 and 11, and Christmas Day. Admission: 80 F. Tour starts at reception desk of City Hall. ☎ T.I.B. 513 89 40 or joint educational service for the city's museums, ☎ 279 43 55.

Maison de la Bellone – Mansion, open Tuesdays to Fridays, 1000 to 1800. Closed Sundays, Mondays, public holidays and month of July. ☎ 513 33 33.

Maison Cauchie – Mansion, open on 1st weekend in the month, 1100 to 1800. Closed at Christmas and New Year. Admission: 100 F. ☎ 673 15 06.

Musée d'Art ancien – Ancient Art Museum, open daily (except Mondays) 1000 to 1200 and 1300 to 1700. Closed Mondays, also New Year's Day, May 1, November 1 and 11, and Christmas Day. No admission charge. ☎ 508 32 11.

Carpet of flowers on Grand-Place

Musée d'Art moderne – Modern Art Museum, open daily (except Mondays) 1000 to 1300 and 1400 to 1700. Closed Mondays, also New Year's Day, May 1, November 1 and 11, and Christmas Day. No admission charge. ☎ 508 32 11.

Musée de la Brasserie – Brewery Museum, open daily 1000 to 1700 (including weekends). Closed at Christmas and New Year. Admission: 100 F. ☎ 511 49 87.

Musée Bruxella 1238 – Guided tour only, Wednesdays 1015, 1115, 1345, 1430, and 1515. City Hall, Grand-Place. Admission: 80 F. Joint educational service for the city's museums, ☎ 279 43 55.

Musée du Centre Public d'Aide Sociale (CPAS) – Social Work Museum, open Wednesdays 1330 to 1630. ☎ 535 30 28.

Musée Charlier – Museum open Mondays, Wednesdays and Thursdays 1330 to 1700, Fridays 1400 to 1630 and Tuesdays 1230 to 1700. ☎ 218 53 82.

Musée du Cinéma – Film Museum, open daily 1730 to 2230. Admission: 50 F. ☎ 507 83 70.

Musée du Costume et de la Dentelle – Costume and Lace Museum, open daily (except Wednesdays) 1000 to 1230 and 1330 to 1700 (1600 from beginning of October to end of March) and 1400 to 1700 on Saturdays, Sundays and public holidays. Closed on Wednesdays, also New Year, May 1, November 1 and 11, and Christmas Day. Admission: 80 F (Children : 50 F). ☎ 512 77 09.

Musée de la Dynastie – Royal Family Museum, open daily (except Mondays) Tuesdays to Sundays 1000 to 1600. Closed Mondays, January 1 to 3, May 1, July 21, November 1 and 11, December 24 to 26. ☎ 511 55 78.

Musée de l'Imprimerie – Printing Museum, open daily (except Sundays) 0900 to 1930 (1700 on Saturdays). Guided tours (75 minutes) available by prior arrangement (☎ 519 53 56). Same closure dates as Bibliothèque Albert Iᵉʳ. No admission charge. ☎ 519 53 56.

Musée Instrumental – Museum of Musical Instruments. Open 0930 (1000 on Saturdays) to 1645 Tuesdays to Saturdays. Closed Sundays and Mondays, also January 1, May 1, November 1 and 11, and Christmas Day. No admission charge. ☎ 511 35 95.

Musée du Livre – Book Museum, open 1400 to 1700 Mondays, Wednesdays and Saturdays. Guided tours (1 hour) available by prior arrangement. Same closure dates as Bibliothèque Albert Iᵉʳ. No admission charge. ☎ 519 53 57.

Musée des Postes et des Télécommunications – Postal and Telecom Museum, open 1000 to 1600, Tuesdays to Saturdays. Also open Sundays and public holidays 1000 to 1230. Closed Mondays, also New Year's Day and Christmas Day. ☎ 511 77 40.

Musée royal de l'Armée et d'Histoire militaire – Royal Army Museum, open daily (except Mondays) 0900 to 1200 and 1300 to 1630. Closed Mondays, also New Year's Day, May 1, November 1 and Christmas Day. ☎ 734 52 52.

Musées royaux d'Art et d'Histoire – Royal Museum of Art and History, open 0930 to 1700 Tuesdays to Fridays and 1000 to 1700 weekends and public holidays. Closed Mondays, also New Year's Day, May 1, November 1 and 11, and Christmas Day. Admission: 150 F. ☎ 741 72 11.

Muséum des Sciences naturelles – Science Museum, open 0930 to 1645 Tuesdays to Saturdays, and 0930 to 1800 Sundays. Closed Mondays, also New Year's Day and Christmas Day. Admission: 120 F (Children: 90 F). ☎ 627 42 38.

Musée de la ville de Bruxelles – City Museum, open 1000 to 1230 and 1330 to 1700 (1600 from beginning of October to end of March) Mondays to Thursdays, 1000 to 1300 Saturdays, Sundays and public holidays. Closed Fridays, also New Year's Day, May 1, November 1 and 11, and Christmas Day. Admission: 80 F (Children: 50 F). ☎ 279 43 55.

Musée Wiertz – Wiertz Museum, open 1000 to 1200 and 1300 to 1700, Tuesdays to Fridays and every second weekend. Closed Mondays, also New Year's Day, May 1, November 1 and 11, and Christmas Day. ☎ 648 17 18.

Palais de Justice – Law Courts, open 0900 to 1600 Mondays to Fridays. Closed Saturdays, Sundays and public holidays. ☎ 508 61 11.

Palais de la Nation – Parliament building. Guided tours of Chamber of Representatives for parties only (90 minutes) daily (except Sundays) at 1000, 1100, 1400, 1500 by prior arrangement (book two months in advance). Public and International Relations Department, 1008 Brussels. ☎ 519 81 36. Closed Sundays, January 1, 2 and 3, Easter weekend, Ascension weekend, Whitsun weekend, May 1, July 21, August 14 and 15, November 1, 2, 11 and 15, December 24, 25, 26, and 31. No admission charge.

Palais Royal – Royal palace, usually open 0930 to 1530 from July 21 to September. Closed Mondays. No admission charge. ☎ T.I.B. 513 89 40.

Place du Jeu-de-Balle: flea market – Every morning but main market is held on Sundays 0600 to 1200.

Théâtre de marionnettes de Toone – Puppet theatre, performances throughout the year, Fridays and Saturdays, 2030. For other days, phone for information. ☎ 511 71 37 or 513 54 86. Closed New Year's Day, Easter and Whit Mondays, and Christmas Day.

Théâtre royal de la Monnaie – Guided tours only, Saturdays 1200 to 1330. Educational service, ☎ 229 13 72.

F

FOREST

Eglise Saint-Denis – Church, open 1000 to 1100 Mondays and Wednesdays, 0900 to 1000 Tuesdays, 1500 to 1600 Thursdays and Fridays. Other times, contact Father Wayembergh. ☎ 344 87 19.

G

GAASBEEK

Castle and park – Open 1000 to 1700, Tuesdays, Wednesdays, Thursdays, Saturdays and Sundays, also public holidays April to October. Closed Mondays and Fridays (closed Fridays only in July and August) and from November to March. Admission: 120 F (Children: 60 F). ☎ 532 43 72.

H

HEYSEL

Atomium – Open daily 0900 to 2000 from beginning of April to end of August and 1000 to 1800 from beginning of September to end of March. Admission: 200 F. ☎ 477 09 77.

Mini-Europe – Open daily 0930 to 1800 end of March to end of June and in September; 0930 to 2000 from beginning of July to end of August (late-night opening to midnight from mid-July to mid-August); 1000 to 1800 from beginning of October to beginning of January. The brochure given free with the visitor's ticket contains the names of the models. Annual closure: January 8 to March 29. Admission: 380 F (Children: 290 F). ☎ 478 05 50.

HUIZINGEN

Domaine récréatif provincial – Recreation ground. Admission fee: 80 F (Children: 40F) from beginning of May to end of October and 40 F (children: 20 F) for the remainder of the year. ☎ 383 00 20.

La HULPE

Domaine Solvay

Park – Open daily 0800 to 2100 from beginning of April to end of September and daily 0900 to 1800 for the remainder of the year. ☎ 653 64 04.

House – Closed to the public.

I

IXELLES

Abbaye Notre-Dame-de-la-Cambre (église) – Abbey church, open daily 0900 to 1200 and 1500 to 1830. Closed during services and on public holidays. ☎ 648 11 21.

Musée communal – Municipal museum, open 1300 to 1900 Tuesdays to Fridays and 1000 to 1700 Saturdays and Sundays. Closed Mondays and public holidays. No admission charge for permanent displays (admission fee for temporary exhibitions). ☎ 511 09 84, ext. 1356.

Musée des Enfants – Children's Museum, open 1430 to 1700 Wednesdays, Saturdays, Sundays and school holidays. Open for school parties during the remainder of the year. Closed in August and on public holidays. Admission: 200 F. ☎ 640 01 07.

Musée Constantin Meunier – Open daily (except Mondays) 1000 to 1200 and 1300 to 1700. Closed Mondays, also New Year's Day, May 1, November 1 and 11, and Christmas Day. No admission charge. ☎ 508 32 11.

J

JETTE

Musée national de la Figurine historique – Historical Figurine Museum, open 1400 to 1700 Tuesdays to Fridays, also 1st Sunday in the month (same opening times). Closed Mondays and public holidays. No admission charge. ☎ 479 00 52.

JEZUS-EIK

Église Notre-Dame – Church, open daily 0800 to 1900. ☎ 657 13 46.

K

KOEKELBERG

Basilique nationale du Sacré-Cœur (Basilica church)

Gallery-promenade – Open daily 0800 to 1700 (1800 in summer). ☎ 425 88 22.

Rolland/EUREKA SLIDE

Basilique du Sacré-Cœur

Access to top of dome – Guided tour only, 1100 and 1500 Mondays to Fridays, Easter to mid-October, Saturdays by prior arrangement only. Also open 1400 to 1745 Sundays and public holidays from beginning of May to mid-October. Closed November to end of February, also July 21 and November 15. ☎ 425 88 22.

L

LAEKEN

Église Notre-Dame-de-Laeken – Church, open Sundays 1500 to 1700. ☎ 478 20 95.

Crypte royale – Royal crypt, open 1st Sunday in the month 1500 to 1700 from March to October, 1400 to 1800 on February 17, 1000 to 1700 on July 31, 1000 to 1200 and 1500 to 1700 on August 29, September 25, November 1 and 2, 1500 to 1700 on November 15, and 0930 to 1700 on Heritage Day. ☎ 478 20 95.

Pavillon chinois – Chinese pavilion, open daily (except Mondays) 1000 to 1645. Closed Mondays, also New Year's Day, May 1, November 1 and 11 and Christmas Day. Admission: 120 F. ☎ 268 16 08.

Chinese pavilion

Serres royales de Laeken – Glasshouses, open on a few days in the spring (April and May). The dates change every year so ask for information from the Tourist Office, ☎ 513 89 40. No admission charge during the day. Evening visits: 200 F.

Tour japonaise – Japanese Tower, open daily (except Mondays) 1000 to 1645. Closed Mondays, also New Year's Day, May 1, November 1 and 11 and Christmas Day. Admission: 50 F. ☎ 268 16 08.

M

MEISE

Jardin Botanique – Botanical Gardens, open daily 0900 to 1730 (1800 on Sundays and public holidays) from Easter to end of October and 0900 to 1700 for the remainder of the year. ☎ 269 39 05, ext. 203.

Palais des Plantes – Glasshouses, open 1300 to 1630 Mondays to Thursdays and Saturdays, and 1300 to 1800 on Sundays and public holidays from Easter to end of October (the glasshouses are open to parties only, by prior arrangement, on Saturday and Sunday mornings). The remainder of the year, open 1300 to 1600 Mondays to Thursdays, Saturdays and Sunday mornings for parties (again by prior arrangement). Admission: 120 F (Children: 50 F). ☎ 269 39 05, ext. 203.

Open-air collections – Open daily (except Fridays) 1300 to 1630 (1800 on Sundays and public holidays), Easter to end of October. ☎ 269 39 05, ext. 203.

R

RIXENSART

Castle – Guided tour only (35 minutes) 1400 to 1800 Sundays, from Palm Sunday to end of September. Tour by prior arrangement for parties only during the remainder of the year. Contact the Brabant Tourist Office, ☎ 351 12 00. Admission: 150 F (Children: 100 F). ☎ 653 65 05.

S

SAINT-GILLES

Hôtel Hannon – Hannon Residence, open daily (except Mondays) 1300 to 1800. Closed Mondays, public holidays and July 15 to August 15. Admission: 50 F. ☎ 538 42 20.

Musée Horta – Museum, open daily (except Mondays) 1400 to 1730. Closed Mondays, New Year's Day, Easter, May 1, Ascension Day, Whitsun, July 21, August 15, November 1 and 11 and Christmas Day. Admission: 120 F (Students: 80 F) and 200 F (students: 160 F) at weekends. ☎ 537 16 92.

Hôtel Hannon

T

TERVUREN

Arboretum – Open from sunrise to sunset. Visitors may walk on paths and grass only. No admission charge. ☎ 769 20 81.

Église Saint-Jean l'Evangéliste – Church, open daily 0830 to 1830.

Musée royal de l'Afrique centrale – Central Africa Museum, open daily (except Mondays) 0900 to 1730 mid-March to mid-October and daily (except Mondays) 1000 to 1630 for the remainder of the year. Closed New Year's Day and Christmas Day. Admission: 80 F (Children: 30 F). ☎ 769 52 11.

U

UCCLE

Chapelle Notre-Dame-des-Affligés – Chapel, open daily 1000 to 1700 and 1000 to 1200 Wednesdays and Sundays. ☎ 344 23 65.

Dieweg Cemetery – Open daily 0900 to 1600.

Musée David et Alice van Buuren – Museum, guided tours only 1400 and 1500 Mondays (except public holidays). Also from Easter onwards open Sundays from 1400 to 1800. Open to parties by prior arrangement Tuesdays to Saturdays. Closed between Christmas and New Year. Admission: 300 F (Children: 200 F). ☎ 343 48 51.

W

🅱 Chaussée de Bruxelles 149 – 1410 – ☎ (02) 354 99 10 – Fax (02) 354 22 23

In Waterloo, visitors can buy a *"Ticket Commun"* (Visitors Pass) which gives reduced-rate admission to all the museums on the Battle site. It costs 385 F for individuals and 300 F for visitors in parties. The Pass is on sale in all the museums and in the tourist office and remains valid for one full year as of the date of purchase.

Butte du Lion – Lion Mound, open daily 0930 to 1830 from beginning of April to end of September, 0930 to 1730 in October, 1030 to 1600 from beginning of November to end of February and 1030 to 1700 in March. Closed on New Year's Day and Christmas Day. Admission: 40 F (Children: 20 F). ☎ 385 19 12.

Centre du Visiteur – Visitors Centre, open daily 1030 to 1700 in April, 0930 to 1830 from beginning of May to end of September, 0930 to 1730 in October, and 1030 to 1600 from beginning of November to March. Closed on New Year's Day and Christmas Day. Admission: 300 F (Children: 190 F). ☎ 385 19 12.

Église Saint-Joseph – Church, open daily 0730 to 1900. ☎ 354 00 11.

Musée provincial du Caillou – Le Caillou Museum, open daily (except Mondays) 1000 to 1830 from beginning of April to end of October, and 1330 to 1700 from beginning of November to end of March. Closed Mondays and in January. Admission: 60 F. ☎ 384 24 24.

Musée de Cires – Waxworks museum, open daily 0930 to 1900 from beginning of April to end of October and 1000 to 1800 Saturdays, Sundays, and public holidays during the remainder of the year. Admission: 60 F (Children: 50 F). ☎ 384 67 40.

Musée Wellington – Wellington Museum, open daily 0930 to 1830 from beginning of April to end of October, and daily 1030 to 1700 the remainder of the year. Closed on New Year's Day and Christmas Day. Admission: 80 F (Children aged 6 – 12: 40 F). ☎ 354 78 06.

Panorama de la Bataille – Open daily 1030 to 1600 November to March, 1030 to 1700 in April, 0930 to 1830 May to September, and 0930 to 1700 in October. Closed on New Year's Day and Christmas Day. Admission: 300 F (Children: 190 F) . ☎ 385 19 12.

WATERMAEL-BOITSFORT

Parc Tournay-Solvay – Park, open daily 0800 to sunset.

WOLUWE-SAINT-PIERRE

Bibliotheca Wittockiana – Library, open 1000 to 1700 Tuesdays to Saturdays. Closed Sundays, Mondays, New Year's Day, Easter Monday, May 1, May 25, June 5, July 21, November 1 and 11, and from December 24 to January 2. Admission: 100 F. ☎ 770 53 33.

Musée du Transport urbain bruxellois – Transport Museum, open 1330 to 1900 Saturdays, Sundays and public holidays from beginning of April to beginning of October. ☎ 515 31 08.

Index

MANUFACTURE FRANÇAISE DES PNEUMATIQUES MICHELIN

Société en commandite par actions au capital de 2 000 000 000 de francs

Place des Carmes-Déchaux - 63 Clermont-Ferrand (France)

R.C.S. Clermont-Fd B 855 200 507

© Michelin et Cie, Propriétaires-Éditeurs 1996

Dépôt légal mai 1996 - ISBN 2-06-151301-8 - ISSN 0763-1383

Printed in the EU 4-96

Photocomposition : A.P.S., Tours

Impression et brochage : I.F.C. Imprimeur-Brocheur, St-Germain-du-Puy

Illustration de la couverture par PUBLIMER

Michelin is expanding *its* *English-language* Green Guide collection

- California
- Canada
- Chicago
- Mexico
- New England
- New York City
- Quebec
- Washington DC

EUROPE

- Austria
- Belgium Luxembourg
- Brussels
- France
- Germany
- Great Britain
- Greece
- Ireland
- Italy
- London
- Netherlands
- Portugal
- Rome
- Scotland
- Spain
- Switzerland
- Tuscany
- England : The West Country

FRANCE

- Atlantic Coast
- Auvergne Rhône Valley
- Brittany
- Burgundy Jura
- Châteaux of the Loire
- Dordogne
- Flanders Picardy and the Paris region
- French Riviera
- Normandy
- Paris
- Pyrenees Languedoc Tarn Gorges

To get the most out of your vacation use Michelin Guides and Maps.